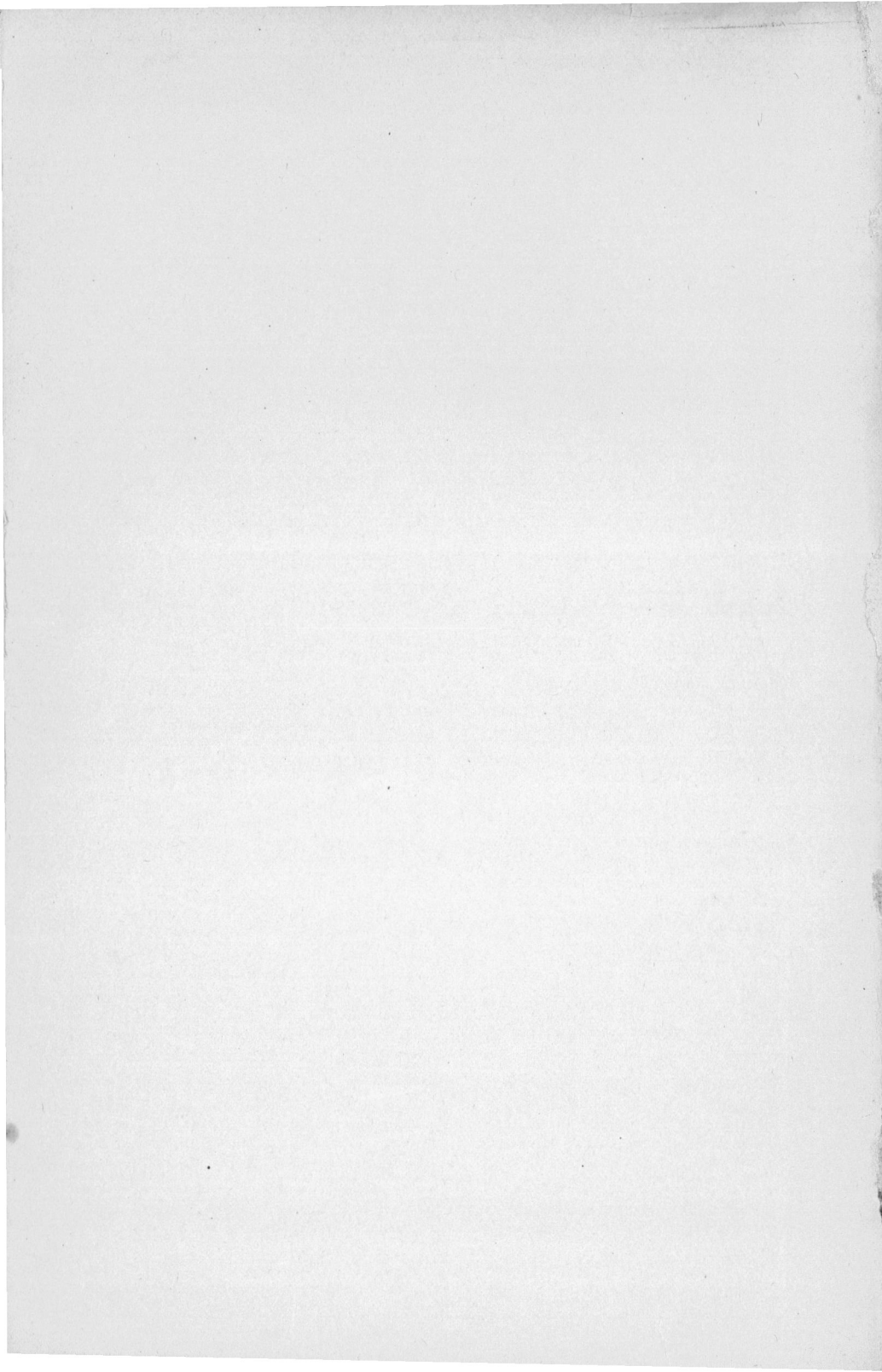

SEVEN GREAT STATESMEN

"The proper study of mankind is man."

Pope.

"For, as I take it, Universal History, the history of what man has accomplished in this world, is at bottom the History of the Great Men who have worked here."

"Great Men, taken up in any way, are profitable company."

"The History of the World is the Biography of Great Men."

Carlyle.

"The true nobility of nations is shown by the men they follow, by the men they admire, by the ideals of character and conduct they place before them."

Lecky.

"The broadest efficiency of great men begins after their death."

Gustav Schmoller.

SEVEN GREAT STATESMEN

IN THE WARFARE OF HUMANITY
WITH UNREASON

BY

ANDREW DICKSON WHITE

LL.D. (YALE AND ST. ANDREWS), L.H.D. (COLUMBIA), PH.DR. (JENA), D.C.L. (OXFORD)
MEMBER OF THE ROYAL ACADEMY OF SCIENCES, BERLIN
LATE PRESIDENT AND PROFESSOR OF HISTORY AT CORNELL UNIVERSITY
AUTHOR OF "A HISTORY OF THE WARFARE OF SCIENCE WITH THEOLOGY," ETC., ETC.

NEW YORK
THE CENTURY CO.
1912

TO
GOLDWIN SMITH
SCHOLAR, HISTORIAN, STATESMAN,
IN REMEMBRANCE OF HIS SELF-SACRIFICING CHAMPIONSHIP
OF THE AMERICAN UNION IN ITS TIME OF PERIL,
OF HIS INSPIRING TEACHINGS AT OXFORD AND AT CORNELL,
AND OF HIS LONG LIFE DEVOTED
TO TRUTH, JUSTICE, RATIONAL LIBERTY, AND RIGHT REASON

TABLE OF CONTENTS

INTRODUCTION

My purpose in writing these essays has been to acquaint men who are interested in the bearings of modern history on public life with sundry statesmen whose time was devoted not to seeking office or to winning a brief popular fame by chicanery or pettifoggery, but to serving the great interests of modern states and, indeed, of universal humanity. I would present these statesmen and their work as especially worthy to be studied by those who aspire to serve their country in any way.

It may be asked why it is that in my list are included neither Americans nor Englishmen. This is mainly because the great leaders of our own country and of Great Britain have already been fully and admirably portrayed for the American student of history, who, while he may know much regarding these, too often knows very little of those who have guided the great peoples of Continental Europe—whom not also to know is a misfortune. But there is another and a more personal reason: my early years abroad were spent mainly upon the European Continent, and public duties since have led me to make prolonged stays in various Continental states—France, Germany, the Netherlands, Italy, Russia—where the study of Continental statesmen has been almost forced upon me.

These studies of European history have been cast into biographical form because it has always seemed to me that Carlyle uttered a pregnant truth when he said that the history of any country is in the biographies of the men who made it.

In dealing with the subjects chosen I have endeavored

to familiarize myself not only with the best authorities, old and new, but, by travel and by acquaintance with men and affairs, to bring myself as much as possible into the atmosphere in which each of these personages lived. With the two who have lived in my own time I have had opportunity for something more. Cavour I never saw; but I knew well the Italy of his time, was present in Paris during the Peace Congress in 1856, knew some of the men who then sat with him, have since talked much with various colleagues of his in the ministries of Piedmont and of Italy, and had frequent conversations regarding him with his near friend and agent, Count Nigra, when we were colleagues at the first Peace Conference of the Hague. Bismarck it was my good fortune in Germany to have under close observation from 1854 to 1856, to be brought into official relations with him at Berlin during the years 1879, 1880, and 1881, to talk with him from time to time, to hear him talk with others, to be present during his discussions of important questions in parliament, to see something of his family life, and, both then and during a later official stay of nearly six years, from 1897 to 1902, to know well many public men who supported him, as well as many who opposed him, and to discuss with them his aims and methods.

While I have given references which will enable historical students to verify my statements and follow them further, I have constantly had in mind the average man intelligently interested in political affairs. It is for this reason that to each of these personages is given a somewhat extended historical setting which may enable any reader to understand his environment, the men and things with which he contended, and the results which he sought and accomplished.

I desire here to acknowledge my especial indebtedness to Professor George Lincoln Burr of Cornell University,

to William Roscoe Thayer, Esq., of Cambridge, Massa-
chusetts, to Professor Edward Payson Evans of Munich,
Germany, and to Mr. Frederick A. Cleveland, now studying at the University of Freiburg, for exceedingly valuable
suggestions as well as for the careful revision of sundry
chapters.

A. D. W.

Cornell University,
    February, 1910.

SARPI

SEVEN GREAT STATESMEN

SARPI

I

A THOUGHTFUL historian tells us that, between the Middle Ages and the nineteenth century, Italy produced three great men. As the first of these, he names Machiavelli, who, he says, "taught the world to understand political despotism and to hate it"; as the second, he names Sarpi, who "taught the world after what manner the Holy Spirit guides the Councils of the Church"; and as the third, Galileo, who "taught the world what dogmatic theology is worth when it can be tested by science."

I purpose now to present the second of these. As a *man,* he was by far the greatest of the three and, in various respects, the most interesting; for he not only threw a bright light into the most important general council of the Church and revealed to Christendom the methods which there prevailed,—in a book which remains one of the half-dozen classic histories of the world,—but he fought the most bitter fight for humanity ever known in any Latin nation, and won a victory by which the whole world has profited ever since. Moreover, he was one of the two foremost Italian statesmen since the Middle Ages, the other being Cavour.

He was born at Venice in 1552, and it may concern those who care to note the subtle interweaving of the warp and woof of history that the birth year of this most resourceful foe that Jesuitism ever had was the death year of St. Francis Xavier, the noblest of Jesuit apostles.

It may also interest those who study the more evident

factors of cause and effect in human affairs to note that, like most strong men, he had a strong mother; that, while his father was a poor shopkeeper who did little and died young, his mother was wise and serene.

From his earliest boyhood, he showed striking gifts and characteristics. Those who knew him testify that he never forgot a face once seen, could take in the main contents of a page at a glance, spoke little, rarely ate meat, and, until his last years, never drank wine.

Brought up, after the death of his father, first by his uncle, a priest, and then by Capella, a Servite monk, in something better than the usual priestly fashion, he became known, while yet in his boyhood, as a theological prodigy. Disputations in his youth, especially one at Mantua, where, after the manner of the time, he successfully defended several hundred theses against all comers, attracted wide attention, so that the Bishop gave him a professorship, and the Duke, who, like some other crowned heads of those days—notably Henry VIII and James I—liked to dabble in theology, made him a court theologian. But the duties of this position were uncongenial: a flippant duke, fond of putting questions which the wisest theologian could not answer, and laying out work which the young scholar evidently thought futile, wearied him. He returned to the convent of the Servites at Venice, and became, after a few years' novitiate, a friar, changing, at the same time, his name; so that, having been baptized Peter, he now became Paul.

His career soon revealed another cause of his return: he evidently felt the same impulse which stirred his contemporaries, Lord Bacon and Galileo; for he began devoting himself to the whole range of scientific and philosophical studies, especially to mathematics, physics, astronomy, anatomy, and physiology. In these he became known as an authority, and before long was recognized as such throughout Europe. It is claimed, and it is not improbable, that he anticipated Harvey in discovering the circulation of the blood, and that he was the forerunner of noted discoverers in magnetism. Unfortunately the loss of the great mass of his papers by the fire which destroyed his convent in 1769 forbids any full estimate of his work; but it is certain that among those who sought his opinion and advice were such great discoverers as Acquapendente, Galileo, Torricelli, and Gilbert of Colchester, and that every one of these referred to him as an equal, and indeed as a master. It seems also established that it was he who first discovered the valves of the veins, that he made known the most beautiful function of the iris,—its contractility,—and that various surmises of his regarding heat, light, and sound have since been wrought into scientific truths. It is altogether likely that, had he not been drawn from scientific pursuits by his duties as a statesman, he would have ranked among the great investigators and discoverers, not only of Italy, but of the world.

He also studied political and social problems, and he arrived at one conclusion which, though now trite, was then novel,—the opinion that the aim of punishment should not be vengeance, but reformation. In these days and in this country, where one of the most serious of evils is undue lenity to crime, this opinion may be imputed to him as a fault; but in those days, when torture was the main method in procedure and in penalty, his declaration was honorable both to his head and his heart.

With all his devotion to books, he found time to study men. Even at school, he seemed to discern those best worth knowing. They discerned something in him also; so that close relations were formed between him and such leaders as Contarini and Morosini, with whom he afterwards stood in great emergencies.

Important missions were entrusted to him. Five times he visited Rome to adjust perplexing differences between the papal power and various interests at Venice. He was rapidly advanced through most of the higher offices in his order, and in these he gave a series of decisions which won him the respect of all entitled to form an opinion.

Naturally he was thought of for high place in the Church, and was twice presented for a bishopric; but each time he was rejected at Rome,—partly from family claims of other candidates, partly from suspicions regarding his orthodoxy. It was objected that he did not find the whole doctrine of the Trinity in the first verse of Genesis; that he corresponded with eminent men of science in England and Germany, even though they were heretics; that he was not averse to reforms; that, in short, he was not inclined to wallow in the slime from which had crawled forth such huge incarnations of evil as John XXIII, Sixtus IV, Alexander VI, and Julius II.

His Jesuit detractors have been wont to represent him as seeking vengeance for his non-promotion; but his after career showed amply that personal grievances had little effect upon him. It is indeed not unlikely that, when he saw bishoprics for which he knew himself well fitted given as sops to poor creatures utterly unfit in mind or morals, he may have had doubts regarding the part taken by the Almighty in selecting them; but he was reticent, and kept on with his work. In his cell at Santa Fosca, he quietly and steadily devoted himself to his cherished studies; but he continued to study more than books or inanimate nature. He was neither a bookworm nor a pedant. On his various missions he met and discoursed with churchmen and statesmen concerned in the greatest transactions of his time, notably at Mantua with Oliva, secretary of one of the foremost ecclesiastics at the Council of Trent; at Milan with Cardinal Borromeo, the noblest of all who ever sat in that assemblage; in Rome and elsewhere with Arnauld du Ferrier, who had been French Ambassador at the Council, with Cardinal Santa Severina, head of the Inquisition, with Castagna, afterward Pope Urban VII, and with Cardinal Bellarmine, afterward Sarpi's strongest and noblest opponent.

Nor was this all. He was not content with books or conversations; steadily he went on collecting, collating, and testing original documents bearing upon the great events of his time. The result of all this the world was to see later.

He had arrived at middle life and won wide recognition as a scholar, scientific investigator, and jurist, when there came the supreme moment of a struggle which had involved Europe for centuries,—a struggle interesting not only the Italy and Europe of those days, but universal humanity for all time.

During the period following the fall of the Roman Empire in the West there had been evolved the temporal power of the Roman Bishop. It had many vicissitudes. Sometimes, as in the days of St. Leo and St. Gregory, it based its claims upon noble assertions of right and justice, and sometimes, as in the hands of Innocent VIII and Pius V, it sought to force its way by fanaticism. Sometimes it strengthened its authority by real services to humanity, and sometimes by such frauds as the Forged Decretals. Sometimes, as under Popes like Gregory VII and Innocent III, it laid claim to the mastership of the world, and sometimes, as with the majority of the pontiffs during the two centuries before the Reformation, it became mainly the appanage of a party or faction or family.

Throughout all this history, there appeared in the Church two great currents of efficient thought. On one side had been developed a theocratic theory, giving the papacy a power supreme in temporal as well as in spiritual matters throughout the world. Leaders in this during the Middle Ages were St. Thomas Aquinas and the Dominicans; leaders in Sarpi's day were the Jesuits, represented especially in the treatises of Bellarmine at Rome and in the speeches of Laynez at the Council of Trent.[1]

But another theory, hostile to the despotism of the Church over the State, had been developed through the Middle Ages and the Renaissance;—it had been strength-ened mainly by the utterances of such men as Dante, Egidio Colonna, John of Paris, Ockham, Marsilio of Padua, and Laurentius Valla. Sarpi ranged himself with the latter of these forces. Though deeply religious, he recognized the God-given right of earthly governments to discharge their duties independent of church control.

Among the many centres of this struggle was Venice. She was splendidly religious—as religion was then under-stood. She was made so by her whole environment. From the beginning she had been a seafaring power, and seafaring folk, from their constant wrestle with dangers ill understood, are prone to seek and find supernatural forces. Nor was this all. Later, when she had become rich, powerful, luxurious, and licentious, her most power-ful citizens, and especially their wives, felt a need of atoning for their many sins by splendid religious founda-tions. So her people came to live in an atmosphere of religious observance, and the bloom and fruitage of their religious hopes and fears are seen in the whole history of Venetian art,—from the rude sculptures at Torcello and the naïve mosaics at San Marco to the glowing altar-pieces and ceilings of John Bellini, Titian, and Tintoretto and the illuminations of the Grimani Psalter. No class in Venice rose above this environment. Doges and

[1] This has been admirably shown by Horatio Brown in his *Taylorian Lecture*, 1895 (pp. 229–234, in volume for 1889–99). For the great speech of Laynez supporting the authority of the Papacy as against the Episco-pate, as well as the discourses on the other side, see Sarpi: *History of the Council of Trent*, Nathanael Brent's translation, London, 1620, lib. vii, pp. 610–614.

Senators were as susceptible to it as were the humblest fishermen on the Lido. In every one of those glorious frescoes in the corridors and halls of the Ducal Palace which commemorate the victories of the Republic, the triumphant Doge or Admiral or General is seen on his knees making acknowledgment of the divine aid. On every Venetian sequin, from the days when Venice was a power throughout the earth to that fatal year when the young Bonaparte tossed the Republic over to the House of Austria, the Doge, crowned and robed, kneels humbly before the Saviour, the Virgin, or St. Mark. In the Hall of the Great Council, the most sumptuous room in the world, there is spread above the heads of the Doge and Senators and Councilors, as an incentive to the discharge of their duties on earth, a representation of the blessed in Heaven.

From highest to lowest, the Venetians lived, moved, and had their being in this religious environment, and, had their Republic been loosely governed, its external policy would have been largely swayed by this all-pervading religious feeling, and would have become the plaything of the Roman Court. But a republic has never been maintained save by the delegation of great powers to its chosen leaders. It was the remark of one of the foremost American Democrats of the nineteenth century, a man who received the highest honors which his party could bestow, that the Constitution of the United States was made, not to promote Democracy, but to check it. This statement is true, and it is as true of the Venetian Constitution as of the American.[1]

But while both the republics recognized the necessity of curbing Democracy, the difference between the means employed was world-wide. The founders of the American Republic gave vast powers to a President and

[1] See Horatio Seymour's noted article in the *North American Review* (1878).

unheard-of authority to a Supreme Court; in the Venetian Republic the Doge was gradually stripped of power, and there was evolved the mysterious and unlimited authority of the Senate and Council of Ten.

In these sat the foremost Venetians, thoroughly imbued with the religious spirit of their time; but men of the world, trained in the politics of all Europe and especially of Italy.

In his "Prince" Machiavelli tells us that "The peoples nearest to Rome are those having least faith in it," and Guizot in his History of Civilization has shown how Crusaders who went to the Orient by way of Italy and saw the papacy near at hand came back skeptics. This same influence shaped the statesmen of Venice. The Venetian Ambassadors were the foremost in Europe. Their "Relations" are still studied as the clearest, shrewdest, and wisest statements regarding the men and events in Europe of their time. All were noted for skill; but the most skillful were kept on duty at Rome. There was the source of danger. The Doges, Senators, and controlling Councilors had, as a rule, served in these embassies, and they had formed lucid judgments as to Italian courts in general and as to the Roman Court in particular. No men had known the Popes and the Curia more thoroughly. They saw Innocent VIII buy the papacy for money. They had been at the Vatican when Alexander VI had won renown as a secret murderer. They saw, close at hand, the merciless cruelty of Julius II. They had carefully noted the crimes of Sixtus IV, which culminated in the assassination of Julian de' Medici beneath the dome of Florence at the moment the Host was uplifted. They had sat near Leo X while he enjoyed the obscenities of the *Calandria* and the *Mandragora*,—plays which, in the most corrupt of modern cities, would, in our day, be stopped by the police. No wonder that, in one of their dispatches, they speak of Rome as "the sewer of the world."[1]

Naturally, then, while the religion of the Venetians showed itself in wonderful monuments of every sort, their practical sense was shown by a steady opposition to papal encroachments.

Of this combination of zeal for religion with hostility to ecclesiasticism we have striking examples throughout the history of the Republic. While most other European powers suffered ecclesiastics to take control of Public Instruction, Venice kept this control in her own hands, only leaving to the Church the direction of theological studies. While, in every other European state, cardinals, bishops, priests, and monks were given leading parts in civil administration and, in some states, a monopoly of civil honors, the Venetian Republic not only excluded all ecclesiastics from such posts, but, in cases which touched Church interests, she excluded even the relatives of ecclesiastics. When Church authority decreed that commerce should not be maintained with infidels and heretics, the Venetian merchants continued to deal with Turks, Pagans, Germans, Englishmen, and Dutchmen as before. When the Church decreed that the taking of interest for money was sin, and great theologians published in Venice some of their mightiest treatises demonstrating this view from Holy Scripture and the Fathers, the Venetians continued borrowing and lending money on usance. When efforts were made to enforce that tremendous instrument for the consolidation of Papal power, the bull *In Coena Domini,* Venice evaded and even defied it. When mediæval and theological preju-

---

[1] For Sixtus IV and his career, with the tragedy in the Cathedral of Florence, see Villari's *Machiavelli and His Times*, English translation, vol. ii, pp. 341, 342. For the passage in the dispatches referred to, *vide ibid.,* vol. i, p. 198.

dice hampered most of the European universities, Venice gave her University of Padua scope and freedom. When Sixtus V, strongest of all modern Popes, had brought all his powers, temporal and spiritual, to bear against Henry IV of France as an excommunicated heretic, and seemed ready to hurl the thunderbolts of the Church against any government which should recognize him, the Venetian Republic not only recognized him, but treated his ambassador with especial courtesy. When the other Catholic powers, save France, yielded to Papal mandates and sent no representatives to the coronation of James I of England, Venice was represented there. When Pope after Pope issued diatribes against toleration, the Venetians steadily tolerated, in their several sorts of worship, Jews and Greeks, Mohammedans and Armenians, with Protestants of every sort who came to them on business. When the Roman *Index* forbade the publication of most important works of leading authors, Venice demanded and obtained for her printers rights which were elsewhere denied.[1]

As to the religious restrictions which touched trade, the Venetians in their public councils, and indeed the people at large, had come to know perfectly what the Papal theory meant,—with some of its promoters, fanaticism, but with the controlling power at Rome, revenue,—revenue to be derived from retailing dispensations to infringe the holy rules.

This peculiar antithesis, nowhere more striking than at Venice—on the one side, religious fears and hopes;

---

[1] For a striking summary, by a devout Catholic, of various other restrictions upon ecclesiastics in Venice, see Cantù: *Les Hérétiques d'Italie*, vol. iv, 117, *et seq.* For a good and short statement regarding the hearty friendship between Venice and Henry IV. of France, despite the Vatican, see De Flassan: *Histoire de la Diplomatie Française*, IVe Période, livre 2. For the Venetian struggle against the Church in the matter of taking interest on loans, see *The Warfare of Science with Theology*, by the present writer, vol. ii, pp. 279 and following.

on the other, keen insight into the ways of ecclesiasticism —led to peculiar compromises. The bankers who had taken interest upon money, the merchants who had traded with Moslems and heretics, frequently thought it best in their last hours to perfect their title to salvation by turning over goodly estates to the Church. Under the sway of this feeling, and especially of the terrors infused by priests at deathbeds, mortmain had become in Venice, as in many other parts of the world, one of the most serious of evils. Thus it was that the clergy came to possess between one-fourth and one-third of the whole territory of the Republic, and in its Bergamo district more than one-half; and all this exempt from taxation. Hence it was that the Venetian Senate found it necessary to devise a legal check which should make such absorption of estates by the Church more difficult.

There was a second cause of trouble. In that religious atmosphere of Venice, monastic orders of every sort grew luxuriantly, not only absorbing more and more property to be held by the dead hand, but absorbing more and more men and women, and thus depriving the state of any healthful and normal service from them. Here, too, the Senate thought it best to interpose a check: it insisted that no new structures for religious orders be erected without consent of the State.

Yet another question flamed forth. Of the monks swarming through the city, many were luxurious and some were criminal. On these last the Venetian Senate determined to lay its hands, and in the first years of the seventeenth century all these burning questions culminated in the seizure and imprisonment of two ecclesiastics charged with various high crimes,—among these rape and murder.

There had just come to the papal throne Camillo Borghese, Paul V,—strong, bold, determined, with the highest possible theory of his rights and duties. In view of

his duty toward himself, he lavished the treasures of the
faithful upon his family, until it became the richest which
had yet risen in Rome; in view of his duty toward the
Church, he built superbly,—evidences of the spirit in
which he wrought being to this day his gorgeous tomb at
Santa Maria Maggiore and his name, in enormous letters, still spread across the façade of St. Peter's. As to
his rights, he accepted fully the theories and practices of
his boldest predecessors, and in this he had good warrant; for St. Thomas Aquinas and Bellarmine had furnished him with convincing arguments that he was
divinely authorized to rule the civil powers of Italy and
of the world.[1]

Moreover there was, in his pride, something akin to
fanaticism. He had been elected by one of those sudden movements, as well known in American caucuses as
in Papal conclaves, when, after a deadlock, all the old
candidates are thrown over, and the choice suddenly falls
on a new man. The cynical observer may point to this
as showing that the laws governing elections, under such
circumstances, are the same, whether in party caucuses
or in Church councils; but Pope Paul saw in this case the
direct intervention of the Almighty, and his disposition
to magnify his office was vastly increased thereby. He
was especially strenuous, and one of his earliest public
acts was to send to the gallows a poor author, who, in
an unpublished work, had spoken severely regarding one
of Paul's predecessors.

The Venetian laws checking mortmain, taxing Church
property, and requiring the sanction of the Republic be-

1 For details of these cases of the two monks, see Pascolato, *Fra Paolo
Sarpi*, Milano, 1893, pp. 126–128. For the Borghese avarice, see Ranke's
Popes, vol. iii, pp. 9–20, also Sismondi, *Républiques Italiennes*, Paris, 1840,
vol. x, pp. 259–260. For the development of Pope Paul's theory of government, see Ranke, vol. ii, p. 345, and note, in which Bellarmine's doctrine is cited textually; also Bellarmine's *Selbstbiographie, herausgegeben
von Döllinger und Reusch*, Bonn, 1887, pp. 181 *et seq.*

fore the erection of new churches and monasteries greatly angered him; but the crowning vexation was the seizure of the two clerics. This aroused him fully. He at once sent orders that they be delivered up to him, that apology be made for the past and guarantees given for the future, and notice was served that, in case the Republic did not speedily obey these orders, the Pope would ex-communicate its leaders and lay an interdict upon its people. It was indeed a serious contingency. For many years the new Pope had been known as a hard ecclesiasti-cal lawyer, and, now that he had arrived at the supreme power, he had evidently determined to enforce the high mediæval supremacy of the Church over the State. Ev-erything betokened his success. In France he had broken down all opposition to the decrees of the Council of Trent. In Naples, when a magistrate had refused to disobey the civil law at the bidding of priests, and the viceroy had supported the magistrate, Pope Paul had forced both viceroy and magistrate to comply with his will by threats of excommunication. In every part of Italy, —in Malta, in Savoy, in Parma, in Lucca, in Genoa, and finally even in Spain—he had pettifogged, bullied, threatened, until his opponents had given way. Every-where he was triumphant; and while he was in the mood which such a succession of triumphs would give he turned toward Venice.[1]

There was little, indeed, to encourage the Venetians to resist; for, while the interests of other European powers were largely the same as theirs, current political in-trigues seemed likely to bring Spain and even France into a league with the Vatican.

Beneficial as was the regeneration which Christianity brought to the world, the Church soon became and long

[1] For letters showing the craven submission of Philip III. of Spain at this time, see Cornet, *Paolo V. e la Republica Veneta*, Vienna, 1859, p. 285.

remained, in two things of vast import, more barbarous than Roman paganism; and about these two things raged during centuries a war for right reason. The first of these was torture. Under the Roman Empire limits to its cruelties had been gradually imposed in obedience to humanity and reason, but the Christian Church, as soon as its priesthood had gained control, cast aside all its previous mild precepts regarding the limitation of torture in legal procedure,—taking the ground that witches and heretics were especially aided by Satan to resist it,— and this cruel doctrine was soon extended into the ordinary courts of law.

The second of these developments of unreason concerned punishment for ecclesiastical offences. The old Roman law had been especially careful not to punish the innocent with the guilty; but the Church, as soon as it had arrived at full power, ceased to content itself with excommunicating the guilty and began laying penalties over large districts and even whole nations.[1]

To a people so devoted to commerce, yet so religious, as the Venetians, the threat of an interdict was serious indeed. Open church services were to cease; the people at large, no matter how faithful, were to be as brute beasts—not to be properly married, to be denied various sacramental consolations, not to be decently buried; other Christian peoples were to be forbidden all dealings with them, under pain of excommunication; their commerce might be delivered over to the tender mercies of any and every other nation; their merchant ships were to be as corsairs; their cargoes, the legitimate prey of all Christendom; and their people, on sea

[1] As to the barbarism fostered by the Church, when it came to full power, as regards torture, see authorities cited in my essay on Thomasius. As to barbarism in the matter of ecclesiastical offences, see E. B. Krehbiel, professor at Stanford University: *The Interdict, Its History and Operation* (Prize Essay of the American Historical Association for 1907), Washington, 1909.

and land, to be held as enemies of the human race. To this was added, throughout the whole mass of the people, a vague sense of awful penalties awaiting them in the next world. Despite all this, the Republic persisted in asserting its right.

Just at this moment came a diplomatic passage between Pope and Senate, like a farce before a tragedy; and it has historical significance, as showing what resourceful heads were at the service of either side. The Doge Grimani having died, the Vatican thought to score a point by promptly sending notice through its Nuncio to Venice that no new election of a Doge could take place if forbidden by the Pope, and that, until the Senate had become obedient to the Papacy, no such election would be sanctioned. But the Senate, having received a useful hint through its own Ambassador, was quite equal to the occasion. It at once declined to receive this or any dispatch from the Pope, on the plea, made with exuberant courtesy, that, there being no Doge, there was no person in Venice great enough to open it. They next, just as politely, declined to admit the Papal Nuncio, on the ground that, the old Doge being dead, there was no longer any one worthy to receive him. Then they proceeded to elect a new Doge who could receive both Nuncio and message,—a sturdy opponent of the Vatican pretensions, Leonardo Donato.

The Senate now gave itself entirely to considering ways and means of warding off the threatened catastrophe. Its first step was to consult Sarpi. His answer was prompt and pithy. He advised two things: first, to prevent, at all hazards, any publication of the Papal bulls in Venice or any obedience to them; secondly, to hold in readiness for use at any moment an appeal to a future Council of the Church.

Of these two methods, the first would naturally seem by far the more difficult. It was not so in reality. In

the letter which Sarpi presented to the Doge, he devoted less than four lines to the first and more than
fourteen pages to the second. As to the first remedy,
severe as it was and bristling with difficulties, it was, as
he claimed, a simple, natural, straightforward use of
police power. As to the second, the appeal to a future
Council was to the Vatican as a red flag to a bull. The
very use of such an appeal was punished by excommunication. To embolden the Doge and Senate in order that
they might consider it as an ultimate possibility, Sarpi
was obliged to show from the Scriptures, the Fathers,
the Councils, the early Popes, that the appeal to a Council was a *matter of right*. With wonderful breadth of
knowledge and clearness of statement he made his points
and answered objections. To this day, his letter remains a masterpiece.[1]

The Republic utterly refused to yield; and now, in
1606, Pope Paul launched his excommunication and interdict. In meeting them, the Senate took the course
laid down by Sarpi: the Papal Nuncio was notified that
the Senate would receive no paper from the Pope; all
ecclesiastics, from the Patriarch down to the lowest monk,
were forbidden, under the penalties of high treason, to
make public or even to receive any paper whatever from
the Vatican; additional guards were placed at the city
gates, with orders to search every wandering friar or
other suspicious person who might, by any possibility,
bring in a forbidden missive; a special patrol was kept,
night and day, to prevent any posting of the forbidden
notices on walls or houses; any person receiving or finding one was to take it immediately to the authorities,
under the severest penalties, and any person found con-

---

[1] As to Sarpi's advice to the Doge, the document is given fully in the
Lettere di Sarpi, Florence, 1863, vol. i, pp. 17 *et seq.;* also in Macchi,
Storia del Consiglio dei Dieci, cap. xxiv, where the bull of excommunication
is also given. Also Cecchetti: *La Republica di Venezia e la Corte di
Roma*, vol. ii, pp. 299 *et seq.*

cealing such documents was to be punished by death.[1]

At first some of the clergy were refractory. The head of the whole Church establishment of Venice, the Patriarch himself, gave signs of resistance; but the Senate at once silenced him. Sundry other bishops and high ecclesiastics made a show of opposition; and they were placed in confinement. One of them seeming reluctant to conduct the usual church service, the Senate sent an executioner to erect a gibbet before his door. Another, having asked that he be allowed to await some intimation from the Holy Spirit, received answer that the Senate had already received directions from the Holy Spirit to hang any person resisting their decree. The three religious orders which had showed most opposition— Jesuits, Theatins, and Capuchins—were in a semi-polite manner virtually expelled from the Republic.[2]

Not the least curious among the results of this state of things was the war of pamphlets. From Rome, Bologna, and other centres of thought, even from Paris and Frankfort, polemic tractates rained upon the Republic. The vast majority of their authors were on the side of the Vatican, and of this majority the leaders were the two cardinals so eminent in learning and logic, Bellarmine and Baronius; but, single-handed, Sarpi was, by general consent, fully a match for them.[3]

Of all the weapons then used the most effective throughout Europe was the solemn protest drawn by Sarpi and issued by the Doge. It was addressed nominally to the Venetian ecclesiastics, but really to Christendom, and both as to matter and manner it was Father

[1] For a multitude of comical details in this struggle, made all the more comical by Cantù's devout and doleful recital of them, see his *Hérétiques d'Italie*, vol. iv, pp. 124 and following.

[2] For interesting details regarding the departure of the Jesuits, see Cornet, *Paolo V e la Republica Veneta*, pp. 277–279.

[3] In the library of Cornell University are no less than nine quartos filled with selected examples of these polemics on both sides.

Paul at his best. It was weighty, lucid, pungent, and deeply in earnest,—in every part asserting fidelity to the Church and loyalty to the papacy, but setting completely at naught the main claim of Pope Paul: the Doge solemnly declaring himself "a prince who, in temporal matters, recognizes no superior save the Divine Majesty."

The victory of the friar was soon recognized far and near. Men began to call him by the name afterward so generally given him,—the *"terribile frate."* The Vatican seemed paralyzed. None of its measures availed, and it was hurt, rather than helped, by its efforts to annoy and pester Venice at various capitals. At Rome, it burned Father Paul's books and declared him excommunicated; it even sought to punish his printer by putting into the *Index* not only all works that he had ever printed, but all that he might ever print. At Vienna, the Papal Nuncio thought to score a point by declaring that he would not attend a certain religious function in case the Venetian Ambassador should appear; whereupon the Venetian officially announced that he had taken physic and regretted that he could not be present,—whereat all Europe laughed.

Judicious friends in various European cabinets now urged both parties to recede or to compromise. France and Spain both proffered their good offices. The offer of France was finally accepted, and the French Ambassador was kept running between the Ducal Palace and the Vatican until people began laughing at him also. The emissaries of His Holiness begged hard that, at least, appearances might be saved; that the Republic might undo some of its measures before the interdict was removed, or at least might seem to do so, and especially that it might withdraw its refusals before the Pope withdrew his penalties. All in vain. The Venetians insisted that they had committed no crime and had nothing to retract. The Vatican then urged that the Senate consent to receive absolution for its resistance to the Pope's authority. This the Senate steadily refused. It insisted: "Let His Holiness put things as before, and we will put things as before; as to his absolution, we do not need it or want it; to receive it would be to acknowledge that we have been in the wrong." Even the last poor sop of all was refused: the Senate would have no great "function" to celebrate the termination of the interdict; they would not even go to the mass which Cardinal Joyeuse celebrated on that occasion. The only appearance of concession which the Republic made was to give up the two ecclesiastics to the French Ambassador as a matter of courtesy to the French king; and, when this was done, the Ambassador delivered them to the Pope; but Venice especially reserved all the rights she had exercised. All the essential demands of the Papacy were refused, and thus was forever ended the Papal power of laying an interdict upon a city or a people. From that incubus, Christendom, thanks to Father Paul and to Venice, was at last and forever free.[1]

The Vatican did, indeed, try hard to keep its old claim in being. A few years after its defeat by Fra Paolo, it endeavored to reassert in Spain the same authority which had been so humbly acknowledged there a few years before. It was doubtless felt that this most pious of all countries, which had previously been so docile, and had stood steadily by the Vatican against Venice in the recent struggle, would again set an example of submission. Never was there a greater mistake: the Vatican received from Spanish piety a humiliating refusal.

---

[1] For an acknowledgment of the fact that interdicts have been permanently given up by the Church—with a solemnly humorous reason for it —making a virtue of necessity, see Addis and Arnold, *Catholic Dictionary*, Art. "Interdict."

Next it tried the old weapons against the little government at Turin. For many generations the House of Savoy had been dutifully submissive to religious control; nowhere out of Spain had heresy been treated more cruelly; yet here, too, the Vatican claim was spurned. But the final humiliation took place some years later under Urban VIII,—the same pontiff who wrecked Papal infallibility on Galileo's telescope. He tried to enforce his will on the state of Lucca, which, in the days of Pope Paul, had submitted to the Vatican decrees abjectly; but that little republic now seized the weapons which Sarpi had devised, and drove the Papal forces out of the field: the Papal ban was, even by this petty government, annulled in Venetian fashion and even less respectfully.[1]

Thus the world learned how weak the Vatican had become as a political power. Even Pope Paul learned it, and, from being the most strenuous of modern pontiffs, he became one of the most moderate in everything save in the enrichment of his family. Thus ended the last serious effort to coerce a people by an interdict, and so, one might suppose, would end the work of Father Paul. Not so. There was to come a second chapter in his history, more instructive, perhaps, than the first,—a chapter which has lasted until our own day.[2]

[1] The proofs—and from Catholic sources—that it was the Pope, not merely the Congregation of the Index, who condemned Galileo's doctrine of the earth's movement about the sun, the present writer has given in his *History of the Warfare of Science with Theology*, vol. i, chap. iii.

[2] Since this chapter was penned, there come tidings which seem to show the Interdict less a thing of the distant past than the world had supposed. In October, 1909, the present Pope laid on the little town of Adria, in Italy, an interdict of a fortnight, for the wounding of its Bishop by a street mob excited by the transfer of his residence to a neighboring city. It is very mild, far less harsh and high-handed than those of former days, and seems but the last feeble muttering of the thunder which rolled through the earth in the days of the Leos and Innocents and Pauls. (See the London *Times* for Oct. 8, 1909, and the official *Acta Apostolicæ Sedis* for Oct. 15, 1909, which gives in full the provisions of the interdict.)

THE Venetian Republic showed itself duly grateful to
Sarpi. The Senate offered him splendid gifts and
entitled him "Theologian of Venice." The gifts he refused, but the title, with its duty, which was mainly to
guard the Republic against the encroachments of the
Vatican, he accepted, and his life in the monastery of
Santa Fosca went on quietly, simply, laboriously, as before. The hatred now felt for him at Rome was unbounded: it corresponded to the gratitude at Venice.
Every one saw his danger, and he well knew it. Poten-
tates were then wont to send assassins on long errands,
and the arm of the Vatican was especially far-reaching
and merciless. It was the period when Philip the Second from his lair in Spain murdered William of Orange
in the Netherlands, and when Pius V, a Pope whom the
Church afterwards proclaimed a saint, commissioned an
assassin to murder Queen Elizabeth.[1]

But there was in Father Paul a trust in Providence
akin to fatalism. Again and again he was warned, and
among those who are said to have advised him to be
on his guard against assassins was no less a personage

[1] This statement formerly led to violent denials by Ultramontane champions; but in 1870 it was made by Lord Acton, a Roman Catholic, one
of the most learned of modern historians, and, when it was angrily denied,
he quietly cited the official life of Pope Pius in the *Acta Sanctorum*,
published under the highest Church authority. This was final; denial
ceased, and the statement is no longer questioned. For other proofs in
the line of Lord Acton's citation, see Bellarmine's *Selbstbiographie*, ed. by
Döllinger, Bonn, 1887, pp. 306 *et seq.* Unable longer to controvert Lord
Acton's statement, the Jesuit Father Campbell asserts that he was not
a *Roman* Catholic, but an *Old* Catholic. The statement is refuted by a
far more eminent authority, the Abbot Gasquet, of the Order of St. Benedict. See Gasquet: *Lord Acton and His Circle*, p. 371 and elsewhere.

than his greatest controversial enemy—Cardinal Bellarmine. It was believed by Sarpi's friends that Bellarmine's humanity prevailed over his fealty to the Vatican, and we may rejoice in the hope that his nobler qualities did really assert themselves against the casuistry which sanctioned assassination.

These warnings were but too well founded. On a pleasant evening in October, 1607, a carefully laid trap was sprung. Returning from his day's work at the Ducal Palace, Father Paul, just as he had crossed the little bridge of Santa Fosca before reaching his convent, was met by five assassins. Two of his usual attendants had been drawn off by the outburst of a fire in the neighborhood; the other two were old men who proved useless. The place was well chosen. The descent from the bridge was so narrow that all three were obliged to march in single file, and just at this point these ruffians sprang upon him in the dusk, separated him from his companions, gave him fifteen dagger thrusts, two in his throat, and one—a fearful gash—on the side of his head, and then, convinced that they had killed him, fled to their boats, only a few paces distant.

The victim lingered long in the hospital, but his sound constitution and abstemious habits stood him in good stead. Very important among the qualities which restored him to health were his optimism and his cheerfulness. An early manifestation of the first of these was seen when, on regaining consciousness, he called for the stiletto which had been drawn from the main wound and, running his fingers along the blade, said cheerily to his friends, "It is not filed." What this meant, any one knows who has seen in various European collections the daggers dating from the "ages of faith" cunningly filed or grooved to hold poison.[1]

---

[1] There is a remarkable example of a beautiful dagger, grooved to contain poison, displayed in the imperial collection of arms at Vienna.

As an example of the second of these qualities, we may take his well-known reply when, to the surgeon, who in dressing the wound made by the "style," or stiletto, spoke of its "extravagance," rudeness, and yet ineffectiveness, Fra Paolo quietly answered that in these characteristics he recognized "the *style* of the Roman Curia."

Meantime the assassins had found their way back to Rome; but it is some comfort to know that later, when such conscience as there was throughout Italy and Europe showed intense disgust at the whole proceeding, the Roman Court treated them coldly and even harshly.

The Republic continued in every way to show Sarpi its sympathy and gratitude. It made him splendid offers, which he refused; but two gifts he accepted. One was full permission to explore the Venetian archives, and the other was a little doorway, cut through the garden wall of his monastery, enabling him to reach his gondola without going through the narrow and tortuous path he had formerly taken on his daily journey to the public offices. This humble portal still remains: beneath few triumphal arches has there ever passed a greater conqueror.[1]

Efforts were also made to cajole him,—to induce him to visit Rome, with fine promises of recognition and honor, and with solemn assurances that no harm should come to him; but he was too wise to yield. Only a short time previously he had seen Giordano Bruno, after seven years spent in the dungeons of the Inquisition at Venice and Rome, burned alive on the Campo dei Fiori. He had seen his friend and correspondent, Fra Fulgenzio Manfredi, yield to similar allurements and accept a safe conduct to Rome, which, though it solemnly guaranteed

[1] The present writer has examined with care the spot where the attack was made, and found that the plot was as cunningly conceived as it was fiendishly executed. He also visited what was remaining of the convent in April, 1902, and found the little door as serviceable as when it was made.

him against harm, proved as worthless as that of John Huss at the Council of Constance; the Inquisition torturing him to death on the spot where, nine years earlier, it had burned Bruno. He had seen his friend, the Archdeacon Ribetti, drawn within the clutch of the Vatican, only to die of "a most painful colic" immediately after dining with a confidential chamberlain of the Pope, and, had he lived a few months longer, he would have seen his friend and confidant, Antonio de Dominis, Archbishop of Spalato, to whom he had entrusted a copy of his most important work, enticed to Rome and put to death by the Inquisition. Though the Vatican exercised a strong fascination over its enemies, against Father Paul it was powerless; he never yielded to it, but kept the even tenor of his way.[1]

In the dispatches which now passed, comedy was mingled with tragedy. Very unctuous was the expression by His Holiness of his apprehensions regarding "dangers to the salvation" and of his "fears for the souls" of the Venetian Senators, if they persisted in asserting their own control of their own state. Hardly less touching were the fears expressed by the good Oratorian, Cardinal Baronius, that "a judgment might be brought upon the Republic" if it declined to let the Vatican have its way. But these expressions were not likely to prevail with men who had studied Machiavelli.

Uncompromising as ever, Father Paul continued to write letters and publish treatises which clenched more and more firmly into the mind of Venice and of Europe the political doctrine of which he was the apostle,—the doctrine that the State is rightfully independent of the Church,—and throughout the Christian world he was recognized as victor.

---

[1] A copy of Manfredi's "safe conduct" is given by Castellani, *Lettere Inedite di Fra Paolo Sarpi*, p. 12, note. No guarantee could be more explicit.

Nothing could exceed the bitterness of the attacks upon him, though some of them, at this day, provoke a smile. While efforts were made to discredit him among scholars by spurious writings or by interpolations in genuine writings, efforts equally ingenious were made to arouse popular hostility. One of these was a painting which represented him writhing amid the flames of hell, with a legend stating, as a reason for his punishment, that he had opposed the Holy Father.

Now it was indeed, in the midst of ferocious attacks upon his reputation and cunning attempts upon his life, that he entered a new and most effective period of activity. For years, as the adviser of Venice, he had studied, both as a historian and as a statesman, the greatest questions which concerned his country, and especially those which related to the persistent efforts of the Vatican to encroach upon Venetian self-government. The results of these studies he had embodied in reports which had shaped the course of the Republic; and now, his learning and powers of thought being brought to bear upon the policy of Europe in general, as affected by similar Papal encroachments, he began publishing a series of treatises, which at once attracted general attention.

As early as 1608 he was at work on his "History of the Controversy between Pope Paul V and Venice," which was well known in manuscript long before it found a printer in 1624. With relentless pungency it laid bare the whole tissue of papal and Jesuit intrigue. In this work, as a historian, he clenched his effort as a statesman; from that day forward no nation has even been seriously threatened with an interdict.[1]

Subsidiary books followed rapidly from his pen,

[1] There is a quaint old English translation of this book. It is entitled a *History of the Quarrels of Pope Paul V with the State of Venice*, and was printed in 1626.

strengthening the civil power against the clerical; but in
1610 came a treatise which marked an epoch,—his History of Ecclesiastical Benefices.[1]   In this he dealt with a
problem which had become very serious, not only in Venice, but in every European state, showed the process by
which vast treasures had been taken from the control of
the civil power and heaped up for ecclesiastical pomp
and intrigue, pointed out special wrongs done by the
system to the Church as well as the State, and advocated
a reform which should restore this wealth to better uses.
His arguments spread widely and sank deep, not only in
Italy, but throughout Europe, and the nineteenth century
has seen them applied effectively in every European
country within the Roman obedience.

In 1611 he published his treatise on the Inquisition at
Venice, presenting historical arguments against the uses
which ecclesiasticism had made of that tribunal.   These
arguments spread far, and developed throughout Europe that opposition to the Inquisition which finally led
to its destruction.   Minor works followed, dealing with
state questions arising between the Vatican and Venice,
each treatise—thoroughly well reasoned and convincing
—having a strong effect on the discussion of similar public questions in every other European nation.

In 1613 came two books of a high order, each marking
an epoch.   The first of these was upon the Right of
Sanctuary, and in it Sarpi led the way, which all modern
states have followed, out of the old, vicious system of
sanctioning crime by sheltering criminals.   The cogency
of his argument and the value of its application gained
for him an especial tribute by the best authority on such
questions whom Europe had seen—Hugo Grotius.

---

[1] The old English translation of this book, published in 1736 at Westminster, is by no means a rare book, and it affords the general reader
perhaps the most accessible means of understanding Fra Paolo's simplicity,
thoroughness, and vigor.

The second of these books dealt with the Immunity of the Clergy. This work belonged to the same order of ideas as the earlier, and the second fastened into the European mind the reasons why no state can depend upon the Church for the punishment of clerical criminals. His argument was a triumphant vindication of Venice in her struggle with Paul V on this point; but it was more than that. It became the practical guide of all modern states. Its reasoning aided powerfully in overthrowing throughout Europe the legal distinction, in criminal matters, between the priestly caste and the world in general: that "benefit of clergy" which had for centuries been so subversive of justice.

Among lesser treatises which followed is one which has done much to shape modern policy regarding public instruction. This was his book upon the Education given by the Jesuits. One idea which it enforced sped far,— his statement that Jesuit maxims develop "sons disobedient to their parents, citizens unfaithful to their country, and subjects undutiful to their sovereign." Jesuit education has indeed been maintained, and evidences of it may be seen in various European countries. The traveler in Italy constantly sees in the larger Italian towns long lines of young men and boys, sallow, thin, and listless, walking two and two, with priests at each end of the coffle. These are students taking their exercise, and an American or Englishman marvels as he remembers the playing fields of his own country. Youth are thus brought up as milksops, to be graduated as scapegraces. The strong men who control public affairs, who lead men and originate measures in the open, are not bred in Jesuit forcing-houses. Even the Jesuits themselves have acknowledged this, and perhaps the strongest of all arguments supplementary to those given by Father Paul were uttered by Padre Curci, eminent in his day as a Jesuit gladiator, but who at last realized the impossibility of ac-

complishing great things with men moulded by Jesuit
methods.

All these works took strong hold upon European
thought. Thoughtful men in all parts of Europe recognized Sarpi as both a statesman and a historian.
Among his English friends were such as Lord Bacon and
Sir Henry Wotton; and his praises have been sounded
by Grotius, by Gibbon, by Hallam, by Ranke, and by Ma-
caulay. Strong, lucid, these works of Father Paul have
always been especially attractive to those who rejoice in
the leadership of a master mind.

But in 1619 came the most important of all,—a service to humanity hardly less striking than that which he
had rendered in his battle against the Interdict,—his
History of the Council of Trent.

His close relations to so many men of mark who sat
in that Council and his long study in public archives and
private libraries bore fruit in this work, which takes
rank among the few enduring historical treatises of the
world. Throughout, it is vigorous and witty, but at the
same time profound; everywhere it is pervaded by sobriety of judgment. Its portraits of leading men; its
revelation of the efforts or threats by representatives of
various great powers to break away from the Papacy
and establish national churches; its presentation of the
arguments of anti-papal orators on one side and of Laynez and his associates on the other; its coupling of acts
with pretexts; its penetration into the whole network of
intrigue, and its thorough discussion of underlying principles,—all are masterly.

Though the name of the author was concealed in an
anagram ("Pietro Soave Polano'"—i. e. Paolo Sarpi
Veneto), the book was felt, by the Vatican party, to be
a blow which only one man could have dealt, and the
worst blow which the party had received since its author
had defeated the Interdict at Venice. Efforts were made,

by outcries and calumnies, to discredit the work, and they have been continued from that day to this, but in vain. That there must be some gaps and many imperfections in it is certain; but its general character is beyond the reach of ultramontane weapons. The blow was felt to be so heavy that the Jesuit Pallavicini was empowered to write a history of the Council to counterbalance it, and his work was well done; but Ranke, the most unprejudiced of judges, comparing the two, assigns the palm to Father Paul.

For his was the work not merely of a minute scholar but of a broad-minded statesman,—of a man who had known intimately and conversed freely with many of those who knew the Council best,—a man who had studied the reports of the quick-witted Venetian ambassadors and who had gathered from the most dissimilar sources masses of information at first hand.

Dry and crisp as is its style, it is lighted up here and there by humor: noteworthy examples are his accounts of the discussions in the Council on *"Limbo,"* the place assigned to the departed spirits of unbaptized infants—the Dominicans holding it to be a dark place under the earth, and the Franciscans, more kindly, declaring it to be a well-lighted place above the earth. It is a comfort to acknowledge that in this Catholic Council of the sixteenth century no one was found so inhumane as to assign to unapproved infants a place as evil as that to which sundry Protestant divines predestined them in the early days of the nineteenth.

A subtle humor pervades Sarpi's story—as in his account of the quarrels for precedence between the Spanish and French ambassadors and his quotation from a French ambassador that a proposed reform was "not a plaster of Isaiah to heal the wound, but of Ezekiel to make it raw." [1]

[1] For examples of style and treatment above given, see *History of the*

Of all modern historians he possesses in largest measure those qualities which have given immortality to Tacitus. Not at all seeking popularity, his power is seen by the simple fact that this work of his has elicited the praises of historians so different as Gibbon and Ranke.

The book was immediately spread throughout Europe; but, of all the translations, the most noteworthy was the English. Sarpi had entrusted a copy of the original to his friend, Antonio de Dominis, Archbishop of Spalato, and he, having taken refuge in England, had it translated there, the authorship being ascribed, as in the original, to "Pietro Soave Polano." This English translation was, in vigor and pith, worthy of the original. In it can be discerned, as clearly as in the original, that atmosphere of intrigue and brutal assertion of power by which the Roman Curia, after packing the Council with petty Italian bishops, bade defiance to the Catholic world. This translation, more than all else, has enabled the English-speaking peoples to understand what was meant by the Italian historian when he said that Father Paul "taught the world how the Holy Spirit guides the Councils of the Church." It remains cogent down to this day; after reading it one feels that such guidance might equally be claimed for Tammany Hall. The claim that the Council represented the Universal Church is perhaps best answered by a simple presentation of figures. The number of Italian bishops in attendance during the culminating sessions was 187. The number of bishops from all the world beside was 81. Of these, Ireland sent but three, Germany but two, and England but one.[1]

Council of Trent, as above, Brent's translation, 1620, lib. ii, p. 178, and lib. viii, pp. 727, 728.

[1] For the numbers of the bishops at the Council of Trent, as given by the best Catholic authorities, see the Acta Conciliorum, edit. by Hardouin, vol. x, pp. 418–438, Paris, 1714. Also, the Concilium Tridentinum, edit. by the Görres Soc., vol. iv, pp. 529–532. As to Germany, it is true that

Although Father Paul never acknowledged the authorship of the History of the Council of Trent, and although
the original copy, prepared for the press, with his final
corrections, still remains buried in the archives at Venice,
the whole world knew that he alone could have written it.

But during all these years, while elaborating opinions
on the weightiest matters of state for the Venetian Senate, and sending out this series of books which so powerfully influenced the attitude of his own and after generations toward the Vatican, he was working with great
effect in yet another field. With the possible exception
of Voltaire, he was the most vigorous and influential
letter-writer during the three hundred years which separated Erasmus from Thomas Jefferson. Voltaire certainly spread his work over a larger field, lighted it with
more wit, and gained more brilliant victories by it; but
as regards accurate historical knowledge, close acquaintance with statesmen, familiarity with the best and worst
which statesmen could do, sober judgment and cogent
argument, the great Venetian was his superior. Curiously enough, Sarpi resembles the American statesman
more closely than either of the Europeans. Both he and
Jefferson had the intense practical interest of statesmen,
not only in the welfare of their own countries, but in
all the political and religious problems of their times.
Both were keenly alive to progress in the physical sciences, wherever made. Both were wont to throw a light
veil of humor over very serious discussions. Both could
use, with great effect, curt, caustic description: Jefferson's letter to Governor Langdon satirizing the crowned
heads of Europe, as he had seen them, has a worthy pen-
dant in Fra Paolo's pictures of sundry representatives of
the Vatican. In both these writers was a deep earnest-

the Emperor was also represented by an embassy, but it will hardly be
claimed that this was inspired by the Holy Ghost.

3

ness, which, at times, showed itself in prophetic utterances. The amazing prophecy of Jefferson against American slavery, beginning with the words, "I tremble when I remember that God is just," which, in the light of our civil war, seems divinely inspired, is paralleled by some of Sarpi's utterances against the unmoral tendencies of Jesuitism and Ultramontanism; and these, too, seem divinely inspired as one reads them in the light of what has happened since in Spain, in Sicily, in Naples, in Poland, and in sundry South American republics.

The range of Sarpi's friendly relations was amazing. They embraced statesmen, churchmen, scholars, scientific investigators, diplomatists in every part of Europe, and, among these, Galileo and Lord Bacon, Grotius and Mornay, Salmasius and Casaubon, De Thou and Sir Henry Wotton, Bishop Bedell and Vossius, with a great number of others of nearly equal rank. King James I showed an especial interest in him, and wrote to obtain his portrait. Unfortunately the greater part of his correspondence has perished. In the two small volumes collected by Polidori, and in the small additional volume of letters to Simon Contarini, Venetian Ambassador at Rome, unearthed a few years since in the Venetian archives by Castellani, we have all that is known. It is but a small fraction of his epistolary work, but it enables us to form a clear opinion. The letters are well worthy of the man who wrote the History of the Council of Trent and the protest of Venice against the Interdict.

It is true that there has been derived from these letters, by his open enemies on one side and his defenders of a rather sickly conscientious sort on the other, one charge against him: this is based on his famous declaration, "I utter falsehood never, but the truth not to every one." ("La falsità non dico mai mai, ma la verità non a ogniuno.") [1] Considering his

---

[1] For this famous utterance, see notes of conversations given by Christoph,

vast responsibilities as a statesman and the terrible dangers which beset him as a theologian;—that in the first of these capacities the least misstep might wreck the great cause which he supported, and that in the second such a misstep might easily bring him to the torture chamber and the stake, normally healthful minds will doubtless agree that the criticism upon these words is more Pharisaic than cogent.

Sarpi was now spoken of, more than ever, both among friends and foes, as the *"terrible frate."* Terrible to the main enemies of Venice he indeed was, and the machinations of his opponents grew more and more serious. Efforts to capture him, to assassinate him, to poison him, to discredit him, to lure him to Rome, or at least within reach of the Inquisition, became almost frantic; but all in vain.

One precaution of his during this period throws a vivid light upon his character and his time. His main fear was that if kidnapped by the Inquisitors he might, under unbearable torture, reveal important secrets of State; he therefore always carried the means of ending his own life.

He still continued his work at the monastery of Santa Fosca, publishing from time to time discussions of questions important for Venice and for Europe, working steadily in the public service until his last hours. None of the attacks by his enemies embittered him. He remained gentle and kindly to the last. Sir Henry Wotton, English Ambassador at Venice, writing to the Earl of Salisbury, says of Sarpi: "He seemeth in countenance, as in spirit, liker to Philip Melanchthon than to Luther." [1]

Burggraf von Dohna, in July, 1608, in *Briefe und Acten zur Geschichte des Dreissigjährigen Krieges*, ii, München, 1874, p. 79.

[1] For the correspondence between Wotton and King James, regarding Sarpi's portrait, and for Wotton's comparison between the great Venetian and Melanchthon, see the very interesting original letters found at

In spite of his excommunication and of his friendships with many of the most earnest Protestants of Europe, he remained a son of the church in which he was born. His life was shaped in accordance with its general precepts, and every day he heard mass. So his career quietly ran on until, in 1623, he met death calmly, without fear, in full reliance upon the divine justice and mercy. His last words were a prayer for Venice—*"Esto perpetua."*

Venice, a few years since, and published in the London *Athenæum*, Sept. 2, 1905.

To any who may have been interested by the foregoing essay and desirous of a more minute and detailed account of Sarpi's life, excellently given and indeed the best of accessible sources known to me in English, see the Reverend Alexander Robertson, D.D., *Fra Paolo Sarpi,—The Greatest of the Venetians, London, Sampson, Low, Marston & Co., 1893.* I desire to express here my indebtedness to Dr. Robertson for especial aid during my last two visits in Venice in finding localities and obtaining information regarding Sarpi's life from various sources difficult of access. I am glad to know that a new edition of his excellent work, with revisions and additions, is to appear during the present year. Its author has lived in Venice during many years and has had exceptional facilities for studies in Venetian history, to which he has so long been earnestly and, in the best sense, fruitfully devoted.

III

SARPI'S battles for right reason had apparently ended. The world might well say,

> "Nor steel nor poison,
> Malice domestic, foreign levy, nothing
> Can touch him further."

Yet now came a new warfare upon him—one of the most virulent in human history, which lasted more than two hundred years. It contains especially instructive lessons for modern states which may have to deal with problems created by priestly power.

Sarpi had, indeed, fought the good fight—and had won it for his country and for humanity. For all this the Venetian Republic had, in his later years, tried to show its gratitude, though he had quietly and firmly refused the main gifts it offered him. At his death came a new outburst of gratitude.

The Republic sent notice of his death to other powers of Europe through its Ambassadors in the terms usual at the death of royal personages; in every way, it showed its appreciation of his character and services, and it crowned all by voting him a public monument.

Hardly was the decree known, when the Vatican authorities replied by a threat that, should any monument be erected to Sarpi, they would publicly declare him excommunicate as a heretic. At this, the Venetian Senate hesitated, waited, delayed. Whenever afterwards the idea of carrying out the decree for his monument was revived, opposition from Rome was bitter.

Time went on, and generations came which seemed to

forget him. Still worse, generation after generation came, carefully trained by clerical teachers to misunderstand him.

How careful this training was may be seen from one instance, typical of many. In 1719, nearly a century after Sarpi's death, the Papal Nuncio at Venice, Aldobrandini, having secured information that there was preparing in that city a new edition of the great patriot's writings, wrote to Rome, and the machinery of the Vatican was immediately set in motion. Both the Roman and the Venetian Inquisitions intervened vigorously. First, an endeavor was made to stop the printing of the work, and this seemed, for a time, successful; but, the printer having got the better of the inquisitors, Pope Clement XI sent a certain Father Bertolli to take charge of the business, and this emissary proved his cunning and zeal by buying up all the copies of the new edition he could find, and so the peril seemed ended.[1]

Three years later came another alarm. In some alterations at the old Church of the Servites, the body of Fra Paolo was found, and, for a wonder, all in excellent preservation save that part of the face which had been injured by the assassin. This aroused deep feeling. There were some who saw in this condition of Sarpi's remains an evidence of his sainthood, and at least one person was so convinced that she had been cured by pray-

[1] Original records of the Roman Inquisition and the Dataria, seventy quarto volumes in all, containing most curious documents regarding the dealings with Sarpi's memory, trials and executions of various heretics, and the like, having been among the papers carried off to France in 1809 under the direction of Napoleon, were not returned at the restoration of the Bourbons, but, by a curious stroke of fate, found their way into the library of Trinity College, Dublin, and there they remain. They are especially rich in details concerning the finding of the body of Father Paul, and the curious chain of circumstances which thence arose, including various matters mentioned above in the text. For the full details, see Ugo Balzani, *Di Alcuni Documenti dell' Archivio del Santo Uffizio di Roma, relativi al Ritrovamento del Cadavere di Paolo Sarpi*, Rome, 1895.

ing at his shrine that she hung up a votive tablet recording this exhibition of divine grace.

A vigorous correspondence ensued. The Holy Inquisition at Rome bestirred itself and soon secured information from the best source, namely, from Father Gennari of the Inquisition in Venice. His letters, now preserved in the library of Trinity College, Dublin, inform us that the chief medical authorities had made examination and that the remarkable statement regarding the preservation of the corpse was true; but the astuteness of the Inquisitor was equal to the occasion: he informed the Roman authorities, among other consoling things, that sundry noble persons had declared that the corpse "could not be the body of Father Paul, since his soul and body were in Hell."

And now a new personage comes upon the scene, no less than that Father Bertolli who, a few years before, having been sent by Pope Clement XI, had succeeded in suppressing the reprint of Father Paul's works. By dint of diligent spying, he was able to report to the Roman authorities that a document had been placed in the coffin, at Father Paul's reinterment, reverently praising his character, and stating that his body had been found incorrupt, that this inscription was signed by the Prior and a number of eminent theologians of the Order, and that at the end of it was written a very significant quotation from the 109th Psalm, at the 28th verse, "Let them curse, but bless Thou" (*Maledicent illi, et Tu benedicas*).

The Holy Inquisition, having read the letter of Bertolli, rose to the height of the great argument, and proposed sundry persecutions against those who had signed this document; but Innocent XIII, who had now come to the Papal throne, seems to have preserved more common sense: he ordained that all persecution in the matter be deferred.

The Papal Nuncio, the Inquisitor, and Father Bertolli

now made another effort. There, in the sacristy of the
Church of the Servites, was the votive tablet of Elizabeth
Gabrielli, declaring that by the intercession of Fra Paolo
she had been cured of a serious disease. A new series
of letters passed to and fro, Father Bertolli especially
insisting that the Inquisitors should proceed in the matter, and he was finally successful. The tablet and one
or two other tributes to Fra Paolo's memory were removed.

Now occurred to the Papal Nuncio another happy
thought. In a letter to the Papal Secretary of State
he made a promise as follows: "I will still give all my
attention, in connection with the intelligence of the Father
Inquisitor and of the Father Provincial Bertolli, to an
endeavor to have the corpse confused with others in the
church." In answer to this the Holy Inquisition at Rome
wrote, approving this idea, and expressing the hope that
the signed document might be removed from the coffin,
and that the body of Father Paul should be "confused
with others."[1]

This attempt to destroy the identity of the corpse of
the great Venetian citizen failed, but Father Bertolli's
effort to remove the laudatory document from the coffin
was at first more successful, and in his letter from Venice
to the Procurator General at Rome, having made a statement to this effect, he piously adds the words, "*Te Deum
laudamus.*"

But, after all, his victory turned out to be incomplete.
To his infinite disgust, one member of the Venetian Council of Three, which had ordered the document to be removed from the coffin, was patriotic and manly enough
to insist that "an honorable record" of the discovery of
Father Paul's remains be placed in the coffin, and in this
he was successful. This was a bad blow to Father Bertolli, to the Inquisitor General, and to the Papal Nuncio,

[1] See Balzani, pp. 16-19, as above, citing the letters now at Dublin.

for it brought to naught the only thing of importance to them—namely, the plan of destroying the identity of Fra Paolo's corpse. A lively correspondence between the Roman and Venetian ecclesiastical authorities ensued; but, alas, there remained in the coffin the "honorable record,"—an inscription quite as evil as the former document. It ran as follows: "The altar of the Blessed Virgin of Sorrows having been restored, this corpse has been found, which, on account of various conformities, is believed to be that of Fra Paolo, a man learned in all sciences." All that had been gained was that, whereas the old document was engrossed on parchment in letters of red, black, and gold, the new record was inscribed on ordinary paper with ordinary ink. The vexation of the baffled fathers breaks out in letters declaring that the patriotic member of the Council of Three is "little inclined to piety."; but the belief is expressed that, with a change at the coming election of the Council and "with dexterity and a little time," this new paper may be got out of the coffin and abolished.

Again Father Bertolli set at work, in an attempt to secure and make away with the corpse of Father Paul, and to suppress the new "honorable record" in his coffin.

But the zealous father had at last fallen on evil times: the Venetian government, vexed at his intrigues, banished him from Venice. Now came his great mistake: in order to make good his standing at Rome, Bertolli forged a letter and signature from the Secretary of the Supreme Tribunal at Venice. The arm of the dead Fra Paolo seemed to reach forth at once from his coffin to seize his enemy, for the law which asserted the right of the Republic to punish criminal priests, and which the monk-statesman had vindicated against Pope Paul V, was immediately put in force:—Bertolli was seized at Padua, brought to Venice, and condemned to five years' imprisonment "in one of the dark dungeons beneath the tribunal.'' Any one of the thousands who have visited those noisome cells must confess that the poor zealot was at last dealt with in full measure. Fortunately for him, after three years of this imprisonment he was pardoned, and thenceforth appears to have passed his time mainly in seeking recognition or remuneration from the Vatican authorities, who, as they did not wish to irritate the Venetian Republic farther, appear to have treated him coldly,—as coldly, indeed, as they had treated the Roman assassins after their failure to kill Fra Paolo a century before.

So disappears from the scene the great effort of the two Inquisitions and Bertolli, with all their innumerable cipher dispatches, reports of spying, assurances of success, clever forgery, and Jesuitry of various sorts, the only result having been to increase among thinking Venetians veneration and love for the memory of their ''Brother Paul.'' [1]

Fifty years more now rolled over the dead patriot's coffin, and in 1771 another campaign was begun against his memory. The former effort was directed to making the Venetians *forget* Father Paul; now the attempt was to make them *despise* him, and the monk Vaerini gathered together, in a pretended biography, masses of scurrility and endeavored to bury the memory of the great patriot beneath them. This was too much. The old Venetian spirit, which had so long lain dormant, now asserted itself: Vaerini was imprisoned and his book suppressed.

A quarter of a century later the Republic fell under the rule of Austria, and Austria's most time-honored agency in keeping down subject populations has always been the priesthood.[2] Again Father Paul's memory was

---

[1] The full account, with citations from the letters and documents, is given by Balzani, p. 22, *et seq.*, as above.

[2] See, for example, the "*Catechismo Politico*," promoted by King "Bomba"

virtually proscribed, and in 1803 another desperate attempt was made to cover him with infamy. In that year appeared a book entitled "The Secret History of the Life of Fra Paolo Sarpi," and it contained not only his pretended biography, but what claimed to be Sarpi's own letters and other documents showing him to be an adept in scoundrelism and hypocrisy. Its editor was the archpriest Ferrari of Mantua; but on the title-page appeared, as the name of its author, Fontanini, Archbishop of Ancira, a greatly respected prelate who had died nearly seventy years before, and there was also stamped, not only upon the preliminary, but upon the final page of the work, the approval of the Austrian government. To this was added a pious motto from St. Augustine, and the approval of Pius VII was distinctly implied, since the work was never placed upon the Index, and could not have been published at Venice, stamped as it was and registered with the privileges of the University, without the consent of the highest church authority.

The memory of Father Paul seemed likely now to be overwhelmed. There was no longer a Republic of Venice to guard the noble traditions of his life and service. The book was recommended and spread far and wide by preachers and confessors.

But at last came a day of judgment. The director of the Venetian archives discovered and had the courage to announce that the work was a pious fraud of the vilest type; that it was never written by Fontanini, but that it was simply made up out of the old scurrilous work of Vaerini, suppressed over thirty years before. As to the correspondence served up as supplementary to the biography, it was concocted from garbled letters

of Naples and Archbishop Apuzzo of Sorrento, but really written before their time by Leopardi, father of the philosopher of that name, as described in the article in this volume on Cavour.

already published.[1] Now came the inevitable reaction, and with it the inevitable increase of hatred for Austrian rule and the inevitable question, how, if the Pope is the infallible teacher of the world in all matters pertaining to faith and morals, could he virtually approve this book, and why did he not, by virtue of his inerrancy, detect the fraud and place its condemnation upon the Index. The only lasting effect of the book, then, was to revive the memory of Father Paul's great deeds and to arouse Venetian pride in them.

But the same sort of hatred which, in our own day, grudged and delayed due honors at the tombs of Copernicus and Galileo among Catholics, and of Humboldt among Protestants, was still bitter against the great Venetian scholar and statesman. It could not be forgotten that he had wrested from the Vatican the most terrible of its weapons, and, as a result of this remembrance, even rest in the grave had been for some years denied him. The Church of the Servites, where he had been first buried and reburied, having been demolished, a question had arisen as to the disposition of his remains. To bury them openly outside the old convent was certain to arouse a storm of ecclesiastical hostility, which would have dispersed and desecrated them: therefore it was that his admirers took them from place to place, sometimes concealing them in the wall of a church here, sometimes beneath a pavement there, and, for a time, keeping them in a wooden box at the Ducal Library. Six times were they thus buried and reburied, and the place where they rested became to most Venetians unknown. All that was left to remind Italy of him was the portrait in the Ducal Library, showing the great gash made by the Vati-

---

[1] For a full and fair statement of the researches which exposed this pious fraud, see Castellani, Prefect of the Library of St. Mark, preface to his *Lettere Inedite di F. P. S.*, p. xvii. For methods used in interpolating or modifying passages in Sarpi's writings, see Bianchi-Giovini, *Biografia di Sarpi*, 2d ed., Zurich, 1847, vol. ii, pp. 135 *et seq.*

can assassins. But this spoke ever more and more eloquently, and so it was that patriotic men throughout the
peninsula joined in proposing a suitable reburial. The
place chosen was the beautiful island of San Michele.
Thither had for many years been borne the remains of
eminent Venetians. There, too, in later days, have been
laid to rest many respected and beloved in other lands,
including our own. This movement met the usual clerical
hostility, and a long correspondence between the leaders
in it and the Papal Consul at Venice ensued. But patriotic pride was strong, and finally a compromise was
made: it was arranged that Sarpi should be buried and
honored at his burial as an eminent man of science, and
that no word should be spoken of his main services to the
Republic and to the world.

Soon, however, began another chapter of hatred.
There had come a Pope who added personal to official
hostility. Gregory XVI, who in his earlier days had been
abbot of the monastery of San Michele, was indignant that the friar who had thwarted the Vatican should
lie buried in the convent which he himself had formerly
ruled, and this feeling took shape, first, in violent
speeches at Rome, and next, in brutal acts at Venice.
The monks broke and removed the simple stone placed
over the remains of Father Paul, and, when it was replaced, they persisted in defacing and breaking it, and
were only prevented from dragging out his bones, dis-
honoring them, and casting them into the lagoon, by the
weight of the massive, strong, well-anchored sarcophagus,
which the wise foresight of his admirers had provided for
them. At three different visits to Venice, the present
writer sought the spot where they were laid, and in vain.
At the second of these visits, he found the Patriarch of
Venice, under whose rule various outrages upon Sarpi's
memory had been perpetrated, pontificating gorgeously
about the Grand Piazza; but at his next visit there had

come a change.   The monks had disappeared.   Their insults to the illustrious dead had been stopped by the
Kingdom of Italy, which had expelled them from their
convent, and there, near the vestibule and aisle of the
great church, were the tombs of Father Paul and of the
late Patriarch side by side; the great patriot's simple
gravestone was now allowed to rest unbroken.[1]

Better even than this was the reaction provoked by
these outbursts of ecclesiastical hatred.   It was felt, in
Venice, throughout Italy, and indeed throughout the
world, that the old decree for a monument should now
be made good.   The first steps were hesitating.   First,
a bust of Father Paul was placed among those of great
Venetians in the court of the Ducal Palace; but the inscription upon it was timid and double-tongued.   Another
bust was placed on the Pincian Hill at Rome, among
those of the most renowned sons of Italy; but this was
not enough: a suitable monument must be erected.   Yet
it was long delayed, timid men deprecating the hostility
of the Roman Court.

This hostility burst forth at various centres.   There
came the old "fool fury," with new spasms of hatred.
If the fanatics could not tear the great statesman's body
from its last resting-place, they might possibly tear respect for him from Italian hearts by reviving old calumnies and inventing new.

The great mass of these were contemptible, but two of
them, having been reiterated here and there even to this
hour, seem to deserve mention.

First of these was the charge that Fra Paolo was a
hypocrite; that he was at heart a Protestant; that he
sought to undermine the faith he practiced.

---

[1] The present writer was shown, by the late Lord Acton, and allowed
to read many of the original documents in the correspondence between the
Papal council and the Venetian authorities regarding Brother Paul's reburial.

Various proofs were alleged. One of these was his association with Sir Henry Wotton, Bishop Bedell, and other leading Protestants who visited Venice. Another was his correspondence with learned men throughout Europe without regard to creed. Most important of all was the testimony of Lebret, who in his *Historical Magazine* had reported that one Linckh, an agent of the German Elector Palatine, had reported that one Pessenti had told him that at Venice there existed a secret society plotting disruption from Rome, and that this society was mainly directed by Sarpi. Lebret also reported that Linckh claimed to have obtained additional proofs of this conspiracy in conversation with the British ambassador at Venice and indeed with Sarpi himself; that Sarpi had shown dislike of sundry Church dogmas, desire for reforms, and inclination to Protestant methods.

But, on the other hand, Diodati, a most devout Italian Protestant and noted Italian translator of the Bible, always lamented that Sarpi, despite his nobility of character and breadth of view, could not be induced to become a Protestant or to countenance any effort to establish Protestantism in Italy. Even more convincing was the testimony of all those nearest Sarpi at Venice: without exception they testified to his determination not to separate himself from the Mother Church.

Most convincing of all is the fact that, resting mainly on hearsay evidence of a very worthless kind, this charge contradicts the whole testimony of Sarpi's life. As a politician, in the highest sense, he was of all men least likely to give away to a foreign emissary thoughts and plans as perilous to his country as to himself.

As a statesman, he knew well that Protestantism in Venice would be an exotic; that the Venetian atmosphere would stifle it; that the attempt to introduce it would provoke civil strife, reaction, and massacre, thus giving to the Vatican and Spain the best excuse possible for intervention,—thus making his beloved country, to which he so fully and freely gave his life, their easy prey.

As a man, while he undoubtedly longed for large reforms in the Church, there were many reasons why Protestantism as it existed in his time must be repulsive to him. He was a thoughtful, quiet scholar—large-minded and tolerant. If he looked toward Great Britain he saw Protestant quarrels leading to unreason, riot, and murder. If he looked toward France he saw the nobler qualities of the reformed faith hopelessly alloyed with a bigotry often cruel and sometimes vile. If he looked toward the Netherlands he saw Calvinists and Arminians, Remonstrants and Contra-Remonstrants, anxious above all things to cut each other's throats, and he also saw his admired Grotius only escaping death first by imprisonment and next by exile. If he looked toward Germany he saw Lutherans and Calvinists thwarting, denouncing, and persecuting each other; he remembered how the deathbed of Melanchthon, whose memory as a scholar he must have cherished, had been embittered by Protestant heresy-hunters; he must have regarded with loathing the men then dominant in the German Protestant Church— whose ideal was Carpzov, with his boast that he had read the Bible through more than fifty times, had brought torture to perfection, and had sent witches to the scaffold by thousands. Sarpi must have seen what Thomasius, the leader in the second great reformation in Germany, saw and stated to a later generation—that under those who bore rule after the death of Luther "the wooden yoke of the Papacy had been changed into a yoke of iron." That feelings of this kind came over the great Venetian appears not only in his recorded conversations but in his letters.[1]

Naturally, then, does Daru declare the whole charge to rest on evidence which lacks authenticity and which, if

[1] See Klemperer Ch. Thomasius, chap. ii, p. 21.

authentic, would be inconclusive. Naturally also does Cantù, a devout Catholic prejudiced strongly against Sarpi, dismiss the whole charge with evident contempt: in a masterly summing up of the whole matter he shows that Sarpi's attitude was that of a Venetian Catholic patriot defending his country against the Vatican and Spain,—that he was a political genius far too shrewd to throw himself into a movement so fatal to his country.[1]

The second charge appears, at first sight, much more serious.

It is founded on a document ascribed to Fra Paolo giving general advice to the Venetian government as to the best methods of governing and perpetuating the Republic.[2]

The work shows insight and foresight. Passages in it are well worthy of the great statesman; and one of them, especially, seems to mirror his spirit. It reads: "Whenever the word of a sovereign power is given, it must be made good, no matter at what cost. Breaches of faith cost dear. How can a second promise be of use when the first has been broken?"

But the work, as a whole, is thoroughly Machiavellian. It advises transferring power, insensibly, by every sort of artifice, from the many to the few; undermining the influence of the people by creating divisions among them; weakening colonies by whatever form of inhumanity may serve best; weakening Italian States in which Venice had a foothold by bribing popular leaders, and, if necessary, exterminating them; and as to this extermination the au-

---

[1] For a full statement of the Linckh matter, see Daru, *Histoire de Venise*, Paris, 1819–21, t. iv, pp. 315 *et seq.*, and note. For Cantù's treatment of the subject, see his *Hérétiques d'Italie*, tome iv, pp. 149 *et seq.* For the testimony of Fra Paolo's letters, see especially that to Leschassier of Jan. 23, 1610.

[2] The title of this document is "Opinione del Padre Fra Paolo Servita . . . in qual modo debba governarsi la Republica Veneziana internamente e esternamente per aver perpetuo dominio," etc., etc. See Daru, as above, vol. v, pp. 574 *et seq.* There is an old English translation, 1693.

4

thor says, "Let poison do the work of the executioner. It is less odious and more serviceable."

If this work were authentic it should be remembered that it was written in the heat and passion of the struggle of Venice against Europe and especially of its hand to hand fight for life against the Vatican and Spain. It might thus be classed with sundry extravagant utterances of Luther in the fury of mortal combat. It should also be remembered that it appeared at a time when the ideas of Machiavelli were very generally adopted both in theory and practice, forming the basis of international rights,— the period before the *De jure belli ac pacis* of Grotius had brought into public law the nobler ideas and methods which have rendered diplomacy less scoundrelly and war less cruel.

But it is far from probable that Father Paul wrote the book. The better opinion seems to be that he did not. His authorship of the work is, indeed, loosely taken for granted by Daru, Cantù, and sundry others; but, on the other hand, so eminent an authority as Romanin dissents from this view, with the result that the latest Jesuit opponent of Sarpi does not insist upon the point. The treatise does not appear in the standard edition of Sarpi's works, and is to be found only at the end of a collection thrown together by a Venetian publisher, and even this publisher, in reprinting the collection five years later, speaks of it as "falsely attributed to Fra Paolo." Sundry special editions of it have been issued from time to time, among them one in English, but none of them in the slightest degree authoritative. To all this should be added the fact that the Doge Marco Foscarini and the biographer Griselini denied strongly Sarpi's authorship of any such work. Professor Emmanuel Cicogna, an authority of the highest rank, states cogently the reasons for believing it to be a forgery, and gives the name of one Casale as the probable forger. Bianchi-Giovini points out a number of peculiarities, in the arrangement and style of the work, differing totally from those of Fra Paolo. Castellani, head of the City Library at Venice, one of the foremost living authorities regarding Venetian matters, in a contribution to his official work on Venetian history, the *Lettere Inedite di Sarpi,* puts the "Advice" aside as utterly discredited, and attributes Cantù's opinion of it to carelessness.

It dates from a time when nothing was more common than forging documents and interpolating false passages in authentic documents, in order to aid special interests or movements. Cantù himself on this ground throws doubt upon another publication ascribed much more generally, and with much more reason, to Fra Paolo.[1]

So much for these two specific charges. But, beside these, writers holding a brief for Ultramontane ideas have repeatedly uttered vague calumnies upon his general character, calling him a "bad priest" who "hated the Vatican because he had not been made a Bishop."[2]

That his character was infinitely above unworthy motives is testified by all who knew him best, by the evidently noble aim of his works, by the whole tenor of his life. They who slander him really slander the Church which gave him his environment, and also slander such great figures in the history of the Church as the men who at one time or another rejoiced in his acquaintance or companionship or friendship:—churchmen like St. Charles Borromeo and Bellarmine; statesmen like

---

[1] For various facts controverting the theory that Sarpi wrote the book, see Bianchi-Giovini, Florentine edition of 1849, vol. i, pp. 425 *et seq.* Also, article in Westminster Review, vol. xxix, p. 146. For the testimony of Cicogna, see his *Iscrizioni Veneziane,* vol. iii. For Cantù, see his *Hérétiques,* as above, vol. iv, p. 130. For Romanin, see his *Storia Documentata,* and, for the recent view referred to, see the Jesuit Father T. J. Campbell, in *The Messenger* for March, 1904.

[2] The main source of these slanders—the central "mud volcano," as Carlyle would have called it—seems to have been in recent years the main Jesuit organ at Rome: the *Osservatore Romano.*

Leonardo Donato and Morosini; men of science like Galileo, Acquapendente, and Battista Porta; and, besides these Italians, foreigners of the highest character in all these fields, like Wotton, Bedell, and Gilbert in England, Mornay and Asselineau in France, and many others of similar character throughout Europe.

Despite, then, all calumnies, hysterics, and pressure—largely, indeed, on account of them—the patriotic movement under the new Italian monarchy now became irresistible. It swept Italy; but it was much more than a mere wave of popular sentiment. It was the result of deep feeling based upon patriotism and love of humanity: the same feeling which erected, despite similar opposition, the splendid statue to Giordano Bruno in the Campo dei Fiori at Rome, on the spot where he had been burned, and which adorned it with the medallions of eight other martyrs to ecclesiastical hatred.

So it came that in 1892, two hundred and seventy years after it had been decreed, there rose a statue—to Paolo Sarpi—on the Piazza Santa Fosca at Venice, where he had been left for dead by the Roman assassins. There it stands, noble and serene: a monument of patriotism and right reason, a worthy tribute to one who, among intellectual prostitutes and solemnly constituted impostors, stood forth as a true man, the greatest of his time—one of the greatest of all times—an honor to Venice, to Italy, to the Church Universal, and to Humanity.

GROTIUS

GROTIUS

I

OF all tyrannies of unreason in the modern world, one holds a supremely evil preëminence. It covered the period from the middle of the sixteenth century to the middle of the seventeenth, and throughout those hundred years was waged a war of hatreds,—racial, religious, national, and personal;—of ambitions, ecclesiastical and civil;—of aspirations, patriotic and selfish;—of efforts, noble and vile. During all those weary generations Europe became one broad battlefield,—drenched in human blood and lighted from innumerable scaffolds.

In this confused struggle great men appeared—heroes and martyrs, ruffians and scoundrels: all was anarchic. The dominant international gospel was that of Machiavelli.

Into the very midst of all this welter of evil, at a point in time to all appearance hopeless, at a point in space apparently defenseless, in a nation of which every man, woman, and child was under sentence of death from its sovereign, was born a man who wrought as no other has ever done for a redemption of civilization from the main cause of all that misery; who thought out for Europe the precepts of right reason in international law; who made them heard; who gave a noble change to the course of human affairs; whose thoughts, reasonings, suggestions, and appeals produced an environment in which came an evolution of humanity that still continues.

Huig de Groot, afterward known to the world as Hugo Grotius, was born at Delft in Holland on Easter day of

1583. It was at the crisis of the struggle between Spain and the Netherlands. That struggle had already continued for twenty years, and just after the close of his first year, in the very town where he was lying in his cradle, came its most fearful event, that which maddened both sides—the assassination of William of Orange, nominally by Balthazar Gerard, really by Philip II of Spain.

It was, indeed, a fearful period. From Spain, fifteen years before his birth, the Holy Inquisition had sent forth, with the solemn sanction of Philip II, the edict which condemned all the inhabitants of the Netherlands to death as heretics. In France, eleven years before his birth, the Massacre of St. Bartholomew had stimulated religious wars, interspersed with new massacres, the sacking of towns, the assassination of rulers and leaders. Less than seven years before his birth this French example had been followed in the great massacre of Antwerp, which filled his country with horror. In Italy a succession of pontiffs and princes, moved sometimes by fanaticism, but generally by greed, were carrying out their plans with fire and slaughter. In Great Britain Elizabeth was in her last days—but still great, gifted, and cruel. Throughout Germany were threatenings of a storm worse than any which had preceded it: for, though the religious Peace of Augsburg in 1555 had established toleration, it was a toleration which, being based upon the whims of individual rulers, settled nothing; all Europe was darkened by the shadow of the great coming calamity, the Thirty Years' War.

The child had from his birth the best of all heritages. For he came of a good, pure, sound ancestry. Among his great-grandfathers were the De Cornets,—driven from France by religious persecution—among those Huguenots who proved of such immense value to every country which received them. Among his immediate ancestors was a line of state servants brave and true. His father was four times Burgomaster of Delft, one of the Curators of the University of Leyden, and a Councilor of State.

But barely had the child begun to lisp when a great danger beset him—his precocity. All his powers, moral and intellectual, seemed developed preternaturally. In his tenth year his Latin verses won the applause of scholars; in his eleventh year poets addressed him as a second Erasmus; at twelve years he was admitted to the University of Leyden. The chances seemed that he would bloom out as a mere prodigy—an insufferable prig; then fade, and never be heard of more.

But his parents seem to have been more sensible than is usual in such cases: they sent him early from home and placed him among men to whom he was sure to look up with reverence. At the University he fell under the influence of Joseph Justus Scaliger. The genius of the youth bridged the chasm of years which separated him from the renowned scholar, and they became intimate friends.

Two years after his entrance at the University he threw learned Europe into astonishment by a work which would not have been unworthy of a veteran in the republic of letters—a revision of the old encyclopædia of Martianus Capella, made up of "The Marriage of Mercury with Philology" and "The Seven Treatises on the Liberal Arts." This labor was great. The subjects treated by Capella covered the whole range of education, and to each the young scholar gave most thorough study, finding what every ancient author had thought upon them.

In rapid succession he also published a translation of Simon Stevin on Navigation, and an edition of Aratus on Astronomy, which gave the young man repute as a mathematician; and at the same time he continued writing Latin verses which increased his fame as a classical scholar and poet,—as scholarship and poetry were then understood.

At the age of fifteen, after the fashion of the period, he held public disputes in mathematics, philosophy, and jurisprudence. His fame spread far and wide. He was recognized as the wonder of the University.

In 1598, the Netherlands sent an embassy to King Henry IV of France. It meant much, for it seemed to bear the fortunes of the Republic. Hitherto France had sheltered the Netherlands by her own war with Spain, but now there was talk throughout Europe of peace between the two great powers, and, if this peace were not prevented, or if a treaty were not most skillfully made, the Netherlands might awake some morning to find themselves exposed to the whole might of Philip II,—to his hatred of their heresy and to his vengeance for their rebellion. To meet this emergency the Dutch Republic sent to Paris the Admiral of Zealand, Justin of Nassau, and John van Barneveld, its greatest statesman; with these went Grotius as an *attaché*.

He now incurred a new risk. His reputation had reached France. Men of high position crowded about him, and Henry IV with his own hand hung his portrait upon the youth's neck; but the moral powers of Grotius were as fully developed as his intellectual gifts: his sober judgment shielded him from flattery; all this distinction, instead of spoiling, stimulated him; he did not loiter among flatterers, but returned to Holland and again took up his work as a scholar.

And he avoided another danger as serious as his precocity had been. He steered clear of the quicksands of useless scholarship, which had engulfed so many strong men of his time. The zeal of learned men in that period was largely given to knowing things not worth knowing, to discussing things not worth discussing, to proving things not worth proving. Grotius seemed plunging on, with all sails set, into these quicksands; but again his good sense and sober judgment saved him: he decided to bring himself into the current of active life flowing through his land and time, and with this purpose he gave himself to the broad and thorough study of jurisprudence.

He was only in his seventeenth year when he was called to plead his first case. It gained him much credit. Other successes rapidly followed and he was soon made Advocate General of the Treasury for the Provinces of Holland and Zealand.

A new danger now beset him,—the danger of becoming simply a venal pleader, a creature who grinds out arguments on this or that side, for this or that client:—a mere legal beast of prey. Fortunately for himself and for the world he took a higher view of his life-work: his determination clearly was to make himself a thoroughly equipped jurist, and then, as he rose more and more in his profession, to use his powers for the good of his country and of mankind.

But he made no effort to attract notice, and one striking evidence of his reserve and modesty was discovered only after more than two centuries, when, in 1868, there was found, in a bookshop at The Hague, an old manuscript never before published, but written by Grotius in 1604, its title being *De jure prædæ*. In this manuscript, prepared during his twenty-second year, were found not merely the germs but, in large measure, the bloom of many ideas and trains of thought which gave to his later works such vast value.

He had evidently felt that his thought on these great subjects was not sufficiently mature; but five years later, in 1609, when a conflict of interests between the Netherlands and Portugal seemed to demand it, he developed a chapter of this unpublished work into his first book of world-wide fame: the *Mare Liberum*. It was a calm, powerful argument against one of the most monstrously absurd claims ever put forth: a claim which at that time clouded the title of humanity to our planet. This was nothing less than the pretense of dominion over the high seas insisted upon by various nations,—a claim which had in days gone by been of some use against piracy, but which had finally become fruitful in wrong. The government which he nominally had in view was Portugal, but there doubtless lay deep in his thought also the claim of England. Her main contention was that the narrow seas—all the seas lying about Great Britain, even up to the shores of Norway, of Holland, and of France—were her own; that she was alone entitled to fish in them or freely navigate them; that other nations could do so only by her permission; that her ships in these waters were entitled to lord it over all other ships; that, as the mistress of these seas, her flag was to be saluted by the vessels of all other powers; and, beside all this, she made a vague claim to the Bay of Biscay and to the ocean north of Scotland.

There was strong warrant for pretensions of this sort. As far back as 1493, Pope Alexander VI had settled disputes between Spain and Portugal arising out of their rivalry in the Orient and the Occident by drawing a line from pole to pole one hundred leagues west of the Azores, giving all west of it to the Spanish, all east of it to the Portuguese. Both these nations attempted more or less persistently to exercise the sway thus given over the oceans as well as over the continent. The Portuguese forbade under heavy penalties any person, whether native or alien, to pass through the waters off the African and Brazilian coasts without special permission; the Spanish were hardly less severe toward those who without leave approached their dependencies. But, though the realization of the earth's rotundity renewed the old difficulty, and Spain and Portugal discovered that the Papal decision was futile, since all their new dominions could be approached both from the east and the west, both nations continued to maintain, as best they could, their sovereignty over the vast oceans.

Other nations followed these examples. France asserted proprietary rights in the seas off her coasts. Denmark claimed the ocean between Norway and Iceland, and, with Sweden, she insisted on the ownership of the Baltic.[1] Venice, upon her mudbanks at the northwestern corner of the Adriatic, insisted upon a similar control over that open sea—the annual marriage of the Doge with the Adriatic being the symbol of this dominion. Genoa and Pisa put in similar claims on the west side of Italy. Against all these assertions Grotius published to the world a demonstration that no such rights could exist.

His whole argument was mainly a development of two postulates. The first of these was that the right of nations to communicate with one another had been universally recognized; that it was based on a fundamental law of humanity; that, the liberty of the sea being necessary to enable nations to communicate with one another, it could not be taken away by any power whatever. The second was that every attempt to make an ocean highway a monopoly of any single nation is forbidden by the immensity of the sea, its lack of stability, its want of fixed limits. This argument in places seemed thin. The book, after the custom of the time, was filled with an array—far more than sufficient—of learned citations; but its most significant feature—that which went to make it the herald of a new epoch—was that it took its stand upon the inalienable rights of mankind,—that it mainly deduced these rights neither from revelation nor from national enactments, but from natural law as ascertained by human reason.

This book was nominally leveled at the pretensions of

---

[1] See Hall: *International Law*, Part II, Chapter 2, § 40.

Spain and Portugal, but the leading spirits in England
soon saw its bearing, and although Queen Elizabeth,
when the Spanish demanded tribute of Sir Francis Drake
in the ocean adjacent to their dominions, had made an
answer appealing to the natural rights of all men upon
the high seas, all this was conveniently forgotten, and
King James I, the crowned pedant of Great Britain, immediately gave orders to his ambassador in Holland to
take measures against the young publicist.

These measures having proved futile, John Selden, a
great legal authority in England, a man well fitted for
the task, was led to write a reply to Grotius. For nine
years he busied himself in bringing his authorities together; and in 1618 the book was ready, but it was not
then published. It was evidently feared that certain
concessions in it might thwart the interests of England
in sundry quarters, so that it did not see the light until
1635, and then on account of the direct necessities of
England in her trouble with the Netherlands.

In his *Mare Clausum* Selden began, as was then usual,
with the Bible. In order to refute Grotius' idea that the
ocean cannot be made the property of any one nation he
cites the twenty-eighth verse of the first chapter of Genesis, which declares that God said to Adam, "Have dominion over the fish of the sea." "Now," continues
Selden, "the fish are the living revenue,—the usufruct of
the sea. If these be given, the property itself may be
considered as given. Again God said to Noah and his
descendants, 'Your fear shall be upon the fish of the sea'
(Genesis ix. 2)." Selden in like manner laid stress upon
the declaration of the Almighty to the Israelites, "Thy
borders are in the midst of the sea," and he argued that
of course dominion was given them within these borders,
and therefore that this dominion extended over the ocean.
He even pressed into his service the poetry of Isaiah,
who, as he says, called Tyre "the might of the seas," and

Selden argues that "might," in this case, implies possession. He declares that the Red Sea is called Edom, which means red, simply because it belonged to the descendants of Esau.

With the same pedantic fullness Selden ransacked the Talmud, the writers of classical antiquity, the records of mythology, theology, and philology. Neptune, god of the seas, he insists, is only a king who really existed and had the right to rule the sea; stress is laid on the binding of the Hellespont by Xerxes; and following these examples are a multitude of others from modern history equally cogent.

Having thus gone through history, sacred and profane, to show that divine and human authority are on the side of political sovereignty over the seas, he turns to logic, and produces a series of arguments still more extraordinary. He argues that if nations can own land they can own water; that if they can own a little water they can own much; that it is as conformable to reason for a nation to control an ocean as a river. All this was enforced with whole regiments of categories and syllogisms.

Such was the work of a dictator of English learning, a man of great powers of thought, of real independence, of true nobility of character. His only defect was the pedantry which was the bane of his time and from which Grotius, though not wholly free, did so much to emancipate the world.

The book of Selden was hailed in England as the great work of the age; its doctrines determined English theory and practice as long as England thought it wise to apply them. The world was made to feel them far into the nineteenth century. The treaty attempted by Mr. King, the American Minister to London in 1803, failed because England would not give up the right to impress seamen from foreign ships upon the high seas; and about the same period she applied her doctrine regarding the control of the narrow seas to the control of the broad seas, up to the very shores of America. Even within the shallow waters of Long Island Sound she seized an American vessel, attempted to take therefrom the French Minister to the American Government, and, having failed to take him, seized his papers. Still later, an English man-of-war, in time of profound peace, attacked an American frigate almost within sight of the American coast, took from her four seamen, hanged one of them as a deserter, and forced the other three into the British service.

But the doctrines of Grotius made their way. Spain, Portugal, Sweden, Denmark, Venice, Genoa, Pisa, and, last of all, Great Britain, were forced to yield by the combined opinion of the whole world.[1]

The *Mare Liberum* was followed by works from Grotius' pen in many fields, among the most important being those upon the history of his own country; and he received the title of Public Historiographer. About the same time he reached the first rank in his profession and was made Attorney General of the Province of Holland, Councilor and Pensionary of Rotterdam, with the right of sitting not only in the provincial legislature of Holland, but also in the States General of the United Provinces. He was also sent as one of a commission to England charged to watch over the maritime rights of his country. James I, who had formerly tried to crush him, now flattered him.

On his return in 1616 greater honors awaited him. He was made Grand Pensionary of Holland and West Fries-

---

[1] For this doctrine of dominion over the sea, see Wheaton, *Histoire du Progrès du Droit des Gens*, première période, par. 17, 18; Woolsey, *Introduction to the Study of International Law*, chap. ii; also Hall, *International Law*, pp. 146, *et seq.* For curious applications of the old doctrine and reasons for them, see Walker, *Science of International Law*, chap. v. As to the Chesapeake outrage, see H. Adams, *History of the United States*, vol. ii, chap. i; also Schouler's *History of the United States*, vol. ii, pp. 163, *et seq.*

land. But this culmination of civic honors in his own country proved to be a beginning of calamity.

Nothing is more wretched in the history of Europe in the period which followed the Reformation than the sectarian quarrels which cursed every country. No theological question seemed too slight a cause for bitter hatred and even for civil war. Germany, England, France, were convulsed with squabbles between various sects and factions, about questions really contemptible. In each of these countries Protestants were not only in a life and death struggle with Catholics, but were seeking to exterminate one another. The Netherlands were no exception to the rule. A professor at the University of Leyden, Arminius, happening to take a different side on the eternal question of fate and free will, his colleague Gomarus became vitriolic; his disciples caught the spirit of their master, and soon the Reformed Church in Holland was split into two hostile sects,—each heaping syllogisms and epithets on the other,—Arminius preaching free will, Gomarus predestination.

The debate went on from bad to worse; it could hardly be pretended that salvation was dependent upon holding the right metaphysical theory upon this question, and Arminius had the rashness to urge toleration; but his foes found this idea yet deadlier. Gomarus declared that Arminius was a supporter of the Roman Catholic Church, and that his doctrine led to skepticism and infidelity. It was difficult for reasoning men to see how the same man could be a Roman Catholic and an infidel, but the vast majority did not reason,—they only believed. Heavy words were hurled: "supralapsarian," "infralapsarian" and the like; and these crushed out the common sense of the populace. Gomarus won the victory.

The majority of the pulpits reiterated the charges or flung back the epithets—until finally the controversy be-

5

came a disease, a disease which speedily took an acute form, breaking out here and there into mob murders. It seemed to warrant fully the declaration of Bishop Butler as to a "possible insanity of states."

In this condition of things, the Arminians, led by Uytenbogaert, a theologian at The Hague, drew up in 1610 a protest stating fully their principles. It was known as the "Remonstrance," and from this the Arminians received their party name of Remonstrants. Upon this the followers of Gomarus, devoted to the doctrine of predestination, drew up a vigorous rejoinder, and so obtained their party name of Contra-Remonstrants. Such mouth-filling party names increased mob violence rapidly. The States General, mainly a body of educated, thoughtful men, seeing the necessity of calming the country, now issued an Edict of Pacification enjoining tolerance and forbearance, and largely permeated by the just and kindly ideas of Grotius.

The Edict of Pacification was supported by one of the most eloquent appeals ever composed,—it came not only from Grotius' head, but from his heart. But all this was outclamored by the Gomarist clergy. They cited from Scripture the words, "Ye must obey God rather than man," by which they simply meant, "Ye are to accept our theory as God's command." This carried the great majority of the population.

With this religious question was complicated a political struggle. The Stadtholder and Captain-General of the United Provinces was Prince Maurice of Orange,—the second son of the murdered William the Silent. He had great qualities, military and administrative, but he had also an evident purpose to make himself virtually a monarch. We need not suppose him merely selfish in this matter; there was in him a mixture of motives. He doubtless knew that what was needed to enable the Netherlands to hold their own against Spain, their religious foe, France, their political foe, and England, their commercial foe, was a strong, concentrated government, and of this he was the natural head. He had encountered much opposition and at the very time when the action of all the provinces under his leadership was the first thing needful.

On the other hand, a small body of enlightened but patriotic men of great influence loved republican institutions and believed in them, feared the monarchical trend, dreaded a dictatorship, and struggled against every effort of the prince which tended toward it. In this they had some success, and in 1609, fearing that the continuance of war and the increasing dependence of the Provinces upon Maurice would result in his dictatorship, they brought about with Spain the famous Truce of Twelve Years. This led to bitter hatred between Maurice, the Stadtholder, on one side, and the leaders of republican tendency on the other. Foremost among these latter was John of Barneveld, a statesman renowned throughout Europe, his whole life full of high service to his country, his religious views tolerant,—and closely attached to him was Grotius.

In this wretched struggle between Calvinism and Arminianism, Maurice saw his opportunity. Had he been a greater genius or of a nobler nature, he might have called Grotius to his aid and fused both these elements into one strong national force. Such a fusion was made most happily when in England the Church was united by combining "a Catholic ritual, Calvinistic articles, and an Arminian clergy," and at a much later period a similar happy compromise was made when Frederick William III of Prussia stood by the more tolerant thinkers and brought together Calvinists and Lutherans into a single body, on whose banner was inscribed the shibboleth "Evangelical." But Maurice did not take so large a view. He saw that the Gomarists had the populace on their side. He cared nothing for their doctrines as such; there is evidence that he did not even understand them; but they were the predominant force, and he took pains to attend their churches, tied his cause to theirs, became the firm ally of fanatical peasants and their clerical managers against the Edict of Pacification. Thus was he able to wield an overwhelming power against Barneveld, Grotius, and their compeers.[1]

The course of Maurice was simple. By virtue of his authority as Stadtholder he had merely to forbid obedience to the orders of Barneveld, Grotius, and others in their respective provinces, and when these men attempted to enforce their authority it was easy to raise the fanatical Calvinists in revolt.

The efforts of Grotius for peace now became heroic. At the head of a deputation of the States of Holland he publicly addressed the authorities of Amsterdam in favor of toleration. He showed that the highest authorities agreed that either of the two theological opinions might be held without danger of perdition; that the earlier reformers had tolerated both opinions. He besought his countrymen most earnestly and eloquently, in view of the political danger to the country and of the religious danger to Protestantism, to allow toleration and peace. All in vain. On the great mass of his countrymen the modern idea of toleration had not even dawned. He and his associates were dismissed with contempt, and his address was suppressed by force.

Weary nigh unto death, he was besought by his family and friends to give up the struggle. But he would not. He would make another exertion, and he drew up a new formula of peace to be signed by both parties. It contained nothing contrary to Calvinism; it proposed to leave to a council the matters at issue, and in the mean-

---

[1] Motley gives a curious story illustrating the ignorance of Maurice regarding the doctrines he supported.

time pledged all to peace. This, too, was in vain. The fanatics would have none of it, and Maurice stood by them.

Matters were soon beyond any peaceable solution. Maurice, with the Gomarists, took such measures that Barneveld, Grotius, and their associates were obliged to summon the Provinces to resist. But resistance was futile. Maurice was a successful soldier with a great name, and behind him were strong currents of patriotism and an overwhelming tide of fanaticism. In August, 1618, he was able to send Barneveld and Grotius to prison. Everything favored Maurice: the death of his elder brother during these events gave him the crowning honor, and he became the head of his family,—Prince of Orange.

And now was set in motion a prodigious piece of machinery,—the Synod of Dort. It embraced the leading theologians of Holland, with delegates from various parts of Protestant Europe. Their weary discussions dragged along through the entire following winter. The result was a foregone conclusion. As in nearly all the greater councils of the Church, Catholic or Protestant, its proceedings were determined by intimidation and intrigue rather than by discussion. Episcopius and the Arminians at the Synod of Dort had as little chance as the opponents of Athanasius at the Council of Nice; or as the Bishop of Braga at the Council of Trent; or as Archbishop Kenrick and Bishop Strossmayer at the Council of the Vatican. They were simply out-intrigued, out-clamored, and voted down. The whole decision was in accordance with the direction of Maurice and the Gomarists. It was now declared that the Remonstrants must submit to the Synod; that to oppose the Synod was to rebel against the Holy Spirit; that if they persisted in disobedience they would incur not only the censures of the Church, but punishment from the State. Against this the Arminians tried to make a stand, and solemnly appealed to their brethren; but at last, in April, 1619, the Synod declared them guilty of pestilent errors and corrupters of the true faith, their doctrines damnable, and deprived Episcopius, with his associates, of their positions. This being accomplished, Barneveld and Grotius were dealt with. The court had been assembled in February. It was composed largely of the enemies of the accused; the proceedings lingered until the Synod of Dort had made its main decision and denunciation. Barneveld was sentenced to death on the 12th of May, 1619, and was executed on the day following, bearing himself nobly on the scaffold, and neither asking, nor allowing any of his family or friends to ask, pardon from Maurice.

A few days later Grotius was sentenced to imprisonment for life, and transferred to the castle of Loevestein. Vigorous measures ensued against lesser offenders; such Arminian ministers as could be seized were torn from their pulpits, stripped of their property, banished, or imprisoned. From all parts of the Netherlands they were driven to neighboring countries, Catholic and Protestant. It was a story like that of the Puritans driven from England, the Huguenots from France, the Moriscoes from Spain, the Protestants from Salzburg, the Finlanders and Jews from Russia in our day;—the same old story,— unreason, bigotry, party passion, individual ambition, all masquerading as "saving faith."

All this work having been set in motion, on the 29th of May, 1619, the Synod of Dort was closed.

The imprisonment of Grotius was not the worst that now befell him. His enemies sought to rob him, not only of his liberty, but of his honor. His request to present his defense to Prince Maurice, as he truly says, "was afterward misinterpreted as if I had had wonderful things to reveal.'' The fact that he thought of offering his services as a councilor to Prince Maurice will not prejudice against him any American who remembers how statesmen in our own country like Daniel Webster and William Henry Seward sought most patriotically to redeem administrations which they may have disliked for the sake of principles which they held dear. Not only was Grotius refused, during the weary months of trial, any opportunity to draw up a defense in writing, but when it was granted he was allowed only a single sheet of paper and four hours of time. After the manner of that period in treason trials, he was not permitted to summon counsel or to consult documents; worst of all, the utterances of Barneveld were evidently presented to him in a false light, so that, in repelling charges against himself, Grotius was made to appear as if attacking his friend. Thus were set in motion the calumnies which have been reëchoed from that day to this, and to which even our eminent American historian of the Dutch Republic has given an attention which they do not deserve. Looking over the whole matter dispassionately, the conclusion seems irresistible that Grotius, in prison, was deceived, and his utterances misinterpreted. Nothing else in his life warrants the belief that he could have been for a moment disloyal to Barneveld. That Groen van Prinsterer repeats these charges in our day adds nothing to their strength. No one can read the attack made by this modern enemy of Arminianism and of Grotius without seeing at once that its charges are vitiated by its sectarian bitterness. Grotius' attitude in those most trying hours was not that of a determined, uncompromising ruler of men, like Barneveld, but that of a scholarly statesman, honest and straightforward, seeking to serve his country. He may have been for a moment deceived by the intriguers who sought to separate him from his friend, but his conduct, taken as a whole, was that of a patriot and a true man.[1]

Shut up in the castle of Loevestein, during nearly two years Grotius found consolation in his studies. At the end of that time he was rescued by a stratagem. His wife, who had shown a most touching devotion to him from first to last, who had shared his captivity, and done all in her power to make it tolerable, made friends with the wife of the jailer and others who might be of use, smuggled her husband into a case supposed to contain borrowed books, and thus had him conveyed from the fortress. After several hairbreadth escapes the box was carried to the house of a friend, and Grotius, escaping from it, fled in the disguise of a brick-layer into France. One thing in his departure did him special honor. This was his letter to the authorities of the Netherlands declaring that no person had been bribed to aid him, that he himself was not guilty of any crime against his country, and that nothing that had taken place had diminished his love for it.

Arriving in France, he was welcomed on all sides as a great European scholar. Louis XIII settled upon him a pension, which, unfortunately, was small and rarely paid; luckily friends were found to give him shelter, and he continued his devotion to his studies. Among other treatises which attracted general notice he wrote a defense of his course,—straightforward, with no bitterness; various works calculated to diminish intolerance; and, in 1622, at the Château of Balagny, he began giving final shape to the great work of his life, the *De Jure Belli ac Pacis*, and for three years it occupied his best thought.

Few more inspiring things have been seen in human

---

[1] As regards the charge that Grotius was disloyal to Barneveld, see Motley, *John of Barneveld*, vol. ii, pp. 396, *et seq.;* and for echoes of the old attacks, resentful and bitter, see Groen van Prinsterer, *Maurice et Barnevelt*, Utrecht, 1876, pp. ccv, *et seq.*

history. He had apparently every reason for yielding to pessimism, for hating his country, and for despising his race. He might have given his life to satirizing his enemies and to scolding at human folly: he did nothing of the sort, but worked on, day and night, to bestow upon mankind one of the most precious blessings it has ever received.

The great work of Grotius was published in 1625. Its reception must have disappointed him; for, while thoughtful and earnest men in various parts of Europe showed their appreciation of it at once, the mass of men were indifferent, and their religious leaders, as a rule, hostile. The condemnation of it at Rome, the fact that it was placed upon the Index of works which Catholics were forbidden to read, and that this Index bore the sanction of a Papal bull, was at first a great barrier. So, too, the distrust felt by the leaders of the Protestant Church checked its progress. But more and more it made its way. In every nation were jurists and statesmen who, while they acquiesced nominally in the teachings of the church in which they had happened to be born, did some thinking on their own account; and in the minds of such the germs of the better system planted by Grotius took root. Many, too, whose belief was in accordance with the dominant ecclesiastical ideas, had hearts better than their heads, and on those the eloquence of Grotius wrought with power. In various universities, his doctrines began to be commented upon and taught, and notably at Heidelberg, where Pufendorf became Grotius' first great apostle. His ideas found their way into current discussion, into systems of law, into treaties; and, as generations rolled by, the world began to find itself, it hardly knew how, less and less cruel, until men looked back upon war as practiced in his time as upon a hideous dream,—doubtless much as men in future generations will look back upon the wars of our time.

Most notable among those who were immediately influenced by Grotius' work were his two foremost contemporaries, one a Protestant and the other a Catholic.

First of these was Gustavus Adolphus. He was by far
the greatest and bravest leader of his time. Grotius'
work became his favorite study; he kept it by his bedside; it was found in his tent after his death on the field
of Lützen. Despite the atrocities of the opposing commanders, he constantly stood for mercy and began on a
large scale the better conduct of modern war: his most
impassioned speeches were made to his soldiers in dis-
suading them from cruelty or in rebuking them for it.

And there was another great example. Three years
after the appearance of Grotius' book, Cardinal Richelieu, who then governed France in the name of Louis
XIII, took La Rochelle. It was the stronghold of French
Protestantism; it had resisted as few fortified places have
ever resisted; the Protestants gathered there had been
guilty of high treason in its worst degrees: they had
called in England to their aid, they had rebelled so madly
that they were outside the pale of mercy, the greater part
of the city population had been destroyed, and among
those who were left there had been recourse to canni-
balism.

The whole civilized world expected to see a frightful
example made; and in view of the ferocious instructions
which at the beginning of the wars thus ended had been
given by Pius V and other pontiffs, in view of the savage
practice general throughout Europe, and above all that of
Philip II and Alva in the Netherlands and of Tilly in
Germany, there was every reason to expect a massacre
of the inhabitants with the plunder and destruction of the
city. All Europe held its breath in anticipation of cruelties befitting the long and bitter rebellion of the Huguenots against their sovereigns in Church and State.

Richelieu was a devoted believer in the dogmas and

authority of the Church—he had begun his literary life by polemics against Protestantism, and his first act after his great victory as a general, was, as a bishop, to celebrate a high mass of thanksgiving. He had received his education in an atmosphere of cruel intolerance of which we can now hardly dream. It was the period when the teachings of the sainted Pope Pius V were in all their vigor,—the teachings of the pontiff who wrote letters to Catherine de Medici, to Charles IX, to the Duke of Anjou, and to other leaders in France, commanding them not merely to persecute, but to massacre, forbidding them to spare a single Huguenot prisoner, citing to King Charles the example of King Saul, and holding up to the most Christian king, as the punishment he would merit and receive from the Almighty if he showed mercy to the Huguenots, the punishment received by that Jewish king for showing mercy to the enemies of Israel. Still dominant were the teachings of Gregory XIII, who had celebrated the Massacre of St. Bartholomew with thanksgiving at Rome, commemorated it in magnificent pictures at the Vatican, and struck a medal in its honor for circulation throughout Europe. Not only did the early education and environment of Richelieu seem to presage a fearful treatment of La Rochelle, but his own conduct in other matters seemed to insure it. As a rule, toward those guilty of treason he was ever merciless, and for crimes against public order he sent members of the highest families in France to the scaffold.[1]

But, to the amazement of the world and to the intense disgust of the fanatics who thirsted for vengeance, Richelieu now did none of the terrible things expected of him.

[1] For the full text of the letters of St. Pius V, commanding massacre and forbidding mercy, see De Potter, *Lettres de St. Pie V*, Paris, 1830. Those especially citing the punishment of King Saul for his mercy to the Amalekites were addressed to King Charles and Catherine de Medici (nos. xii, xiii). For copious citations, see Laurent, *Hist. du Droit des Gens*, tome x.

He indeed swept away a mass of dangerous party privileges which the Calvinistic sect had enjoyed, but even to the most bitter of the Huguenots he was merciful. He allowed no massacre, no destruction, no plunder. After he had summoned into his presence Guiton, the Huguenot mayor of the city, who had stood out against him so long and so desperately, he treated him with respect and inflicted upon him merely a short banishment. The Huguenots, though broken as a party, were not even excluded from civil office or debarred from the exercise of their religion; everywhere was lenity. The fanatics of his own church bestowed on him such names as "Cardinal of Satan," "Pope of the Atheists."

How was it that in this case Richelieu showed a toleration and mercy so at variance with everything in his previous career? All the circumstances of the case enforce the conviction that, during the three years between the publication of Grotius' book and the taking of La Rochelle, the cardinal had been influenced by it. It had arrested the attention of thinking men in all parts of Europe, and must have been known to the foremost statesman of France, living in the very city where it was published. Throughout his whole career, Richelieu showed an especial respect for scholars and scholarly work, as his monument in the Sorbonne bears witness to this day. At a later period, even when there was much official friction between the two statesmen, Richelieu freed Grotius' writings from the French censorship, and declared him one of the three great scholars of his time. Even if the cardinal knew the book merely as Nicholas II of Russia knew the epoch-making work of Jean de Bloch against war,—the book which in our own days led that czar to call the Peace Conferences of The Hague,—that is, merely by report, by quotations, by discussions, he could not fail to have grasped its main purport. There seems, indeed, no other way to account for the fact that from one of the most devoted of ecclesiastics and most merciless of statesmen there came, during this vast temptation to cruelty, so benign a treatment of subjugated heretics and rebels.

But a striking proof that Grotius had brought in a new epoch was shown three years after his death. In 1648 plenipotentiaries from the great states of Europe signed at Münster the Treaty of Westphalia, which closed the Thirty Years' War in Germany, the Eighty Years' War in the Netherlands, and a long era of savagery in all parts of the globe. This instrument embodied principles which Grotius had really been the first to bring into the thought of the world. At its base was his conception of the essential independence and equality of all sovereign states,—all its parts were riveted together by his conceptions of eternal justice,—the whole structure was permeated by his hatred of cruelty and love of mercy. To the signing of this treaty the Papal authorities at Rome had constantly shown themselves bitterly opposed; all that intrigue, bribes, and threats could do, they had done; and, as the congress at Münster went on more evidently toward a merciful issue, this violence at Rome became more and more marked. As the climax of the whole, Pope Innocent X issued his bull, *Zelo Domus Dei,* absolving the signatories of the treaty from the oaths they had taken when affixing their signatures to it; and not only this, but virtually commanded them to break their oaths. But a new time had come. The signers, having foreseen this exercise of the Papal power "to bind and loose," made a solemn pledge and vow not to avail themselves of any such absolution. The book had indeed begun its work.

In the next chapter we shall examine the teaching of Grotius, note the proofs of its influence on the two centuries following, and mark the latest exhibition of its power in the International Peace Conferences of The Hague in 1899 and 1907.[1]

[1] I. For a striking example of the hatred felt by bigots toward Richelieu's tolerance, see Henri Martin, *Histoire de France*, tome xi, p. 278. As to diplomatic friction between Richelieu and Grotius, see Burigny, *Vie de Grotius*, Amsterdam, 1754, tome i, pp. 248–258. For Richelieu's order relieving Grotius' works from the censorship, *ibid.*, tome ii, p. 110. For Richelieu's estimation of Grotius as one of the three foremost savants of his time, *ibid.*, tome ii, p. 208.

II. For proofs that Richelieu, worldly wise as was his policy, was at heart a devout believer, see Hanotaux, *Histoire du Cardinal de Richelieu*, tome ii, 2me partie, chapitre 2; Avenel, *Richelieu et la Monarchie Absolue*, Paris, 1887, tome iii, pp. 393–421; also Perkins, *France under Richelieu and Mazarin*, vol. ii, p. 128, note.

III. For an admirable brief summary of Grotius' relation to the Treaty of Westphalia, see Walker, *Science of International Law*, chap. iv.

IV. For Pope Innocent X and the bull *Zelo Domus Dei*, see Laurent, *Histoire du Droit des Gens*, vol. x, pp. 174, *et seq.*

II

THE first characteristics which the book of Grotius revealed were faith and foresight. Great as it was,—the most beneficent of all volumes ever written not claiming divine inspiration,—yet more wonderful than the book itself was the faith of its author. In none of the years during which he meditated it, and least of all during the years when it was written, could any other human being see in the anarchic darkness of the time any tribunal which could recognize a plea for right reason in international affairs, or enforce a decision upon it. The greatness of Grotius lies, first of all, in the fact that he saw in all this darkness one court sitting supreme to which he might make appeal, and that court—the heart and mind of universal humanity.

What the darkness was which his eye alone could pierce was shown in his preface. He says: "I saw many and grave causes why I should write a work on that subject. I saw in the whole Christian world a license of fighting at which even barbarous nations might blush. Wars were begun on trifling pretexts or none at all, and carried on without any reverence for law, Divine or human. A declaration of war seemed to let loose every crime."[1]

To understand the significance of Grotius' work, let us glance over the evolution of international law up to his time.

The Hebrews, in their wars with their neighbors, considered themselves bound by hardly any of the rules of humanity which in these days prevail as axioms. On sundry neighboring nations they thought themselves com-

[1] *De Jure Belli ac Pacis, Prolegomena*, par. 28.

manded by the Almighty to exercise merciless cruelties: "to save nothing alive that breatheth;" to burn cities; to mutilate and murder captives; to spare neither men, women, nor children. Any exceptions to this barbarity were, as a rule, confined to populations which would consent to be enslaved.

Exhortations to cruelty are not only constant in the laws of Moses, but they ring loud and long through the Psalms and Prophecies. Yet here and there we see an evolution of a better view: out of this mass of savagery there were developed some regard for treaties and for the persons of ambassadors, and from time to time precepts and examples of mercy.

During the Hellenic period, germs of humanity had appeared. Among themselves, the Greek states observed truces and treaties, took pains at times to make war less barbarous, occasionally gave quarter, substituted slavery or ransom for the murder of prisoners, spared public monuments, respected the persons of heralds and ambassadors. Such, with exceptions many and cruel, was their rule among themselves; but, in dealing with those not of Hellenic origin, their rule, in peace and war, was outrage and slaughter.

The Roman Republic, struggling constantly with tribes, nations, and races not bound to it by any recognized tie, acknowledged, as a rule, no claims of humanity. In conquering the world, it demanded none, and, as a rule, granted none.

Under the Roman Empire a better evolution was seen. The Roman feeling for system and order took shape in their municipal law, and this was extended largely and wisely over their conquests. Though it was really a law imposed by conquerors upon conquered, it came to have many characteristics of an international law between the subject states. Law *to* nations began to look much like a

law *of* nations: the *jus gentium* came to be mistaken by
many, then and later, for a *jus inter gentes.*

In the confusion which followed the downfall of the
Roman Empire, there was one survival to which the world
seemed likely to turn at once, and this was the idea of
an imperial power giving laws to the nations. The heir-
ship of this power was naturally claimed by the mediæval
empire in northern Europe, based upon German characteristics but permeated by Roman ideas; and, had the successors of Charlemagne proved worthy of him, there
might have been imposed upon Europe a *pax Germanica*
as strong and as durable as the *pax Romana* had been.
But the German Empire, fallen to weaklings and broken
into discordant states, lost more and more its power to
enforce a mediating will upon Europe; and, though at the
Reformation it still called itself "Holy" and "Roman"
and an "Empire," it had become merely a single party
in a great struggle of warring religions and policies.

But there had arisen another power, which soon appeared even more likely to inherit the old Roman mission
of enforcing peace and law throughout the world. For
this mission the Papacy seemed to fulfill every require-
ment. Seated on the hills once occupied by the Cæsars,
representing an unquestioned spiritual authority, it
seemed, even more than the German Empire, fitted to impose upon Europe, and indeed upon all mankind, a true
law of nations, or at least to establish a court before
which the nations should appear.

Great pontiffs came, like the early Gregories and Leos
and Innocents, who worthily proclaimed this high mission. The Church at large, in the eleventh and twelfth
centuries, was clearly ready to join in it, and at various
centres throughout Europe the spirit of the blessed
Founder of Christianity asserted itself in efforts to check
the mediæval flood of cruelty in war. Most striking

6

among these efforts was the "Truce of God," which condemned and largely prevented war at various sacred seasons and on certain days of the week. But, unfortunately, the central hierarchy began to show an alloy of human weakness which gradually deprived the Papacy forever of this splendid and beneficent function.

The first element in this alloy was the lust for an earthly dominion. There came the pretended "Donation of Constantine," the false Decretals, the struggles with sword and pen to despoil this petty prince, to win that petty territory, to establish a petty temporal throne, in the shade of which grew luxuriantly and noxiously nepotism and scoundrelism.

A far more serious obstacle in the way of the Papacy to recognition as a mediator and moderator between states was its doctrine regarding dealings with unbelievers and misbelievers. For the fundamental doctrine which permeated theological thought and ecclesiastical action was condensed into the statement that "no faith is to be kept with heretics." Throughout the Middle Ages, and afterward, this doctrine steadily undermined confidence in the Papacy as an international umpire. The burning of John Huss by the Emperor Sigismund at the behest of ecclesiastics in violation of a solemn promise and safe conduct, the advice to Charles V to violate the safe conduct he had given Luther, and various similar cases quietly had their effect. Memorable was the solemn declaration, just after the Reformation, made by the Bishop of Augsburg: "There can be no peace between Catholics and heretics; as well attempt to make agreements between light and darkness." Significant, too, in Grotius' own time, was the declaration of an eminent professor of theology at Mainz, the seat of the German Primate, that "a peace which permits men to be Catholic, Lutheran, or Calvinist is absolutely null, because it is contrary to the law of God." Even in 1629, four years after the appearance of Grotius' work, came a treatise, eminently approved by the older Church throughout Europe, which taught that any treaty between Catholics and heretics is fundamentally void. Indicative of a recognized fact was the declaration of the Jesuit father, Ribadeneira: "If Catholics sometimes make agreements with Protestants, it is solely in order to gain time and to get forces together with which to overwhelm them." [1]

But that which most fatally undermined the Papal position as a law-giving and moderating umpire in Europe was its assertion, loud and frequent, of its power to break treaties and annul oaths. The fundamental doctrine of the Church on this subject, which theologians had devised and which ecclesiastics had enforced, was laid down in the decretal which declared in express terms that "an oath contrary to the interests of the Church is void." [2]

What this meant was seen when Clement VI gave to the confessors of a French king power to give releases from various oaths and vows which it might be found "inconvenient to keep"; when Eugenius IV released Nicholas Piccinino from his solemn agreement with Francis Sforza; when Julius II released Ferdinand of Spain from the oath sworn upon his treaty with Louis XII of France; and, above all, when the Papal absolution, and indeed persuasion, led Francis I of France to break his solemn oath and pledges to the Treaty of Madrid, and to renew the war which desolated France, Germany, and Spain. So fearful had this evil become in Grotius' own land and time, that William of Orange made a solemn protest against the annulling of oaths and treaties as "leaving nothing certain in the world." [3]

[1] See citations in Laurent, *Histoire du Droit des Gens,* Paris, 1865, vol. x, p. 439.

[2] For the Latin text of this decretal, see Laurent, as above, vol. x, p. 429, note.

[3] For the Latin text of the permission to absolve from oaths which were found "inconvenient to keep," see Laurent, vol. x, p. 432, note.

War to extermination thus became the only means of obtaining peace. This was the strictly logical basis of the decree of the Holy Inquisition, which Philip II solemnly approved, condemning to death the entire population of the Netherlands. All treaties had thus become illusory.

Nor was there any possibility, after the Reformation, of a Protestant international tribunal. For the breaking of oaths was sanctioned also by the Reformed Church. Noteworthy was the case of the Count of Nassau, a member of the great Protestant house of that name. He had sworn to a treaty tolerating the worship of his Catholic subjects, but the Calvinist theologians insisted that he must violate his oath on the ground that Catholics were idolaters. It is something, however, that his brother, William of Orange, and Beza opposed this decision.[1]

In another important respect, Protestant practices were less excusable than Catholic. The Roman authorities and all that obeyed them throughout Europe felt themselves, in all their cruelties, to be striving for the "salvation of souls." The Protestants had no such excuse. They waged war, not only against conscientious Catholics, who, as they thought, came under the Old Testament denunciation for idolatry, but also against their Protestant brethren, who differed from them on merely metaphysical points not involving salvation. The only thing to be said in mitigation of Protestant intolerance is that, though more inexcusable than the intolerance of the older Church, it was less inexorable: for in the Protestant Church there was no dogma of infallibility which prevented an open modification or even reversal of any teachings which the evolution of humanity had gradually proved false and noxious.

---

[1] For the case of John of Nassau, see Groen van Prinsterer, *Archives de la Maison d'Orange*, t. vii, pp. 127 ff. For Beza's view, *ibid.* pp. 248–254. For William of Orange, *ibid.* p. 133, note.

But, despite this mitigation, the Protestants found, as they thought, a sure warrant for cruelties quite as great as any practiced by Catholics. By all who broke away from Papal authority in the sixteenth century, there was made an especial appeal to the Jewish and Christian sacred books. These books were read as never before. From the Protestant pulpit, whether Lutheran, Calvinist, or Anabaptist, constant appeals were made to them as final in the conduct of war. On both sides of the great controversy which had taken such fearful shape in the middle of the seventeenth century, but especially on the Protestant side, the minds of men were devoted, not to promoting that peace which was breathed upon the world by the New Testament, but to finding warrant for war—and especially the methods of the Chosen People in waging war against unbelievers—in the Old Testament. Did any legislator or professor of law yield to feelings of humanity, he was sure to meet with protests based upon authority of Holy Scripture. Plunder and pillage were supported by reference to the divinely approved "spoiling of the Egyptians" by the Israelites. The right to massacre unresisting enemies was based upon the command of the Almighty to the Jews in the twentieth chapter of Deuteronomy. The indiscriminate slaughter of whole populations was justified by a reference to the divine command to slaughter the nations round about Israel. Torture and mutilation of enemies was sanctioned by the conduct of Samuel against Agag, of King David against the Philistines, of the men of Judah against Adoni-bezek. Even the slaughter of babes in arms was supported by a passage from the Psalms,—"Happy shall he be, that taketh and dasheth thy little ones against the stones." Treachery and assassination were supported by a reference to the divinely approved Phinehas, Ehud, Judith, and Jael; and murdering the ministers of unapproved religions, by Elijah's slaughter of the priests of Baal.

But while the Germanic Empire and the Papacy had proved their unfitness to mediate between the nations of Christendom, and while the Reformation had shown itself utterly unable to diminish the horrors of war or to increase the incentives to peace, there had been developed some beginnings of an appeal to right reason.

The first of these were seen in the Middle Ages, when plain merchants and shipmasters devised such maritime codes as the *Jugemens d'Oleron*, the *Consolato del Mare*, the *Laws of Wisby*, the *Customs of Amsterdam*, and others. Still more important, there had come, during the closing years of the Middle Ages and at the beginning of the modern period, even more hopeful evidences of a growth of better thought. Men like Vittoria, Soto, Vasquez, and Suarez in Spain, Conrad Bruno in Germany, Ayala in the Netherlands, and, above all, Albericus Gentilis in England, were the main agents in this evolution of mercy. But the voices of these men seemed immediately lost in the clamor and confusion of their time. And yet their efforts were not in vain.

> "One accent of the Holy Ghost
> The heedless world hath never lost."

The ideas of these men, no matter how imperfect and inadequate, were received into the mind of Grotius. He himself makes ample acknowledgment of this throughout his writings.

But, as the Renaissance progressed, the system developed in diplomacy, and war became more and more vile. The fundamental textbook was Machiavelli's *Prince*. Lying and treachery were the rule. Assassination by poison and dagger, as supplementary to war, was frequent. Catherine de Medici, Philip II, Alva, Des Adrets,

Tilly, Wallenstein, were simply incarnations of the Machiavellian theories which ruled this period.[1]

The treatment of non-combatants is perhaps the most fearful element in all this chaos. The unspeakable cruelties of the war in the Netherlands, spread along through more than half a century, the world knows by heart.

The Thirty Years' War in Germany was in many respects worse. Apart from a few main leaders, of whom Gustavus Adolphus was chief, the commanders on both sides prompted or permitted satanic cruelties. Ministers of religion were mutilated in every conceivable way before murder; the churches were drenched in the blood of non-combatants and refugees; women treated with every form of indignity and cruelty; children hacked to pieces before their parents' eyes; the limbs of non-combatants nailed to the doors of churches; families tied together and burned as fagots; torture used to force revelations regarding buried treasure; whole city populations put to the sword; people of great districts exterminated; those not exterminated by the sword swept off in vast numbers by pestilence and famine. At the taking of Magdeburg by Tilly, six years after the publication of Grotius' book, the whole city was burned,—only the cathedral and a few houses being left,—and from twenty to thirty thousand inhabitants were massacred. Other captured cities were reduced to one-fourth their original population; hundreds of towns disappeared from the map of the empire. During all that period men might cry, with the king's son in Shakespeare's *Tempest*,—

"Hell is empty,
And all the devils are here."

[1] For excellent brief statements regarding the development of the Machiavellian doctrines, see David J. Hill, *History of European Diplomacy*, vol. ii, pp. 316, 317, and Lord Acton's introduction to Burd's translation of *Il Principe;* for valuable suggestions to thought, J. N. Figgis, *From Gerson to Grotius*, Lect. iii, Ferrari, *Histoire de la Raison*

Two hundred and fifty years after the Treaty of Münster, Germany had not fully recovered the prosperity which she enjoyed before this war of thirty years.

Especially to be noted in Grotius' work are the sources from which he develops it. These are two. The first is the principle of natural morality,—the commands of justice written, as he claims, by God on the hearts and minds of men. These, he says, are to be ascertained by right reason,—by the powers of discernment which God has given; thus is obtained what he calls the "Law of Nature." His second source he finds in the institutions, or enactments, or ideas, which the nations or gifted men have agreed upon as right, necessary, or final; thus is obtained what he calls the "Law of Nations."

Difficulties and dangers, many and great, meet him at once. Frequently the elements obtained from these sources did not at all agree;—indeed, in some cases could not by any ordinary means be made to agree. As regarded the "Law of Nature" there were struggles with theologians who pointed triumphantly to texts of Scripture; as regarded the "Law of Nations" there were conflicts with jurists who showed that what he maintained was by no means what had been held "always, everywhere, and by all."

No man of less splendid powers, intellectual and moral, could have grappled with such opponents and triumphed over such difficulties. His genius as a reasoner, his scholarship so vast in range, his memory bringing to him the best thoughts of the best thinkers in all literature, sacred and profane, ancient and modern, his skill in applying the doctrines of Roman jurisprudence, enabled him to develop out of these elements a system. But his main guide through all this labyrinth of difficulties was his own earnestness and unselfishness, his nobility of mind, heart,

d'État, pt. 2, sect. iii, chaps. i and ii, and Dunning, *History of Political Theories*, vol. i, chap. xi.

and soul. He fused together right and authority on
every fundamental question, and with precious results.

Some of the elements he cast into his crucible were
doubtful, and some of his reasoning faulty; yet, when all
were submitted to the fervor of his love of justice, the
result was always the same,—a new doctrine, clear and
lustrous, a new treasure for humanity.

Take, for example, the fundamental question which
met him at the outset, regarding the right of waging
war. He declares that war is legitimate if just, and in
answer to the question what is a just and proper motive
for war, he allows simply one cause,—a sincere desire
for justice. To those who confront him with the Sermon
on the Mount, he answers that similar arguments can
be drawn from the Gospels against civil and penal justice,
and concludes that the doctrines alluded to were ideals
and not intended for literal embodiment in actual law.[1]

As another example of his method, take his dealing
with the question of wars for religion. He gives many
reasonings which are precious, but, with them, some which
seem to us in these days fallacious and even dangerous.
He contends, for example, like all men of his time, that
war is lawful to avenge insults offered to God, and brings
this contention into accord with his fundamental assertion
as to the proper motive for war by arguing that when
any nation insults the Almighty it endangers the very
foundations upon which all nations repose, thus violating
the rights of all, and that war to maintain these rights is
of course allowable.

The danger of this concession is evident, for who is to
decide what constitutes an insult to God? In one country, men see such an insult in a neglect to kneel before the
consecrated wafer; in another country they see it in disrespect to the sacred cattle; here, in eating flesh on Fri-
day; there, in catching fish on Sunday. But to this con-

[1] *De Jure Belli ac Pacis*, lib. ii, cap. i.

cession Grotius adds deductions from natural law which, in connection with his previous statements, give a noble product, for he arrives at the conclusion that war against infidel nations or against heretics as such is unjust. He says, ''Christianity consists of mysteries which cannot be established by material proof, and therefore nations cannot force them upon any man's conscience, or make disbelief in them, by any person, a crime.'' He reminds his readers that all cannot believe who would gladly believe, that belief comes by the grace of God; and, if war against infidels cannot be justified, still less, he says, can we justify war against heretics, who have separated themselves from the Church on merely secondary beliefs; and he cites the words of Christ, of St. Paul, of St. John, and of various fathers and doctors of the Church, as disapproving forced conversions.[1]

A striking example of Grotius' method, both in its weakness and in its strength, is his discussion of the question how far war shall be extended as to methods and persons. This was a question of capital importance. In his time, the theory and practice of antiquity and the Middle Ages were in cruel force. A vast array of authorities, from the commands of Jehovah to the children of Israel down to the latest orders in the Thirty Years' War, were frightfully cruel. Not only might combatants who had laid down their arms be massacred, but non-combatants; and not only men, but women and children. To the question—where is the limit to what is lawful and unlawful?—he answers: ''The substance of the evil ought to be in proportion to the right sought and the culpability of the enemy refusing to grant the right.'' From this it is easy for any one to follow him to the conclusion that, in modern times, the criminality of the enemy can rarely, if ever, be so great as to war-

[1] *De Jure Belli ac Pacis,* lib. ii, cap. xx, par. 48–50.

rant the massacre of prisoners, and never so great as to warrant such reprisals as the slaughter and outrage of innocent non-combatants.

That some of his concessions were dangerous was the fault of the age. Grotius could not, in the seventeenth century, have solved the questions at issue otherwise. Had he not paid every respect to the Old Testament authorities, he would not only have done violence to his own convictions, but would have insured the suppression of his book, by both Catholics and Protestants, as blasphemous. But, even in the midst of these concessions, he seeks to deduce from its best sources a "Law of Nations" distinct from the "Law of Nature," yet combining with it. He brings a mass of arguments to bear against assassination, against dishonor and cruelty to women and children, against plunder, against the whole train of atrocities common in his time; and finds authority for his declaration after his usual method: by citing the ideas and practice of the noblest warriors and thinkers of all nations and periods, thus stimulating the leading warriors and statesmen of his time, of whatever creed or party, to admire and imitate the noblest examples. The Renaissance had not spent its force. It was a period when, as never since, statesmen and generals emulated the great men of antiquity,—and Grotius' method proved fruitful in clemency.[1]

Among a vast number of difficult questions, comes up the limit of a conqueror's rights over the conquered. First, as to property, shall he reimburse himself by stripping individuals and reducing them to poverty, or by levying contributions on the entire nation? Grotius concedes that the authorities warrant either of these methods, but his noble instincts again lift him to a height from which he discerns a solution, and he declares

[1] *De Jure Belli ao Pacis,* lib. iii, cap. xii.

strongly in favor of the modern and more merciful system of not ruining individuals, but of taxing the entire
hostile nation.

Then the second part of the question comes up. What
is the right of the conqueror as regards the persons
vanquished? Here, too, his sane instincts have to meet
terrible precedents both in sacred and profane history,
but he falls back on his argument that the penalty should
be brought into proportion with the offense, preaches
clemency and moderation, applies his method of ascer-
taining the Law of Nations from the noblest utterances
and examples, and leaves in his reader the conviction
that there are few, if any, offenses in modern times of
a nature which can justify extreme retaliation.

Such is an outline of Grotius' main positions regarding a few of the larger practical questions of that and
after ages. That the solutions are at times inconclusive, especially in the domain of what he calls "Natural
Law," is the fault partly of his age, in which it was
vain to deny or combat authorities held sacred, and
partly of sundry limitations in his own reasoning; but
his work had, none the less, vast results,—the *De Jure
Belli ac Pacis* is the real foundation of the modern science of international law.

And here should be mentioned the most penetrating
of all its doctrines.

For a question of more practical importance than any
other arises,—the nature of the tribunal in case of an
infringement by one nation of the rights of another.
His answer has been fruitful in the past and is to bear
still greater fruit in the future. In his usual way, he
points first of all to authority, and quotes Cicero as
follows: "There are two ways of ending a dispute,—
discussion and force; the latter manner is simply that of
brute beasts, the former is proper to beings gifted
with reason: it is permitted then to recur to violence only

when reason is powerless." He then takes up various methods by which international questions may be settled without war, and from these he deduces naturally the idea of conferences and international arbitration. Here is the culmination of his services to mankind. Others, indeed, had proposed plans for the peaceful settlement of differences between nations, and the world remembers them with honor; to all of them—from Henry IV and Penn and St. Pierre and Kant and Bentham down to the humblest writer in favor of peace—we may well feel grateful; but the germ of arbitration was planted in modern thought when Grotius wrote these solemn words: "But especially are Christian kings and states bound to try this way of avoiding war." Out of the arguments of which this is the culmination has arisen the greatest hope of mankind in its dealings with international questions.[1]

The whole work of Grotius has been often censured, and harshly. Some religionists have insisted that his use of reason unduly tempered the authority of Scripture; some anti-religionists, that he yielded unduly to Scripture. Others have complained of the arrangement of the work, of its immense number of citations, of what they call its "pedantry"; and among these are Voltaire and Dugald Stewart. It must be confessed that, wonderful as the book is, its arrangement, style, and sequence of thought are at times vexatious. Yet these are but the defects of its qualities. In the midst of masses of learning which not infrequently cloud the main issue, and fine-spun arguments which seem to lead nowhither, there frequently comes a pithy statement, an illuminating argument, a cogent citation, which lights up a whole chapter. It reminds an American of Emerson. Grotius has even more than Emerson's power of pithy citation,— a power which any one who studies Pufendorf's clumsy

---

[1] *De Jure Belli ac Pacis,* lib. ii, cap. xxiii, viii, 3.

efforts to imitate it will appreciate painfully. As to
the charge based on the number of citations, nothing
can be more unjust: that charge arises from a complete
misapprehension of Grotius' method; the brilliant ref-
utation of it by Sir James Mackintosh is convincing.
These citations were in accordance with the fundamental
plan of the work, which was to formulate the decisions
of right reason by showing its action in countries most
diverse in situation and history, and among men most
different in habits and opinions. Grotius' own statement is conclusive. He says: "In order to give proofs
on questions respecting this Natural Law, I have made
use of the testimonies of philosophers, historians, poets,
and, finally, orators. Not that I regard these as judges
from whose decision there is no appeal, for they are
warped by their party, their argument, their cause,—
but I quote them as witnesses whose conspiring testimony, proceeding from innumerable different times and
places, must be referred to some universal cause which,
in the questions with which we are here concerned, cannot be any other than a right deduction proceeding from
the proofs of reason or some common consent. The
former cause of agreement points to the Law of Nature,
the latter to the Law of Nations." [1]

It has also been objected that Grotius made a concession fatal to humanity, in palliating slavery. Rousseau
was especially severe upon him for this.

But, in the atmosphere of Grotius' discussions of
slavery, an evolution of ideas destructive to all involun-
tary servitude was sure. Starting with the idea that
slavery is the first step from the massacre of prisoners,
he limits and modifies it in ways which lead more and

---

[1] *De Jure Belli ac Pacis, Prolegomena*, par. 40, Whewell's translation.
For the admirable defense of this method by Sir James Mackintosh, see
Pradier-Fodéré, French edition of Grotius' work, Paris, 1867, tome i, p.
39, note; also, Hallam, *Lit. of Europe*, part iii, chap. iv, with Hallam's
impressive assent to it.

more clearly to its abolition. He constantly finds miti-
gations of the Law of Nations in the Law of Nature,
and of the Law of Nature in the Law of Nations; he dissents from a theological argument that slaves have, by
the Law of Nations, no right to escape; he limits the
right of the master in administering punishment; he
insists that the private acquisitions of a slave, by economy or donation, are his own; that his ransom should
be moderate; that his children should be free save as
they are held for debts due for sustenance during their
minority. In behalf of justice and mercy, he cites
Seneca, St. Paul, Clement of Alexandria, and many others, until he finally rises to a conception of human brotherhood in which the whole basis of slavery, and indeed
its whole practice, must soon dissolve away.[1]

Another of his conclusions which has repelled, and
even angered, many critics is embodied in his statement
that to save the state or the city an innocent citizen might
be delivered into the hands of the enemy. But, when
closely scrutinized, we find it an extreme statement due
to his horror of war,—much like' that attributed to
Franklin, that there could not be a good war or a bad
peace. Grotius' statement was evidently based on a very
high conception of the duty of the individual to the state,
namely, that to save the state the individual should be
ready to sacrifice himself, and that the state had a right
to presume on this readiness.[2]

Another charge which has been made against him is
that he committed himself virtually to the doctrine of a
primitive contract and was thus a forerunner of Rousseau
and Robespierre. This charge has been made in many
forms and reiterated, even in our own time, by sundry

[1] For Grotius' discussion of slavery, see mainly the *De Jure Belli ac
Pacis*, lib. iii, cap. vii and xiv.

[2] See Hallam's wise remark, but especially the brief argument of
Whewell in a note on his translation of Grotius' statement, *De Jure Belli ac
Pacis*, lib. ii, cap. xxv, 3, iii, 1 and 2, note.

countrymen of Grotius, in whose hearts there still linger the old sectarian hatreds.[1]

Nothing can be more superficial or unjust. The "social contract" theory was not invented by Rousseau; a long series of men had labored at it, and, among them, Hobbes and Locke, with enormously different results. Grotius' theory is entirely different from that of Rousseau, both in its essence and outcome. To Rousseau's mind, as to that of Robespierre, human beings in a "state of nature" were good, and the generality of mankind, if freed from the ideas and institutions of civilized society, would return as a whole to this native goodness. The most effective appeal of Rousseau's disciples was to the Parisian mob,—the same mob which had applauded the St. Bartholomew massacres,—the same which, two hundred years later, applauded the September massacres and the cruelties of the Reign of Terror, and which adored *la sainte guillotine,*—the same which glorified Napoleonism, deifying the man who trampled on their earlier ideal and sent them to slaughter by myriads,—the same which upheld the Commune with all its absurdities and atrocities. On the other hand, while Grotius accepted the hypothesis which for so long a time proved so serviceable, namely, the idea of original human consent to law, his appeal was not to "man in a state of nature" or to a mob of men in a "state of nature," whether that mob tyrannized a village or an empire. As a student of classical antiquity, he knew that some of the worst of the Roman emperors had been adored by the people; as a student of modern history, he knew that Henry VIII of England had been one of the most popular of monarchs; he knew but too well that Philip II of Spain, the monarch against whom his people had

[1] For a very striking, and even painful, example of this prejudice in an eminent and otherwise excellent Netherlandish historian, see Groen van Prinsterer, *Maurice et Barnevelt,* chap. xiii.

revolted,—narrow, bloodthirsty, brutal,—was yet considered, by the vast majority of his subjects, as an exponent of the Divine Will; he knew that Barneveld, one of the strongest and noblest men Europe had ever seen, who had served the Netherlands faithfully in the most difficult of all emergencies at home and abroad for forty years, had against him the vast majority of the people of the Dutch Republic simply because he had dreaded absolutism and loved toleration; and, could he have looked forward an hundred years, he would have seen two other great Netherlandish statesmen, the De Witts, murdered by "the people" at The Hague, within a stone's throw of the spot where Barneveld had been put to death. The real appeal of Grotius was not to "man in a state of nature," but to the sense of justice, humanity, righteousness, evolved under the reign of God in the hearts and minds of thinking men. His appeal was not to a "contract made in the primeval woods," but to the hearts, minds, and souls of men, developed under Christian civilization.

Grotius' appeal was not to a mob; it was not, indeed, to the average man of the mob; it was to the thinking man, whether educated or uneducated, whether Protestant or Catholic, whether Lutheran or Calvinist, whether Gomarist or Arminian. One feature of Grotius' great inspiration was his faith that there were such men, and that an appeal to them would be of use to the world. The result of Rousseau's idea was seen in the excesses of the French Revolution, which led to new deluges of bloodshed, both during the Revolution and the reaction which followed it; the result of Grotius' theory was seen in the beginning of a new era of mercy to mankind, an era in which wars became infinitely less cruel both to combatants and non-combatants.[1]

[1] For Rousseau's theory and the better character of Montesquieu's view, see Pollock, *Introduction to a History of the Science of Politics*, p. 81.

Again, it has been said that Grotius, in his great work, devoting himself, as he did, to the rights and obligations of belligerents, indicated too superficially the rights of neutrals.

No doubt this statement, made at the Hague Peace Conference of 1899 by one of the most eminent compatriots and admirers of Grotius, is entirely true. It was made in giving point to a most earnest appeal for the preparation of a code of neutrality to be considered at some future meeting of the conference. But every student should be on his guard against considering this statement, in the slightest degree, a reproach to Grotius.

For the simple truth is that Grotius did the work which was set before him, in view of the necessities of the world in his time. The first thing to be done was to make a presentation of the rights and duties of belligerents. If he passed rapidly over the rights and duties of neutrals, it was because the time had not arrived for their full discussion, and also because a neutrality code was sure to be evolved at a later period, out of his work, if it should accomplish his purpose. Frederick the Great once said that his great reforming contemporary, Joseph II, usually made the mistake of taking the second step before the first. This mistake Grotius avoided. He simply took the first step, no doubt with a feeling of certainty that if he could maintain his foothold the second step must follow.

It did follow; but not until the next century, when

For Rousseau's hostility to Grotius' ideas, see *Le Contrat Social*, especially the opening chapters. For Rousseau's minute description of the process and results of forming the "social contract," *ibid.*, chap. vii.

The translation by Whewell of the words *ex consensu obligatio,* in the *Prolegom.* xvi, by the words "obligation by mutual compact" seems somewhat likely to mislead. Pradier-Fodéré's translation runs "l'obligation que l'on s'est imposée par son propre consentement," and this does not seem so suggestive of the Rousseau "contract" theory.

Bynkershoek, inspired by Grotius, began that long series of discussions which, we may hope, are soon to result in articles on the rights and duties of neutrals, presented by future peace conferences, and accepted by all the civilized nations.[1]

But the good results of Grotius' book were at first veiled. Except Gustavus Adolphus and Richelieu, no commander of that time seems to have read it. In France, its influence seems manifest in the mercy shown to the Huguenots after the siege of La Rochelle, but in Germany the Thirty Years' War dragged on more and more cruelly for over twenty years after its publication. Commanders on both sides, Protestant and Catholic, seemed to become more and more merciless. Arson, bloodshed, torture, and murder became more and more the rule. But at the close of the war, as we have seen, in the Treaty of Westphalia, some of the fundamental ideas of Grotius had evidently taken hold of the plenipotentiaries at Osnabrück and Münster, and were wrought into their work.

During the fifty years which followed that great treaty, the book, thanks to disciples like Pufendorf and Thomasius, became more and more known; but at first there was little to show that its ideas had taken practical hold on Europe. Louis XIV, in his policy at home and in his wars abroad, showed little trace of Grotius' ideas on either toleration or peace: *le Grand Monarque,* under the inspiration of his bishops and his confessor, did his worst in revoking the Edict of Nantes and in laying

[1] See the address by Mr. Asser before the Hague Con. ~ence and others at Delft, July 4, 1899, as given in Holls: *History of the Peace Conference at The Hague,* pp. 558, 559. For a very complete statement, see Woolsey: *Introduction to the Study of International Law,* Revised Edition, 1895, chap. ii. Also, Hall: *International Law,* Oxford, 1895, part iv. Also, for a more brief, but especially lucid statement, see T. J. Lawrence: *Principles of International Law,* Boston, 1895, part iv.

waste the Palatinate; but in spite of his cold-blooded cruelty there was a steady diminution in military ferocity.

Early in the first days of the eighteenth century came the War of the Spanish Succession, spreading over much of the same German and Dutch territory which had suffered during the Thirty Years' War; but a great change was now evident. Instead of leaders like Mansfield, Wallenstein, Christian of Brunswick, and so many others, who had led in the old atrocities, there now came Marlborough, Eugene, Villars, and other commanders on both sides, who, as a rule, repressed pillage, murder, and arson, paid for supplies taken from the inhabitants, levied their contributions upon governments and not upon individuals, cared for their prisoners, were merciful to non-combatants, and in every way indicated an immense progress in mercy and justice. Here and there, it is true that, in spite of all that commanders could do, cruelties took place, as in the devastation of Bavaria in 1704; but, as a rule, the ideas advocated by Grotius had begun to take strong hold upon the world's best thought.

It has been claimed that credit has been bestowed upon Grotius for much that had been given to the world by men of earlier periods. No one will think of denying that there has been a great evolutionary process as regards international law and especially during the last three or four centuries, and that in this development men like Vittoria, Soto, Ayala, Gentilis, Suarez, and others, have rendered noble services. But the thoughtful student of European history sees in Grotius the first who rightly discerned the best in the thought of all these men,—increasing it from his own thought, strengthening it from his broad knowledge, enriching it from his imagination, glorifying it by his genius, and bringing it to

bear upon the modern world,—in a new work creative
and illuminative.[1]

And finally as to the statement that of all works not
attributed to divine inspiration Grotius' book has been
the most fruitful in blessed results to mankind. The
same claim has been made by one distinguished historian
for Beccaria's *Crimes and Punishments,* and by another
for Adam Smith's *Wealth of Nations.* It is true that
these three books represent such precious conquests of
thought that they seem to stand by themselves, and it is
true that all three went through purging fires,—the *De
Jure Belli ac Pacis* and the *Crimes and Punishments*
being placed upon the Roman Index and the *Wealth of
Nations* being condemned by the Spanish Inquisition.
But, effective as Beccaria's book was in the long struggle
of humanity against torture in procedure and penalty, it
was but one of many as strong or stronger—among these
being the works of Thomasius and Voltaire. And powerful for good as Adam Smith's work has been against
unreason in legislation and administration, the claims
put forth for it in the middle of the nineteenth century
will hardly be renewed in the twentieth. To say nothing
of doubts regarding the system of political economy
which Adam Smith advocated, it is more and more evident that the work of Grotius was on a yet higher plane,
was obedient to more lofty ideals, and is to-day produc-
ing wider and deeper results for the good of all mankind.[2]

[1] For excellent studies of the work of Grotius' predecessors above named,
see Wheaton: *Histoire des Progrès du Droit des Gens,* Introduction; and
especially D. J. Hill's *History of European Diplomacy,* ii, Dunning's *Political Theories,* ii, and Walker's *History of the Law of Nations,* i. It may
also be mentioned that the Carnegie Institution at Washington is now
publishing a monumental edition of what may be called "Classics of
International Law," including those above named and others, each in its
original and its translated form.

[2] As to Grotius and the Index, his various theological and historical
writings were naturally prohibited. So too his *Mare Liberum,* doubtless
because it attacked Pope Alexander VI's comical bull dividing the world

between east and west. The *De Jure Belli ac Pacis* was placed on the Index, but only "until corrected." No corrected edition was ever published, and the prohibition of it was not removed until Leo XIII, the wisest of the popes since Benedict XIV, in 1901 cleared from the Index this and many other books of which the prohibition, sanctioned by previous infallible popes, had provoked scandal.

Pope Leo had earnestly sought admission for a delegation representing him at the Hague Conference of 1899, but he had been unsuccessful. Among various arguments against the admission of his representatives was the fact that the very book which lay at the foundation of arbitration by an international tribunal was still prohibited by the Church.

Beccaria's *Dei Delitti e delle Pene*, though one of the books most fruitful in good ever written, and though its author was a devout churchman, was put on the *Index* February 3, 1766, within two years after its first issue, and is there yet. See the various editions of the *Index*, also the books of Reusch and Hilgers on the *Index* and Putnam's *The Censorship of the Church of Rome*.

III

WE may now return to Grotius' personal history and to his fruitful labor in another field of humanitarian effort.

Until 1631, he remained in Paris, greatly honored, yet often suffering from poverty. The pension granted him by Louis XIII was rather honorable than useful; it was rarely paid.

Interwoven throughout all his efforts for peace and mercy was his continuous labor for RELIGIOUS TOLERATION. A great publicist has said that "intolerance was then the common law of Europe." More than any other of his contemporaries, Grotius wrought to undermine it. Neither triumphs nor sufferings abated his steady labor. Treatises philosophical and historical, translations and commentaries in which the first rank in the scholarship of his time was reached, came constantly from his pen; but his great work during this period was one which he had begun during his imprisonment at the Castle of Loevestein,—his *Truth of Christianity*. Though in advance of his time, its success was enormous. Five times it was translated from the original Latin into French, three times into German, and, beside this, into English, Swedish, Danish, Flemish, Greek, Chinese, Malay, Persian, and Arabic. Its ideas spread widely among European Christians of every name, Catholic and Protestant, Arminian and Calvinistic, Lutheran and Anglican. The reason was simple. It was a Christian book, but not sectarian. It was written with full belief in the fundamental doctrines of Christianity, with but slight regard for the questions which divided Christians. At first it succeeded, but at last came the inevitable outcry. Narrow men on either side insisted that the book was not sufficiently "positive." Bigoted Protestants began to express hatred of it because it was not more "positive" in showing the weakness of Catholicism; bigoted Catholics because it was not more "positive" in showing the weakness of Protestantism; bigoted Lutherans because it was not more "positive" in argument against Calvinism; bigoted Calvinists because it was not more "positive" in denunciation of Lutheranism.

All insisted that Grotius neglected many of the great doctrinal statements developed by theologians. On the fact that Grotius evidently preferred the simple teaching of the Founder of Christianity were based the strongest charges against him. Voetius, an especially bitter foe, in answer to Grotius' assertions of Christian truth declared that "to place the principal part of religion in the observance of Christ's commands is rank Socinianism." This book, too, was put upon the Index at Rome, and its use discouraged by various eminent Protestant authorities. Still, it was effective. Its plan of defense has long since been abandoned; the work begun by Erasmus has brought the world beyond it. Biblical criticism was then in its infancy, and the growth of it has made necessary different methods and new statements; but Grotius' book on the Christian religion does its author none the less honor. None the less, too, has the book been a blessing to mankind in calling the attention of the Christian world to religious realities and away from theological subtleties. In this, as in all his writings, Grotius struggled as a peacemaker, and in his dedication to King Louis XIII he especially pleads for toleration. In one of his letters to his brother, he says, "I shall never cease to do my utmost for establishing peace among Christians, and if I do not succeed it will be honorable to die in such an enterprise." And again, "If there were no

hopes of success at present, ought we not to sow the seed
which may be useful for posterity?" And again, "Even
if we should only diminish the mutual hatred among
Christians, would not this be worth purchasing at the
price of some labor and reproach?" [1]

In 1631, Maurice of Orange having died five or six
years before, and his successor, Prince Henry, seeming
inclined to lenity, Grotius endeavored to return to Holland. But his reception was disappointing:—at first
merely chilly; but erelong the Calvinist bigots of the day
bestirred themselves, and in March, 1632, to such purpose that the States-General offered a reward of two
thousand guilders to any one who should deliver him up
to them. Again he became an exile. His first place of
refuge was Hamburg, and there, giving himself to literary work, he waited again for the return of reason
among his countrymen; though flattering offers were
now made him by the King of Denmark, by Spain, and
even by Wallenstein, who was the real dictator of Germany, he refused them all. He still looked lovingly toward the little Dutch Republic; and it was only after two
years of weary waiting that he gave up that hope and
entered the service of Sweden.

The invitation to this service was honorable both in
its character and its source. Gustavus Adolphus had
fallen at Lützen, but he had left a request that Grotius
be secured for his kingdom; his great chancellor, Oxen-
stiern, bore this in mind, and in 1635 sent Grotius as
Swedish Ambassador to Paris. The position was important, for Sweden was then one of the leading militant
powers of Europe; but the task of the new ambassador
soon became trying. Though the French government
was at heart almost as jealous of Sweden as of Austria,
he was expected to keep France and Sweden active allies;
and, in the Thirty Years' War, the government of his

---

[1] See his *Epistolæ,* 363, 494, 1706, cited by Butler.

native country, both for public and private reasons, endeavored to thwart him. In all the more important part of his mission, Grotius succeeded well; in the lesser parts he was not so happy. There were questions of etiquette and form: Richelieu must be flattered; various parties must be petted or bribed. For such service Grotius was ill fitted: it is related that, while waiting in the anterooms at Court, instead of chattering nonsense, he studied his Greek Testament.

During his final stay in Paris he employed his leisure in various works, among them an investigation as to the origin of the American tribes and an exegetical study upon the Bible; but, though this latter showed good scholarship, its significance in modern criticism is small. He did, indeed, declare his conviction that sundry prophecies in the Old Testament, generally supposed to refer to the coming of the Messiah, had reference to events accomplished before that event, and this brought upon him much obloquy; but, however discredited by this audacity, his work was useful. At this time, too, he wrote his history of the Netherlands, and from it one of his best traits shines forth brightly: he was called, as historian, to discuss the character and services of Maurice of Orange; Maurice had unjustly deprived him of home, property, and freedom, and sought to deprive him of life;—but Grotius points out none the less fully his services as a commander and patriot; not a trace of ill will appears in any of his judgments.

The Swedish government showed erelong, not unnaturally, the belief that one who did so much literary work could hardly do the political work required in such stirring times; his personal relations to Richelieu and Mazarin had become irksome to him; and, in 1645, he resigned his ambassadorship and returned, first to Holland, where, at last, he was more kindly received. Thence he went to Sweden, took formal leave of Queen

Christina, and started upon his return voyage, hoping to pass the remainder of his life in his native country. But it was not so to be. The ship was thrown by a storm upon the Pomeranian coast, and Grotius, having after great suffering reached Rostock, lay down to die.

The simple recital of the Lutheran pastor, Quistorp, who was with him in his last moments, touches the deep places of the human heart. The pastor made no effort to wrestle with the dying scholar and statesman, but simply read to him the parable of the Pharisee and the publican, ending with the words, "God be merciful to me, a sinner." And the dying man answered, "I am that publican."

On the 28th of August, 1645, he breathed his last. It had not been given to him to see any apparent result of his great gift to mankind. From his childhood to his last conscious moments, he had known nothing but war, bigoted, cruel, revengeful war, extending on all sides about him. The Peace of Westphalia, which was to be so largely influenced by him, was not signed until three years after his death. One may hope that the faith which led him to write the book gave him power to divine some of its results.

His first burial was at Rostock, the German town where he died, and there, before the high altar of its great church, to-day is sacredly preserved, as a holy place, the tomb in which his body was then enshrined.

But his wish had been to rest in his native soil, and, after a time, his remains were conveyed to the Netherlands. It is hard to believe, and yet it is recorded history, that as his coffin was borne through the city of Rotterdam stones were thrown at it by the bigoted mob. Finally, it was laid in a crypt beneath the great church of Delft, his birthplace.

Few monuments are more suggestive to the thinking traveler than that ancient edifice. There lie the bones of men who took the lead in saving the Dutch Republic and civil liberty from the bigotry of Spain. Above all, in the apse, towers the canopied tomb of William the Silent,— sculptured marble and molten bronze showing forth the majesty of his purpose and the gratitude of his people. Hard by, in a quiet side aisle, is the modest tomb of Grotius, its inscription simple and touching. Each of these two great men was a leader in the service of liberty and justice; each died a martyr to unreason. Both are "risen from the dead, and live evermore" in modern liberty, civil and religious, in modern law fatal to tyranny, in modern institutions destructive to intolerance, and, above all, in the heart and mind of every man who worthily undertakes to serve the nobler purposes of his country or the larger interests of his race.

Thrice during the latter half of the century just closed did the world pay homage at this shrine. The first occasion was on April 10, 1883,—the three-hundredth anniversary of Grotius' birth, when the people of the Netherlands honored themselves and mankind by a due celebration of it. The second act of homage took place three years later, at the erection of the bronze statue to his memory in front of the church where he lies buried. Most worthily did the eminent Minister of the Netherlands, M. de Beaufort, dwell on the services thus commemorated, and the vast audience showed that the country at last recognized its illustrious servant. Yet there came one note of discord. A touching feature in the tribute was the singing of simple hymns by a great chorus of school-children; but in this chorus a section of the more determined adherents of the old rigid Calvinist orthodoxy refused to allow their children to join. One of their representatives, indeed, declared that the statue was fitly placed, since its back was turned to the Church; to this it was rejoined that the statue was indeed fitly placed, since its face was turned towards Justice. The allusion was to the fact that the monument faced the Palace of Justice and the effigy of Justice adorning it.

The third of these recognitions was on the Fourth of July, 1899. On that day, the American delegation to the Peace Conference of The Hague celebrated the anniversary of American independence by placing, in behalf of the Government of the United States, which had especially authorized and directed it, a wreath of oak and laurel leaves, wrought in silver and gold with appropriate inscriptions, on the tomb of Grotius. The audience filling the vast church comprised not only the ambassadors and other delegates to the conference, but the ministers of the Dutch Crown, professors from the various universities of the Netherlands, and a great body of invited guests from all parts of the world. A letter was read from the King of Sweden and Norway, expressing the gratitude of the power which Grotius had so faithfully served; the ministers of the Netherlandish Crown and the delegates of the American Republic united in presenting the claims of Grotius to remembrance; the music of the chimes, of the great organ, and of the royal choir rolled majestically under the arches of the vast edifice: all in tribute to him who, first among men, had uttered clearly and strongly that call to arbitration which the conference at The Hague was then making real.

And it may well be hoped that early in the twentieth century there will come yet another recognition. By the gift of an American citizen, provision has been made for a Palace of International Justice in which the Court of Arbitration created by the Hague Conference may hold its sessions. Thanks to the munificence of that gift, the world has a right to expect that this temple of peace will be worthy of its high purpose: its dome a fitting outward and visible sign to all peoples that at last there is a solution of international questions other than by plunder and bloodshed; its corridors ennobled by the statues,

busts, and medallions of those who have opened this
path to peace; its walls pictured with the main events in
this evolution of Humanity. But among these memorials,
one monument should stand supreme,—the statue of
Grotius. And in his hand may well be held forth to the
world his great book, opened at that inspired appeal in
behalf of international arbitration:—

" Maxime autem Christiani reges et civitates tenentur
hanc inire viam ad arma vitanda."

THOMASIUS

THOMASIUS

I

THE year 1688 is memorable for two revolutions—one in England, the other in Germany. In England a conspiracy,—partly patriotic, partly rascally,—dethroned the last of the Stuarts; in Germany a young Leipzig professor began giving lectures, not in Latin but in German.[1]

Each of the revolutions thus begun ended an evil phase of history which had lasted during centuries; each began a better phase which lasts to-day. A plausible argument might be made to show that of these two revolutions the act of the German professor was really the more important. For, if the work of William of Orange and his partisans was to destroy Stuartism, with all its lying kingcraft, and to set in motion causes which have directly developed the constitutionalism of England, of the United States, and of many other modern nations, the work of this young professor and his disciples was to dethrone the heavy Protestant orthodoxy which had nearly smothered German patriotism, to undermine the pedantry which had paralyzed German scholarship, to substitute thought

[1] Luden, the biographer of Thomasius, assigns this act to 1688, and in this he has been followed by most modern writers on Thomasius. The latest students, however (Nicoladoni, Landsberg, Hoffmann), point out that Thomasius himself—in his "Lesser German Writings" (1701), and in his "Thoughts and Reminiscences" (1721)—names 1687 as the date when these German lectures were announced. But the course belonged mainly to the following year, and it was then, with the appearance in January of his German magazine, that the struggle was fairly begun. The best guide to the growing literature on Thomasius is now the bibliographical note of Landsberg, in Stintzing and Landsberg's *Geschichte der Deutschen Rechtswissenschaft*, iii, 2.

for formulas, to bring right reason to bear upon international and municipal law, to discredit religious intolerance, to root out witchcraft persecution and procedure by torture from all modern codes, and to begin that emancipation of public and especially university instruction from theological control which has given such strength to Germany, and which to-day is invincibly making its way in all other lands, including our own.

That we may understand this work, let us look rapidly along the century and a half which had worn on since the time of Luther and Melanchthon.

Even before Melanchthon sank into his grave, he was dismayed at seeing Lutheranism stiffen into dogmas and formulas, and heartbroken by a persecution from his fellow-Protestants more bitter than anything he had ever experienced from Catholics.[1]

Luther had, indeed, been at times intolerant; but his intolerance towards Carlstadt was simply the irritation of a strong man at nagging follies,—the impatience of a sensible father with a child who persists in playing with firebrands. Far worse was his intolerance toward Zwingli. That remains the main blot on his great career —and a dark blot; yet, with all this, he was in breadth and fairness of mind far beyond his associates. But the theologians who took up the work which the first reformers had laid down soon came to consider intolerance as a main evidence of spiritual life: erelong they were using all their powers in crushing every germ of new thought. Their theory was simply that the world had now reached its climax; that the religion of Luther was the final word of God to man; that everything depended upon keeping it absolutely pure; that men might comment upon it in hundreds of pulpits and lecture rooms and in thousands

[1] For a most eloquent reference to Melanchthon's last struggle with Lutheran bigotry and fanaticism, see A. Harnack, *Address Before the University of Berlin*, 1897, pp. 16 and following.

of volumes; but—change it in the slightest particle—
never.

And in order that it might never be changed it was
petrified into rituals and creeds and catechisms and statements, and, above all, in 1579, into the "Formula of
Concord," which, as more than one thoughtful man has
since declared, turned out to be a "formula of discord."

For ten years the strong men of the Lutheran Church
labored to make this creed absolutely complete; to
clamp and bind it as with bonds of steel; to exclude from
it every broad idea that had arisen in the mind and soul
of Melanchthon; to rivet every joint, so that the atmosphere of outside thought might never enter. At last,
then, in 1579, after ten years of work, the structure was
perfect. Henceforth until the last day there was to be
no change.

But, like all such attempts, it came to naught. The
hated sister sect grew all the more lustily. When the
"Formula of Concord" was made, Calvinism was comparatively an obscure body in Protestant Germany, but
within a generation it prevailed in at least one quarter of
the whole nation, and had taken full possession of the
dominant German state of the future, the Electorate of
Brandenburg.[1]

The result, then, of all this labor was that the Protestants quarreled more savagely than ever; that, while
they were thus quarreling, Protestantism largely lost its
hold upon Germany; that Roman Catholicism,—no
longer dull and heavy, but shrewd, quick, aggressive,—
with the Jesuits as its spiritual army and Peter Canisius
as its determined head,—pushed into the territory of its
enemies, reconverted great numbers of German rulers
and leaders of thought disgusted at the perpetual quarreling in the Protestant body, availed itself skillfully of

[1] See Biedermann: *Deutschland im Achtzehnten Jahrhundert*, vol. ii,
pp. 291 *et seq.*

Protestant dissensions and waged the Thirty Years' War —thus bringing back to the old faith millions of Germans who had once been brought under the new.

Yet, even after these results were fully revealed, and despite most earnest pleas for concord by, many true men, clerical and lay, a great body of conscientious ecclesiastics continued to devote themselves to making the breach between Lutherans and Calvinists ever wider and deeper. Various leading theologians gave all their efforts to building up vast fabrics of fanaticism and hurling epithets at all other builders. Their bitterness was beyond belief. Just before the beginning of the Thirty Years' War, Paræus, a Calvinistic divine of great abilities and deeply Christian spirit, proposed that Lutherans and Calvinists unite in celebrating the hundredth anniversary of the Reformation. Both sides denounced him. The leaders at the Lutheran universities of Tübingen and Wittenberg united in declaring the scheme "a poisonous seduction of hell."

Still later, when the Thirty Years' War was showing the monstrous results of Protestant bigotry and want of unity, the leading court preacher of Saxony thundered from the pulpit the words:—"To help the Calvinists to free use of their worship is against God and Conscience, and nothing less than to do homage to the founder of the Calvinistic monstrosity—Satan himself." [1]

When Tilly began the siege of Magdeburg, which ended in the most fearful carnival of outrage and murder the world had seen since the Massacre of St. Bartholomew, efforts to relieve that city were cruelly hindered by these same Protestant dissensions. At about the same time, the period when peasants began to declare their doubts of the existence of a God who could permit such terrible evils as were brought upon them by the Thirty Years' War, the magistracy, at a religious discussion in

[1] See Biedermann, as above, vol. ii, pp. 291 *et seq.*

Thorn, in 1645, having forbidden blackguardism and calling of names and hurling of epithets from the pulpit, the eminent Calovius, with two other Lutheran divines, protested so vigorously that the order was revoked. And when the evil consequences of discord had been stamped into men's minds even more deeply, and various statesmen and even ecclesiastics sought to promote more kindly views, John Heinzelmann, eminent as pastor of the Nicolai-Kirche in Berlin, declared, "Whosoever is not a Lutheran is accursed." [1]

All attempts by wise men to put an end to this scandal seemed utterly in vain. The Great Elector of Brandenburg having published a decree exhorting all the clergy, both Lutheran and Calvinistic, to keep the peace, Paul Gerhard, a gentle and deeply religious soul, whose hymns Christians are singing to-day in all lands, declared that he could not conscientiously obey—that he could not consider Calvinists his brother Christians. Against this decree of the Elector sundry clergy appealed to the theological faculties of Helmstädt, Jena, Wittenberg, and Leipzig, and to the clergy of Hamburg and Nürnberg, to know whether the order of the Elector was to be obeyed; and very nearly all these bodies answered, "No; ye are to obey God rather than man." The University of Wittenberg went a step further and showed that while the duty of Calvinists was to tolerate Lutheranism, the duty of Lutherans was to persecute Calvinism, because, as they said, "the Lutherans can prove Calvinism to be false." [2]

A justly eminent Protestant theologian of the 17th century, George Calixt, exerted himself for peace; and on him was fastened the epithet "Syncretist." The mean-

[1] See Biedermann, as above, vol. ii, pp. 272, 291–293; Landwehr, *Die Kirchenpolitik des Grossen Kurfürsten*, Berlin, 1894, p. 197; also citations from Hagenbach, Ranke, and others in Klemperer, *Christian Thomasius*, Landsberg, 1877.

[2] See Biedermann, ii, 294.

ing of this terrible word was, virtually, harmonizer; but, when repeated in the ears of the people, it aroused as much horror and brought as much persecution as the epithet "atheist" would have done.

And Spener came,—seeking to revive devotion in the Church. He urged Christianity as a life and not a repetition of formulas; his personal creed was "orthodox" in every particular, his life was saintly, his words wrought as a charm on multitudes to make them more true and noble—all to no purpose. He was driven by the ecclesiastical authorities out of pulpit after pulpit, and his own goodness and the goodness produced in his disciples were held by his clerical superiors to increase his sin. August Hermann Francke began the career which resulted in the creation of the most magnificent charity ever established by a German Protestant—the Orphan House at Halle—but for years he was driven from post to post for his lack of fanatical zeal. Generation after generation raised men who labored in vain for peace; they were simply denounced as shallow, impious, and the epithet "Syncretist" was hurled at them as a deadly missile. The greatest German philosopher of the century, Leibnitz, attempted to find some common ground and was declared to be "worse than an atheist."

Hardly better was it in science and literature. The universities were fettered by theological clamps; professors, instructors—even fencing masters and dancing masters—were obliged to take oath to believe and support the required creed in all its niceties. Galileo's discoveries were received by the ruling Protestant ecclesiastics with distrust and even hostility. When Kepler began to publish the results of his researches, the Stuttgart Consistory, on September 25, 1612, warned him "to tame his too penetrating nature, and to regulate himself in all his discoveries in accordance with God's word and the Testament and Church of the Lord, and not to trouble them with his unnecessary subtleties, scruples, and glosses.'' The standing still of the sun for Joshua was used against Galileo by the Protestant authorities in Germany as it was used against him by the Inquisition at Rome. The letter of the Reformation Fathers was everything; their real spirit nothing.[1]

Another crushing weight upon Science and Literature was the dominant pedantry. The great thing was to write commentaries upon old thought, and diligently to suppress new thought. The only language of learned lecturers was a debased Latin. During the 17th century pedantry became a disease in every country. In England a pedant sat on the throne, and Walter Scott has mirrored him in the ''Fortunes of Nigel.'' In Italy and Spain the same tendency prevailed: the world now looks back upon it sometimes with abhorrence, sometimes with contempt, as pictured by Manzoni in the ''Promessi Sposi.'' In the American colonies it injured all thinkers; two of the greatest—the Mathers—it crippled. In France there was resistance:—Montaigne had undermined it, and it was the constant theme of his brightest wit; Labruyère presented it in some of his most admirably drawn pictures; Molierè, who had occasion to know and hate it, never tired of holding it up to ridicule.[2]

Bad as that 17th-century pedantry was in France, England, Italy, and Spain, each of these countries had a literature of which thinking men could be proud, and a language in which its most learned men were glad to write. Not so in Germany. The language of learned Germans had become mainly a jargon; their learning owlish; their principal business disputation.

The same spirit was seen in the whole political and

[1] See Günther, *Kepler und die Theologie*, Giessen, 1905. The ruling of the Stuttgart Consistory is printed in full on pp. 125–133.

[2] Doubtless the wittiest example of this ridicule was Molierè's *Mariage Forcé*.

civil administration. The Thirty Years' War had left the country in a fearful state; the population of great districts had been nearly rooted out; powerful cities had been reduced to a third of their former population; wealthy districts had been brought to utter poverty. Then, if ever, the country needed good laws and a wise administration. But nothing could be worse than the system prevailing. In its every department pedantry and superstition were mingled in very nearly equal proportions; everywhere was persecution; everywhere trials for witchcraft; everywhere criminal procedure by torture, though the futility of torture had been demonstrated nearly two thousand years before.

The lower orders of society had been left by the war in a state of barbarism, and their Protestant leaders, while struggling with one another on points of dogma, found little, if any, time to instruct their flocks in anything save antiquated catechisms.

Into such a world, in 1655, was born Christian Thomasius. The son of a professor at the University of Leipzig, his early studies, under his father's direction, comprised nearly all the sciences then taught at that centre of learning and at that of Frankfort-on-the-Oder, in the neighboring Brandenburg, where he learned respect for Calvinists; but he finally settled upon the Law as his profession, and, after having done thorough work both in study and practice, he began lecturing at the University where his father had lectured before him, but not upon the same subject.

In order to understand the work which Thomasius thus began, we must review, briefly, the development of International Law just before the time at which he found it.

In ancient history, as we have seen, we have no great treatises on the subject,—no one body of thought. We have merely, here and there, utterances more or less happy by leading thinkers, and improvements in practice by enlightened rulers.

Throughout the Middle Ages, thanks to the spirit of Christianity, more rays of justice and humanity shone forth; but Ecclesiasticism triumphed over Christianity by establishing the doctrine that "an oath contrary to the interests of the Church is void."

As we go on through that period, matters seem at their worst. Such actions as those of Pope Julius II releasing Ferdinand of Spain from his treaty with France; of Pope Clement V allowing the King of France to break an inconvenient oath, and violate a solemn treaty; of Pope Pius V destroying the sanctity of treaties in order to revive civil war in France, had seemed to tear out the very roots of International Law. But, bad as these acts were, they were followed by worse. The conduct of Pope Innocent X, denouncing the Treaty of Westphalia and absolving its signers from their oaths, thus seeking to perpetuate the frightful religious wars which had devastated Germany for thirty and the Netherlands for eighty years; this and a host of similar examples, Protestant as well as Catholic, seemed to fasten that old monstrous system upon the world forever. So far as nations had any views regarding their reciprocal duties, these were practically expressed in Machiavelli's *Prince,* which, whatever may have been its author's intent, had become the gospel of State Scoundrelism. All was a seething cauldron of partisan hostilities, personal hatreds, and vile ambitions—scoundrelism coming to the surface more evidently than all else.[1]

But under this cloud of wretchedness an evolution of

---

[1] For Innocent X and the Treaty of Westphalia, see Gieseler, *Kirchengeschichte*, translated by H. B. Smith, vol. iv, p. 239, where citation from original sources is made. For previous cases mentioned, see Laurent, *Études sur l'Histoire de l'Humanité*, vol. x, *passim*. For additional and more complete citations, see the preceding article on Grotius.

better thought had been going on. Amid the mass of
mere dry lawyers and venal pettifoggers had arisen jurists, men who sought to improve municipal and international law; until finally, in 1625, amid all the horrors
and atrocities of the Thirty Years' War, was published
at Paris the great work of Grotius—the *De Jure Belli
ac Pacis*. This became the foundation of modern
thought in that splendid province. With perfect justice
does an eminent English authority of our time declare,
"It is scarcely too much to say that no uninspired work
has more largely contributed to the welfare of the Com-
monwealth of States; it is a monument which can only
perish with the civilized intercourse of nations, of which
it has laid down the master principles with a master's
hand. Grotius first awakened the conscience of Governments to the Christian sense of international duty." [1] It
confronted the unreason of the world with a vast array
of the noblest utterances of all time; it enforced these
with genius; it welded the whole mass of earlier ideas,
thus enforced, into his own thought, and put into the
hands of those who followed him a mighty weapon
against the follies of rulers and the cruelties of war.

We have seen, in the foregoing chapter, that the fundamental thought of Grotius was that international law had
a twofold basis: first, the "Law of Nature," the moral
commands of God to the human family, as discerned by
right reason; secondly, the "Law of Nations,"—or
"Positive Law,"—the law which results from the actual
enactments and agreements of nations, and that, as between these two divisions, his clear tendency was to give
supremacy to the "Law of Nature" and to bring the
"Law of Nations" more and more into conformity with
this.[1]

[1] See Phillimore, *Commentaries upon International Law*, London, second
edition, 1871, preface, p. 50.
[1] See Phillimore, *Commentaries upon International Law*, London, second

The first eminent apostle of Grotius was Pufendorf, who, in 1672, published his *De Jure Naturæ et Gentium.* He was at once confronted, as Grotius had been, by a large part of the clergy. At that period International Law, and, indeed, all law, was kept well in hand by theology, and theology discovered in the views of these new thinkers, a certain something which weakened sundry supposed foundations of law as laid down in our sacred books.

Was any attempt made to mitigate the horrors of war, the Old Testament was cited to show that the Almighty commanded the Jews in their wars to be cruel. Was any attempt made to mitigate persecution for difference in belief, the New Testament was opened at the texts, "Compel them to enter in," and "I came not to send peace, but a sword." Was any attempt made to loosen the shackles of serfs, both Old and New Testament were opened to show that slavery was of divine sanction. Was any attempt made to stop the witchcraft trials which during yet a century continued destroying hundreds of innocent persons in Germany every year, an appeal was made to the text, "Thou shalt not suffer a witch to live," in the Old Testament, and to the blinding of Elymas and the everlasting damnation of sorcerers, in the New. Was an attempt made to abolish torture, the eminently orthodox Carpzov and his compeers cited the detection of Achan, the lot which fell on Jonathan, the "inquisition" made by King Ahasuerus.

The teachings of Grotius and Pufendorf cut to the heart of all this, and therefore, as the work of Grotius had been placed on the Index for Catholics, the works of Pufendorf were put under the ban by a large body of Protestants.

edition, 1871, preface, p. 50; and, for the beginnings of the application to government of the theories of natural law, Gierke, *Johannes Althusius und die Entwicklung der naturrechtlichen Staatstheorien,* Breslau, 1880.

Into the war thus begun, Thomasius, faithful to the views of his teachers, entered heartily by lecturing against Grotius and Pufendorf. He himself tells us, later, that he did not at first separate the questions of legal philosophy from those of theology; that, in his judgment at that early period, to doubt the principles laid down by theologians was to risk damnation; that, so great was his trust in the authority of so many excellent men, he would have exposed himself to the charge of ignorance sooner than to the slightest suspicion of separating himself from the dominant teaching.[1]

But there came in his thinking a great change. With that impartiality which is one of the rarest virtues in strong men, he studied carefully the writings of his adversary and was converted by him; and, having been converted, felt it a duty to be even more earnest in supporting than he had been in opposing him. More than this, he thereby learned the great lesson of relying upon his own powers. He declares, "I now saw that any being gifted by God with reason sins against the goodness of

[1] See Biedermann, *Deutschland im Achtzehnten Jahrhundert*, vol. ii, p. 349, Leipzig, 1880. For excellent accounts of the relative position of Grotius, Pufendorf, and Thomasius, see Heffter, *Droit International*, troisième édition, 1875, par. 10; also Phillimore, *Commentaries on International Law*, second edition, London, 1871, p. 50; also Wheaton, *Elements of International Law*, introduction; Woolsey, *International Law*, introduction, and appendix I; for extended and interesting accounts of the historical development, see Wheaton, *Histoire du Progrès du Droit des Gens*, introduction and first chapters. And, for a close discussion of the main points involved, see Franck, *Reformateurs et Publicistes de l'Europe, Dix-septième Siècle*, Paris, 1881, chap. iii. For excellent brief summaries, see Walker, *History of the Law of Nations*, Cambridge (England), 1899, vol. i, pp. 162–164, and D. J. Hill, introduction to Campbell's translation of the *De Jure Belli ac Pacis*, Washington, 1901; also the *History of European Diplomacy*, by the same author. For the interesting personal relations which were developed between Pufendorf and Thomasius, see Gigas, *Briefe Pufendorfs und Thomasius*, Leipzig, 1897; this work contains thirty-four letters hitherto unpublished, lately discovered in the Royal Library at Copenhagen,—only five others having been previously known.

his Creator when he allows himself to be led like an ox by any other human being"; and he adds, "I determined to shut my eyes against the brightness of human authority, and to give no more thought to the question, *who* supports any doctrine; but only to weigh fairly the grounds for and against it."

The earlier views of the young instructor had been well received; but, as he developed these later ideas, his audiences became alarmed and "before long," as he tells us, "I was left alone in my lecture room with my Grotius."

Yet he was not discouraged. Having given two years to study, thought, and travel, he began again, and now drew large audiences. The inert mass of German law began under his hands to throb with a new life.[1]

At first his zeal and ability carried all before him, and despite the grumblings of his opponents he was in 1685 admitted to membership in the learned society which edited the literary journal of the University—the *Acta Eruditorum*.

But matters became speedily worse for him. The young instructor's facility in lecturing and publishing was as great as his zeal, and his every book and every lecture aroused new distrust in the older race of theologians and jurists. Enemies beset him on all sides; now and then skirmishes were won against him, resulting in condemnation of this or that book or prohibition of this or that course of lectures.

But for his real genius he would have lost the battle entirely. He committed errors in taste, errors in tact, errors in statement, errors in method, more than enough to ruin a man simply of great talent; but he was possessed of more than talent, of more than genius. For

[1] For interesting details of Thomasius' struggle against the ideas of Pufendorf and of his final conversion to them, see Stintzing and Landsberg, *Geschichte der Deutschen Rechtswissenschaft*, part ii, chap. iii.

there was in him a deep, earnest purpose, a force which obstacles only increased; and so, as preparatory to his lectures of 1687–8 came the startling announcement that they were to be in the spoken language of his country. This brought on a crisis.   To his enemies it seemed insult added to injury.   Heretofore Thomasius had developed the ideas of Grotius and Pufendorf; this was bad enough; but now his opponents declared that he purposed to disgrace the University and degrade the Faculty.   In vain did Thomasius take pains to make his views understood.   In vain did he admit the worth of Greek and Latin to those aiming at ripe scholarship; in vain did he show the great advantages which France had reaped from the cultivation of her own language; in vain did he show that through the modern languages those aiming only at a practical career could be given a far wider and more useful education than through a tongue which they could never know with thoroughness; that a flexible modern language is the best medium in which new thought can be developed—all in vain.[1]

The opposition became more and more determined; but he stood none the less firmly.   More and more he labored to clear away barbarisms and to bring in a better philosophy; and, while he continued to deliver some of his lectures and write some of his books in Latin, he persisted in using German in those lectures and books which

[1] This opening lecture of Thomasius (the "programme" which served as an announcement of his course) was reprinted by himself in 1701, and has again been reprinted in our day, under the title of "Christian Thomasius on the Imitation of the French," as No. 1 of the new series of *Deutsche Litteraturdenkmale*, Stuttgart, 1894.

For a striking example of his errors in taste and method, see the very curious and comical statement of a speech before the professors and students of Halle in 1694, in Tholuck, *Vorgeschichte des Rationalismus,*— second part, *Das kirchliche Leben des Siebzehnten Jahrhunderts,*—Berlin, 1861, part ii, pp. 71 *et seq.;* and for other examples, see pages following. For an open confession of what he considered his own too great indulgence in cutting speech, see especially p. 72.   For complaints by others against his too great sharpness and severity, see pp. 74 *et seq.*

appealed to his audiences more directly and fully. This brought more and more intrigues, more and more pressure; every sort of authority, lay and ecclesiastic, was besought to remove him.

As we have seen, he had been one of the editors of a Latin literary journal; he now established a literary journal in German,—the first of any real value ever known. Thomasius was the first to found a German literary journal in any true sense of the word.[1]

Not only did he give up the old language of literary criticism, but he relinquished its old paths. The time-honored methods in criticism were simple. They were largely those of a mutual admiration society—each professor sounding in sonorous Latin the glories of his sect or his clique, and showing in pungent Latin the futility of all others. With all such Thomasius made havoc; discussed the works of his colleagues and of others impartially; asked no favors and showed none. He was the sworn foe of intolerance, of abuses rooted in prejudice, of all mere formulas and learned jargon.

Nor did he confine himself to that easiest and cheapest of all things—destructive criticism; he determined not merely to criticise, but to create,—not merely to destroy, but to build; he showed, distinctly, power to develop new good things in place of old bad things.

This work of his, then, apparently revolutionary, was really evolutionary: he opened German literature to the influences of its best environment; he stripped off its thick, tough coatings and accretions of pedantry, sophistry, bigotry, and conventionalism, and brought it into clean and stimulating contact with the best life of Germany and of Europe.

[1] For a brief but excellent statement of the relation of this new journalism to the advancement of German thought, see Kuno Francke, *Social Forces in German Literature*, p. 176 (note). For a fuller treatment, see Prutz, *Geschichte des Deutschen Journalismus*, and the histories of German literature by Hettner and Julian Schmidt.

While opposing the unfit use of the ancient languages, he never ceased efforts to improve his own language. Luther had, indeed, given it a noble form by his translation of the Bible; but pedantry was still too powerful: the vernacular was despised. All care was given to Latin. At sundry schools of high repute children were not only trained to speak Latin, but whipped if they spoke anything else. Learned schoolmasters considered it disgraceful to speak their own language, or to allow their pupils to speak it. The result was that the German language had become a jargon. Even Thomasius himself never fully freed his style from the influence of his early teachers: much as he did to improve German literature by calling attention to the more lucid French models, he never could entirely shake off the old shackles.[1]

Nor less striking were his efforts in behalf of a better system of instruction. He insisted that so much useless matter was crammed into scholars' minds that there was little place for things of real value. He urged the authorities to give up the debased Aristotelianism still dominant, quickened thought on subjects of living interest, and declared that "the logic of the schools is as useless in prying into truth as a straw in overturning a rock."[2]

The evil was deep-seated. Candidates for degrees in his time discussed such subjects as the weight of the grape clusters which the spies brought out of the promised land; one professor lectured twenty-four years on the first chapter of Isaiah; another lectured an equal time on the first ten chapters of Jeremiah; still another gave thirteen years to an explanation of the Psalms;

[1] See curious examples in Räumer, *Geschichte der Pädagogik*, cited in Klemperer. On the general change from Latin to French in intercourse between nations, see Paulsen, *Die Deutschen Universitäten*, pp. 47, 48.

[2] As to Thomasius' plan to give something better than the usual subjects of study, see Dernburg, *Thomasius und die Stiftung der Universität Halle*, pp. 8 et seq.

Gesner, the philologist, tells of another who devoted four lecture-hours to one word in Aristotle's "Rhetoric." [1]

To all the objections of Thomasius against this sort of learning, his opponents made easy answer:—that his arguments were shallow, and he himself a charlatan. But he committed still another crime. Spener having continued his efforts to bring peace between the warring factions in the Church and to arouse Christian effort, Thomasius defended him, made common cause with him, and, indeed, for a considerable time, became milder in character and utterance. Hence it was that, though for his views on the source of public law he had been called an "Atheist," he was now stigmatized as a "Pietist."

And soon came another charge, even worse. A Danish Court Preacher, Masius, had put forth a treatise to prove Lutheranism the form of religion most favorable to princely power; most clear in teaching the divine authority of princely government, the necessity of passive obedience on the part of the governed, the absolute authority conferred on government directly from God, and without any necessary consent of the people. No argument could appeal more strongly to the multitude of princelings, great and small, who then ruled every corner of Germany. These statements and arguments, Thomasius, in the regular course of his work as Professor and Journalist, brought under criticism; stigmatized them as attempts to curry favor with the ruling class; and finally declared that, although the powers that be are ordained of God, various rights on the part of the governed must be supposed. This threw the opposing theologians and jurists into new spasms. They had previously, without much regard for consistency, declared Thomasius guilty of atheism and pietism; they now de-

---

[1] See citations from Tholuck and others in the admirable summary of Klemperer.

9

clared him guilty of disrespect to majesty: the Danish
Government made a solemn complaint to the Government
of Saxony; and his book was burned by a Danish hangman, while the Elector of Saxony, the palace clique, and
the authorities of the Church at Dresden, were more
loudly than ever besought to remove him.

Against all this he stood firm. But at last fortune
seemed to desert him. His love of justice plunged him
into apparent ruin. The Duke of Sachsen-Zeitz had
chosen to marry a daughter of the Elector of Brandenburg. The reasons for the marriage were many and
weighty. The alliance was a happy one for the two
states, and the Prince and Princess loved each other;
but Saxony was Lutheran, and Brandenburg Calvinistic:
the marriage was, therefore, denounced from the leading
Lutheran pulpits. Against these Thomasius began another struggle. On grounds of simple justice, of public
right, and of opposition to intolerance he defended the
marriage. This angered the Saxon Court and brought
fresh complaint from his theologic colleagues at Leipsic.
The other great Saxon university, at Wittenberg, was
not less indignant, and was further angered by his ex-
posure of a gross misstatement by one of its great Lutheran theologians regarding the Calvinist teaching. The
two Faculties vied in denouncing him to the authorities.
This led to a catastrophe: he was forbidden until further
orders to lecture either in public or in private or to print
anything whatsoever, and a warrant was issued for his
arrest. Deprived thus of all his means of support, and
with his family looking to him for bread, he did not
await the service of the warrant: baffling his foes by
his very boldness, he shook from his feet forever the
dust of Saxony and sought refuge at the capital of the
Elector of Brandenburg.

Thus, in 1690, apparently ended all his opportunities
to better his country. At the age of thirty-five years, he

saw his enemies triumphant;—every cause for which he had struggled apparently lost;—himself considered, among friends, and enemies alike, as ruined, discredited, and ridiculous.[1]

[1] As to all this, seè Thomasius' own account, appended to his *Das Recht evangelischer Fürsten in theologischen Streitigkeiten*, Halle, 1696, and his yet fuller narratives in his *Juristische Händel*, ii (Halle, 1721), pp. 1–167, and in his *Gemischte Händel*, ii (Halle, 1723), pp. 44–558; iii, 625–768.

AS we have seen, Thomasius had been driven, under a serious charge, from a leading chair in a renowned university, to seek whatever chance might offer in a town comparatively unimportant.

To his contemporaries, clearly viewing the whole field, the future of his reforms, as well as his own personal prospects, must have seemed poor indeed. And yet, to us, looking along that chain of cause and effect which spans the abyss separating the American civilization of the twentieth century from the German civilization of the seventeenth, it is now clear that this catastrophe was but a prelude to that great series of victories for justice, right reason, and mercy, which have brought vast blessings to his country and to humanity.

There was at Halle what was known as a "Ritterschule": an intermediate academy for young nobles. It seemed but a dull centre of thought as compared with that which Thomasius had left, but he took service in it, and began a new career even more strenuous than the old. Discouraging prophecies were many, but all were soon brought to naught; the best of his old Leipsic students followed him; others flocked in from other parts of Germany, and soon he was more influential than ever: speaking to larger audiences and taking stronger hold.

The sovereign under whom he had thus taken refuge was the Elector Frederick III of Brandenburg, who afterward made himself the first king of Prussia: thus beginning that line of monarchs which has since won the sovereignty of the present German Empire.

The Elector saw his opportunity. True to those same instincts which have made the Hohenzollerns the ruling

family in Europe, true to the policy which led King
Frederick William III, after his defeat by the first Napoleon, to establish the University of Berlin, and the Emperor William I, after his victory over the third Napoleon,
to reëstablish the University of Strasburg, Frederick III,
in 1694, made the Academy of Halle a university, gave it
a strong faculty, named Thomasius a full professor in it,
and a few years later placed him at its head.

The new institution was at once attacked from all sides,
and especially by its elder sisters. Intrigues were set
on foot to induce the Emperor at Vienna to abolish it.
Every attempt was made to stir sectarian hate against
it. A favorite reference to it among its enemies was a
play upon words: naming it the University of Hell
(Hölle), and alluding to it as "ein höllisches Institut." [1]

But these attacks helped Thomasius's work rather than
hurt it. To understand the causes and results of such
attacks an American in these days has only to recall the
articles in very many sectarian newspapers and the sermons in numberless sectarian pulpits during the middle
years of the nineteenth century against Cornell University and the State Universities of our Western commonwealths; very good examples may also be seen to-day in
similar diatribes upholding the sectarian colleges of various Southern States against their state universities. But
in that, as in more recent cases, the Darwinian theory
seemed to apply: for, while these diatribes kept many
sons of timid parents away from Halle, there seemed a
survival of the fittest: the more independent and thoughtful youth flocked to Thomasius's lecture-room in ever
increasing numbers. Erelong, his university rivaled
Leipzig and Wittenberg, and became a leading centre of
German thought. It became almost what Wittenberg had
been in the days of Luther. Well has Thomasius been

[1] See Dernburg, pp. 23 *et seq.;* also Guericke and others cited by Klemperer.

called by an eminent authority "the cornerstone of the new university," for during forty years his spirit was its main inspiration.[1]

The basis of all his teaching was his development of the ideas of Grotius and Pufendorf: making law an evolution of right reason as against that survival of mediæval ideas which mainly promoted conformity with the letter of the sacred books and especially with the laws of Moses. But this was by no means all. More and more he strove to bring order out of chaos. The main material of law as then presented in Germany was an incoherent mass drawn not only from the Bible, but from the Roman Law, the Canon Law, and from decisions, glosses, notions, whimsies,—of authorities here, there, and everywhere, often irreconcilable,—the breeding-ground of pedantry and the happy hunting-ground of venal ingenuity.

The spirit which permeated the teaching of Thomasius gave him a special power. The foremost purpose of his predecessors and rivals was the maintenance of dogma; their principal means being hair-splitting definitions, distinctions, subtleties, and pedantries. Through all these the young professor broke boldly. His evident ambition was to distinguish himself, not by buttressing outworn beliefs, but by infusing into the younger generation a love for truth;—a straightforward use of right reason in seeking it and a manly courage in defending it. His clear purpose was to give his country deeper foundations of justice, and on these to begin a better superstructure of law. He was by no means contemptuous of ancient sources. If right reason was embodied in an Old or New Testament declaration, or in a Roman code, or in the decision of a mediæval

[1] For the hard names hurled at the new institution, and for the reasons which led parents to send their sons to it, in spite of these attacks, see Ludewig's history of the founding of the University of Halle, prefixed to the second volume of his *Consilia Hallensium Jurisconsultorum*, Halle, 1734—especially pp. 44 ff.

court, or in the better thought of a contemporary pedant,
he was glad to make use of it; but he was, of all things, and
in the highest sense, practical: anxious to set men, not at
spinning new theories to cover old abuses, but at thinking out better theories and working out better practice.
So vigorous a teacher was a marvel in that age of pedantry.
He dressed like a man of the world, and lectured to his
students as if he were chatting with them. He encouraged them to interrupt him with questions. He depre-
cated their taking of notes—he had noticed, he said, that
the most industrious note-takers were often the poorest
listeners: they took down things which had never entered his head; and, satisfied with their notes, they gave
the subject no thought or study of their own. Instead he
gave them printed outlines of his lectures—terse and
pithy summaries, the "kernel and basis," as he said, of
his teaching—and, with these in his own hands as well as
in his students', he made the rest of his work extempore.
He threw open to his students his home and cultivated
their personal acquaintance. Yet he would have no abject disciples: they must be independent even of him—
he wanted no "Thomasites," he said.

Amazing was the ground he covered. What the pedants had dawdled over for months he despatched in a
week. Yet he found time for excursions into every field
of practical interest—Manners, Morals, Politics, Economics. Long before Halle, at his instance, established the
first chair of Economics and Administration and entered
consciously on the career which has long made it so pre-
eminent a school for students of government, he was
teaching there the elements of all the political sciences.
But, above all, he tempered everything with History.
To him things were intelligible only in their historical
growth and their setting; and, following the best tradition of the great sixteenth-century jurists, he made his
courses in Law courses also in History—national, eccle-

siastical, universal. Thus far, in the universities, History, if taught at all, had been almost a monopoly of the theologians,—set forth, with Daniel's interpretation of the vision of Nebuchadnezzar as an outline, to illustrate the divine government of the world or demonstrate some scheme of redemption. Thomasius freed it from its supernatural background, made its theme the affairs of states and of society, and showed its use as a discipline for practical men. His pithy summaries strayed far beyond his classroom. A generation later Frederick the Great still urged that History be studied with the outlines of Thomasius.[1]

The main result of all this was soon seen in the new sort of professional men who went forth from Halle. That University became, under his direction, the training school for the state officials of Prussia. Instead of pedants discoursing endlessly in wretched Latin on the weight of the grapes of Eshcol, or on the meaning of this or that word in Aristotle, or on the sin of "syncretism" and the like, we find men under his guidance learning to think upon municipal and international law, on public economy, on state administration, and, none the less for all of this, on a new and nobler literature. No wonder that Paulsen, the eminent historian of German higher education, calls Halle "the first really modern university."

As the years went on, increasing numbers of young men were sent out from this seat of learning to lay foundations

[1] For the work of Thomasius as a teacher, see not only the books of Ludewig and Dernburg already cited, and the great history of the University of Halle by Schrader (Halle, 1894), but Paulsen's *Geschichte des gelehrten Unterrichts,* and especially an article in the Preussische Jahrbücher (vol. cxiv, 1903), by Schiele, *Aus dem Thomasischen Collegio.* A set of the printed outlines of Thomasius—that for his course on the History of German Law (we should call it Constitutional History)—may be seen in the library of Cornell University. Especially rich in detail as to the teaching of Thomasius is an address by Frensdorff on *Halle und Göttingen* (Göttingen, 1894); and a study of the same year by Rauch, *Thomasius als Gast in Erhard Weigel's Schule zu Jena* (printed in the *Symbola Doctorum Jenensis Gymnasii in honorem Gymnasii Isenacensis*), shows his warm interest in secondary as well as in higher education.

for Prussian administration, and thus to prepare the ground for the House of Hohenzollern, and for the present German Empire.[1]

Nor did science, literature, or theology suffer. Better progress was made in each of these. Into every one of these fields great men went forth from the new university, especially into theology. Such men in our own day, from Tholuck and Julius Müller to Harnack and Pfleiderer,— who have been and are leaders of religious thought in Germany, and indeed throughout Christendom,—are the legitimate results of Thomasius's influence: without him, so far as we can now see, they would have been impossible.

But, while thus building up his department and the University, he did not forget his duty to the German people at large. He ceased, indeed, to publish his literary journal; but this was only that he might give all his time to works of greater importance. He never forgot that his main effort must be to lay better foundations of principle, to bring in better modes of thought, and to stimulate a more practical performance of duty. In 1691 was published his *Doctrine of Common Sense;* in 1692, his *Doctrine of Morals;* and, after a number of other treatises designed to uplift the character and conduct of the whole nation, appeared, in 1705, his work on *Natural and International Law.*

Yet all this was but a part of his activity. While doing university work, and writing treatises, learned and popular, he plunged more and more into great living questions,—the greatest on which any man of his time could be engaged, and in which he rendered more direct service to mankind than did any other German between Luther and Lessing.

First of these was THE BELIEF IN WITCHCRAFT. To un-

---

[1] For an excellent summary of the services rendered by Thomasius to German literature and to the House of Hohenzollern, see Julian Schmidt, *Bilder aus dem Geistigen Leben,* Leipzig, 1870, vol. i, pp. 42, *et seq.*

derstand the work of Thomasius toward finally destroying a growth so widespread, so noxious, and so tenacious
of life, we must look back over its history.

Its roots ran deep into the earlier strata of human civilization, and especially into the mythologies and theologies of Babylonia, Persia, Judea, Rome, and the rude
tribes of early Europe.   In the early days of Christianity
a rank growth had come from sundry passages in our own
sacred books; above all from the command in the Mosaic
law, "Thou shalt not suffer a witch to live," and from
the declaration in the Psalms that "All the gods of the
heathen are devils." [1]

Various great fathers and doctors of the Church, with
St. Augustine, St. Gregory the Great, and St. Thomas
Aquinas at their head, strengthened this growth, and it
was more and more bound on the consciences of the
faithful by various pronouncements of the infallible head
of Christendom.

First among these may be noted the bull *Super illius
specula,* issued in 1326 by Pope John XXII.   In this
solemn utterance, addressed to the universal Church and
to all future times, the Holy Father grieves at the increase of those who make a pact with hell and pay worship to demons, shutting up devils in finger-rings and
mirrors and phials that they may extort their aid, and
making waxen images of their fellow Christians in order
to bewitch them.   Pope John believed that his own life
had thus been attempted by piercing a waxen image of
him with needles; and not only in this bull but in brief
after brief to bishop and inquisitor he urged the prosecu-
tion and extirpation of these miscreants by all the penalties prescribed for heresy.

---

[1] So Psalm xcvi, 5, was translated by the Vulgate and by all the early
versions; and so the early Christian church unquestioningly believed, as is
clear, for example, from I. Cor., x, 20, 21: "The things which the Gentiles
sacrifice, they sacrifice to devils," etc.

His successors shared his alarm, and in 1437 Pope Eugene IV addressed a general letter to all the inquisitors, recapitulating for them the horrid deeds of the witches and how by mere word or touch or sign they can bewitch whom they will, inflict or cure disease, or call down storms, and exhorting the guardians of the Holy Faith to greater rigor, even though it should be necessary to enlist the aid of the secular power. Such utterances, issued, as devout Christians believed, under the infallible guidance of the Holy Spirit, led to new carnivals of judicial murder in various parts of Europe; but it was left to Pope Innocent VIII to lend the culminating sanction of the Church both to the superstition and to the cruelty of the witch-persecution. The inquisitors commissioned for Germany found in many quarters of that rational and liberty-loving land, both lay and clerical, a slowness to accept either their startling teaching or their summary procedure. Turning, therefore, to Pope Innocent, they won from him, in 1484, the famous bull *Summis desiderantes,* which, of all edicts ever sent forth under Paganism or Christianity, has doubtless caused the most unlimited cruelty and the most profuse shedding of innocent blood. Setting forth at much length and in hideous detail the orgies of crime in which throughout Germany men and women sold to Satan were revelling, it empowered the inquisitors to proceed, in spite of the opposition of those who "think of themselves more highly than they ought to think," with all the authority of the Church, and instructed the Bishop of Strasburg to put down by force any attempt to hinder or annoy them, authorizing them to use, where necessary, excommunication and interdict or to call in the help of the State.[1]

[1] As to these papal utterances, see especially Hansen, *Zauberwahn, Inquisition und Hexenprozess im Mittelalter;* and, for the text of the documents, his *Quellen und Untersuchungen zur Geschichte des Hexenwahns.*

Even thus equipped the inquisitors were not content. They now set themselves at compiling a code of witch-persecution which should leave no excuse for delay or laxity. They called it *"Malleus Maleficarum,"*—*"The Witch Hammer."* At the head of it, to give it authority, they printed the papal bull, and to the bull they added a writ of approval from the Emperor and a commendation, genuine or forged, from the eminent Theological Faculty of Cologne.[1]

This work, thus written and thus vouched for, was received as almost divinely inspired, and its teachings soon became fruitful in horrors throughout Germany, and, indeed, throughout Christendom. Its doctrines were preached in thousands of pulpits, spread by myriads of traveling friars, and soon, through all central Europe, came wide and systematic spying, torture, strangling, and burning. The victims were numbered by thousands. They included many men and children, but the overwhelming majority were women. Typical of the reasoning in the *Witch Hammer* may be noted a most cogent argument for seeking the main culprits among women: a rare bit of philology. It asserted that the word *femina* (woman) was a compound of *fe* (faith) and *minus* (less); therefore that women had less faith than men, and hence were especially prone to alliances with Satan.

From diocese to diocese, from village to village, the

An English translation of the bull *Summis desiderantes* may be found in the little body of extracts on *The Witch Persecution*, edited by Professor Burr in the University of Pennsylvania's *Translations and Reprints*. As to the rise of the witch persecution in general, compare also Soldan, *Geschichte der Hexenprozesse*, Lea, *History of the Inquisition of the Middle Ages*, iii, Riezler, *Geschichte der Hexenprocesse in Bayern*, and Hinschius, *Kirchenrecht*, vi, i. What can be said in defense of the Church's relation to it—and more—has been said by Diefenbach, *Der Hexenwahn vor und nach der Glaubensspaltung.*

[1] On the composition of the *Witch Hammer* a flood of light has been thrown by the researches of Hansen. See not only his two works, mentioned above, but also his article in the *Westdeutsche Zeitschrift*, 1898.

witchcraft procedure spread, and the torture chambers were soon in full operation everywhere. The victims, writhing under torture, anxious only for death to end their sufferings, confessed to anything and everything. All that was needed was that the inquisitors should hint at the answers desired, and, there being no limit to the torture, there was no limit to the folly of the confessions. The agonized victims confessed readily to raising storms, spreading epidemics and cattle pests, riding on broomsticks to the Blocksberg, doing homage to Satan, signing Satanic compacts in their own blood, taking part in every sort of vile rite which the imagination of the inquisitors could conceive, and even to bearing children to Satan. Confessions of this latter sort were forced by torture from the lips not only of women, but of children; and then, for this preposterous crime, thus absurdly proven, they were strangled and burned, if not burned alive.

The main agents in carrying on this sacred work in Germany were, first, the Dominicans, and, at a later period, the Jesuits. They did it thoroughly. Especially during the later sixteenth century and the earlier seventeenth we find them pushing it everywhere.

Leaders of a forlorn hope against this folly and cruelty arose in Teutonic lands as elsewhere,—such as Cornelius Agrippa, John Wier, Dietrich Flade, and Cornelius Loos. All were persecuted for their boldness, and the last two effectively silenced; Loos, indeed, escaped capital punishment, but only, after repeated imprisonment, by being carried off by the plague, while Flade, though Chief Justice of the old city of Treves and ex-Rector of its University, was put on trial by the Archbishop, tortured until he confessed everything suggested to him, and then strangled and burned.[1]

---

[1] The original manuscript records of the trial of Flade, including the questions of his inquisitors and his answers while under torture, as well as a copy of the manuscript of Loos's suppressed and long-lost book against the persecution, may be seen in the library of Cornell University.

To maintain this system, there had continued a stream of teachings from infallible Rome. The successors of Pope Innocent—Alexander VI, Julius II, Leo X, Adrian VI, Clement VII—had all found occasion to urge on the pious work; and, to deepen and broaden it, new treatises were written by theologians and jurists in various parts of Europe, the most learned and most cruelly potent being the new manual for witch finders and witch murderers put forth, just at the opening of the seventeenth century, by the Jesuit Delrio.[1]

Despite all this incitement to persecution, opposition to it continued. Even among the Jesuits themselves, who had furnished so many leaders for these atrocities and follies, there arose a few men who dared to harbor doubts and to seek to open the eyes of others. Two of these, Tanner and Laymann, whose pleas for hesitation and moderation found place mainly in heavy tomes of theology, reaped only suspicion and abuse. A third, Father Friedrich Spee, tried a different method. Deputed to hear the final confessions of witches before their execution, he had learned from them that their previous confessions to the inquisitors had been due simply to unbearable torture; and he had thenceforth been obliged to see multitudes of men, women, and children whom he knew to be absolutely innocent consigned to torture and death. To reveal the truth to their judges, even could he thus have betrayed the secrets of the confessional, could have resulted only in a repetition of the torture, in a renewal of the lying confession, and in suspicion of himself as an accomplice. The strain of this fearful dilemma made him prematurely old and gray; and, during a respite from his frightful duty, he prepared a most eloquent treatise against the whole delusion, the *Cautio Criminalis*. Even

---

[1] For the deliveries of the Popes, see Hansen and the other authorities named in an earlier note. The influence of Delrio's book is best shown by its many editions.

this he dared not publish, but circulated it only in manuscript till some friend, perhaps not without the author's connivance, secured its publication at the Protestant university town of Rinteln. It found a wide, and in many quarters, a sympathetic hearing; yet, in spite of its convincing statement of facts and its eloquent arraignment of the whole procedure, a change came but slowly. The persecutions raged on much as before. Spee had, indeed, imparted his secret to a young student—Johann Philipp von Schönborn—who afterward rose to be Bishop of Würzburg, Bishop of Worms, Archbishop of Mainz, Primate of Germany; but, though von Schönborn did untold good by checking the persecution throughout his dioceses so long as he lived, and confided to such friends as the philosopher Leibnitz the secret of his opposition, he dared not take open ground against the superstition, and could effect no permanent reform.[1]

Nor had the Reformation brought to Protestant lands any alleviation of these follies and cruelties. The leading reformers, both Lutheran and Calvinist, accepted the whole monstrous system as grounded, infallibly, in Holy Scripture. The great body of Protestant theologians and ecclesiastics, as soon as they had obtained power, exerted themselves to prove their orthodoxy by making their procedure even more searching and cruel, if possible, than that in Catholic states.

[1] How far from thoroughgoing was the skepticism of Tanner and Laymann has been pointed out by Riezler (*Geschichte der Hexenprozesse in Bayern*, pp. 248–267). His doubts as to the praise due Laymann, however, have been partly annulled by the studies of Duhr (his *Die Stellung der Jesuiten in den deutschen Hexenprozessen* and his article, in the *Zeitschrift für Katholische Theologie*, 1899, on *Paul Laymann und die Hexenprocesse*). As to Tanner, see also Rapp, *Die Hexenprozesse und ihre Gegner in Tirol*. On Spee (his latest biographer prefers to spell his name Spee) see, beside Duhr's book just named, the same writer's *Neue Daten und Briefe zum Leben des P. Friedrich Spe* (in the *Historisches Jahrbuch* of the Görres-Gesellschaft, 1900) and his revision of the life of Spee by Diel.

In small towns, whether Catholic or Protestant, more executions sometimes took place in a single year for this imaginary crime than are now allowed in the whole German Empire for capital crimes during decades of years. The statement has never been disproved that in the century previous to the birth of Thomasius—the hundred years between the middle of the sixteenth and the middle of the seventeenth century—more than a hundred thousand persons were put to death in Germany alone for witchcraft, confessed under torture; and, though there had gradually come some diminution in the number of victims, it remained a fearful curse even in Thomasius's time—accepted largely by the best men, and, among these, by Thomasius himself.[1]

But in 1694 he was called, as a member of the Halle faculty of law, to take part in a discussion on the procedure to be used against an alleged witch. Basing his decision upon the doctrines and methods of the great theologians and jurists of Germany, and indeed of the world, he gave his vote for the use of the torture, against the supposed criminal. Happily the accused was saved by the verdict of the majority of Thomasius's associates, led by the vote of Professor Stryk, his principal rival in the Halle Faculty of Law.

Had Thomasius been a mere dogmatist, or a logical gladiator, or a sensation-monger, or simply opinionated or selfish or conceited, he would have plunged into the

---

[1] In addition to the authorities already given, see Klemperer; Soldan, *Geschichte der Hexen-Processe in Deutschland;* Scherr, *Kulturgeschichte Deutschlands,* chap. v; Henne-am-Rhyn, *Kulturgeschichte der neuern Zeit,* etc. For profound, and at the same time interesting discussions based on the results of the superstition, see Wächter, *Beiträge zur Geschichte des Deutschen Strafrechts;* and, in English, the admirable summary given in Lecky's *History of Rationalism in Europe.* For exact statistics and details, see, in either edition of Soldan, chapters giving the lists of the condemned, with their ages, at Würzburg, Bamberg, Salzburg, and elsewhere; also Horst's *Zauber-Bibliothek,* and a mass of other authorities cited by the present writer in his *History of the Warfare of Science with Theology.*

fray, and, with pen and tongue, shown himself right and
his opponents wrong. It was a fine opportunity for
noise, for popularity, and for victory over Stryk, his
great rival. But he spurned all such temptations; put
aside all hostile feeling toward Stryk; bore his mortifica-
tion without complaining; began studying the whole subject more thoroughly; examined with the utmost care all
the cases he could hear of; and the result was that he not
only acknowledged himself wrong, but, having begun by
declaring against the torturing of witches, he soon took
a step further, for which the whole world is to-day his
debtor: he declared his disbelief in the whole superstition,
and especially in a devil—hoofed, horned, and tailed—
who whisks wretches through the air, assembles them
upon the Blocksberg, accepts their homage, and makes
those compacts with them which formed the foundation of
the witch trials.[1]

Thomasius's position was now full of peril. Indeed,
he seems himself to have felt this, and he was careful to
define it. He stated, no doubt with perfect honesty, that
as the Bible, both in Old Testament and New, declares
the existence of witches and sorcerers, and also declares,
"Thou shalt not suffer a witch to live," he did not presume to deny the existence of witches or their criminality; but what he protested against was the mode of action
usually attributed to Satan, and especially the existence

---

[1] For Thomasius' own account of this part of his life, see his *Juristische
Handel* (Halle, 1720, I. Theil, xviii).

For light upon Thomasius' first utterances against the prevailing
witchcraft theory, see the *Programmata Thomasiana*, Halle and Leipzig,
1724, pp. 351–355. They present a picture, at times pathetic, and at
times comic, of a strong man seeking to rend his fetters.

For the growth of Thomasius' theories on this subject, see Stintzing and
Landsberg, *Geschichte der deutschen Rechtswissenschaft*, iii, especially pp.
91, 92, which show that he speedily went beyond Stryk, who simply
denied the existence of any proofs of the alleged diabolical mode of action,
and denied the *possibility* of such relations between devils and human
beings.

10

of Satanic compacts and that mass of unreason which the great theologians and ecclesiastics of the Middle Ages and the Reformation period, Catholic and Protestant, had for so many generations developed and defended.

This disclaimer helped him little. Catholic writers denounced it as only one more example of the skeptical tendencies of Protestantism; Protestants denounced it as bringing disgrace upon their Church. Both the old theologians and the new pointed out the fact that he impugned not only the judgments of the most learned and pious authorities, Catholic and Protestant, but that he defied the clear statements of Holy Writ, the beliefs of the primitive Church, the assertions of the Fathers, the decisions of Councils dictated by the Holy Spirit, the infallible decrees of a long line of Popes, the whole mass of theological wisdom, past and present, and therefore the voice of the Holy Church Universal as uttered ''always, everywhere, and by all.''

Remembrances of the fate of many who had made a similar fight might well haunt him, and especially of the trial of Dietrich Flade, who, like him, had at first believed in the punishment of witches, like him had learned to doubt the evidence against them, like him had said so, and then, though like him an eminent jurist and a university professor, had been tortured and put to death.

Since that judicial murder a century had passed, and a series of champions had won various strong positions for humanity; but, though the defenders of the superstition could no longer send their enemies to the stake, they had fallen back into strong entrenchments, and were well armed.

The first of his main attacks on the whole witchcraft position were made by Thomasius during the opening years of the eighteenth century, and the earlier of these were curious in that they appeared as the theses of students under his presidency: notable among them being one by

Johann Reiche in 1701 and another by Johann Paul Ipsen in 1712. Thomasius freely acknowledged his controlling part in these, and during the remainder of his life followed them up with lectures, treatises, tracts, discussions of trials, translations of foreign works,—all in the same direction against this theological and judicial monstrosity.[1]

The air was thick with missiles, theological and judicial. In the Protestant church, there was cited against him that colossus of theology and ecclesiastical law, Benedict Carpzov—the man who boasted that he had read the Bible through fifty-three times; that he took the Holy Communion at least once a month; that he had sentenced or caused to be sentenced to death over twenty thousand persons; that he had devoted his life to strengthening the foundations of witchcraft procedure, and to increasing the severity of torture. In the older church, at the head of Thomasius's innumerable adversaries, as regarded theory, sat a multitude of the most eminent theological writers; and, as regarded practice, such prelates as the Archbishop of Salzburg and most of the other ecclesiastical princes of South Germany, who quietly ignored all argument, and went on torturing and burning as of old.

But the work of so many heroic champions and martyrs, now crowned by the efforts of Thomasius, began to bear abundant fruit. When, in 1679, the Archbishop of Salzburg sent in one year to the stake ninety-seven persons for witchcraft, he ended the series of greater burn-

---

[1] In the library of the Cornell University are not only copies of the original theses of Reiche and Ipsen, but a mass of publications and manuscripts of all sorts relating to the whole struggle. For a good detailed statement, see Luden, *Christian Thomasius*, p. 274 and note.

"In general," writes Riezler, one of the latest and most eminent of the German historians who have studied this subject, "Rationalism (*die Aufklärung*) in the Protestant lands of the Empire, for which especially the literary activity of Christian Thomasius was decisive, conquered the witch-delusion about one or two generations earlier than in the Catholic." See his *Geschichte der Hexenprozesse in Bayern*, p. 282.

ings; when the Bishop of Würzburg brought Maria Renata Sänger to scaffold and stake in 1749, and when in 1775 the courts of the Prince Abbot of Kempten beheaded Anna Maria Schwägelin, they ended judicial executions for witchcraft in Germany; and when Anna Göldi was executed at Glarus, Switzerland, in 1782, and two witches were judicially burned in Poland in 1793, the whole series was ended in civilized Europe.

III

B UT, perhaps, even greater were Thomasius's services in another field. Closely allied with the witchcraft superstition was the system of PROCEDURE BY TORTURE, then prevalent throughout the Continent. The connection between torture and witchcraft was logical. In England, where torture was rarely used, witchcraft never produced any such long series of judicial murders as on the Continent; but in Scotland and Continental Europe, wherever torture was applied, it came to be an axiom that a person charged with witchcraft who once entered the torture chamber was lost.[1]

The system of procedure by torture in securing testimony regarding crime had lingered along with more or less vitality ever since the days of the Roman Republic. One of the strongest arguments against it had been made by Cicero, though it is only fair to state that, on another occasion, Cicero, after the fashion of men like him, argued on the other side. In the latter days of the Roman Empire, largely under the influence of the Stoics, it had nearly died out. Successive Pagan Emperors had ameliorated it; had, indeed, abolished its worst features, and its destruction seemed certain. The barbarians of Europe, with few exceptions, ignored it in their codes; from the Vehmgericht it was absolutely excluded.

[1] For a most masterly essay, by a great jurist, on the connection between wholesale witchcraft convictions and procedure by torture, see Wächter, *Beiträge zur Geschichte des Deutschen Strafrechts*, especially in the appendices. For Thomasius' special arguments, made in legal treatises of 1711 and 1712, showing the logical and historical connection between the inquisitorial procedure, as sanctioned early in the 13th century by Pope Innocent III, the use of torture, and the witch trials, see Stintzing and Landsberg, *Geschichte der Deutschen Rechtswissenschaft*, iii, pp. 97, 98.

The Christian Church, too, in its days of comparative weakness, seemed to pronounce against it. In the fifth century St. Augustine, in the sixth century St. Gregory, and in the ninth Pope Nicholas I, were among great church leaders who denounced it, and during the early Middle Ages it fell comparatively into abeyance.

But the great misfortune was that the Church, after arriving at power, abjured the mild policy which it had supported during its weakness, gave torture new vitality, found cogent reasons for it, and introduced it in a far more cruel form and to a far greater extent than had ever before been known under Greeks, Romans, or barbarians.

For, under the Greeks and Romans, and in the ancient world generally, the cruelties of torture were *limited*. It was from this fact, indeed, that Cicero drew one of his strongest arguments against it, namely, that a criminal, if robust, could resist torture and avoid confession, but that an innocent man, if physically weak, might be forced to confess crimes which he had never committed.

But in the Christian Church, during the Middle Ages, there was developed the theory of "excepted cases." Under the belief that heresy and witchcraft were crimes especially favored by Satan, and that Satan would help his own, the old Roman procedure by torture was not only revived, but at last made unlimited. It was held that no torture could be too severe in suppressing these crimes. Every plea against the most extreme torture was met by the argument that Satan would of course strengthen heretics and witches to resist ordinary torture. The restraints of the earlier Pagan civilization were therefore cast aside. In trials for heresy and witchcraft there was absolutely no limit to torture. This new evolution of cruelty received the highest infallible sanction when in 1252 Innocent IV issued his directions to the Inquisition in Tuscany and Lombardy that confession should be extorted from heretics by torture, and this sacred precedent was followed for centuries by new and even more cruel decrees of Popes, Councils, and Bishops regarding procedure against both heretics and witches throughout Europe.

This procedure by torture naturally passed from the ecclesiastical into the lay courts, and all the more so because a method which was considered reasonable in one court seemed reasonable in another.

From time to time noble voices were raised in the Church against it, and among these that of Geiler of Kaisersberg,—the most popular of preachers at the beginning of the sixteenth century,—whose warnings against it resounded under the arches of Strasburg Cathedral, and along the upper Rhine.

But all in vain. During generation after generation procedure by torture was extended and systematized. In the sixteenth century the great "Caroline Code" of Charles V gave it new life. In the seventeenth century the codes of Louis XIV gave it new life in France. In the eighteenth century the code of Maria Theresa gave it new sanction in Germany.

In Great Britain, it long flourished noxiously in Scotland, and especially during the reign of James VI. Fortunately England remained comparatively free from it, the main exceptions to the milder English practice, strange to say, having occurred under Lord Coke and Lord Bacon.

Strong thinkers, indeed, arose from first to last against it. But when such philosophers as Montaigne and Bayle and Voltaire, and such jurists as Pussort and Sonnenfels and Beccaria, would have abolished torture, the whole Church influence, as well as the vast conservative authority in the legal profession, was against such an innovation, and this procedure steadily maintained its hold upon the world.[1]

It was widely argued that, since the Almighty punishes the greater part of mankind with tortures infinite in severity and eternal in duration, men might imitate the divine example by administering tortures which at the worst can only be feeble and brief as compared with the divine pattern. It was also held, as a purely practical view, by the great body of the ecclesiastics and lay lawyers that torture was the only effective method of eliciting testimony. Among the monuments of this vast superstition which exist to this day, the traveler sees the "witch towers," the torture chambers, and the collections of instruments of torture in various towns on the Continent: notably at Nuremberg, Ratisbon, Munich, and The Hague; but perhaps nothing brings the system more vividly before us than the executioners' tariffs still preserved. Four of these may be seen in the library of Cornell University, and, among them, especially that issued by the Archbishop Elector of Cologne in 1757. On four printed folio pages, it enumerates in fifty-five paragraphs every sort of hideous cruelty which an executioner could commit upon a prisoner, with the sum allowed him for each, and for the instruments therein required. Typical examples from this tariff are the following:—

[1] For a general statement of the history and development of torture, especially on the Continent, see Wächter, *Beiträge zur Geschichte des Römischen Strafrechts*, as already cited. For an excellent statement of its general development, see Lea, *Superstition and Force*, edition of 1892, pp. 477, 478, also 575, 576. For the history of procedure by torture in England, see Jardine's essay, also Pike, *History of Crime in England*, and for means of tracing out the historical development of English and Scotch ideas regarding it, see the index to Howell's *State Trials*, under the word "Torture." For the Church's use of it, see also Lea, *The Inquisition of the Middle Ages*, i, 421 ff; or, if a Catholic authority be preferred, the chapter on "Innocent IV and the Torture" in the Abbé Vacandard's *L'Inquisition*.

		Thalers.	Alb.
1.	For tearing asunder with four horses	5	26
2.	For quartering	4	
5.	For beheading and burning	5	26
7.	For strangling and burning	4	
8.	For cord and for laying the fire and kindling it .	2	
9.	For burning alive	4	
11.	For breaking a man alive on the wheel	4	
13.	For setting up the wheel with the body twisted in it	2	52
19.	For cutting off a hand or sundry fingers, and for beheading,—altogether	3	26
20.	For burning with a hot iron	1	26
22.	For beheading and placing the head upon a stake .	3	26
24.	For beheading, twisting the body in the wheel, and placing the head upon a stake,—altogether . .	5	
28.	For tearing a criminal before his execution with red-hot pincers,—each tearing of the flesh . .		26
31.	For nailing a tongue or hand to the gallows . .	1	26
42.	For the first grade of torture	1	26
44.	For the second grade of torture, including setting the limbs afterward, with salve for same . .	2	26

and so one through the fifty-five items and specifications.

On this whole system also, thus widespread, thus entrenched, thus defended, Thomasius declared war. Again it was through the thesis of a student—one Martin Bernhardi—that, in 1705, he opened the campaign. But this time the student in his zeal went faster than Thomasius could follow. The letter he appended to the youth's thesis shows his practical caution. He commends the student for his courage and echoes his conviction that the torture is a blot upon Christian states; but he counts it rash to sweep it away all at once. Further than this Thomasius seems never to have gone; and there is no reason to doubt the sincerity of his hesitation. Toward the very close of his life, in 1724, he reprinted this letter of caution—by itself and without a word of comment—

in the little volume of "Programmata" into which he gathered the academic utterances of which he was most proud.[1] But in the mean time he had so undermined, even among jurists, the prestige of the torture by his exposures of its cruelty and fallibility, by his researches into its history, by his demonstrations of its responsibility for the witch-panic and other judicial delusions, that, though for a century yet legal conservatism continued to defend it, its abandonment began even before his death. The sovereigns of Prussia and of other German states gradually, under the influence of the new thought, allowed torture to fall into disuse. There were some rare exceptions, but at the close of Frederick the Great's reign it had virtually ended.[2]

The influence of Thomasius soon spread throughout other parts of Europe. Though torture lingered in France, and was only fully swept from the statute books by the Revolution of 1789, and though it prevailed in vari-

---

[1] For the letter in which Thomasius expressed his doubts, see Biedermann, as above. Bernhardi's thesis was itself often reprinted. Three impressions may be found in the library of Cornell University—the original of 1705, one of 1743, and one of 1759. In the second the letter of Thomasius is still appended; in the third it has been dropped. Strangely enough, it is lacking in this copy of the original impression, the two final pages being filled instead with laudatory verses by friends of Bernhardi. As, however, the letter of Thomasius was written before the publication of the thesis, and expressly for inclusion in it, and as the official catalogue of his writings published just after his death (in the *Wohlverdientes Denkmal*, Halle, 1729), just as expressly describes the original edition as containing it, it can only be inferred that a part of the impression was printed without it.

[2] As a curious and painful monument of the occasional use of torture in Prussia, even at a late period, see, in the Cornell University library, the contemporary account of the trial and punishment of sundry servants who robbed the royal palace at Berlin. It contains illustrations representing various administrations of torture. For the horrors of torture in its prime, see, in the same library, the trial of the "Anointers" at Milan (a mass of men and women who were tortured until they confessed that they had caused the plague there by anointing the city walls)—the *Processo dei Untori*—with even more fearful illustrations.

ous other parts of Continental Europe until even a later
period, it had mainly vanished before the end of the
eighteenth century, under the antagonism of Thomasius
in Germany, Voltaire in France, and Beccaria in Italy.

In still another great struggle Thomasius did heroic
work.   While in the thick of this war against witchcraft
and torture, he fought no less bravely against INTOLER-
ANCE.

Very early in his career he laid down certain fundamental ideas on the subject, and these frequently reap-
pear in his writings.   He declared against all state
interference with religious convictions; he formulated
the theory that human law deals with men's wills, and
not with their consciences; and from these germs there
bloomed forth essays, dialogues, satires, every form of
attack upon every form of intolerance, culminating in
1722 in his *History of the Struggle between the Empire
and the Church in the Middle Ages* and in the appended
study on Church and State in later centuries.   From the
first word of this book he goes straight to the mark.   He
points out errors of the Fathers of the Church, displays
the futility of persecution, and makes clear the necessity
of proclaiming religious liberty.   All this gave great
offense, and especially were his enemies shocked by one
pungent expression: "The duty of Princes is not to
save souls, but to preserve peace."   This was denounced
as rank heresy, and even as blasphemy.

In Germany the idea of toleration had hardly begun
to dawn.   Religious persecution had indeed been condemned by the early Church, but only while the Church
was herself persecuted.   When she became able to persecute, she quickly changed her view.   Nothing could seem
more tolerant than the eloquent protests of Tertullian
and Lactantius when the Church was weak; nothing was
more fruitful in cruelty than the arguments for persecution by Firmicus Maternus, St. Augustine, and the great

theologians who followed them, when the Church had become strong. The same must be said of Protestantism. During its brief period of weakness its leaders urged tolerance; in the long period of power it was intolerant. When, at last, war forced on Germany a sort of tolerance, it was in a form which to us now seems incredible. The religious peace of Augsburg in 1555 established a toleration expressed in the maxim, "To whom the territory belongs, the religion belongs": *Cujus est regio ejus est religio.* Toleration extended only to allowing subjects who dissented from the religious ideas of their ruler to emigrate from his dominions. Even into minds blessed with the largest and most liberal instincts,—minds like those of Luther and Melanchthon,—no full ideas of toleration, much less of religious liberty, had really entered. But Thomasius followed out his principle logically. He stood not merely for toleration, but for religious liberty. Whoever was oppressed for conscience' sake found in him a defender. Spener and his disciples were glad to avail themselves of his aid against oppression, and he stood by them firmly, receiving more than his share of the epithets hurled at them; and it should also be said to his honor that, when the followers of Spener, at last, in their turn, became powerful, and therefore intolerant, he left them forever.[1]

Just at the close of his life—in 1723—the old Titan girded himself for yet another thrust at legal superstition. The very title of his scathing dissertation is an

[1] For Thomasius' main line of argument in favor of Toleration, see *Das Recht evangelischer Fürsten in theologischen Streitigkeiten*, etc., etc. (arguments by himself and Brenneysen), Halle, 1696. On the whole subject of the earlier tolerance and later intolerance of the Church, see the admirable chapters on Persecution in Lecky's *History of Rationalism in Europe.* On the reasons for Thomasius' changed attitude toward the Pietists, see especially the annotated reprint of Joachim Lange's attack upon him (1703). If these annotations are not from his pen, they were certainly inspired by him.

argument: "Whether penalties upon the living which disgrace them for life are absurd and to be put away." The laws of all states then abounded with such punishments, which, by attaching some permanent stigma to those who had once been convicted of a crime, made them outcasts among their fellows and forced them to turn to crime as their only means of livelihood. Their abolition, now begun, was one of the first steps in the substitution of reformation, as an aim of penalty, for retribution or mere deterrence.[1]

All along in Thomasius's career we see him putting forth ideas of vast use to the world: germ ideas, some of which have been obliged to wait for centuries before coming to full bloom and fruitage in institutions and laws. He did not hesitate to declare in Germany—groaning under Princes by the grace of God—that men were created naturally equal. He asserted the rights of women to a higher education and to the individual possession of property. His impartiality was judicial, and to the last he continued his various methods of work. In 1720–21 he published four volumes and in 1723–25 three more of *Thoughts and Reminiscences* of his legal life, an admirable mixture, profound and comical, grave and gay; but all pervaded with love of truth and hatred of tyranny.

His old enemies remained bitter; but a new generation was coming on, and the strongest men in it were his friends. Supporters came when least expected. The University of Leipsic, from which he had been forced to flee, later made amends by calling him to one of its most honored professorships. This he declined, and was soon afterward made Director of the University of Halle, and first Professor of Jurisprudence. His work ended only with his life. His manner of attack in his later years

---

[1] See Stintzing and Landsberg, *Geschichte der Deutschen Rechtswissenschaft*, iii, 105.

became less unsparing than in his youth; but what he lost in vigor he gained in authority.

As we look back over his life, so full of blessings to mankind, we can now see clearly one result of his activity to which no reference has hitherto been made, yet which was in some respects the most permanent of all;—a result so fruitful that it has acted and is still acting powerfully in our own time, and above all in France, Great Britain, and the United States.

This was his general influence on the higher education,—an influence in favor of FREEDOM FROM SECTARIAN INTERFERENCE OR CONTROL. Down to the time of his work at Halle, German universities had been mainly sectarian, and their sectarian character, whether frankly brutal and tyrannical, or exercised deftly and through intrigue, held back science and better modes of thought during many generations.

Theology, as the so-called "queen of the sciences," insisted on shaping all teaching in the alleged interest of "saving souls." Innumerable examples of this in the dealings of the older universities might be cited. But Thomasius's work at the University of Halle began the end of it. By him, more than by any other, was that institution brought out of the old sectarian system. In the environment of right reason which he there promoted, and which was spread throughout his fatherland, was evolved that freedom of research and instruction which has made the German universities the foremost in the world, and has given to Germany a main source of strength,—and not less in theology than in other fields.

His effort against witchcraft, torture, religious persecution, and various cruelties and pedantries, was triumphant long ago, but the struggle began by him against sectarian control of instruction still continues, and nowhere more steadily than in the United States. Evidences of it in Great Britain are the liberalizing of her great universities, and the election of laymen to so many positions in the higher instruction to which only ecclesiastics were formerly eligible. Evidences of it in France are the successful efforts to wrest the control of primary education from various monkish orders. In our own country it is seen in the escape of various older universities from sectarian control, and in the establishment of new universities, especially in our Western states, freed from this incubus,—and all, whether East or West, more and more under the management of laymen rather than of ecclesiastics. The clauses in various state constitutions, notably that recently inserted in the constitution of the state of New York, forbidding appropriations to institutions under sectarian management, and the exclusion from Mr. Carnegie's fifteen million pension fund of universities under the rule of a sectarian majority in their boards of control, testify to the continuance of this movement. Sectarian hostility is, indeed, still strong in some parts of our country. It resists somewhat the proper development of the state universities of the North, and thus far absolutely prevents adequate legislative appropriations to the state universities of the South. It has also been a main source of opposition to the establishment of a university at the city of Washington, which, though proposed by Washington himself, and supported by nearly every president since his time, still remains in abeyance. But the ideas of Thomasius will yet bear fruits in these fields as in others.[1]

His death came in 1728. He had looked forward to it without fear. All that the Church, with the dogmas then in vogue, could do to increase the terrors of death failed to daunt him. Striking was his selection of a text for his own funeral sermon. It began with the words of St. Paul

[1] For a brief but excellent treatment of Thomasius' work in emancipating the higher instruction in the German universities generally from ecclesiasticism and theology, see Dernburg, pp. 16, *et seq.*

before Felix: "Neither can they prove whereof they now accuse me; but this I confess unto thee, that after the way which they call heresy so worship I the God of my fathers." [1]

So ended a life precious not merely to Germany, but to universal humanity. Many have thought it unlovely. We naturally expect little kindliness or serenity of temper in a man so continually belligerent. As we hear of struggle after struggle, fight after fight—of war perpetual—we begin to suspect him as a dyspeptic, or an Ishmaelite. To the present writer, standing before his portrait in the great hall of the University of Halle, and before his bust in the University of Leipsic, the falsity of this theory was revealed. The face is large, kindly—even jovial: it is the face of a man keen enough to see far into the unreason of his time, and bold enough to fight it; not dyspeptic, never vexed, never peevish, never snappish; but large, fearless, strong, determined, persistent.[2]

From first to last he was a warrior. Many have thought his methods too drastic. But his was a period when, as a rule, only drastic methods could avail—a time like that when Luther began his work; when Richelieu and Mirabeau grappled with the enemies of France; when Cromwell took the helm in England; when Washington led in establishing our republic and Lincoln led in saving it. At such times measures apparently the most humane are often in reality the most cruel. When Christian Thomasius began his work, "sweet reasonableness" was absurd; mild methods futile. Only a man who could fling himself, and all that he was, and all that he hoped to be, into the fight—who could venture every-

---

[1] Acts xxiv, 13, 14.

[2] An excellent copy of the Halle portrait, painted by Charles Burleigh, hangs in the law library at Cornell,—between the portraits of Grotius and Lord Mansfield.

thing and continue venturing everything until the last—could really be of use. He had, doubtless, the defects of his qualities; but he did his work for Germany and for mankind. He was the second of the three great reformers in Germany; and, at his death, there seemed to come a transmigration of his soul to the third; for, a few months later, in that same part of Germany in which he died, was born Gotthold Ephraim Lessing.

TURGOT

TURGOT

I

When the flood which sweeps through modern society, and which still carries with it good and evil, shall have deposited its impurities, what names will float on the surface of the quiet waters? Who will then be considered the true precursors of the modern world?—those who gave the terrible signal call for revolution, or those who have wished to found the progressive reign of liberty and fraternity among men by peace, by the power of natural order, and by universal harmony?

—Leonce de Lavergne.

I PRESENT to-day one of the three greatest statesmen who fought unreason in France between the close of the Middle Ages and the outbreak of the French Revolution—Louis XI and Richelieu being the two others. And not only this: were you to count the greatest men of the modern world upon your fingers, he would be of the number—a great thinker, writer, administrator, philanthropist, statesman, and, above all, a great character and a great man. And yet, judged by ordinary standards, a failure. For he was thrown out of his culminating position, as Comptroller-General of France, after serving but twenty months, and then lived only long enough to see every leading measure to which he had devoted his life deliberately and malignantly undone; the flagrant abuses which he had abolished restored, apparently forever; the highways to national prosperity, peace, and influence, which he had opened, destroyed; and his country put under full headway toward the greatest catastrophe the modern world has seen.

165

Anne Robert Jacques Turgot, Baron de l'Aulne, was born in 1727, of a family not only noble but of characteristics which had become very rare among the old French nobility.

Several of his ancestors had been distinguished for public spirit and for boldness in resisting tyranny. His father had been Provost of the Merchants of Paris, or, as we might say, mayor of the city, for a longer term than had any of his predecessors, and had won fame not only by enterprise in works of public utility but by resisting the fury of mobs.

The son, at an early age, showed himself worthy of this lineage. As a boy at school he was studious, thoughtful, modest, dutiful, firm in resisting evil; and it throws light on personal tendencies which continued through his life to learn that his pocket money was quietly lavished upon those of his fellows who were meritorious and needy.

Yet his condition was not at first entirely happy. He was diffident, shy, and greatly lacking in the manners necessary to social success. In all lands and times, simple, easy, good manners have been of vast value to any young man, but in the first years of the reign of Louis XV, manners were everything. Reversing the usual rule in such cases, his father appreciated and admired him, but his mother misunderstood him and had, apparently, little hope for his future.

Being the youngest of three sons, and not having the qualities necessary to success at court, it was thought best to make him a priest; and, after a very successful course in two of the best lyceums of Paris, he was sent to the seminary of Saint-Sulpice. That divinity school included among its professors, then as ever since, many noble and earnest men, but it was, of course, mainly devoted, not to the unbiased search for truth, but to the buttressing of dogmas.

With ninety-nine young men in a hundred, the régime

then applied to Turgot produced the desired effect. The young man destined for an ecclesiastical career was placed within walls carefully designed to keep out all currents of new thought; his studies, his reading, his professors, his associates, all were combined to keep from him any results of observation or reflection save those prescribed: probably, of all means for stifling healthy and helpful thought, a theological seminary, as then conducted —whether Catholic or Protestant, Jewish or Mohammedan—was the most perfect.

The greatness of Turgot now began to appear: while he performed all the duties of the seminary and studied thoroughly what was required, he gave himself to a wide range of other studies, and chiefly in two very different directions—to thought and work upon those problems in religion which transcend all theologies, and upon those problems in politics which are of vast importance in all countries, and which especially needed discussion in his own.

But the currents of thought which were then sweeping through Europe could not be entirely kept out of Saint-Sulpice. The French philosophy of the eighteenth century was in full strength. Those were the years in which Voltaire ruled European opinion, and Turgot could not but take account of his influence. Yet no one could apparently be more unlike those who were especially named as the French philosophers of the eighteenth century. He remained reverential; he was never blasphemous, never blatant; he was careful to avoid giving needless pain or arousing fruitless discussion; and, while the tendency of his whole thinking was evidently removing him from the orthodoxy of the Church, his was a broader and deeper philosophy than that which was then dominant.

As to the two main lines of his thinking, it is interesting to note that his first important literary and scholastic

effort was a treatise *On the Existence of God*. Few
fragments of it remain, but we are helped to understand
him when we learn that he asserted, and to the end of his
life maintained, his belief in an Almighty Creator and
Upholder of the Universe. It did, indeed, at a later
period, suit the purposes of his enemies, exasperated by
his tolerant spirit and his reforming plans, to proclaim
him an atheist; but that sort of charge has been the
commonest of missiles against troublesome thinkers in all
times.

Theology becoming less and less attractive to him, he
turned more and more toward his other line of thought—
upon the amelioration of the general wretchedness in
French administration; and he now, in 1749, at the age of
twenty-two, wrote to one of his school friends a letter
which has been an object of wonder among political
thinkers ever since. Its subject was paper money. Discussing the ideas of John Law, and especially the essay
of Terrasson which had supported them, he dissected
them mercilessly, but in a way useful not only in those
times but in these.

Terrasson's arguments in behalf of unlimited issues
of paper had been put forth in 1720. He revived the old
idea which made the royal mint mark the essential sign
and source of value, and he declared that the material
used for bearing the sign of value is indifferent, that it
pertains to the ruling monarch to determine what the
material object bearing this sign shall 'be, and that, if
there be placed in circulation a sufficiency of such objects
thus authorized, the people thereby secure the capital
necessary for commercial prosperity.[1]

Warming with his subject, Terrasson claimed that
paper money is better than any other, and that, if a

---

[1] For a very early cropping out of this error, see Duruy, *Histoire des
Romains*, tome iv, chapter upon Nero. For the latest appearances of it,
see sundry American publications of recent years.

sovereign issues enough of paper promises, he will be able to loan or even to give money in unlimited amounts to his needy subjects.[1]

The French have generally, and unfortunately, gone to the extreme length of their logic on all public questions, and Terrasson showed this national characteristic by arguing that, as business men constantly give notes for very much greater sums than the amount of money they have on hand, so the government, which possesses a virtually unlimited mass of property, can issue paper to any amount without danger of depreciation. One premise from which this theory was logically worked out was the claim asserted by Louis XIV, namely, that the king, being the incarnation of the State, is the owner of all property in the nation, including, to use Louis's own words, "the money we leave in the custody of our people." [2]

Terrasson also made the distinction between the note of a business man and notes issued by a government, that the former comes back and must be paid, but that the latter need not come back and can be kept afloat forever by simple governmental command, thus becoming that blessed thing—worshiped widely, not many years since, in our own country—"fiat money."

This whole theory, as dear to French financial schemers in the eighteenth century as to American "Greenbackers" in the nineteenth, had resulted, under the Orleans Regency and Louis XV, in ruin to France financially and morally, had culminated in the utter destruction of all

---

[1] For the arguments of Terrasson and other supporters of John Law's system, see the *Collection d'Économistes Français*, Paris, 1851, tome i, pp. 608 *et seq.* For his "fiat-money" idea, see Léonce de Lavergne, *Les Économistes Français du Dix-Huitième Siècle*, pp. 220, 221.

[2] For the theory of Louis XIV regarding his ownership of the property of his subjects, see his own full statement in *Les Œuvres de Louis XIV*, Paris, 1806, tome ii, pp. 93, 94. And for a full statement of his whole doctrine regarding his relations to the State, see Laurent, *Études sur l'Histoire de l'Humanité*, tome xi, pp. 9 *et seq.*

prosperity, the rooting out of great numbers of the most important industries, and the grinding down of the working people even to starvation.

Never was there a more perfect demonstration of the truth asserted by Daniel Webster, that, of all contrivances for defrauding the working people of a country, arbitrary issues of paper money are the most effective.

Turgot's attempt was to enforce this lesson. He showed how the results that had followed Law's issues of paper money must follow all such issues. As regards currency inflation, Turgot saw that the issue of paper money beyond the point where it is convertible into coin is the beginning of disaster—that a standard of value must have value, just as a standard of length must have length, or a standard of capacity, capacity, or a standard of weight, weight. He showed that if a larger amount of the circulating medium is issued than is called for by the business of the country, it will begin to be discredited, and that paper, if its issue be not controlled by its relation to some real standard of value, inevitably depreciates, no matter what stamp it bears.[1]

Out of this theory, simple as it now seems, Turgot developed his argument with a depth, strength, clearness, and breadth which have amazed every dispassionate reader from that day to this. It still remains one of the best presentations of this subject ever made; and what adds to our wonder is that it was not the result of a study of authorities, but was worked out wholly from his own observation and thought. Up to this time there were no authorities and no received doctrine on the subject; there were simply records of financial practice more or less vicious; it was reserved for this young student, in a letter not intended for publication, to lay down for the first time

[1] See Turgot, *Œuvres*, in the *Collection d'Économistes*, Paris, 1844, tome iii, pp. 94 *et seq.;* also, Neymarck, *Turgot et ses Doctrines*, Paris, 1885, pp. 10, 11.

the great law in which the modern world, after all its puzzling and costly experiences, has found safety.

His was, indeed, a righteous judgment on the past and an inspired prophecy of the future. For, refusing to heed his argument the French people had again to be punished more severely than in John Law's time: the over-issue of *assignats* and *mandats* during the Revolution came forty years after his warning; and paper money inflation was again paid for by widespread bankruptcy and ruin.[1]

For similar folly, our own country, in the transition from the colonial period, also paid a fearful price; and from a like catastrophe the United States has been twice saved in our time by the arguments formulated by Turgot.[2]

Having taken his bachelor's degree in theology at Saint-Sulpice, he continued his studies at the Sorbonne, the most eminent theological institution in Europe. The character of this institution was peculiar. It had come to be virtually a club of high ecclesiastics united with a divinity school. Around the quadrangle adjoining the sumptuous church which Richelieu had made his mausoleum, were chambers for a considerable number of eminent theologians, and for a smaller number of divinity students of high birth, great promise, or especial influence. Though fallen from its highest estate, its prestige was still great. Its modes of instruction, its discussions, its public exercises, futile though they often

---

[1] For a short account of the Assignats and Mandats of the French Revolution, see *Fiat Money Inflation in France, How it Came, What it Brought, and How it Ended*, by Andrew D. White (New York: D. Appleton & Co. 1896). For a more extended treatment of the subject, see Levasseur, *Histoire des Classes Ouvrières âvant 1789*, liv. i, chap. vi.

[2] The very remarkable speeches of Mr. Garfield, afterward President of the United States, which had so great an influence on the settlement of the inflation question throughout the Union, were on the main lines laid down in Turgot's letter.

were, certainly strengthened many men intellectually, but
generally in ways not especially helpful to their civic
development. With Turgot it was otherwise. He soon
won the respect and admiration of all in the establishment
by his moral earnestness, by his intellectual vigor, by the
thoroughness of his general studies, and by his devotion
to leading lines of special study, theological and political.

So rapid was this recognition that within six months
of his entrance at the Sorbonne his position as a scholar
and thinker was recognized in a manner most significant:
he was elected by his associates to be their Prior—the
highest distinction they could offer.

It thus became his duty to deliver two discourses: one
on taking office, and one several months later.

The subject of the first of these was "The Services
rendered to the World by Christianity." In this he laid
stress upon the morality developed by the Christian
religion, upon its ideals and its practices as compared
with those of the pagan world, upon its nobler view
of the relations of mankind to God and to one another,
upon the beneficent impulses which had proceeded from
it, upon the salutary restraints it had imposed, upon
its incidental benefits to science, and upon the new fields
it had given to literature and art. But to its theological
garb—its dogmas, forms, observances, and even to its
miraculous sanctions—there was hardly a reference.

His environment did, indeed, cause him to make a few
perfunctory limitations and concessions, but throughout
the whole discourse he showed clearly that he disliked
proselytism, and abhorred intolerance. Noteworthy was
it that his tributes were paid, not to churchmanship, but
to Christianity. Curious, as showing the ideas of his
time, is his reference to the architectural triumphs of
the Roman Empire. Speaking especially of the circus
and amphitheatre as monuments of Roman skill, power,
greatness, and inhumanity, he bursts forth into an apos-

trophe: "How much more I love those Gothic edifices designed for the poor and the orphans! Monuments of the piety of Christian princes and of religion: even though your rude architecture repels us, you will always be dear to tender hearts." Here is manifest the spirit shown at that same period by the wife of John Adams, who, when she passed Canterbury Cathedral, had no thought of entering, but compared it, in appearance, to a prison; and the spirit of Thomas Jefferson, who, while he adored a ruined classic temple—the *Maison Carrée* at Nimes—drove for days through eastern France, so rich in cathedrals and churches, and never noticed them.

Many expressions give evidence of Turgot's keen vision. Of certain philosophers he speaks as "indifferent to the gross errors of the multitude, but misled by their own, which had only the frivolous advantage of subtlety."

This discourse, while causing misgivings among the older theologians, increased his influence among the younger; even sundry bishops and archbishops expressed almost boundless admiration for him. But their tributes seem to have had no injurious effect upon him; they seem only to have increased his zeal in seeking truth and his power in proclaiming it.

Some months later came his second discourse—its subject being "The Successive Advances of the Human Mind."

This was vastly superior to his earlier effort, especially in originality, breadth, and clearness. Its fundamental idea was that the human race, under the divine government, is steadily perfecting itself. In view of the discouragements and disenchantments the world has encountered since that day, it is difficult to appreciate the strength of this belief; but there can be no doubt that it inspired and sustained him throughout all his labors and disappointments, even to the end of his life. In combination with this was his fundamental idea on the philosophy of history, given in these words: "All the ages are linked together by a sequence of causes and effects which connects the existing state of the world with all that has preceded it."

No doubt that, as to its form, there was a hint from Bossuet's famous discourse on universal history; but in Turgot's work one finds a freedom and breadth of vision greater by far than had been shown in any other historical treatise up to his time. In every part of it were utterances which, though many of them have now become truisms, were then especially illuminative. One passage shows a striking foresight. Speaking of colonial systems, he develops an idea of Montesquieu, and says: "Colonies, like fruits, are only held fast to the trees up to the time of their maturity. Having become ripe, they do that which Carthage did, and which America will one day do." Thus was the American Revolution prophesied by Turgot in 1750, nearly a quarter of a century before leading American patriots began to foresee it. Bear in mind that Franklin denied a tendency in America toward independence very nearly up to the time of the Declaration, and that, less than two years before the Declaration, Washington wrote that independence was desired by no thinking man in America.[1]

In close relations with this second discourse were Turgot's sketches in Universal History and Geography. Only fragments of these remain, but they give us the torso of a great philosophic and historic creation. As

[1] For the famous prophecy regarding America, see Turgot, *Œuvres*, tome ii, p. 602, in the *Collection d'Économistes*, tome iv.

For an excellent statement regarding the reluctance of leading American thinkers—both Whigs and Tories—to foresee independence, and especially for the attitude of Franklin and Washington toward the question, see M. C. Tyler, *Literary History of the American Revolution*, vol. i, pp. 458 ff.

in all his writings in this field, the fundamental idea was
that the development of the human race goes on, ever,
by the methods and toward the goal fixed by the Almighty, and is proof of the divine forethought and wisdom. While one does not find in it the confident theological statements of the first Sorbonne discourse, the
theistic view is never lost. Regarding this work, the most
sober and restrained among all the modern historians of
France declares, "There is nothing greater in the eighteenth century than Turgot's plea against Rousseau, regarding the tendency and high destiny of universal humanity." [1]

In taking account of Turgot's writings, both at this
period and during his after life, his early training may
well be noted. It not only included a vast range of general reading, but the foundation of the whole was the best
discipline and culture to be obtained from mathematical
and classical studies, while not neglecting natural history. Like Lord Bacon, he seemed "to take all knowledge for his province." With leading philosophers of
his time he corresponded on even terms. As to mathematics and astronomy, he occupied himself at various
periods, even to the end of his life, with the works of
such princes in that realm as Newton, Euler, and their
disciples; as to natural science, he interested himself
especially in geology and kindred studies, and corresponded with Buffon; as to the classics, the range of his
reading was astonishing, and, as to his facility in Latin,
it may be mentioned that the two great discourses at the
Sorbonne, as well as other writings during his scholastic
life, were first written and delivered in that language.
In this field bloomed one of the flowers of modern Latin
poetry: his tribute to Franklin,—

"Eripuit caelo fulmen sceptrumque tyrannis."

[1] Henri Martin, *Histoire de France*, tome xvi, p. 186.

Of all tributes ever paid to the American philosopher, this line undoubtedly sped farthest and struck deepest.

As to modern languages other than his own, he made extended translations of leading English and German writers. Light is thrown upon his character by the fact that he wrote out, carefully, Pope's *Universal Prayer*.

On leaving the Sorbonne, at the age of twenty-three years, he was confronted by the question as to his future profession. This he solved at once, declaring that he could not enter the priesthood, and that he purposed devoting himself to the law and the civil service.

From this decision several of his companions sought to dissuade him. They had, apparently, no more belief in the dominant theology than had Turgot. Though they were under the influence of the eighteenth-century philosophy, they evidently held that the great mass of people can never rise above the current beliefs of their time, and that certain men are appointed to control them by means of these beliefs, and to be well rewarded for this control. They held up to Turgot the prospect of wealth and power in the ecclesiastical career, showed him that the most lofty positions in the Church would be his, and, knowing his patriotic aspirations, they especially displayed his opportunities in these positions to be of use to his country.

To all this Turgot made a reply which has passed into history. Thanking his friends for their efforts, he said, "Take for yourselves, if you like, the counsels which you give me, since you feel able to do so. Although I love you, I cannot understand how you are able to do it. As to myself, it is impossible for me during my whole life to wear a mask." [1]

___

[1] Various efforts have been made to show that this reply by Turgot, in view of his Sorbonne discourse and other contemporary utterances, is probably legendary; but the testimony of Dupont de Nemours is explicit, and there is no better authority. The statement made by Condorcet in his

Here these friends separated. Of those who became ecclesiastics, and sought to persuade Turgot to do likewise, were Véry, later Grand Vicar of Bourges; De Cicé, afterward a bishop; Boisgelin, who became an archbishop and a cardinal; and, above all, Loménie de Brienne, who secured the utmost of place and pelf which an ecclesiastic could obtain in France: two archbishoprics, a cardinal's hat, the post of Prime Minister, and, finally, retirement after merited political failure, with the plunder of several abbeys and the unbounded scorn of every right-thinking Frenchman from those days to these.

It may be remarked here that Brienne's effort to combine his "philosophic" views with the duties of a high ecclesiastic brought him to ruin. Rebuked by Pius VI, he flung back to the Pope his cardinal's hat; but not all his concessions to the Revolution could save him from its devotees; he died in 1793 in prison at Sens, the seat of his second archbishopric, after cruel insults from his revolutionary jailers,—the only doubt being whether he died as a result of their cruelty or by his own hand.[1]

On the announcement of Turgot's decision, he was, to all appearance, speedily left behind by his old associates; but, in his new field, his moral and intellectual force rap-

Vie de Turgot seems to strengthen rather than to weaken Dupont's account. Strangest of all, on the side of those who prefer to think these words legendary, is the argument by August Oncken, Professor at Berne, who urges that, as Turgot was not an atheist, and, as some of the highest dignitaries in the Church at that time did not hesitate to avow atheism, there was no reason why Turgot should make such a remark. This argument would seem fully to refute itself. Nothing, in view of Turgot's moral character, could be more likely under these very circumstances than such an utterance. It ought, also, to be said that, valuable as Oncken's book may be, there is, in all its treatment of the physiocrats and Turgot, far too much of that de haut en bas style so often to be observed in references to a Frenchman of genius by a German of talent. See Oncken, Geschichte der Nationalökonomie, Leipzig, 1902, p. 436.

[1] See Biographie Universelle, article "Loménie." Also Rae, Life of Adam Smith, pp. 177, 178.

12

idly won him promotion. Modest and quiet though he was, he must have had from the first a consciousness of his abilities. This was never shown offensively—indeed, it may be justly said that it was never shown at all; but one thing he could not but show, and this was his deep sense of responsibility for the use of his powers in every station to which they lifted him. Never at any time was he the prostitute attorney who from that day to this has burdened the world, never a venal defender of criminals, never a partner of marauders, never a hireling supporter of men and measures injurious to his country or to mankind. Well did Malesherbes say that devotion to the public good was in him "not merely a passion, but a *rage.*"

Higher and higher positions were opened to him. In accepting them, there is ample evidence that his motives were patriotic; but one such acceptance cost him dear. The Parliament of Paris, which had played so large and so noxious a part in French history, had become intolerable. Like the twelve other French parliaments, its real functions were judicial; yet, in spite of this, it had long usurped legislative and, at times, something very like executive functions. With occasionally a good thing to its credit, it had long been a curse to the country. When the sovereign was strong it had usually groveled; when he was weak it had usually rebelled. It had finally endeavored to block a series of absolutely necessary reforms, had been banished from Paris, and a new court had been established in its place. Into this court Turgot had been called, and had accepted the position; but thereby he aroused the bitter hatred of various old members and parasites of the Parliament, and among these was no less a personage than Choiseul,—perhaps the most powerful intriguer since Cardinal Mazarin.

Engrossing as was his professional work, Turgot still devoted himself to the study of all questions whose solution was important for France,—whether within or without his official duties. We find him constantly engaged in thorough research and profound thought, not only on political and administrative problems, but on great questions in science, in philosophy, and in literature.

Of all he wrote at that early period, by far the most interesting to the general scholar were his discourses and his drafts of elaborate treatises upon universal history and political geography. These show an amazing breadth of knowledge, and a no less wonderful grasp of the significance of events, especially in their bearing on human progress. They impress themselves deeply on the reader, not only by their matter, but by their style. Out of the innumerable pungent expressions of weighty truths in them, one may be cited as containing food for reflection in America of the twentieth century,—''Greed is the ambition of barbarians.''

He did not lose himself in these broader views of human destiny; he constantly studied the practical problems rising in his own country,—most of all, those which pertained to public administration; and in this latter field also he became more and more widely known throughout France, and indeed through Europe. The French *Encyclopédie,* so powerful in bringing in a new epoch, gives striking evidence of the vastness of his fields of thought and of his thoroughness in cultivating them. He wrote several of its most valuable articles, and, while their subjects lay in widely differing provinces, all were recognized as authoritative, and each took high rank as combining the best results of wide observation, wise reflection, close criticism, illuminating thought, and thorough sympathy with the best currents of opinion flowing through his time.

But the most directly important in the series of writings thus begun were those upon TOLERATION.

About the year 1753 the ecclesiastical power in France

was making every effort to restore the old persecuting policy of Louis XIV. That policy had culminated in the Revocation of the Edict of Nantes, involving enormous cruelty to the best part of the middle classes, the exile of the most thoughtful manufacturers and their adherents, with a transfer of various great industries to rival nations. Thus began an evil epoch in France, which is, indeed, not yet fully finished. The injury thereby done has been not only material, but, even to a greater degree, political and moral. When one considers the history of Germany, England, and the United States, it seems certain that, had that vast body of Huguenots who were driven by the bigotry of Louis XIV into those countries been allowed to remain in their own, the Jacobin phase of the French Revolution and all the ruin and misery which that and the various despotisms following it inflicted upon France would have been impossible.[1]

After that monstrous intolerance there had, indeed, come a milder policy, but in Turgot's time there had set in a reaction against this, and a large body of courtiers were, by clerical influence and ecclesiastical pressure, brought over to the idea of restoring the old system of persecution, and were doing their best to bring Louis XV into it. Against all this Turgot wrote his *Letters on Toleration,* and his *Conciliator.* As a motto for the latter he took the noble words of Fénelon: "No human power can destroy the liberty of the affections. When kings interfere in matters of religion, they do not protect it,—they enslave it." He then showed cogently the reasons why toleration was true statesmanship: that in matters of belief neither right nor expediency sanctions

[1] For a most careful and thorough statement of the injury done to French interests by the Revocation of the Edict of Nantes, see Levasseur, *Histoire des Classes Ouvrières et de l'Industrie en France, avant 1789,* deuxième édition, vol. ii, pp. 344 *et seq.*

state interference, and that toleration should be carried
to the farthest point possible.

Especially characteristic are the first words of his first
letter. They embody the doctrines which in the nineteenth and twentieth centuries have taken possession of
all the really great powers of the world. These words
are as follows: ''You demand 'what is the protection
which the state ought to give to the dominant religion?'
I answer, speaking exactly to the point, 'No religion has
the right to demand any other protection than liberty,
and it loses its rights to this liberty when its doctrines
or worship are contrary to the interest of the state.' '' [1]

He then goes on to argue that the only cases in which
the State has a right to take cognizance of dogmas are
those where clear, direct results upon the public safety
are concerned. Hence, he argues the right to exclude
polygamy. But he constantly takes pains to show that
a government should be slow in concluding that the practical results of any dogma are injurious. While constantly respectful to the religion in which he had been
nurtured, he urges the establishment of a system of
education which shall make moral men and good citizens,
leaving to the Church the teaching of religion.

Of course, all this led to resistance. In spite of his
efforts to make every possible concession to the clergy
consistent with the welfare of his country, their leaders
now began to treat him as an enemy. Despite his deeply
religious nature, which always kept him from the aggressive excesses of Voltaire, and the French philosophers
generally, he was none the less marked as an object of
ecclesiastical hatred; and from that day to this he has been
maligned by the representatives of those he thus angered.
Even in recent years, a venomous biography of him in
pamphlet form has been spread throughout France. The

[1] See Turgot, *Œuvres,* tome ii, p. 675.

men who accomplished this piece of work thought, doubt-less, that they were doing a service to the Church. Possibly they were; for this libel upon Turgot, revered as he finally is by every thinking French patriot, is un-doubtedly one of the causes which have in our own time produced the most effective of all French revolts against clerical sway,—the abolition of the teaching congrega-tions and the divorce of the French Church from the State.

 In all these writings Turgot was at his best,—clear, strong, and effective. His plea for toleration became at once a main agency in ending all plans and intrigues to entangle Louis XV in the persecuting policy of Louis XIV. In this, as in his other arguments, there was a remarkable depth and breadth of thought, with quiet force in expression. Here and there they take an epi-grammatic form, but never at the cost of truth. There are pithy statements, cogent phrases, illuminating sum-maries, but all permeated by an earnestness which forces conviction,—as no utterances of a venal advocate could ever do. Their ability and honesty carried them far. Through Frederick the Great they made a triumphant entrance into Germany; through Franklin and Jefferson they entered America; through Cavour they took pos-session of Italy; and through Waldeck-Rousseau and Combes they have won France.

Mention should be made here of Turgot's ideas on EDUCATION. His presentation of this subject, like that of his views on many other subjects, had begun in private letters to honored friends; his earlier thoughts upon it being given in his correspondence with a gifted writer, Mademoiselle Graffigny. The roots of many of them are to be found in Locke, but their best development is his own. Very striking is his treatment of the Rousseau ideas which became such an affliction to the world a few years later. With his usual clearness of vision, Turgot forewarned France against that hotbed of folly, the "State of Nature" theory, in which were to sprout the sentimentalism and ferocity of the Reign of Terror, with Robespierre as its most gaudy flower.

During this period, also, Turgot was deepening and extending his study of political economy. Up to his time hardly a germ had appeared of the modern science of economics, and little if any practical recognition of those truths in political economy which are considered in this century as fundamental. These problems had now become crucial. The fate of the monarchy was hanging upon them. Colbert, the greatest of the ministers of Louis XIV, and the most devoted to French interests, had, indeed, carried on what was called the "mercantile system," but that was simply the building up of favored industries,—a makeshift system which considered all competing nations as enemies to be bullied, cajoled, or crushed.

Colbert, as Comptroller-General, had stood at the head of French industry as a great manufacturer stands at the head of his mill; grasping, conceding, using cunning or force as the case might seem to need. His was a system carried out by innumerable edicts, decrees, regulations, often conflicting, always leading to much trouble within France, planting the seeds of terrible war between France and her neighbors. This system it was which had most to do with bringing on the exhausting war with the Netherlands, which finally entangled and embarrassed every leading European power, and brought France to the verge of bankruptcy.[1]

Bad as this system was, its evils were mitigated as long as a really great man like Colbert stood at its

[1] For a brief but fair judgment of Colbert and his policy, see Adam Smith, *Wealth of Nations*, chap. ix; and for a not less impartial but far more thorough judgment, see Levasseur, *Histoire des Classes Ouvrières*, as above, tome ii, chap. iii.

centre; but after him its results speedily showed themselves to all men; and finally, under the Regency and
Louis XV, his successors, without either his genius or
his honesty, brought France to wretchedness. Of these,
the Abbé Terray was an example. Terray's only effort
had been to squeeze out of the nation the largest sums
possible for the king and court, without regard to the
public interest. Some industries were protected into
debility, others were taxed out of existence. Loans were
raised without regard to the danger of bankruptcy; more
and more, under him, was developed utter carelessness
regarding national financial honor.

One of the consequences of this system is especially
instructive. Certainly no system is so costly as one
which tampers in the slightest degree with national
credit. So it proved in this case. State loans could be
obtained only at rates of interest which would make up
to the lender not only the proper usance, but the risks
rising from the caprices of ministers, the trickery of
courtiers, and the general want of financial probity.

Even while this system held full sway, various thinkers had stirred new thought on economic doctrines as
applied to the national administration. Early among
these was Locke, but the first man who began effectively
to lay a basis for the modern science of political economy in France was Quesnay. He had contributed articles to the *Encyclopédie,* especially upon agriculture and
the regulation of the grain trade; and these articles
attracted attention and formed a school of thinkers.
Gradually there was brought together a body of patriotic
and thoughtful men who cared little for the prizes held
out by court favor, but much for the substantial prosperity of their country: these were known as the "Economists," or, more widely and permanently, as the
"Physiocrats."

In the thinking of these men lay some fallacies. A

natural reaction from the mercantile policy of Colbert led them to lay stress almost entirely upon the agricultural interest.   They believed the soil the only source of real wealth, agriculture the only productive labor, and all other forms of labor to be essentially different from agriculture, as not adding to real values.

Mistaken as their theory was, and injurious as it at times became in the legislation of the years following, its defects were far more than atoned for by the real contributions which they made to economic science.   In their whole history we see a striking evidence of the truth that exact statements of fact do far more good than mistaken theories can do harm.   Indeed, their mistaken doctrine was vastly outweighed for good by another on which they laid special stress: this was that the main trust of nations should be, as far as possible, in individual initiative,—in the general good sense and ability of men to look better after their own interests than any government or any functionary can do.

This idea, that governments should govern as little as possible, was a force sure to produce good effects in that chaos of general and local powers, general and provincial tariffs, monopolies, special privileges, interferences of functionaries, and governmental meddling of every sort.   The Economists first planted in the modern world the idea of commercial and industrial liberty as both right and expedient; more than any other thinkers they enforced the statement that "every man should be allowed to buy or sell when he pleases, where he pleases, as he pleases, and as much or as little as he pleases."   They first gave to the world that formula which has since exercised such power in the political economy of France and of the world: *"Laissez faire, laissez passer."*

With Colbert, carefully planned regulation from the centre of government had been everything; with Quesnay and his followers toward the end of Louis XV's reign,

liberty for manufactures and trade was everything. With
men of the former school, that government was best
which governed most; with men of this new school, that
government was best which governed least.

The Economists naturally won Turgot's sympathy.
In that seething mass of courtiers, ecclesiastics, sham
statesmen, tax contractors, venal lawyers, and mistresses,
—all pushing for place and pelf without regard to the
future of their country—it was inevitable that he should
turn to the only body of true men and strong thinkers
who really had at heart the interests of France. One of
these, Gournay, had an especially happy influence upon
him. Gournay had been made Intendant of Commerce,
and his duties obliged him to travel through various
provinces of France, in order to study commercial interests, and the condition of the people. During two years
Turgot accompanied him on these journeys and devoted
himself to the practical questions constantly arising, thus
becoming familiar with the needs of all classes and the
best ways of meeting them. Although Gournay died a
few years later, his influence over Turgot remained.
Well has one of Turgot's recent biographers said: "Almost every social and every economic improvement in
Europe and America for the last hundred years or more
has had its germ in the teachings of men who belonged
to that early school of French Economists."[1]

And here let me commend the example of Turgot and
Gournay to American students who may be ambitious to
take part in public life. To such I would say, having
developed your powers by the best means accessible, bring
yourselves early in touch with men as they are, with
facts as they are, with problems to be actually solved,
and with practical solutions of them. As early in your
career as possible get yourselves placed on town boards,

[1] See Stephens, *Life of Turgot*, p. 65.

county boards, grand and petit juries. De Tocqueville was right when he pointed out jury duty as a great political education in this republic. Study men and things in town meetings, in county sessions, in public institutions created to deal with evil and develop good. But, while thus keeping in relations with every-day practice, do something by reading and reflection to keep yourselves abreast of the higher thinking on political and social questions. Mingle with your practical observations study and reading in history, political economy, and social science, under the best guides you can find. In these days our leading universities, seeking to send out into public service men who shall unite practical knowledge with the higher thinking, seem our best agencies for sane progress and our best barriers against insane whimsies. James Bryce, the most competent foreign observer of American affairs since De Tocqueville, has cogently supported this view.

But, while Turgot sympathized with the Physiocrats, even in some of their errors, he never surrendered to them or to any sect, religious, philosophical, or economic, his full liberty of thought. One of the most striking passages in all his writings is his discussion of the sect spirit, and it can be read with quite as much profit in the twentieth century as in the eighteenth. He says: ''It is the sect spirit which arouses against useful truths enemies and persecutions. When an isolated person modestly proposes what he believes to be the truth, he is listened to if he is right, and forgotten if he is wrong. But when even learned men have once formed themselves into a body, and say 'we,' and think they can impose laws upon public opinion, then public opinion revolts against them, and with justice, for it ought to receive laws from truth alone, and not from any authority. Every such society sees its badge worn by the stupid, the crackbrained, and the ignorant, proud in joining themselves to it to give themselves airs." [1]

In 1761 came one of the main turning points in Turgot's career. His merits had so generally aroused attention that the ministry now determined to avail themselves of them, and he was made Intendant of Limoges.

The "intendancies," or "generalities," were among the most effective organizations developed by the absolute monarchy in France in its effort to make head against the manifold and monstrous confusions which finally brought on the Revolution.

To all appearance, the old provinces—dating from the Middle Ages, and earlier—were the important divisions of France, and the men placed over them as governors were the most showy figures in local administration; but, in fact, these governors were, as a rule, courtiers sent to the various provincial capitals, sometimes as a reward, sometimes as a riddance. The really important divisions had become the "generalities," or "intendancies," which had been carved out of the old provinces. To take charge of these it was thought best to have men who knew something and could do something. Turgot, though hampered badly by the central authority at Paris and Versailles, thus became, in a sense, viceroy over an important part of central France. Though the work set before him in this capacity might well seem thankless, he gladly embraced it. With his ability and knowledge he might have shone in the salons of the capital as a man of science or letters,—but there was a chance here to render a service to his country by showing what could be done in carrying out better ideas of administration, and this determined his choice.

[1] See quotation in Higgs, *History of the Physiocrats*, p. 14.

II

THE district to which Turgot now gave thirteen of the best years of his life was one of the poorest and most neglected in France. Authentic pictures of it during the period before his intendancy are distressing: the worst abuses of absolutism and feudalism had enjoyed full and free course,—with poverty, ignorance, and famine as their constant results. The Marquis de Mirabeau declared that the food of the peasantry, as a rule, was buckwheat, chestnuts, and radishes; that there was no wheat bread, no butcher's meat; that at best the farmer killed one pig a year; that the dwellings of the peasantry were built of raw clay roofed with thatch,—without windows, with the beaten ground as a floor,—and that their clothes were rags. Taine tells us that there were no ploughs of iron, that in many cases the plough of Virgil's time was still in use.[1] Boudet declares: "Everything in these God-forsaken countries reflected the image of ignorance and barbarism, in the middle of the eighteenth century." One expression in a letter from Turgot to a rural functionary throws light upon the intellectual condition of the people: he says, "I have seen with pain that in some parishes the curate alone has signed, because no one else could write." And Turgot follows this with exhortations to spread the rudiments of an ordinary education.[2]

His first care in this new position was to secure thorough and trustworthy information. To this end he set at work every agent under his control or influence, and

[1] This may well be; for the present writer saw, in 1856, in various parts of Italy, the plough described by Virgil.

[2] See citations in Stephens, *Life of Turgot,* pp. 26–32.

sought not only accurate knowledge of conditions, but the widest possible acquaintance with men. Especially striking were his friendly letters to the parish priests: though differing from them in religious theories, he besought their aid in behalf of a better system among the people at large. Nothing could exceed his kindly sympathy with them and the shrewdness and tact of his questions; and to the credit of the French rural priesthood it must be said that they were won by Turgot's evident devotion to their poverty-stricken parishioners, and that they effectively aided him in his efforts to know the exact condition of every part of the intendancy and to secure acquaintance with vast numbers of men, even among the humblest, who had ability or real character.

He infused his spirit also into his official agents. Addressing the officers of police of Limoges, he said, "The way to succeed is to reply with suavity and in detail to the popular complaints you every day hear,—to speak more in the language of reason than in that of authority."

Turgot's first grapple was with the *taille,* or land tax. No tax could have been more unjustly laid: the nobility and clergy virtually escaped it, and it therefore fell with crushing force upon the middle and lower classes.

He was powerless to abolish it, but, in every way possible, he mitigated it. It had become absurd, both in its character and administration. Local men of influence used every sort of intrigue to escape it; inequalities and injustice made it especially obnoxious to the poorer and weaker classes. Turgot wrought steadily to mitigate the exactions of the central government, and, though his representations were never wholly yielded to, they at least lightened the burden. He also sought to secure real information as to the exact ability of every community, and, indeed, of every unit in each community throughout his intendancy, to bear taxation; but efforts to abolish the *taille* he was obliged to reserve for a later period.

Not only were these great taxes imposed with injustice; they were collected with inhumanity. The duty of collecting this and other taxes known as "direct" was forced upon unpaid peasants and other men of small means in a way which often brought them to ruin. Fundamental in the practice of the time was the personal responsibility of collectors for the whole tax of their districts, and the added responsibility of selected taxpayers for the total amount required: all being responsible for the taxation of each, and each for the taxation of all. For this state of things Turgot substituted within his jurisdiction a system of collectors carefully selected and suitably paid, and in various other ways he greatly mitigated the hardships of the older practice.[1]

Still another of his efforts, which proved to be far more successful, and which set an example to France and, indeed, to the world, was his dealing with the royal *corvée* for public works. It had been devised first under feudalism; it had then been carried still further by the central monarchical government as an easy means of financial oppression. Against feudal *corvées*, Turgot could do little or nothing, but his main attack was upon the royal *corvée*. This consisted mainly of two parts: first, the making and repairing of the public roads, and, secondly, the transportation of military stores—and all by the forced labor of the peasantry. The immediate result of this system as regards the public works had been that they were wretched,—the roads almost impassable in bad weather,—and their cost enormous. This outcome of that old French system we can understand by looking at a similar method in various parts of our own country. Probably in few other parts of the civilized world have

[1] For a very full and lucid statement of the classification and imposition of the taxes before the Revolution in France, see Esmein, *Histoire du Droit Français*, Paris, 1901, pp. 573 *et seq.* For a brief but especially clear summary, see Rambaud, *Histoire de la Civilisation Française*, Paris, 1897, chap. ix.

roads been so bad as in the state of New York, and the main cause of this is a survival of this same old system by which the rural population were required to construct the highways, and allowed to make them as badly as the most narrow-minded of them pleased.

But this was the least of evils under the French system. Bad as was the condition of the public roads, it was better than the condition of the peasants themselves: they were liable to be withdrawn from their work at any moment in order to repair the roads for the passage of this magnate or that body of soldiers. To make matters worse, there came the transportation of military stores and munitions,—an even more disheartening burden: no matter how occupied their farm animals might be, army material of every sort must be transported at a moment's warning, nominally at about one-fourth of what would have been a fair compensation,—really, in most cases, without compensation at all. The loss of effective labor and the disabling of their beasts of burden became fearfully oppressive: cases are authentically mentioned where the farmers of large districts were left after such *corvées* virtually without draught animals.

Against this whole system Turgot won a victory. For the *corvées* he substituted a moderate tax, and, instead of building roads after the old shiftless plan, he had them made in accordance with the specifications of good engineers, under carefully drawn contracts; with the result that throughout his intendancy a network of highways was developed better than any others then known in France, and at a cost far below the sums which had previously been wasted upon them.

Closely connected with these measures was the breaking down of barriers to internal commerce. One can hardly believe in these days the perfectly trustworthy accounts of the French internal "protective" system in those. Typical is the fact that on the Loire between

Orleans and Nantes, a distance of about two hundred miles, there were twenty-eight custom-houses; and that between Gray and Arles, on the rivers Saone and Rhone, a distance of about three hundred miles, the custom-houses numbered over thirty, causing long delays, and taking from twenty-five to thirty per cent in value of all the products transported.

Pathetic and farcical is the story of M. Blanchet's wine,—a true story. M. Blanchet bought a quantity of wine in the extreme south of France, intending to bring it to Paris. At the chief village of each little district duties were levied upon it, not only for the municipality, but for various individuals. At Nevers five separate and distinct tariffs were levied,—one for the Duc de Nevers, one for the mayor and town council, one for each of two privileged nobles, and one for the bishop. At Poids de Fer four different tariffs were imposed, at Cosne two, and so on, at place after place, single, double, triple, or even more numerous duties by towns, lords spiritual, lords temporal, monasteries, nunneries, and the like, along the whole distance.[1]

To break down such barriers as these, Turgot exerted himself to the utmost; and, in logical connection with these efforts, he obtained in 1763 a declaration from the king permitting free trade in grain, followed during the next year by another edict to the same purpose. In thus declaring against an internal protective system, especially as regards agriculture, he braved a deep-seated public opinion. Every province insisted that, when Heaven had given it a good crop, it should have the main enjoyment of that crop, and that, whether crops were

---

[1] For the customs duties on the Loire and elsewhere, see Levasseur, *Histoire des Classes Ouvrières*, etc., as above, tome ii, p. 83. For a multitude of instructive details, see Taine, *The Ancient Régime*, Durand's translation, book v, chap. ii. For Blanchet's wine, see the detailed account given in Stourm, *Les Finances de l'Ancien Régime et de la Révolution*, tome i, pp. 473–474.

good or bad, the only safety from famine was in the existing system of "protection."

To educate public opinion, Turgot wrote, in 1764, his *Letters on Free Trade in Grain*. They were mainly prepared during official journeys, and dashed off at country inns. It was a hard struggle. Of all things done by him during the Limoges period these letters and the effort to put their ideas into practice brought upon him the most bitter opposition. From the Abbé Terray down to the people who suffered most by the old order of things, all attacked him. There came mobs and forcible suppression of them. But Turgot, braving the bitter opposition both of theorists and of mobs, insisted that the consecrated system of interfering with the free circulation of grain throughout the kingdom was one of the greatest causes of popular suffering; and while this argument of his had but a temporary effect at that period, it afterward did more than anything else to prepare the French mind for the final breaking up of that whole system of internal protection,—with the result that famines disappeared from France forever.

In close relation to this was his direct grapple with famine, in 1771 and 1772. Famines in various parts of continental Europe were frequent throughout the Middle Ages and, indeed, down to the French Revolution; and they were produced by the same causes which underlie the frequent and terrible famines in Russia to-day: ignorance, superstition, want of public spirit, want of that knowledge in agriculture and political economy necessary to maintain a suitable supply, want of discernment between harassing regulations which increase the evil and the liberty which prevents it.

The measures which Turgot took in his house-to-house and hand-to-hand struggle against peasant starvation are given in detail by various biographers, and they present a wonderful combination of sound theory with

common-sense practice. These measures proved to be
more successful than those of any other intendant in
France; and it is worthy of note that, in the midst of
all the severe labors which this effort imposed upon him,
he was steadily on his guard to prevent the people from
becoming beggars. The ingenuity of his devices to avoid
this evil makes them worthy of study even in our day.
Nor should his private efforts to aid the starving be forgotten: in these he not only exhausted his own immediate
resources, but incurred personal debts to the amount of
twenty thousand livres.

Of especial value also were his exertions to improve
the wretched agriculture of the country. In various ways
he stimulated agricultural studies; he introduced new
food plants and grasses, and, with these, the potato.
Here came curious opposition, not only in France, but in
other countries. It was claimed that potatoes ought not
to be eaten, because they produced leprosy, and also
because no mention of them was made in Scripture. By
a world of pains, and especially by inducing the upper
classes to adopt potatoes as a part of their diet, he at last
wore away these prejudices; but to aid in overcoming
them finally no less a personage than the king himself
was induced to order the new vegetable served at his own
table.

An evil with which he then grappled—in some respects
the most serious of all—was the prevailing militia
system. It greatly injured not only the industry, but
the personal character, of the people. Its whole administration by the nobility who commanded in the various
regiments was barbarously cruel, and of all the evils
which beset the peasantry of France this service was the
most detested. Exemptions from it were, indeed, many,
but they were entirely in favor of the upper classes.
So dreaded did the drawing of militiamen become that
young men, in great numbers, deserted the villages, and

large country districts were at times thus crippled for want of laborers. Those who had been so fortunate as not to be chosen then joined in the chase of those who had drawn unlucky numbers, and innumerable petty wars were thus promoted.

Turgot dealt with this subject after his usual fashion: he studied it carefully, appealed to the peasantry judiciously, secured volunteers by bounties, and made the whole system not only less obnoxious, but appreciated as never before by those whose temperaments best fitted them for army life. Closely connected with the other evils of the militia system was the custom of billeting troops upon the inhabitants—resulting in endless conflicts and immoralities. Turgot constructed barracks, kept the troops in them, and thus relieved his people materially and morally.[1]

Hardly less fruitful were his efforts to stimulate and extend manufactures. To him, in large measure, is due the creation of that vast porcelain industry at Limoges, which, in our own time, largely in the hands of Americans, has produced works of ceramic art hardly equaled in beauty or value by those of any nation outside of France.

But his efforts had a wider scope. While struggling thus to save and improve the people of his intendancy, he was constantly writing reports, most carefully thought out, to clear the vision and improve the methods of the ministry at Paris, and these have remained of great value ever since. Noteworthy is the fact that when Napoleon took in hand the administration of France his main studies, in preference to all else that he had received from the old French monarchy, were these reports and discussions of Turgot.[2]

[1] For striking revelations of the militia horrors, see Taine, *Ancient Régime*, book v, chap. iv.

[2] See Daire, Introduction to the *Œuvres de Turgot*, p. lviii; and, for Turgot's Reports on Mines and Quarries, etc., etc., see the *Œuvres*, tome ii, pp. 130, *et seq.*

So great was Turgot's success in making his government an oasis in the desert of French rural misery that it finally became a matter of interest, not only in France, but throughout Europe. This led his friends to urge upon him other and more lucrative positions, among these the intendancy of Lyons. But all such attempts he discouraged. He felt that it was more important to show France what could be done by carrying out a better system in some one province, no matter how poor; and all personal considerations yielded to this feeling.

While thus abolishing throughout his intendancy some of the worst oppressions of the absolute monarchy, he was steadily mitigating feudal evils. Worthy of special note is it that down to this period, hardly twenty years before the Revolution, the nobility not only persisted in all the monstrous exactions which had been developed during the Middle Ages, but took advantage of famine to sell agricultural produce to their peasants at starvation prices, to break the agreements which they had made with them, and to evade contributing to save them from starvation. Against this Turgot exerted himself to the utmost, straining his authority even beyond its legal limits, until he had forced the great landed proprietors to treat their peasantry with more humanity. To do this, of course, endangered his position. The nobility naturally had friends at court, and through these they made the corridors and salons of Versailles resound with their outcries against his interference.

It would seem that in all this heavy work he would have found full scope for his ability. Not so. During this period he found time to write essays and treatises which have exerted a happy influence upon France and upon Europe from that day to this.

As the first and greatest of these should be mentioned his treatise, "On the Formation and Distribution of Wealth." It was written in 1766 and published about three years later. Though he accepted the fundamental fallacy of his fellow economists in making agriculture the sole source of real production, this work was fruitful in good. Even his errors, resulting, as they did, from honest thinking, led men to the discovery of new truths.

Perhaps its greatest result was the stimulus it gave to Adam Smith, who shortly after it was written visited France, made acquaintance with leading Physiocrats, including Turgot, and about ten years later, in 1776, published that work which Buckle declares "probably the most important book ever written," the *Wealth of Nations*.[1]

Regarding the relations of Turgot to Adam Smith growths of partisanship have sprung up, many of them, on either side, more rank than just. Of this there is not the slightest need. While we may recognize the fact that Buckle, in his panegyric of Smith's *Wealth of Nations,* forgot Grotius's *De Jure Belli ac Pacis,* and while one of the latest and most competent editors of the *Wealth of Nations* acknowledges that its author "was greatly indebted to the Economists," and that "in the first book, important passages will be found which are almost transcripts from Turgot's divisions and arguments," we must agree that Smith's place is secure among the foremost benefactors of the modern world, and that Turgot, though his arguments were presented in a different form and manner, stands close beside him.[1] But, while a place in the front rank must be assigned to Adam Smith, and while it must be conceded that he

[1] Buckle makes this assertion twice, and to his first declaration adds that the work "is certainly the most valuable contribution ever made by a single man towards establishing the principles on which government should be based." (*History of Civilization in England*, American Edition, vol. i, chap. iv; vol. ii, chap. vi.) For interesting particulars of the intercourse between Adam Smith and the Physiocrats, including his opinion of Turgot, see Rae, *Life of Adam Smith*, London, 1895, chap. xiv.

[1] See Thorold Rogers, Introduction to Smith's *Wealth of Nations*, Oxford, 1880, chap. xxiii.

cleared political economy of Physiocratic error regarding the relation of agriculture to the production of wealth, it is only just to keep in mind that, ten years before Adam Smith's book appeared, Turgot, as one of the most fair and competent of American economists has shown, made the first analysis of distribution into wages, profits, and rent, discussed the distribution of labor, the nature and employment of capital, and the doctrine of wages, gave the main arguments for free trade and free labor, laid down some of the fundamental principles of taxation, and asserted very many other doctrines precious to the modern world—and that he did this with a force and clearness to which Smith never attained.

In forming an opinion of the characteristics and claims of these two great men, it may well be taken into account that while Smith's work was the result of inductions from facts observed during his whole life and passed upon during twenty years of steady labor on these and similar subjects, the work with which Turgot preceded him was struck out in the thick of all his vast labors as Intendant of Limoges and as adviser to the central government of France on a multitude of theoretical and practical questions, and that it was written, not as an elaborate treatise, but simply as a letter to two gifted Chinese students, who, having studied for a period in France, were returning to their native land. Each of the two works has vast merits, but, as an exhibition of original power, that of Turgot unquestionably stands first.[1]

---

[1] For the statement above referred to, see Seligman, review of Léon Say's "Turgot," *Political Science Quarterly,* vol. iv, p. 180, cited by R. P. Shepherd in his *Turgot and the Six Edicts,* p. 32, which also contains a short but able discussion of the arguments between the partisans of Smith and of Turgot. Also John Morley, *Crit. Misc.,* vol. ii, p. 149. For perhaps the most magnanimous, concise, and weighty of all tributes to Adam Smith, see E. Levasseur, *L'Économie Politique au Collège de France,* in *La Revue des Cours Littéraires* for December 20, 1879. For details regarding the two Chinese students, see Neymarck, *Turgot et ses Doctrines,* tome ii, pp. 345, 346.

Still another treatise in this same field of Turgot's activity was his *Loans at Interest,* published in 1769. An attempt made within his district to defraud sundry bankers by accusing them of charging too high a rate of interest caused him to take up the whole subject of usance. For ages, France, like the rest of Europe, had suffered from the theological theory opposed to the taking of interest for money. From sundry texts of Scripture, from Aristotle, from such fathers of the Eastern Church as St. Basil, St. Chrysostom, and St. Gregory of Nyssa, from such fathers of the Western Church as St. Ambrose, St. Augustine, and St. Jerome, from St. Thomas Aquinas, the foremost of mediæval thinkers, from Bossuet, the most eminent of all French theologians, from Pope Leo the Great and a long series of Popes and Councils, and from a series almost as long of eminent Protestant divines, had come a theory against the taking of interest for money, and this had been enforced by multitudes of sovereigns in all parts of Christendom.

The results had been wretched. The whole policy of the Church having favored the expending of capital, there was far less theological opposition to waste and extravagance than to that investment of capital at interest without which no great progress of industry is possible.

Turgot's method of dealing with this question took high rank at once, and, despite the authoritative treatises of Bentham and of Jean Baptiste Say, which appeared more than twenty years afterward, his may be accounted, on the whole, the most original and cogent work in the whole series of arguments which have obliged all branches of the Christian Church to change their teachings, and all civilized governments to change their practice, regarding the taking of interest for money.[1]

[1] See Léon Say, *Turgot,* Anderson's translation, p. 88; also Morley and Stephens.

For the passages from which the theological doctrine regarding interest

The last of Turgot's important writings during the Limoges period was his letter to Terray on protection to the French iron industry. In the course of this, not foreseeing the use of mineral coal in the manufacture of iron, he fell into a curious error. His theory was that only nations in an early stage of development, with great forests at their disposal for conversion into charcoal, can make iron. Strange as this idea seems to those who have observed the growth of the great iron industry in the leading modern nations, it must be confessed that his conclusion was better than some of his premises. His arguments favoring more freedom to the admission of iron may be read to good purpose even now, and one sentence, regarding protective duties between nations, may well be carefully pondered. It is as follows: "The truth is that in aiming to injure others we injure ourselves."

As time went on, Turgot's work at Limoges became more and more known and admired. Arthur Young, whose personal observations give us the best accounts of French agriculture before the Revolution, visiting the Limousin shortly after Turgot left it, dwelt upon the results of his administration as the best ever known in France up to that time; and Young's picture of the transformation of the whole region under Turgot's control produced a marked effect on public opinion, not only in France, but throughout Great Britain and in Continental Europe.

During the last years of Louis XV, recognition had come to Turgot as never before. To men of public spirit,

was developed, see Leviticus, xxv: 36, 37; Deuteronomy, xxiii; Psalms, xv: 5; Ezekiel, xviii: 7, 17; St. Luke, vi: 35. For a detailed account of the long struggle against this form of unreason, and citations from a long line of authorities, see *A History of the Warfare of Science with Theology in Christendom,* by the present writer, vol. ii, chap. **xix**, on "The Origin and Progress of Hostility to Loans at Interest."

and especially to the philosophers who had long dreamed
of a better government and a more prosperous people,
he had become an idol. Even many who had mobbed
him for his interference with agricultural protection in
the provinces now became his strong supporters.
Though he was intensely hated by a vast body of reactionaries, self-seekers, and graspers of place and pelf,
the great majority of thinking Frenchmen loved him
all the more for the enemies he had made.

Turgot had fought and wrought thirteen years at the
head of the Limoges government when, on a beautiful
May day in 1774, the long reign of Louis XV was ended.
Ancestors of the dead king—like Charles IX and Louis
XIV—had dealt more evident and direct blows at the
well-being of France, but never since the foundation of
the monarchy had any sovereign so debauched the whole
national life; and not only France, but the world at large,
began to take account of the legacies he had left.

First of these were his character and example, the
worst since the most degraded of the Cæsars; next was
his court, unmoral and immoral, from which corruption
had long welled forth over and through the nation. In
civil matters, there had prevailed the rule of the worst;
in military matters, defeat and dishonor; in finance,
constantly recurring deficits and an ever-nearing prospect of bankruptcy; among the higher clergy, luxury
and intolerance; among the nobility, the sway of cynics
and intriguers; among the middle classes, unreasoning
selfishness; among the lower classes, pauperism, ignorance, frequent famines, a deep sense of injustice, and
a rapidly increasing hatred for those who had so long
oppressed them. Imbedded in this enormous legacy of
corruption, misrule, misery, and hate, were two sayings
with which the late king and his most intimate adviser
had been wont to repel pleas for reform—"This will

last as long as I shall," and "After me the deluge." [1]

The deluge had come: a flood of resentments for old wrongs, of hatred for wrong-doers, of new thought boding evil to all that was established, of sentimentalism likely to become cruelty. [2]

To withstand this deluge had come Louis XVI, twenty years of age, kindly at heart, hating the old order of things, longing for something better, but weak, awkward, mistrusting himself and all about him; and, at his side— destined to be more fatal to him and to France than all else—his beautiful queen, Marie Antoinette, sometimes kindly, sometimes selfish, but always heedless, frivolous, lavish, never strong and persistent, save against those who sought to shield her husband and herself from the approaching catastrophe.

First of all there must be a prime minister. Reflecting upon this fact, and calling in the advice of those whom he thought his friends, Louis named Maurepas—a decayed fop, seventy-three years of age, whose life had been mainly devoted to cultivating useful acquaintances and scattering witticisms among courtiers, but who, on account of quarrels with some of the women about Louis XV, had several years before been banished to his country seat. Maurepas promptly reappeared, and to him was entrusted the duty of selecting a new ministry.

He would doubtless have preferred to call men of his own sort; but, being shrewd enough to see that this was hardly possible, he began gradually replacing the old

---

[1] The latter utterance is attributed by Sainte-Beuve to Madame de Pompadour, but there is ample evidence that the king adopted it.

[2] See a remarkable citation from Burke in Alison's *History of Europe*, vol. i, chap. i, on the natural transition from sentimentality to cruelty. A curious inversion of this is seen in our own country, where the same men who will risk their lives to lynch a murderer just after his crime is committed will, as jurymen, a few months later, after hearing a cunning speech, acquit him,—and with tears of joy.

ministers with better. In this he had a system:—the
selection of men who could make a reputation likely to
give him popularity, but who were without any ambitions
which might endanger him.

Foremost among these men was Turgot. The story of
his success in the intendancy of Limoges had spread far.
Even amidst all the scoundrelism of the time there was
a deep respect for his character, and an admiration for
his services. Yet Maurepas, thinking it perhaps not best
to trust him very far at first, made him simply Minister
of Naval Affairs, and this office Turgot held for just five
weeks and three days. Even during this time he showed
his good qualities, by casting out evils and suggesting
reforms; but Maurepas, feeling it necessary to yield to
the universal hatred against the Abbé Terray—everywhere recognized as a main centre of evil under the late
king—removed him from the great office of Comptroller-
General—at that time the most important position under
the monarchy—and in his place set Turgot.

This nomination gave universal satisfaction, and most
of all to the new king. He received the new Comptroller
with open arms; and during their first interview Turgot
made his famous proposal: "No bankruptcy, no increase
of taxation, no new debts; economy and retrenchment."
At this the king was overjoyed, gave his heart to Turgot,
and pledged his honor to support him.

That this confidence was well placed was shown by
Turgot's first budget; it was made with such genius that
it ended the deficit, extinguished a great mass of debt,
and set the nation on the road to prosperity.

This practical financial policy was but part of a plan
far deeper and wider. Turgot clearly saw that the old
system was outworn, that its natural result must be a
catastrophe, that in place of it must be developed a
system to meet the needs of the new time, that whatever
was to be done must be done promptly and thoroughly,

and that the only question was, whether this new system should come by evolution or by revolution.

Like heavy drops of rain before a shower came various suppressions of old abuses, including the monstrous *droit d'aubaine,* dismissals of incapables, abolitions of sinecures, arrests of peculators, freedom of internal trade in grain, and freedom of the press in matters pertaining to financial and general administration. Everything began to tend away from the old rule of secrecy, in which all noxious growths flourished, and toward throwing public business open to the light of public opinion.

All these things were contrary to the genius of Maurepas, and he gave as little help as possible; but during the following year he strengthened Turgot by the appointment of a true statesman as Minister of the King's Household. This statesman was Malesherbes, a man holding high judicial position—neither ambitious nor especially hopeful, but of great capacity and of noble character. His new office was of vast importance, for its occupant had large control of the court, of ecclesiastical affairs, Catholic and Protestant, of the city of Paris, and of various districts and institutions throughout the kingdom. Observing Turgot's preliminary reforms and the appointment of Malesherbes, good men and true throughout the realm took heart. The king, Turgot, and Malesherbes stood together—apparently a great force. Maurepas, encouraged by this success, gradually added other ministers; some, like Vergennes, strengthening the effort toward a better era; others, like Saint-Germain, holding back or going astray.[1]

Meanwhile came two things of ill omen. First was the recall of the Parliament of Paris, which had been suspended in 1771, and which had been superseded, as we have seen, by a new royal court. The parasites of the banished Parliament besought Louis to restore it; the

[1] See Foncin, *Le Ministère de Turgot,* livre ii, chap. x.

queen strongly seconded these efforts; Maurepas, with
the great mass of time-servers, took the same side; and
the mob hurrahed for it.   Opposing the recall of this old,
selfish, tyrannical body were Turgot, Malesherbes, Vergennes—Minister of Foreign Affairs—and two powers
which it surprises us to find in such company—first, the
king's next brother, the Comte de Provence, and
secondly, the clergy.   This position of the Comte de
Provence was doubtless due to his clear conviction that
the Parliament injured the royal power; the position of
the clergy was due to the only good thing in the recent
record of the Parliament, namely, its opposition to the
French prelates, and especially to the Jesuits, in their
attempts to revive religious persecution.[1]

The second thing of ill omen was the coronation oath.
The king must be crowned; and, costly as this solemnity
was, and empty though the treasury was, it seemed best
to give the monarch the prestige of the old ceremony—
the stately journey to Rheims, the largess of all sorts,
the coronation by the archbishops and bishops of France
in the most splendid of French cathedrals, the anointing
with oil from the sacred ampulla brought from heaven
by a dove more than a thousand years before, and first
used by St. Remy in crowning the founder of the French
monarchy.   Turgot had advised a coronation like that
of Henry IV, and that of Napoleon afterward, before the
high altar of Notre Dame, at Paris.   This would have
saved millions to the treasury, would have brought to
France multitudes of visitors whose expenditures would
have enured to the benefit of the country; and all this, in
the fearful condition of French finances, was much.

But in Turgot's mind this financial consideration was
of comparatively small account.   For, in the coronation
oath, the French kings had been made to swear to exterminate all heretics, and this oath Turgot—in the inter-

[1] The recall took place November 12, 1774.

est of justice, peace, and prosperity—sought to modify. But the clergy were too strong for him. They insisted that the king must, above all things, take the old oath, and Louis yielded to them; yet amid all the pomp of the coronation it was observed that, when his majesty arrived at the part of the oath which referred to heretics, his words were incoherent and nearly inaudible.

Soon came a new trial of strength between Turgot, representing what was best in the new epoch, and the recalled Paris Parliament, adhering to what was worst in the old. We have already seen what the old system of internal protection of agriculture had done for France. Its main result had been frequent famines, but even more evil had been its effects on the king, court, and high financiers. For there had been developed a practice of deriving profit from famine and starvation; and a leading feature in this was the sale of privileges to escape the protective duties. Out of these had grown an enormous system of monopoly and plunder,—what, in modern days, would be called a "grain ring," including not only petty intriguers throughout the nation, but very many of the highest personages. Even King Louis XV had been besmirched by it. This monopoly had power to keep grain cheap in sundry parts of the nation, and there to buy it; power to keep grain dear in other parts of the nation, and there to sell it. There was an unlimited field for intrigue and greed; and for the tillage of this field was developed a strong and shrewd monopoly. Efforts were made to expose this; but to criticise a minister was considered akin to treason. Significant was the case of Prévost de Beaumont. He had discovered sundry misdoings of the grain monopolists and endeavored to expose them; no doubt with a bitterness which led to exaggeration; as a result he was thrown into prison, where he remained over twenty years, until the outbreak of the Revolution and the destruction of the

Bastile set him free.[1] Against this whole system of internal protection of agriculture, and against all who profited by it, Turgot stood firmly. As far back as 1763 and 1764 royal decrees had been put in force abolishing it; but, with his invincible tendency toward cheatery, the Abbé Terray, Turgot's immediate predecessor in the comptrollership, had suspended these decrees, and the old system with all its evils had again settled down upon France. Now came a new struggle. Turgot induced the king to revive the old decrees giving internal free trade in grain, and, although protection of agriculture from foreign grain remained, the whole system of internal protection was abolished. This aroused bitter opposition; first, of course, from the grain ring and its satellites. Unfortunately, bad harvests followed the new decree; during the winter of 1774–75 came scarcity and even famine, and, as a result, bread riots and insurrections in various parts of France, notably beginning at Dijon near the eastern frontier, but steadily drawing near the centre of government, and finally, in April and May, 1775, appearing in Versailles and in Paris. The result was much pillage of bakers' shops in the towns, burning of barns in the country, and sinking of cargoes of grain in the rivers, with here and there wholesale plunder and occasional murder. At Versailles, poor Louis tried to win the mobs by harangues, but these being unheeded, he thought it best, in the absence of Turgot, to lower arbitrarily the price of bread.

Turgot saw in this a beginning of new evils. Clearly, if the king lowered the price of the loaf at Versailles, every other province, every other district, every other city, every other hamlet, had a right to demand a similar

---

[1] For the alleged *Pacte de Famine*, and the history of Prévost de Beaumont, the most complete account I have found is in Afannassiev, *Le Commerce des Céréales en France au 18ième Siècle*, chaps. xiv, xv. For Louis XV's interest in the grain monopoly, and for Prévost, see also Henri Martin, *Histoire de France*, tome xvi, pp. 292–296.

favor, and this meant a policy ending in bankruptcy and more helpless famine. Turgot's policy was really more merciful. As preliminary to all else, he insisted on having full powers from the king, suppressed the insurrection, dispersed the mobs, and two of the leaders in plundering and murdering he hanged on a gibbet forty feet high. It was a healthful act. Weak, sentimental people, whose measures in such crises generally turn out the most cruel which can be devised, lamented this severity; but the execution of these two malefactors doubtless prevented the deaths of scores, and perhaps hundreds, of innocent persons, which would have been unavoidable had the insurrection been allowed to rage and spread. What sentimental lenity to crime can do in enormously increasing murder we know but too well in the United States; what manly, prompt, and decisive dealing with crime can do in reducing the number of murders to almost a negligible point we see, to-day, in the administration of criminal justice in Great Britain.

While thus suppressing insurrection, Turgot struck boldly at the centre of the whole evil. The Parliament of Paris, in its general hatred of reforms, in its entanglements with monopolists, and in its dislike for Turgot, had done all in its power to thwart his policy by every sort of chicanery and pettifoggery. Thus they delayed the registration of the decree for reëstablishing freedom to the grain trade within the boundaries of France for three months; but now, near the end of the year 1774, Turgot availed himself of all the resources of French royal power, and forced them to yield.

Unfortunately, he could not get at his worst enemies. The bread riots had been organized to discourage free trade in grain. Behind the mob were the monopolists; the whole movement had a regularity which proved that its leaders were accustomed to command; and in the pockets of insurgents, howling for relief from starvation,

14

were found goodly sums of money. Various clues led back to the Prince de Conti, of royal blood, and to other magnates of position and influence; but Turgot, not wishing to delay other projects for important reforms, or to increase popular feeling, was obliged to abstain from any attempt at punishing them.

III

A T the beginning of the year, 1775, Turgot turned to a new series of great questions, and, most important of all, to a project for reforming the *taille,*—the great land tax,—one of the abuses which weighed most heavily upon the lower orders of the people. It was the principal tax in the kingdom. The old theory was that the nobility upheld the monarchy with their swords, that the clergy upheld it with their prayers, and that the third estate upheld it with their money. This theory had borne a vast fruitage of injustice. The nobility escaped with such comparatively small taxes as the "capitations" and the "twentieths"; the clergy evaded the heavier burdens by so-called "gifts," which they themselves voted from time to time; the monied classes escaped the greater taxes by purchasing a sort of half-caste nobility which freed them entirely from the *taille* and largely from other burdens. Very many of the less wealthy, who could not attain to enrollment among the nobles, were able to buy privileges which exempted them from much taxation. Sundry privileged towns, too, in one way or another, had secured immunities. As a result of all these exemptions, the burdens of the state fell with all the more crushing force upon the class of small peasant proprietors, farmers, and laborers, numbering about one-fourth of the entire population. They were the poorest inhabitants of France, but on them fell the main burden of the *taille,* and to this were added multitudes of feudal and church dues,—to such an extent that throughout large parts of the country men of this poorest class were taxed more than four-fifths of their earnings.

Here, too, it may be mentioned that taxes on articles of ordinary consumption fell upon them as heavily as upon the richest in the land, and in some respects even more heavily. The government duties on salt, which made the price of that commodity eight times as high as at the present day, were levied in a way especially cruel, while monopolies and trade regulations raised the price of every article of use.

The most competent authorities tell us that the deaths of Frenchmen from famine in 1739–40 had been more numerous than those caused by all the wars of Louis XIV, that eight thousand persons died of misery in one month, in one quarter of Paris, that peasants died of want within the precincts of Versailles, that some villages were completely deserted, and that multitudes fled across the frontier. The Bishop of Chartres, being asked by the king how his flock fared, answered, "Sire, they eat grass like sheep and starve like flies." Turgot found that more than half of France was cultivated by peasant farmers who were absolute paupers, and all this within the most fertile, the most healthful, and the best situated state in Europe. Arthur Young tells us that not less than forty million acres of French soil were wholly or nearly waste. Many abuses, royal, feudal, clerical, contributed to this state of things, but among the causes especially prominent was the *taille,* and therefore it was that Turgot, who had endeavored to ease this fearful burden at Limoges, now sought to adjust it fairly throughout France.

The main difficulty dated from Louis XIV. A modern economist states it as follows: "Costly campaigns abroad, ruinous extravagance at home, left the kingdom at his death in 1715 with a debt of 3,460 millions of francs. . . . His murderous wars, reducing the birth-rate, increased the mortality, and the expulsion of the Protestants had reduced the population by four millions, or twenty per cent, since 1660. Agricultural products had fallen off by one-third since he ascended the throne. Burdens increased, while they were diminished who bore them. A competent judge computed that more than half of the taxes were eaten up by the cost of collection."[1]

This condition of things had been made even worse by the Orleans regency and Louis XV. No less cruel than the taxes themselves was the manner of collecting them. The king in council having fixed the amount to be levied every year, an order was issued naming some individual in each community as collector, and making him personally responsible for the whole amount of the direct taxes in his district. In case this official failed under his burden, the other leading taxpayers in his district were made responsible,—all for each and each for all. This system was known as the *contrainte solidaire,* and it was substantially the same which had done so much, nearly fifteen hundred years before, to dissolve the Roman Empire.[2]

Even more cruel were the "indirect" taxes levied upon all the main articles consumed by the peasantry and collected by the agents of the Farmers General. Remembrances of indignities and extortions by these agents were among the leading incentives to the fearful pillage, destruction, and murder with which the Revolution began fifteen years later.[3]

[1] See the admirable little book of Higgs, *The Physiocrats.* For the above statement he cites such eminent authorities as Levasseur and Lavergne. For the best statement known to me on this whole subject, see Taine, *Ancien Régime;* and for the best summary known to me in English, see Lecky, *History of England,* vol. v, citing Rocquain, Doniol, and others.

[2] For the disintegration of the Roman Empire by burdens upon leading tax payers, see Guizot, *Histoire de la Civilisation en France;* and for a comparison of the tax collectors with the Curiales just before the end of the Roman Empire, see E. Levasseur, *Histoire des Classes Ouvrières,* as above, tome ii, p. 710.

[3] One of the most satisfactory accounts, within reasonable compass, of

To meet these evils, Turgot prepared plans for an equitable adjustment of the tax and a better system for its collection, and this, with a multitude of other capital reforms, he elaborated during 1775, although during the first four months of the year he was confined to his bed by a most painful attack of gout. His physical condition did not daunt him: he worked on vigorously despite his suffering, and, so far as the world knew, he was as valiant in grappling with the enemies who had beset him as he had been in the vigor of his early manhood.

Steadily pressing on in his policy of breaking a way out of the mass of old abuses and developing a better order of things, Turgot, in January and February of 1776, took up his most important work for France,— the preparation of "the six great edicts." Their main purpose was to loose the coils which were strangling French activities of every sort; and, of these, two were by far the most important. First, was the edict for the suppression of the royal *corvée*. The character of the *corvée* and the happy result of its suppression France had learned during his administration at Limoges. As we have seen, the purpose of this burden was the making of the royal roads, and the transportation of military stores. Under the old system the peasantry were liable to be called from their farm work during seed time or harvest and made to give many days of hard and exhausting work to road construction or to military transportation,—the main result being that the roads were among the worst in the world and the transportation of military stores anything but satisfactory. The cruelty

the old French system of taxation, which I have found, is in Esmein, *Histoire du Droit Français*, Paris, 1901, pp. 380 ff, 552 ff. For excellent short and clear statements regarding the *taille*, the *contrainte solidaire*, and the "five great *fermes*,"—the latter being the taxes collected by the Farmers General,—see Rambaud, *Histoire de la Civilisation Française*, Paris, 1897, chap. ix. See also, for the best presentation of the subject in its relations to French industry, Levasseur, as above.

and wastefulness of the system had then and there been remedied by Turgot, and for it he had substituted a moderate tax, which being applied to the roads, under proper engineers, and to transportation, under well-guarded contracts, had given infinitely better results, and had relieved the peasantry of these most galling burdens.

But to this system, which succeeded so well in the Limousin, and which Turgot now proposed, by one of the six edicts, to extend throughout France, there soon appeared an ominous opposition. Nobles, clergy, and the Parliament of Paris united to oppose it. Their main argument was that Turgot purposed to degrade the upper classes; that, logically, if government could tax the nobility and the clergy equally with the peasantry for the improvement of the highways of the kingdom, it could tax them equally for any other purpose, and that this would obliterate the essential distinction between nobles and base-born.

It is hard, in the France of these days, to understand the chasm of prejudice between the upper and lower classes which existed in those. There had been in French history before Turgot's time striking exhibitions of this feeling. Significant of much was the protest and complaint solemnly made by the nobility to the king at the States-General of 1614. They complained that the Third Estate, consisting of representatives of the vast body of the French people not noble, had in one of their appeals presumed to speak of themselves as the "younger brothers" of the nobility; and the noble delegates protested against this as "great insolence." Not less striking evidences of this same feeling are to be seen throughout the plays of Molière: in all of them the *gentilhomme* is everything, the *roturier* nothing.[1]

[1] For the protest and complaint of the nobles at the States General of 1614, see Duruy, *Histoire de France*, tome ii, pp. 236, 237.

More extended and hardly less bitter was the opposition to the other great edict,—for the suppression of the *Jurandes* and *Maîtrises*—the corporations which represented the various trades and the wardenships which controlled them. In order to understand this particular complex of abuses which Turgot now endeavored to unravel, it must be remembered that under the old ideas of governmental interference there had grown up in France a system by which the various trades and industries had become close corporations, each having its rights, its laws, its restrictions, its exclusions, its definitions, its hierarchy of officials. No person could exercise such trades without going through a long series of formalities; no person could rise in any of them without buying the right to rise. For some of these features there had doubtless once been a valid reason; but the whole system had finally become one of the most absurd things in all that chaos of misrule. Between 1666 and 1683 Colbert had issued one hundred and forty-nine different decrees regarding various trades; from 1550 to 1776, over two hundred and twenty-five years, there was dragging through the courts and the cabinets of the ministry the great struggle between the tailors and the clothes-menders, the main question being as to what constitutes a new and what an old coat,—the tailors being allowed to work only upon new clothing and the menders upon old. From 1578 to 1767, close upon two hundred years, the shoemakers and cobblers had been in perpetual lawsuits regarding the definition of an old boot,—the regulation being in force that shoemakers were allowed to deal only with new boots and cobblers with old. Similar disputes occurred between the roasters and the cooks as to which should have the exclusive right to cook geese, and which to cook smaller fowls; which the right to cook poultry, and which the right to cook game; which the right to sell simply cooked meats, and which to sell meats prepared with sauces. Beside these were endless squabbles between sellers of dry goods, clothiers, and hatters: wonderful were the arguments as to the number of gloves or hats which certain merchants might expose for sale at one time. In cloth making and selling there were minute restrictions, carefully enacted, as to the width, length, and color of pieces which might be sold. Workmen of one sort were not allowed to do work generally done by another sort in the same trade, and upon all the trades were levied taxes and exactions which they recovered, as best they might, from each other and from the public at large. Underlying and permeating all this tangled mass of evil was the idea of paternal government,—the idea that the duty of a good government is to do the thinking for its subjects in a vast number of matters and transactions on which the individuals concerned would far better think for themselves. As a legitimate consequence of this theory, one regulation required that tailors, grocers, sellers of mustard, sellers of candles, and a multitude of others engaged in various branches of business, carefully specified, should belong to the established church.[1]

This whole system—as crippling French industry and undermining French character—Turgot sought to remedy. There was nothing of the Jack Cade spirit in his policy. He allowed just compensation in every case, but, having done this, he insisted that the trade corporations should be extinguished and all wardenships abolished, except in four industries: in printing, because the nation was not yet ready for the measures which he would doubtless have elaborated later; in pharmacy and jewelry, because these trades need governmental control under all governments,—individuals being unable to exercise it;

---

[1] For special cases in this growth of human folly, see Duruy, *Histoire de France*, tome ii. For the development of the system, see Levasseur, tome ii, *passim*.

and in the barbers' and wigmakers' trade, because, during financial emergencies under previous reigns, so many wardenships, inspectorships, comptrollerships, and minor positions of various sorts in this branch of business had been created and sold to produce revenue that Turgot felt unable to buy them in. Noteworthy is it that when the rights of these barber functionaries were redeemed during the Revolution, the indemnity paid was over twenty millions of francs.

Of course, ingenious and elaborate arguments were made by strong men in favor of that old system, as they have been always made in favor of every other old system. In our days these arguments have been echoed by Alison. As a representative of English High Toryism he naturally declares against Turgot's reforms; and especially striking is the Tory historian's defense of the old French trade corporations in comparison with the trade unions of Great Britain in the early part of the nineteenth century. He exhibits the long series of wrongs and plundering, and even of unpunished murder, by these modern English organizations of labor, and attempts to present them as the only alternative to the French organizations under the Bourbons. But this argument, striking as it was when Alison presented it over fifty years ago, has now lost its force.[1]

The main line of contemporary argument against Turgot was that his reforms "impugned the wisdom of our ancestors," that they swept away all distinctions between expert and worthless artisans, and that they were sure to destroy the supremacy of French industry.

There were long sessions of the Paris Parliament by day and night, with no end of sham patriotic speeches and impassioned debates. Prominent in these was D'Espréménil, big, handsome, oratorical, adored by his party,—ready at any moment to make eloquent harangues

[1] See Alison, *History of Europe,* vol. i, chap. iii.

supporting abuses and denouncing reforms. Little did it occur to him that his own life and the lives of his friends were at stake and that Turgot was doing his best to save them; possibly this thought dawned upon him when, a few years later, he took his way to the guillotine.

Regarding this edict, also, Turgot persevered. The Paris Parliament, making a pretense of fairness, did, indeed, register of its own accord one of the minor edicts, while rejecting the others. All in vain: the king, though reluctant and halting, summoned the Parliament to a "Bed of Justice" and compelled it to register this and all the other edicts.

Closely connected with these reforms were Turgot's dealings with another vast evil. The system of farming the "indirect taxes" of the nation had long been fruitful of corruption among the higher classes and of misery among the lower. In general terms, the system was one in which, the amount of these taxes having been determined, the collection of them was let out to a great combination of contractors, and on terms enormously profitable to them. To secure this monopoly, and to prevent opposition to it, this syndicate kept the hands of the government tied by advancing to it large sums in times of its greatest need; captured influential personages at court, from ministers and mistresses of the king down to the most contemptible of their parasites, by petty offices, pensions, and gifts; secured the services or silence of rogues in all parts of the kingdom by threats or bribery. It assumed the character of what in America of these days would be called a "combine," and at the head of it were the Farmers General,—wealthy, powerful, and, as a rule, merciless. Their power pervaded the entire nation,—from the king's apartments at Versailles to the cottages of the lowliest village. Whenever it was thought best to buy a man, he was bought; whenever it was thought best to discredit him, he was discredited;

whenever it was thought best to crush him, he was crushed.[1]

To these men and their methods, Voltaire had made a reference which ran through France, and, indeed, through Europe. A party of Parisians were amusing each other by telling robber stories. Presently Voltaire, who had been listening quietly, said, "I can tell a robber story better than any of yours." The whole room immediately became silent and listened to the greatest personage in the French literature of the eighteenth century. Voltaire, after clearing his throat, began as follows: "Once on a time there was a Farmer General." Then he was silent. Presently all began to cry out: "Why do you stop? Go on. Tell us the story." "I *have* told the story," said Voltaire; "do you not see that my statement implies the greatest robber story in history?"

The French came to understand the Farmers General perfectly, and twenty years later a class of patriots and reformers differing from Turgot in their methods sent all the Farmers General on whom they could lay hands to the guillotine.

Against that phalanx of injustice Turgot stood forth undaunted. He could not, indeed, completely rout it, but he checked its worst abuses, cut down its illegal profits, and greatly diminished its power to corrupt the nation.

In his own person he set a noble example. For a long time it had been customary for the Farmers General to present to the Comptroller an enormous gift whenever the government contract with them was renewed. This had

---

[1] For a striking, but entirely trustworthy, statement of this system of farming the taxes, see Foncin, *Le Ministère de Turgot*, liv. i, chap. vi. See also Esmein and Rambaud, as above. Also for a very complete, thorough, and critical study, see R. P. Shepherd, in his "Turgot and the Six Edicts," *Political Science Quarterly* of Columbia University, vol. iv. For a list of pensions paid by each of the sixty Farmers General, with names of recipients, and amounts received, see Neymarck, *Turgot et ses Doctrines*, tome ii, appendix.

become a well-known institution, and the so-called "gift" to the Comptroller was regarded as one of his proper perquisites. In Turgot's case it amounted to three hundred thousand livres, equal in purchasing power, very nearly, to the same number of dollars in our own land and time. Turgot utterly refused this gift; he had determined to enter into his great struggle unhampered.

While carrying out these fundamental measures he effected a long series of minor reforms. There was the abuse of the *octroi,* under which taxes were collected on the produce of the peasants at the gates of cities. In this there had come various growths of injustice, notably one in levying high taxes on the sorts of products consumed by the poorer inhabitants of towns, and in levying low taxes on luxuries consumed by the higher classes. At this he struck an effective blow. In sundry cities and districts, especially at Rouen, were special monopolies in the grain trade, and in the business of bakers, which bore heavily upon the poorer classes. These he planned to destroy. At court and throughout the nation were myriads of sinecures; and these he extinguished whenever a chance offered. Throughout the country the system of raising money by lotteries prevailed; he saw—what so few statesmen among the Latin governments have seen from that day to this—the power of lotteries to undermine the financial morality of a people; and he struck effectively at these also. But here it should be especially mentioned that at all times and in all places he was careful to provide compensation to all who had just claims for loss of place or privilege. In this he showed that same wisdom which Great Britain has shown in the history of her reforms.[1]

Turgot now realized that measures to ameliorate feudalism must come. But he saw that the time had not yet arrived for developing them beyond what was abso-

[1] On Turgot's policy regarding lotteries, see Foncin.

lutely necessary in preventing revolution. His main effort in this field was to prepare the public mind for gradual reforms, and therefore it was that, in 1775, he suggested to Boncerf, whom he knew to have thoroughly studied the subject, the publication of a pamphlet on the evils of feudalism. As a respected officer in one of the highest grades of the financial administration, and as a man thoroughly trained in the law, Boncerf was in every way fitted to discuss the subject. Nothing could be more fair, just, and moderate than his book. Even its title was studiously mild. Instead of announcing it as an exhibition of the evils or cruelties or wrongs perpetrated by feudalism, he entitled it *The Inconveniences of Feudal Rights* (*Les Inconvénients des Droits Féodaux*). It was neither drastic nor vindictive. It simply defended, as an experiment, the abolition of feudal rights on the domains of the king, not merely as a matter of justice, but as a matter of policy. Hardly had it appeared, in January of 1776, when the Parliament struck at it venomously. On motion of D'Espréménil the book was ordered burned by the hangman, and indictments were brought against Boncerf which hung over his head until the Revolution swept them away. It is a curious historical detail that Boncerf, after the Revolution had begun its course, was placed by the Constituent Assembly in a position which aided him in destroying the evils he had exhibited in his book, and that he himself sealed up the cabinets which contained the indictments that had been brought against him. Significant also, perhaps, is the further detail that, later in his career, while D'Espréménil was brought to the guillotine, Boncerf escaped the Revolutionary jury by a majority of one.[1]

But it should not be understood that all of Turgot's efforts were given to removing old abuses. He was no

[1] A copy of the rare first edition of Boncerf's book is to be found in the Library of Cornell University.

mere destroyer; he was essentially a builder; all his reform measures had as their object the clearing of a basis for better institutions. Though the shortness of his ministry—only twenty-one months—prevented his putting all into definite form, there were several which have since rendered great services to his country. He vastly bettered the postal system throughout France, not only improving the roads on the plan which had done so much for the Limousin during his intendancy, but developing on these a service of fast coaches and diligences which greatly reduced the time between the most important points in France, and which became the envy of all neighboring nations. Under his direction were also prepared projects for a great network of internal water communications by the improvement of rivers, and the construction of canals; and, to study the problems connected with these, he called to his aid the men most eminent in applied science. He sought to create a scientific system of weights and measures to take the place of the chaos of systems which had come down from the Middle Ages. To aid industry he organized a better system of banking, not only in cities, but in rural centres, thus initiating the ideas which have done so much for French prosperity in these days. As to higher education, he virtually created the Academy of Medicine, which since his time has become the most famous and weighty in the world; and in the Collège de France he established new professorships of law and literature.

Best of all, as revealing his depth and breadth of thought, his insight into the character of the French people, his intuition as to their capacities, his foresight of their dangers, and his desire to create an environment in which a better future might be developed, was the *Memorial on Municipalities*. Among the many evidences of his power as a political thinker and statesman, this is the most striking as showing his ability to bring theory

to bear on practice. He saw what the most thoughtful
men in France have only just begun clearly to see,—that
the greatest defect in that gifted nation has been its
want of practical political education and its consequent
centralization of political power. Therefore it was that,
amid all his pressing occupations in 1775, he, with his
friend Dupont de Nemours, sketched out a plan for the
gradual education of the French people, not only in public
schools, but in the practical management of public affairs, by a system beginning in local self-government and
ending in A CONSTITUTIONAL GOVERNMENT OF THE NATION.

Beginning at the little village communities, he proposed to establish in each a local council elected by peasants and other small taxpayers, to discuss and decide
upon its own local matters, and also to elect delegates
to the councils of the *arrondissements,* or, as we should
call them, the counties. The *arrondissement* councils,
thus elected by the village communities, were to discuss
and decide *arrondissement* matters, and to elect deputies
to the assemblies of the provinces. The assemblies of
the *provinces* were to discuss and decide *provincial* matters and to elect representatives to the *assembly of the
nation.*

Closely connected with this plan was a broad, graded
SYSTEM OF PUBLIC INSTRUCTION for children and youth.
Could he have been given a free hand in accomplishing
this combination, he would have redeemed his promise
that ten years of it would make a new France. In all
this there was no rashness; he expressly declared it his
wish to proceed with the utmost moderation, and that
his main desire was to lay foundations. Had he been
allowed freedom to make a practical beginning of his
work, he would soon have produced an environment in
which Bourbon autocracy and Jacobin mob rule would
have been equally impossible.[1]

[1] For Turgot's plan of political education, see *Œuvres de Turgot,* tome

To a very large body of men in his time the reforms of Turgot, and especially this plan for the political education of the French people, seemed madness; but those who best know France to-day, and who look back upon her history without prejudice, will, as a rule, find in this two-fold plan a proof that Turgot saw farther than any other man of his time into the needs of his country. However we may dislike his temporary restriction of the suffrage, there would seem to be no question that, had his plan been carried forward, the French nation would, within a generation, have attained what a century of alternating revolutions and despotisms is only now beginning to give.

It should be borne in mind that for over a century and a half before Turgot there had not been a meeting of any body of men representing the French nation, that there was not among the French people any idea of the most ordinary public discussion of political matters, and that the holding of a political meeting in accordance with the simplest rules of order was something beyond French comprehension. This should be remembered by those who think that Turgot should have given universal suffrage at the outset. Two things more should not be forgotten: first, that the number of peasant proprietors was large and increasing; and, secondly, that he went farther in giving them power than any other man of note in his time—proposing a beginning from which a

---

ii, pp. 502–550. For a good summary, see Stephens, *Life of Turgot*, pp. 113, 114; and for an eloquent statement of Turgot's *Memorial* and its probable effects, see Duruy, *Histoire de France*, tome ii, p. 567. The present writer had the fortune to take part in discourse with various ministers who served Napoleon III during different epochs of the Second Empire, and afterward, and to observe closely their doings; and never did he find one who, in his department, seemed to embody so thoroughly the spirit of Turgot as did Duruy, who, during more than six years held the Ministry of Public Instruction against the constant attacks of the French clergy.

15

more extended suffrage would have been developed naturally and normally.

This, too, should be said for his system. He clearly saw that matters involving taxation in municipalities should be passed upon by the taxpayers themselves, and in this respect he was beyond the point at which our own nation has arrived. No absurdity in modern government is greater than that seen in the American cities, which permits great bodies of people, very many of them recently from foreign climes, ignorant of American duties, devoid of American experience, and unconscious of paying any taxes at all, to confer franchises and to decide on the expenditures of moneys collected from taxpayers.

On political questions, the rule at which general human experience has arrived is universal suffrage. In municipal matters, which are corporation matters, the rule should be that questions involving the granting of franchises, and the raising and expenditure of taxes, should be settled by taxpayers. Blindness to this fact has made our municipalities the most corrupt in the civilized world. A proper compromise would seem to be the election of mayor and aldermen by the whole body of the people, and the election by taxpayers of a "board of control" or "board of finance," without whose consent no franchise should be granted, and no tax levied.

A natural effect of Turgot's reforms was seen in the increasing number of his enemies and their growing bitterness towards him. First of them all was the queen. She persisted in making enormous pecuniary demands for worthless favorites, and in endeavoring to force into the most important places courtiers absolutely unfit. At the very beginning Turgot had foreseen this, and there still exists the rough draft of a letter to the king, in which, prophesying the dangers which Louis must resist, he had begun a reference to the queen and had then erased

it.[1] No less virulent was the king's brother, the Comte de
Provence,—a prince who made pretensions to wit and
literary ability. He had sided with Turgot in opposing
the recall of the Paris Parliament, but now there came
from his pen attacks on the great minister,—always
contemptuous, and sometimes scurrilous. With the
queen and the king's brother stood the great body of
the courtiers. To understand the reasons for their
resentment, we have only to look into the "Red Book,"
brought to light during the Revolution, and note the
enormous sums which all these people drew from the
impoverished treasury, and which Turgot endeavored to
diminish.[2]

Very bitter also were the prelates of the Church.
Probably the humble rural clergy, who remembered what
Turgot had done for their flocks in the Limousin, felt
kindly toward him; but the hierarchy, with the exception
of two or three who bore him personal friendship, never
relaxed their efforts to thwart him.

At an earlier period it might have been otherwise.
Various writings by Fénelon, in which he braved the hostility of Louis XIV, show that his great heart would
certainly have beat in unison with that of Turgot. Nor
is it difficult to believe that Belsunce, the noble archbishop who stood by his people at Marseilles during the
plague of 1720–21, religious persecutor though he was,
would also have sided with Turgot in a clear question
between the peasantry and their debased masters. But
the spirit of St. Carlo Borromeo, of Fénelon, and of

---

[1] For the striking out of a reference to the queen, see Léon Say's *Life
of Turgot*, Anderson's translation.

[2] For an example of the impudent manner in which the Bourbon princes
of the blood demanded that money should be ladled out to them from the
treasury, see a letter to Turgot from the Comte de Provence, in Levasseur,
Histoire des Classes Ouvrières, tome ii, pp. 611, 612, notes. The "Red
Book" (a copy is in the Cornell University Library) gives monstrous examples of the way in which money was thus demanded and paid.

Belsunce had given place to that of a very different class of prelates. The measure of their fitness as religious teachers had been given in their panegyrics at the death of Louis XV, which, perhaps, did more than all else to undermine their influence.[1]

The hierarchy was still determined to continue the old persecutions of the Huguenots, their hope being that, by annulling Huguenot marriages, rendering Huguenot children illegitimate, and reviving the long series of other persecutions initiated in Louis XIV's time, they might drive those who held the new faith from the kingdom.

Most virulent of all, save the queen and bishops, in opposing Turgot's measures, was the Parliament of Paris. In every way it sought to undermine them. To it are due some of the worst methods of arousing public hate, which later brought the fury of the Revolution upon its members themselves.

To all these should be added the great mass of hangers-on of the court, and of people who profited by the general financial corruption. Typical was the remark of a court lady: "Why these changes? *We* are perfectly comfortable."[2]

On all sides time-servers fell away from the great reformer more and more, his only friends seeming to be the philosophers and a thinking minority among the people. Pressure and intrigue were steadily brought to bear upon the king, and such machinations were as cunning as were similar plans to undermine Prince Bismarck in our own time; but, unlike these, the efforts made against Turgot were not exposed until too late.

More than once Louis declared that only he and Turgot

---

[1] There is in the Library of Cornell University a very remarkable volume in which have been bound together a large number of these sermons at the death of Louis XV, lauding, magnifying, and justifying his character, and, of all things in the universe, his *religious* character, and comparing him to David and other approved personages in Scripture.

[2] See Droz, tome i, p. 206, cited by Alison.

cared for the people; but about a year and a half after Turgot had become Comptroller-General, and the king had pledged to him hearty support, it was clear that this support was rapidly weakening. First came the resignation of Malesherbes. His services in improving the administration had been beyond price, but he at last lost all hope, both for Turgot's reforms and for his own. Naturally pessimistic, he complained that Turgot's desire for the public good was "not merely a passion, but a craze." Now came the crucial test of the king. The court, in view of the immense patronage of the office which Malesherbes had held, urged as his successor Amelot de Clugny, a contemptible parasite of no ability, sure to thwart the reforms of Malesherbes and to restore the old order. On this Turgot wrote letter after letter to the king, pleading most earnestly, not for himself, but for the reforms which had been accomplished under Malesherbes and which must be lost if Clugny came into power. But the king made no answer, save a cool and insulting demeanor whenever he met the great minister who was trying to save him. Finally, Turgot wrote a letter which has become famous and which still exists,—a letter showing entire respect and deep devotion, but solemnly, heroically, with that power of prophecy which was perhaps his most marvelous gift, reminding the king that it was weakness which had brought Charles the First to the scaffold. As a reply to this letter came a dismissal.

This was in 1776. Turgot had held office twenty-one months, and more than four of these months had been passed mainly in bed under acute suffering. He had done his best; but in vain. No man in the whole history of France had labored with more heroism and foresight to save his country.

His death took place in 1781, five years after his retirement, and his life during this period was worthy of him. He never again appeared at court, but gave himself up mainly to scientific work and philosophical pursuits. Only once during that time did he make any appeal to the government, and this took shape in a suggestion that, for the honor of France, Captain Cook, then upon one of his voyages around the world, should be exempt from the disabilities of other Englishmen during the war then raging. To the credit of French chivalry, this advice was taken.

No sooner had Turgot laid down his high office than a policy of extreme reaction set in. His main reforms were joyfully and malignantly undone. Lampoons against him abounded. Queen, court, nobles, and high clergy devoted themselves with renewed vigor to restoring the old abuses. Thenceforward they flourished, until the Revolution, in a way very different from that proposed by Turgot, dealt with them and with those who had restored them.[1]

Various arguments have been made against Turgot. First of these is the reactionary charge, that he favored atheism,—that he brought on the Revolution. Any one who has dispassionately viewed the history of that epoch knows these charges to be monstrously unjust: that Turgot was not an atheist is shown abundantly by his writings and his conduct; that he did not bring on revolution is shown by his myriad efforts to produce that environment which alone could prevent revolution.

Next comes the flippant and cynical argument,—one of those epigrams which for a time pass as truths: the charge that in reforming France he dealt as does an anatomist with a corpse, and not as a wise surgeon deals with a living organism. This has been widely repeated, but its falsity is evident to any one who will study Turgot's

---

[1] For attacks on Turgot before and after his downfall, in the shape of pamphlets, verses, songs, and general ridicule, see Gomel, *Les Causes Financières de la Révolution Française*, pp. 206 ff; also Foncin, as above, liv. iii, chap. xvii.

work at Limoges, and the statements to the French people
which prefaced his most important acts as Comptroller-
General. When one compares his work with that of
Richelieu and Sully, it becomes clear that no statesman
ever realized more deeply than Turgot the needs of all
classes of the people, and the necessity of dealing with
them as moderately and gently as he could. Nor is there
any evidence of any feeling toward the nobility and clergy
save an earnest wish to make the changes, which would
have been so beneficial to them, as satisfactory as possible. But *some* remedy to the evils which were destroying France he *must* administer, and it must be a *real*
remedy. Within twelve years after his death the whole
world saw with horror the results of its rejection.

Again, there is the English High Tory argument, best
stated by Alison. His main charge is that Turgot was
a doctrinaire, who wished to rebuild France "on strictly
philosophic principles" and on no other. So far was
Turgot from being a doctrinaire that he was perhaps the
most shrewd, practical, far-sighted observer of actual
conditions in the entire kingdom. Typical were his long
journeys through the rural districts with Gournay, his
letters to the country curates, his discussions with the
poorest and humblest of peasants who could throw light
on the actual conditions of the country. His own reply
to the charge that he unduly pressed doctrinaire measures may be found in one of his notes to a hostile keeper
of the seals, in 1776, which runs as follows: "I know as
well as any one that it is not always advisable to do the
best thing possible, and that, though we should not tire
of correcting little by little the defects of an ancient constitution, the work must go forward slowly, in proportion
as public opinion and the course of events render changes
practicable." [1]

Closely connected with this charge is the statement that

---

[1] See citation in Say's *Turgot,* Anderson's translation, p. 105.

his insuccess was due to his lack of *finesse* with the king, lack of suppleness with the queen and princes of the blood, lack of deference for the nobility and clergy.

But the fact remains that in such desperate cases applications of rose water and burnings of incense cannot be substituted for surgery and cautery. A sufficient answer to the contention for such pleasing treatment is found in the career of Turgot's successor, Calonne,—the *"great"* Calonne,—who, while evidently believing in the fundamental ideas of Turgot, applied them tactfully, deferentially, and soothingly. He it was who said to the queen, "Madam, if what you ask is possible, it is done; if impossible, it shall be done." He petted and soothed king, queen, court, everybody; delayed every effective operation or remedy, obligingly,—until all found themselves, past help, in the abyss of revolution.[1]

Still another charge has been made against Turgot by sundry fanatics of the sort who believe in bringing in extreme democracy by decree, rather than by education and practice,—whether in France of the eighteenth century or in the Philippine Islands of the twentieth. They dwell upon the fact that he proposed a property qualification for suffrage. A French historian, M. Aulard, dwells on the fact that Turgot composed his village municipalities of land owners, his city municipalities of householders, and made property the base of the right of the citizens generally. And he adds that when France endeavored, in 1787, to make a general application of Turgot's plan, those only were admitted to the Paris elections who paid at least ten francs of direct taxes, and those only were eligible to vote for members of the municipal assemblies who paid at least thirty francs annually of direct taxes.[2]

[1] For an excellent comparison between Turgot and Calonne in this respect, see Say, Anderson's translation, p. 206.

[2] For Turgot's views on a property qualification for suffrage, see

But M. Aulard, without intending it, then gives us an admirable answer to any charge of narrowness or want of foresight based on these facts; for he reminds us that the example of America had fortified these ideas, that the constitutions of the thirteen states were, as a rule, based upon the idea that no man could be free and, consequently, worthy to exercise civic rights, unless he had a certain financial independence. The fact that Turgot was as far advanced as the foremost Americans of his time may well be pleaded in his favor. He advocated evolution rather than revolution. Like the fathers of our own republic, he preferred to make a beginning suited to the time and let future events determine how rapidly and how far the suffrage should be extended. That Turgot was right in this is amply shown by the fact that universal suffrage—shortly afterward adopted in France—led, first, to terrorism and the reign of murder and pillage, and, afterward, at two different epochs, to the return of absolute monarchy under the two Napoleons. And Turgot's wisdom is shown, also, by the contrasting fact that in America the system of a slight restriction of the suffrage has invariably proved to be but a preliminary stage in the steady and inevitable evolution of democracy.

If Turgot erred, he erred in company with the founder of American democracy, Thomas Jefferson, who, in a letter to John Adams, speaking of the French people and of their incapacity for governing themselves in the eighteenth century, virtually approved the ideas of Turgot. So far from laying it down as a universal principle that "everything should be done for the people but nothing by them," Turgot, as we constantly see, proposed by a wide and thorough system of education and by the steady development of a political practice in the

Aulard, *Histoire Politique de la Révolution Française*, Paris, 1901, p. 27, citing Turgot, *Œuvres*, ed Daire, t. ii, p. 511.

French *bourgeoisie* and peasantry, to initiate the entire nation gradually into self-government.[1]

Napoleon did, indeed, openly avow and act upon this doctrine imputed to Turgot; but Napoleon's purpose was not to uplift the French people into fitness for self-government, but to keep them permanently beneath his throne.

The charge of too great haste has also been frequently made against Turgot's measures, and most powerfully of all by M. Levasseur, Professor of Political Economy and Director of the Collège de France—certainly one of the foremost authorities, if not the foremost, on all questions relating to men and measures which concern the commerce and industry of France. While considering Turgot one of the greatest men whom France has produced, he compares him, to his disadvantage, with Richelieu and Colbert. But Richelieu dealt with problems far less complicated than those which fell to the lot of Turgot, and Colbert had twenty-two years in office, under a monarch who stood by him; while Turgot had less than twenty-two months, under a monarch who deserted him. M. Levasseur thinks that Turgot ought to have surmounted the numerous obstacles in his path "little by little and one by one"; but the eminent economist seems to lose sight of the fact that the opposition to each and every one of his measures was practically as great as that to all combined, and that *time* was an element of more essential importance in Turgot's work than it had been in the work of either of the other two great statesmen.

For what Turgot's friends have called the vigor, and what his critics have called the haste, with which he con-

---

[1] For the influence of Turgot on the Constituent Assembly and for John Adams' reply to the criticisms upon Turgot, in 1787, see H. E. Bourne, on "American Constitutional Precedents in the French National Assembly," *American Historical Review*, vol. viii (1903), pp. 466 *et seq.*

ducted public affairs, he often gave, in his discussions
with friends, a pathetic personal reason, namely, that
the Turgots always died in middle life, and that what
was to be done he must do at once; this saying proved
sadly prophetic. But there was a greater, more statesmanlike reason. Turgot's prophetic gift showed him
that what he offered was the best chance for France and
the last chance for the monarchy; that promptness in
decision and vigor in execution had become the only hope;
that reforms, to prevent a wild outburst of revolution,
must be made then or never.[1]

Again, sundry good and true men, like M. Léonce de
Lavergne, point out minor defects in Turgot's manner
and career which they think mistakes, and, as the crowning mistake of all, the fact that he did not summon the
States-General.

All great statesmen have the defects of their
qualities, and all make mistakes; but the refusal
to summon the States-General would probably be
voted by the vast majority of thinking men, not a
mistake, but an evidence of Turgot's wisdom and
foresight. Eight years after Turgot's death the
States-General was summoned, and it plunged France
at once into that series of revolutions which has now
lasted more than a century. Turgot's methods were not
revolutionary, but evolutionary. He did not believe that
a new heaven and a new earth could be brought in by
an illiterate mob, whether let loose in a city or throughout·
a nation. As a historical scholar, he knew that every

---

[1] For M. Levasseur's judgment upon Turgot, in which the above criticism is made, see his *Histoire des Classes Ouvrières*, tome ii, p. 606 *et seq.*
It is, of course, with the greatest diffidence that I presume to differ from
so eminent an authority, but possibly one looking at the history of France
from a distance may occasionally get nearer the truth than would a far
more eminent authority immediately on the ground. The traveler who
looks at Mont Blanc from a distance may obtain a clearer idea of its
relations to the peaks which surround it than can one who dwells nearer
the mountain.

republic ruled by uneducated masses had ended in despotism. As a practical observer of human affairs, he believed that to have anything like a free government, the first requisite is popular moral and intellectual education, and, as we have seen, his system was shaped toward developing a people who might gradually be fully entrusted with political power. Here again we may cite Thomas Jefferson, whose faith in democracy will hardly be questioned. In those most interesting letters, written toward the end of his life, reviewing events which he had known intimately, he admits that the French were not in his time fit for unlimited democracy.[1]

Yet another objection is that Turgot lacked tact; and as proof is adduced his final letter to the king, alluding to the fate of Charles I. The answer to this is simple. That final letter was written when Turgot saw that the end had come, that the king was giving himself into the hands of his enemies, that the only remedy must be heroic. Then it was that, like a great prophet of Israel, he firmly pointed to the past and told the king the truth. Looking across the abyss of revolution which separates the France of to-day from the Bourbon monarchy, the utterance seems divinely inspired. Rightly judged, it presents one of the greatest proofs of Turgot's fitness for his high mission and of his claim upon universal humanity.

And, finally, the objection is made that he failed. As to this, we may simply say that France had come to the parting of the ways. One way seemed hard. It led through reforms soberly planned and steadily developed —over a solid basis of institutions thoughtfully laid and adjusted, hedged in by ideas of duties as well as of rights, lighted by education—towards constitutional liberty. This was the way planned by Turgot. The other way

---

[1] See Léonce de Lavergne, *Les Économistes Français du Dix-Huitième Siècle,* essay on Turgot, *passim,* and especially p. 253.

seemed easy. But it led, first, through the stagnant marsh of unreasoning conservatism;—then through dikes broken by unreasoning radicalism;—then, by a wild rush, through declamation and intrigue; through festivals of fraternity and massacres; through unlimited paper wealth and bottomless bankruptcy; through mob rule and Cæsarism; through sentimentalism and murder; through atheism and fetichism; through the Red Terror and the White Terror; through the First Empire and the Invasion; through the Second Empire, the Invasion, and the Commune; through proscription at home, wars of conquest abroad, and enormous indemnities to be paid for them; through a whole century of revolutions—sometimes tragical, sometimes farcical, but always fruitful in new spawn of declaimers and intriguers. At the parting of these two ways stood Turgot, looking far down along them both;—marking with clearness of vision what lay in either path;—seeing and showing what king, queen, nobility, clergy, and thousands on thousands of French citizens realized only when brought to pauperism, prison, exile, and the guillotine. He wrought and strove like a Titan to mark out the better path,—to fit the French people for it,—to guide his generation into it,—and in this he failed; but, in his failure, he was one of the greatest men the modern world has known.

For, across the revolutionary abyss,—through the storms of demagogism and the conquests of imperialism, —above the noise of orations heralding new millenniums, and of drums and cannon dismissing them,—his calm, strong counsel, rejected by the eighteenth century, has been received and developed by the nineteenth and twentieth centuries. Every régime since that which perished with the king he tried to save—and not only in France but in all other civilized countries—has been made to hear and heed him. His statue, which looks down upon the great quadrangle of the Louvre—the scene of so much glory and folly—fitly represents him. Kings, emperors, presidents, have there been welcomed as saviors and dismissed as malefactors; but Turgot, steadily breasting the tides of unreason, remains to point out those principles of liberty, justice, righteousness, tolerance, education, which alone can give to any nation lasting prosperity and true glory.

STEIN

STEIN

I

MANY events in history show the inherent weakness of absolutism, but none in modern times more vividly than the eclipse of Prussia and the destruction of the old German Empire by Napoleon.

Frederick the Great had taken his father's army (all save "The Tall Grenadiers"), his father's treasury, his father's principles of administration,—had developed and used all these with genius; but there was in his whole work just one fully developed man—himself. He it was who thought out the problems, laid the plans, pushed on work, baffled adversaries; and, despite sundry errors and absurdities, he did all this with genius.

At his command, the nobility marched to death or glory; the middle class manufactured and merchandized to fill his treasury; the peasantry laid down their lives as his soldiers or as serfs in ill-requited toil. The individual was nothing; the state, everything.

In the upper stratum of the population stood army officers, high civil officials, clergy, and men of letters. The army officers had inherited stern ideas of duty, honor, and discipline from the days of the Great Elector and his still greater grandson, but their system and training were outworn; during the last years of the eighteenth and first years of the nineteenth century they had "learned nothing and forgotten nothing." Many of these men were valuable, some of them admirable, but very few were of use in great affairs; their power to originate, to direct, to take responsibility, had been gradually superseded by unreasoning obedience. The clergy had some exceptional men, but in general had become dull, heavy, stupefied by the Protestant orthodoxy and intolerance which set in after the death of Luther. The great German thinkers of the modern epoch were already at work, and powerfully; but as yet they had not taken full hold upon the German mind and heart: Kant and Schiller had begun their message, but their full strength was yet to be revealed.

In the towns remained the mediæval medley of corporations, guilds, classes more or less privileged, but with the old Teutonic spirit of independence long since taken out of them.

Beneath absolutism and various intermediate strata, there remained the lowest and largest stratum of all—two-thirds of the whole population, including, virtually, the whole rural population, subject to mediæval exactions and restrictions—and, among these, a widespread body of serfs.

Even during the lifetime of the great Frederick there had come warnings of European trouble. The French philosophers had begun their work. Voltaire had set in motion currents of thought sure to bring storms; Rousseau had spread new ideas of right very dangerous to despotism, not merely in France, but in all countries; yet Frederick steered his ship of state steadily in spite of these ideas—sometimes, indeed, by means of them.

But in 1786 he died, and the times demanded that his successor be as great as he, or greater. To adjust the old state to the new ideas, there was needed not only a great ruler, but a great reformer, a genius hardly less than miraculous; and, at this time, of all times, Frederick the Great was succeeded by Frederick William the *Fat*.

He was the most worthless of the Hohenzollerns. Herein is seen the fatal vice of absolutism—it demands a constant succession of men of genius on the throne, and such a succession never has been and never will be seen. A Frederick the Great has generally been soon followed by a Frederick William the Fat; a Charlemagne by a Charles the Simple; a Charles V by a Philip II; an Elizabeth by a line of Stuarts; a Henry IV by a Louis XIII; a Napoleon I by a Napoleon III; a Joseph II by a Francis I; a Peter the Great by an Alexis; a Catherine by a Paul; a Nicholas I by a Nicholas II.

The new Prussian king, in essentials, was much like Louis XV of France—perhaps a better-hearted man, but, as a monarch, worse than worthless. Each of these two sovereigns received in early years the title of "well beloved";—the French king being called "Le Bien-Aimé," and the Prussian "Der Viel-Geliebte." Both were good-natured; both lazily wished their subjects well; both firmly believed that their subjects existed for them, and not they for their subjects; both were hopelessly licentious, and at the same time excessively orthodox; both were consequently brought to grief by the wiles of women and priests; each was very anxious, while pampering his body, to save his soul—and to save the souls of his people; each had an instinctive dread of the new philosophy, and both resorted to the same futile means of checking it.

Decay in Prussia, and, indeed, throughout Germany, now became rapid. Most effective of all disintegrating influences were two, and both mainly from France:—the influence of the old French corruption and of the new French freedom. It was like applying to granite first fire, then water.

For the only time in its history, Prussia was now largely influenced by courtesans and favorites, after the Louis XV manner. Frederick I, seventy years before, had shown some tendency toward Bourbon methods, but his good sense, inherited from his father, the Great Elector, prevented their becoming dominant; Frederick

William I had kept them out by brutality; Frederick the
Great, by common sense; and, if either of these committed
sins, they were not flaunted before his people.

The internal administration of the new king, Frederick
William II, soon became, in its essential features, like
that which had impoverished France and almost all the
lesser courts and governments of Germany. For favorites and mistresses he carved estates from the public domain, and lavished treasure, patents of nobility, and
orders of chivalry. His example spread his own view of
life, first through the court and Berlin society, and then
through the higher classes of the whole country. Corruption came, then extravagance, then debts and dishonesty.
Wöllner, a cabinet minister, distinguished himself by
edicts in the interest of the old Protestant orthodoxy,
though expressly allowing the clergy to disbelieve, if they
would keep their disbelief to themselves. He strengthened the censorship of the press, instituted doctrinal test
examinations, and gave special instructions to prevent
any new views filtering down among the people. Kant,
at Königsberg, the future glory of Prussia and of Germany, was, indeed, elaborating a better philosophy; his
work in establishing new foundations for morality was
the greatest single force in human thought during the
nineteenth century; but he showed some tendency toward
freedom of opinion, and this brought from Berlin stern
reproofs; he was told to hold his peace, lest worse befall
him.

The external policy of the new king differed no less
widely from that of his predecessor. The great Frederick had concentrated his efforts upon the safety and
welfare of his own country; but Frederick William the
Fat scattered his forces in efforts, more or less vague, to
accomplish something noteworthy in other countries.
He meddled and muddled and gained neither strength
nor glory. The Prussian army was sent into the Nether-

lands to aid one of the parties there, and won some trifling victories; but the efforts of the Prussian Foreign Office to continue the work of Frederick the Great within the limits of Germany resulted mainly in a series of farces, the dupe being sometimes Prussia and sometimes Austria.[1]

While this was going on, the flood of French liberty, equality, and fraternity seemed about to break over all barriers raised by German officialism. Three years after the accession of Frederick William the Fat, the French Revolution burst forth, showing as yet little of its evil side, but warming and stirring all Europe by its enunciation of new truths. The resistance of the States-General to king and court, the establishment of the National Assembly in apparent harmony with the monarch, the renunciation of privileges by the nobility, the pamphlets of Sieyès, the speeches of Bailly and Mirabeau, leavened German thought.

What was done in Prussia to meet this tide? Worse than nothing. A few concessions as to military service were flung to the privileged classes; a few concessions of milder discipline to the army; a few shiftings of burdens from the upper classes, who made themselves heard, upon the lower classes, who were dumb; but the main mass of abuses in Prussia and in every other German state remained.

The political action of the Prussian Kingdom, both internal and external, at this period was profoundly immoral. In spite of pledges to protect the integrity of Poland, the partitioning of that wretched country went on. No doubt Poland had seemed unfit to exist as a nation; no doubt her government had been the most pre-pos-

[1] For a brief statement of some other differences between Frederick the Great and Frederick William the Fat, see Gneist, *Denkschriften des Freiherrn von Stein*, p. 3. For interesting particulars regarding the rise and progress of Wöllner, see Guy S. Ford, in the *American Historical Review*, Jan., 1910.

terous in Christendom; her nobles anarchic; her labor-
ing classes priest-ridden, and consequently ignorant and
hopeless; no doubt the whole Polish people who came
under Austria, Prussia, and even Russia, were material
gainers; but seizing and appropriating an independent
nation in time of peace was setting a precedent which the
partitioning powers had, and still have, reason to lament
—bitterly.

Meantime, the French Revolution was passing into its
more threatening phase, and Prussia made new blunders.
The crowned heads of Europe took counsel together,
among them, especially, the German Emperor Leopold
and King Frederick William the Fat; and there was
issued the Declaration of Pillnitz, which simply drew
upon Germany the French fury of 1792. In one of his
admirable essays, Von Sybel declares the idea that the
allied monarchs made war against France a popular
fallacy. This assertion seems unworthy of so great a
historian. Technically speaking, the war was made by
France; really, it was made by the powers allied against
her: the French, indeed, declared war, but the declaration by the allied monarchs had made war inevitable;
the Republicans at Paris had the wit to see this; the
Royalists at Berlin and Vienna had not.

The armies of Prussia and Austria were now pushed
against France, and at first the French troops gave way.
In some cases panic seized them: they threw down their
arms and fled for their lives, strikingly like the Union
troops invading the South at the beginning of our own
Civil War. Essentially, their great panic near St.
Menehould was amazingly like our great panic at Bull
Run. But soon all was changed. Prussians and Austrians wore out their strength in intrigues regarding
their shares in the plunder of Poland, and in wretched
squabbles for precedence; worst of all, they issued the
famous Brunswick Manifesto, which, by its threats, in-

fused into every Frenchman the courage of desperation. The Germans now began to be pushed back; better commanders arose among the French, who beat the allies, first at Valmy and Jemappes, and later all along the Rhine, until at last, in 1795, Prussia escaped from the whole complication by making the Peace of Basle—thereby deserting her ally, Austria, allowing France to take all the left bank of the Rhine, including Belgium and Holland, and receiving, as a bribe, permission to deal with the lesser North German States as she chose,—to annex and oppress them to her heart's content.

While Prussia was thus rapidly losing the strength and prestige given her by Frederick the Great, Frederick William, "the well beloved," went on with his pleasures. Our Gouverneur Morris, who was presented to him at court in 1797, wrote home that, robust as the king seemed to be, it was evident that his time was to be short. This prophecy of the shrewd American was realized even more rapidly than he expected, for Frederick William II died that same year, and there came to the throne his son, Frederick William III.

The new king seemed more unpromising than his father in every respect save in morals. He was timid, awkward, undecided, slow. He had been wretchedly educated, partly under bigots, partly under debauchees; his spirit had been crushed by the favorites of his father; he was at first, to all appearance, the most forlorn and hopeless Hohenzollern who ever existed; and yet deep in his heart and mind was a spark of that genius which has given to the Hohenzollerns the German Empire. At his accession this showed itself in some spasmodic attempts at reform: the Countess of Lichtenau, who through his father had ruled the court, he banished, and Wöllner he drove from the service; but soon, though he kept clean and clear from his father's surroundings, he subsided into the hands of the old politicians of his father's time—tricksters like Haugwitz, Lucchesini, and the like.

Meantime history went on in France, also, and a very different history. The French Revolution had raised vast armies and developed great generals, and, among these, Bonaparte. France had thrown off her old shackles, distributed her church lands and the estates of refractory nobles, transformed her serfs into free citizens, and developed the courage of desperation.

Germany and Prussia clung to the old system; even the people refused to accept reforms; Joseph II of Austria, for his efforts to better his country, had gained from the people, apparently, nothing but curses, and died of a broken heart. The game of the French, especially after Bonaparte had arrived as "the man on horseback"—the natural result of liberty gone mad—was easy; they played the continental governments against one another, bribing some, crushing others; and, to prevent the larger states from becoming too powerful, they grouped the smaller states and tied them, by their ambitions, to France—thus, in due time, creating the kingdoms of Bavaria, Würtemberg, Westphalia, the Confederation of the Rhine, and various petty satrapies, in which hopes of gain from France were substituted for loyalty to Germany. In 1803 large parts of Germany, outside of these greater divisions, were divided up to make bribes—for such use among German rulers as the conqueror might think best; fifty thousand square miles, with three millions of inhabitants, were thus appropriated, and in this process over two hundred small German states were deprived of their sovereignty and extinguished. As in the time of Bismarck, sixty years later, princes who had steadily refused to make any concessions to patriotism or right reason were crushed and ground out of existence by men of "blood and iron."

Austria, not being supported by Prussia, was stripped by successive conquests, humiliated at Ulm by one of the most ignominious capitulations in history, and finally, in 1805, crushed at the Battle of Austerlitz, and forced to submit to the terrible Peace of Pressburg, which deprived her of her most important outlying territories on all sides.

Now began a dire series of humiliations for Prussia. Had she joined heartily with Austria and Russia against Napoleon, the result might have been widely different; but she dallied and delayed until the Treaty of Pressburg had ruined her natural allies, apparently forever. As usual in the early days of Frederick William III, before he had been schooled by disaster, he delayed until too late. Before the battle of Austerlitz he had sent Haugwitz to meet Napoleon, with an ultimatum threatening war; but the interview was put off until the battle had been fought, and that changed everything—Napoleon having utterly crushed Austria and driven off Russia, Haugwitz was obliged to put the ultimatum in his pocket and pretend that he had been sent to propose mediation for the benefit of Europe and to congratulate the conqueror on his victory. Napoleon knew that Haugwitz was lying, and Haugwitz knew that Napoleon knew that he was lying; but a private letter from the Prussian king allowing Haugwitz to take the responsibility, they now made the Treaty of Schönbrunn,—a treaty apparently most favorable to Prussia, but really the greatest humiliation in her history. For Napoleon, knowing the Prussian need of peace, promised that, if Prussia would separate herself wholly from the allies, he would give her Hanover. This was a masterpiece of rascality. If any new territory was coveted by Prussia, it was Hanover; but Hanover belonged to the ruling house of Great Britain; for Prussia to take it was to make Great Britain her bitter enemy, and to make all right-thinking Europeans despise her.[1]

The Prussian government was very reluctant to make itself an accomplice in Napoleon's system of robbery; but, as he grew stronger every day, and showed decided signs of offering less favorable terms, the treaty was at last ratified. Napoleon seemed to delight in making it as humiliating as possible—giving Hanover, nominally, but insisting on taking, in return, so much other territory that the advantage to Prussia by this dishonor was, after all, next to nothing.

But this was merely a beginning. Napoleon's genius in scoundrelism was as wonderful as his genius in war; having made the Prussian king his accomplice, he treated him like a lackey, forced him to send away his capable and patriotic foreign minister, Hardenberg, to take back Haugwitz, and to allow Prussian territory to be treated as virtually French.

Worse still, Prussia was openly made a dupe. While carving out of the states on the western side of Germany the Confederation of the Rhine and allying it, with its sixteen millions of Germans, to France, Napoleon soothed Prussia by graciously giving her permission to create a Federation of North German States, and to put herself at its head; but when Prussia attempted this she soon found delays, objections, resistance on all sides, and

---

[1] For a scathing summary of Haugwitz's evil deeds and qualities, see Pertz, *Leben Steins*, vol. i, pp. 137, 138; but the bitter diatribes of German and English historians against the man who played such an important part in Prussia's early struggle against Napoleon should be read in the light of the statement made by Thiers's *Le Consulat et l'Empire*, livre 23, that the proposal to take Hanover was first made by Napoleon and not by Haugwitz. For the good and evil in Haugwitz, see Von Sybel's life of him in the *Allgemeine Deutsche Biographie*. For a brief statement of the real responsibility of Frederick William in the light of documents recently discovered, see Henderson, *Short History of Germany*, vol. ii, pp. 255, 256.

ere long discovered that Napoleon, while allowing her to establish a federation, had virtually forbidden the German states to enter it. But a dupery even more vile followed. Prussia had accepted Hanover, thus breaking with her natural ally, England, and uniting with her natural enemy, Napoleon. She had done so with shame. Judge of the abyss of disgust into which every thinking Prussian was plunged, when, after the treaty was fully made—after England had punished Prussia severely for it on the high seas; after Napoleon, on account of it, had demanded from Prussia great concessions of territory and enormous sacrifices of national respect—it was discovered that Napoleon was secretly treating with England, and offering, on sundry conditions, to restore Hanover to her. Clearly there was no longer honor among thieves.

To cap the climax of degradation, Napoleon, in time of peace, contemptuously marched his troops through Prussian territory, utterly disregarding the simplest principles of international law, and allowed his generals to talk of an approaching war with Prussia.

There was also talk, loud and loose, on the Prussian side. It was reported that a high official at Berlin had openly declared that the King had several generals, each as good as "M. de Buonaparte." Prussia now entered secretly into arrangements with Russia against France, and finally, in the autumn of 1806, the Prussian army was set in motion; in a few weeks Napoleon had met it, had beaten it utterly and easily at Jena, at Auerstadt, at Saalfeld, and the edifice erected by ages of care and sacrifice—from the old Electors of Brandenburg to the death of Frederick the Great—was beneath the conqueror's feet.

Napoleon now rises from glory to glory; enters Berlin amid the applause of its citizens, and from the old palace of the Prussian king dictates the hardest of conditions; then presses on toward Russia, holds his own at the fearful struggle of Eylau, wins the great victory of Friedland, and, having thus triumphed completely over Russia and Prussia, meets the Russian emperor in the summer of 1807 on the Niemen raft and makes the renowned Treaty of Tilsit. By this the two emperors became accomplices in a scheme, more or less definite, for subjugating Great Britain and the European continent, thus depriving Prussia of her former devoted ally, the Russian emperor, and leaving Napoleon free to deal with her as he would—to reduce her one-half in territory and population, to take away her most necessary fortresses, to quarter a vast army upon her, and to use her army, her territory, her finances as his own. Frederick William III now became a sort of discredited hermit prince in the remote northeast corner of his kingdom—a kingdom reduced from five thousand German square miles to a little over two thousand, and from about ten millions of inhabitants to about six millions, and with prospects of even more serious reductions.

Worse than these reductions was the manner of them. Poland was taken from the conquered kingdom, thus making Prussia defenseless on the east; everything between the Elbe and the Rhine was taken from her, and thus she became defenseless on the west; the most important fortresses upon her other frontiers were filled with French troops, so that finally she was left defenseless on all sides. Thus the Prussian realm lay shattered, impoverished, open at any time to the armies of any neighboring states whom Napoleon might choose to set upon it; indemnities to enormous amounts were levied upon the Prussian people, and enforced by every sort of extortion. There were also petty frauds especially exasperating. Typical is the fact that the French authorities at

Berlin, within a year after their arrival, had struck debased coin to the amount of nearly three millions of Prussian dollars.[1]

Hard upon all this spoliation followed galling insults. The great triumphal chariot, with its horses and Winged Victory of bronze, the main ornament of Berlin, was taken from the Brandenburg Gate and sent to Paris. The ingenuity of Napoleon in degrading the Prussian king and people before Europe was only equaled by its folly. He dragged the Prussian Queen Louise into his bulletins and letters; hinted at vileness in her character; set afloat monstrous calumnies regarding her and when he met her was brutal—her only offense being a patriotic devotion to Prussia. She seems to have had an artistic side which afterward reappeared in her eldest son, the next king, Frederick William IV; but she also had that sense of duty, steadfastness, and devotion to country which was destined to develop so beneficially in her second son, then a child at Königsberg, later the conqueror of France and ruler of restored Germany—the Emperor William I.

Napoleon was fond, at times, of cruelty to women. Next to his colossal, ingenious, and persistent lying, this was perhaps the worst trait in his character; and, as regarded Queen Louise, he gave this characteristic full play; she at last died broken-hearted, and was thereupon made a sort of tutelar saint by the Prussian people. Her statues and portraits have become objects of popular worship; the peasants of Prussia have given her, from that day to this, much the same place in their hearts which the same class in another part of Germany gave in the Middle Ages to St. Elizabeth; more than once remembrance of the wrong done the martyred Queen has moved myriads of German households to pour

[1] See Pertz, *Leben Stein's,* vol. ii, p. 110.

forth stalwart peasant soldiers to take vengeance upon France.[1]

But there was a still deeper humiliation. Upon entering the Prussian capital in triumph, as on entering other towns, Napoleon was received by the assembled crowds with applause: German misgovernment had, to all appearance, rooted out patriotism.

Yet from the darkness of the time light began to appear. The hard rule of Frederick the Great had not lasted long enough to crush out all manly vigor; the sensualism of Frederick William the Fat had not lasted long enough to destroy all morality; men who had been known hitherto only as routine officials now began to show the characteristics of statesmen; men who had been known simply as martinets now began to show military genius; in this terrible emergency genius and talent and a deep feeling of duty began to appear in every quarter, but above all in Prussia. A galaxy of great men arose who remind an American of the "war governors"—the great soldiers, the strong counselors, who, during our Civil War, arose in our own country from what had seemed to be a great foul mass of politicians hopelessly corrupted by subservience to slavery.

Foremost of all these great Germans in that fearful crisis was Henry Frederick Charles, Baron vom Stein. Born in 1757, near the old castle where his ancestors had lived as barons of the empire—the Castle of Stein, on the river Lahn, above Ems, in Nassau—he was the youngest but one of ten children. His family, having lived on the rock from which they took their name for seven hundred years—until it was laid waste in the Thirty Years' War

---

[1] For the propensity of Napoleon to lying, and even to forgery, see examples in Lanfrey, *Histoire de Napoléon*. There is a quiet but weighty reference to his persistence in this habit of lying, even until his death, in Emerson's *Representative Men*.

—had then built a house in the little village below, and there their representatives live to this day. Under the old "Holy Roman Empire of the German Nation," they ruled over two villages near them, with various attributes of sovereignty. Most of Stein's brothers showed talent, but he was early recognized as possessing both character and genius, and so, by a family compact, he became the representative of the family name—the family head. He was well brought up. After the old German fashion, he was taught to speak the truth, and was especially made to understand that his position not only gave rights, but imposed duties. The ability of the rest of the family seems to have been often alloyed with something of wildness or sensuality, but *the* Stein continued a steady course —manly, stainless, independent, self-controlled, straightforward, energetic—a power to be reckoned with.

The study which he most enjoyed was history—ancient and modern, and especially English history. From 1773 to 1777 he studied at the University of Göttingen, in the department of jurisprudence; but for this he made preparation, not by scraps of metaphysics or by mere dalliance with literature, but by thorough work in constitutional law and history—chiefly in the law and history of his own country and of England. He revered great men, above all Charlemagne and Luther. His classical scholarship was passable, but his knowledge of French and English he made thorough and practical. Uniting to his historical reading close study of political economy, social science, statistics, and the like, he was deeply impressed by the study of Adam Smith's new work, *The Wealth of Nations,* and, as we note this and its result in the reforms which Stein instituted in Prussia, we gain new light on the contention of Burke and Buckle that Adam Smith's book was the greatest benefaction ever given the world by any man.

After remaining in Göttingen for four years, he traveled extensively through Germany, not merely for pleasure, but to study men and realities. For a considerable time he settled down at Ratisbon, in order to learn the manner of doing legislative business in the Imperial Diet; at Wetzlar, in order to know the mode of doing judicial business in the chief imperial courts; and at Vienna, in order to understand executive methods at the centre of the Empire. All this actual contact with life prevented his becoming pedantic—a man of mere formulas; during all this period he kept his eyes open to realities which a man who hoped to be of service to his country ought to know. He also went outside his country; visited Hungary, Styria, and finally England, looking closely into mining and manufactures—everywhere studying the sources of national strength.

It had been understood from the first that he was to take office in some one of the German states, as men of his standing with small means and large ambitions usually did. Many places were open to him. In almost any of the petty states under the Empire, each with its own civil service demanding men of ability, there seemed some chance for him. His ancestral allegiance was to the house of Austria; but he knew its past well enough and could look far enough into its future to see that there was no hope for Germany from that source, and so, deliberately breaking away from his family traditions and from South German prejudices against North German methods and manners, he chose the service of Frederick the Great and Prussia. Deepest in his thoughts was a desire for German unity; he saw that this unity might be accomplished under Prussia, and it was this feeling that caused him to go to Berlin, where, in 1780, he became an under official in that branch of the administration which had to do with mining—more especially, in Westphalia. His duty was to inspect the mines, to study and report upon the best means of production, and he at once went at this duty in a manner most thorough; made new studies in chemistry, mineralogy, and metallurgy, with the best professors, but prevented such studies from becoming pedantic by close observation of actual conditions and processes. His promotion was rapid, and in 1784 he was made director in the administration of the mines and manufactures of Westphalia—from that day to this one of the leading mining and manufacturing districts of Europe.

He now showed great vigor. The Westphalian functionaries in general had become sleepy; but he pushed and pulled, to advance the public interest, and his skill, energy, and public spirit were at last recognized.

A year later he was suddenly called to a very different field. Frederick the Great, in closing his renewed struggle against Austria, wished to gain over to his League of German Princes sundry leading personages of the old Empire—especially the Archbishop Elector of Mayence; and, breaking away from old traditions, he sent Stein to Mayence as his ambassador. The young man, unaccustomed though he was to this sort of work, cut through the tangled mass of petty lying and cheatery which had so long existed there in such matters, impressed the Archbishop by his honesty, and gained his points by his common sense. This, for so young a man, was counted a great victory.[1]

But he had accepted this diplomatic position with the greatest reluctance—indeed, had at first utterly refused it, and was only led to take it by his sense of loyalty and honor; and, now that his duty was discharged, he determined to have no more of it. One statement of his throws

[1] For curious details regarding the difficulties which Stein had to surmount during this mission, see Pertz, *Leben Steins*, vol. i, pp. 44 *et seq.* The courts of the ecclesiastical Electors seem to have been anything but saintly.

a bright light into his motives, for he speaks with dislike of the "alternation of idleness and crafty, calculating activity"—a sentence in which the whole diplomacy of that period is perfectly summarized.

In 1786, Frederick the Great having died, Frederick William the Fat began his meddlesome policy, and sought to send Stein as ambassador, first to Holland, and then to Russia. These positions were most brilliant, and Stein's career at Mayence seemed a promise of success: all to no purpose; his aversion to this kind of service was unalterable, and he kept on with his work in Westphalia. There are many evidences that in taking this course he was influenced by the example of Turgot, whose life had shown, not only to the province which Turgot ruled and to France, but to all Europe, how much greater is constructive work, even provincial, than the sort of service which merely or mainly enforces the whims of courts and cabinets.

Stein's duties in Westphalia were now rapidly extended, and he was soon devoting himself especially to promoting manufactures and to opening communications by land and water on a great scale. Here came an innovation as startling in his day as, in some parts of our country, in our own; for he did this work in opening roads of the best construction, not by forcing peasants to contribute unskilled labor, after the feudal fashion, but by labor scientifically directed and adequately rewarded. Thus it was that Stein, in 1786, like Turgot a few years before, arrived at the same conclusions and adopted the same methods which the state of New York and other great commonwealths of the American Republic have reached, more than a hundred years later.

He also improved the internal tax system, and thus, during twenty years, wrought, not merely for the Prussian treasury, but for the well-being of the people at large.

During the first war of Prussia with the French Republic, which ended with the Treaty of Basle, he had reason to feel deeply the errors of Berlin statesmen, but steadily attended to his own business: more and more clearly he saw that by developing the resources of the country he could do more for it than by dabbling in foreign affairs. He constantly laid hold on new work, extending important lines of communication, improving roads and waterways, strengthening manufactures, dismissing useless functionaries, stopping peculation; but, what was even better than this, he developed public instruction, and began planning various reforms in the country at large, especially the abolition of the caste system and of serfdom.

His success led to the imposition of more and more duties upon him: he was called upon to superintend the work of incorporating into Prussia the new acquisitions made under her Basle Treaty with the French Republic, and especially to curb the severity of underlings seeking to carry from the capital into these new territories the stiff, stern Prussian system.

His continued success led now to the highest provincial promotion. In 1796 he was made Supreme President of the Provincial Chambers and head of the entire administration in Westphalia. His duties after this promotion can best be understood by an American if we imagine the governor of one of our greatest states called upon to discharge duties, not only executive, but legislative, judicial, and diplomatic, and adding to them various functions of important cabinet officers at Washington. The system was undoubtedly bad, but his genius made it work well. His strength rose with his tasks; it was soon felt that his was a force to be obeyed, and that behind it all was a determined zeal, not for pelf or place, but for the good of the kingdom.

In 1804 he was transferred to a far greater sphere.

He was made minister of state for Prussia, the departments of finance, manufactures, and trade being placed in his hands—his career as minister thus beginning a few weeks before Napoleon's career as Emperor. In this new position, the feeling which inspired all his main efforts was an intense devotion to German unity under the lead of Prussia: both he and the French Emperor, whose most effective enemy in Germany he was destined to become, had the same instinct—Napoleon seeking to prevent German unity by crushing Prussia, Stein seeking to promote this unity by strengthening her.

This feeling in Stein was wedded to an idea then new in political economy. Prussia, like the old French monarchy, was divided into provinces, each, as a rule, with its own historic frontiers and its own manifold vexations and discouragements to manufactures and trade. Against this system Turgot had fought the good fight in France and lost it. The world now sees that the system was absurd, but then it was generally regarded as natural, and indeed essential: the government favored it as giving increased revenue; the people favored it as giving protection to their provincial industries. Most of its absurdities Stein swept away, and all of them he undermined. The old complicated ways of collecting the revenues he made simple; despite most serious opposition, he developed a new system which proved not only less costly but more fruitful, and at the same time he steadily unearthed frauds, stopped abuses, and changed various modes of financiering which tended to scoundrelism.

But the war against Napoleon was now in sight, and Stein, as finance minister, was called upon to furnish money for it. In previous wars, Prussia had adopted the policy of having a standing war fund, and this system remains to this day; so that when she mobilizes her army she can immediately have ready means to tide over monetary disturbance until adequate financial provision is made. This system, which in these days is a subordinate convenience, was then a main reliance. It prevented sudden pressure upon the people. Prussia thus, at the beginning of a war, made business more easy by making money more plentiful. But the unwisdom of Frederick William the Fat had exhausted all such treasure, and more. Various projects were considered. Frederick the Great had accomplished much for a time, though at fearful ultimate cost, by issuing debased coin; this Stein refused to do, and expressed himself to the King regarding his Majesty's great predecessor in terms more honest than complimentary. Though the decision was in favor of paper money, it was paper money carefully controlled; no "fiat money," such as not long since won such wide support in our own country, was thought of. The amount of currency was comparatively small—smaller, indeed, than the King and many of his counselors thought permissible; but Stein utterly refused to go farther than he could go in perfect safety; the fool's paradise of paper money, in which various ministers in France had disported themselves, only to be tormented by it afterward, Stein refused to enter.

The labor henceforth thrown upon him was overwhelming. With the most inadequate machinery, he must provide funds for fighting France; but finance was the smallest of his cares, for he saw swift destruction coming unless the system of government was greatly changed, even in some of its foundations.

Still influential in foreign policy was Haugwitz, a poor creature at best, and now absolutely dazzled and dazed by the Napoleonic glory: him Stein opposed bitterly. Close about the king, standing between him and the ministers of state, was a sort of "kitchen cabinet," its main members being Lombard, a mere trickster belonging to the school which had brought ruin upon France; Beyme, a good sort of man at times, but wrong-headed; Haugwitz, and others like him. On these Stein waged war without ceasing.

Studying the general administration, he found a medley of favorites, ministers, directors, commissions, boards, bureaus, functionaries, with all sorts of titles and attributes, working largely at cross purposes. Studying the country at large, he found the population divided into castes: nobles, burghers, serfs—each tied up by every sort of rusty restriction, all prevented from using their persons or their property according to their needs or the needs of their country. For all this he thought out reforms.

The battle of Jena, terrible as were its consequences, did not shake his purpose. Though various other magnates hastened to declare allegiance to Napoleon, Stein was uncompromising; others gave up national property to the conqueror and took office under him; but Stein seized and sent everything possible beyond the conqueror's reach, refused to submit himself to an enemy of his country, and followed his sovereign into his last refuge—the most woebegone corner of the kingdom.

The king now urged Stein to take the Department of Foreign Affairs, but this he steadily declined, resisting all flattering promises; partly from a belief that his fellow statesman, Hardenberg, was more fit, and partly from an unwillingness to serve before the "kitchen cabinet" had been abolished forever. After various attempts to secure him, and at the same time to hold fast to the old system, his Majesty lost his temper, wrote Stein a bitter letter, referred to one of his remonstrances as a "bombastic essay," called him a "refractory, insolent, and disobedient official, proud of his own genius and talents, inattentive to the good of the state, guided purely by caprice, acting from passion, personal hatred, and rancor," and ended by saying: "If you are not disposed to alter your disrespectful and indecorous behavior, the state will not be able to reckon much upon your future services."

At this, on the 3d of January, 1807, the sturdy patriot resigned his place in the cabinet, returned to his ancestral home in Nassau, and settled there; but not in sloth, for he at once began drawing up plans for various reforms which he saw must come before Germany could throw off the tyranny which had settled down upon her more and more fearfully since the defeat of Austria at Austerlitz, of Prussia at Jena, and of Russia at Friedland— among these plans being one for a better council of ministers, which should forever replace "kitchen cabinets" by known and competent advisers, not only to the king but to the country.

Opportunity to carry out this and other good ideas came sooner than Stein had expected: Hardenberg, driven from office at the command of Napoleon, patriotically besought the king to make Stein his successor, and to this idea support came from another quarter at first sight surprising—from Napoleon himself. The great conqueror, planning to draw heavily upon Prussian finances, favored Stein as a man who could develop them. Thus it was that less than ten months after his ignominious dismissal Stein was requested by the king to resume his old place, and, in addition, to become Minister-President of the kingdom, with full charge of the civil administration, and with great powers in military and foreign affairs—thus becoming a legislator for Prussia, with the duty of meeting the terrible exigencies of the present and of promoting a better system for the future.

There were then in being two great commissions, with which he had long been in touch, one on civil, the other on military matters; his ideas had taken possession of their members, and had wrought on them to good purpose. Stein now became the great man in the first of these bodies, and in the second he had by his side another great man, his friend, General Scharnhorst.

When these men now resumed their work, the half of the Prussian kingdom which had been left by Napoleon to its former government was a wreck—its resources mortgaged to France, its defenders under the command of the conqueror, its people impoverished and benumbed. The spirit of Stein during this period is best described in his own reminiscences:—

"We started," he says, "from the fundamental idea of rousing a moral, religious, patriotic spirit in the nation; of inspiring it anew with courage, self-confidence, readiness for every sacrifice in the cause of independence and of national honor; and of seizing the first favorable opportunity to begin the bloody and hazardous struggle for both."

His greatness in character, in thought, and in work, was recognized by his friends from the beginning. But, as his task grew upon him and his plans unfolded more and more, his brain was recognized throughout Prussia —nay, throughout Europe—as the real centre of German activity against the Napoleonic tyranny. Towering thus above all contemporary growths of Prussian statesmanship, he did not seek to overshadow or wither them. There have been great statesmen dissatisfied until they have received all royal and popular favor: unhappy until all their colleagues have drooped beneath their shadow. Stein was not of these: determined as he always was, and irritable as he frequently was, his activity called into being other activities, and these he favored and fostered; under his influence other strong and independent men grew and strengthened; and of these were such as Hardenberg, Scharnhorst, Gneisenau, and Schön.

While taking care of the complicated and vexatious affairs pressing upon him from all sides, Stein and his compeers promoted a twofold revolution. The first was peaceable, favoring the creation of new institutions from which might grow a better spirit in the German people; the second was warlike, and, for a considerable time, secret and insurrectionary—a revolution against the Napoleonic tyranny, and as truly an effort for rational liberty as had been the American Revolution, or, at its beginning, the French Revolution.

The peaceful revolution naturally comes first in our thoughts, for it was the necessary preliminary of the second. Faithfully Stein and the great men who stood by him thought and wrought; not spasmodically, not by orations to applauding galleries, but quietly and steadily, in the council chamber; and on the 9th of October, 1807, appeared the first of THE GREAT EDICTS OF EMANCIPATION. These had three main purposes—first, to abolish the serf system; secondly, to sweep away restrictions in buying and selling land; thirdly, to prevent the great proprietors from using their position and capital to buy up small farms, after the English fashion—thus rooting out the yeomanry. Underlying, overarching, and permeating all these objects was one great thought and purpose—the intent to create a new people.

First, as to the serf system. It was essentially the same mass of evil which had done so much to bring on the revolution in France. De Tocqueville has shown how the wrongs which grew out of outworn feudalism had separated the French nation into distinct peoples, hating each other more and more, and at last ready to spring at each other's throats. This process had not gone so far in Germany as in France. The French mind, with its clearness and its proneness to carry ideas to their logical results, had moved faster and farther than had the thoughts of the lower classes in Germany; but the German peasantry, and indeed the whole German people beneath the nobility, had become more and more indifferent to the ties which guaranteed national unity.

When we read Arthur Young's indignant accounts of the French peasantry as he saw them just on the eve of the Revolution, we naturally think that France, as regarded her rural population, had sunk to a lower point than had any of her sister nations; but there is ample evidence that rural Germany was at that time even more wretched than rural France. Goethe, who went over the French frontier with the German army in 1792, tells us that he found in cabins of the French peasantry white bread and wine, whereas in those of the German peasantry he had found only black bread and no wine. As to galling oppression, had Arthur Young gone into the Prussian dominions, he would doubtless have given us pictures quite as harrowing as those he brought from France. Take a few of the leading Prussian provinces. In Brandenburg—largely an agricultural region—out of ninety thousand inhabitants, there were hardly three hundred and fifty persons who owned land; these held sway in courts, churches, schools, enjoyed police and hunting privileges, and down to 1799 were mainly exempt from tolls, taxes, and service as soldiers. About one-sixth of the Brandenburg peasantry had, under feudal tenure, the use of a little land, but the great body of peasants were virtually day laborers. In Silesia the peasant was, as a rule, held under strict serfdom: compelled to remain on the land; could only marry by consent of his lord; and his children were obliged to remain on the soil as farm laborers unless graciously permitted by the lord of the land to take up some other occupation. In the principality of Minden, at the death of every peasant one-half of his little movable property went to his lord. In Polish Prussia, the serf, as a rule, could own absolutely nothing. He and all that was his belonged to his lord; the land owners had managed to evade even the simplest feudal obligation, and could throw out their tenants as they chose.

Various Prussian rulers had striven to diminish the pressure of all this wrong. Frederick the Great, cynical as he appeared, sought to mitigate the brutalizing influences of this debased feudalism, and Frederick William III had shown a wish to make some beginning of better things; but the adverse influences were too strong. Nobles and clergy were then in Protestant Prussia what they had been in the days of Turgot in Catholic France, and their orators struck their keynote in declaring this existing order of things "a system ordained by God"; that thereby alone virtue, honor, and property could be secured; that to change it was to give up their beautiful patriarchal heritage. Hearing this utterance, one would suppose that under this system the rule was kind treatment from the upper classes, and love from the lower; but the fact was that while the feudal lord's idea of his right had become grossly magnified his idea of his duty had mainly disappeared; the system had become fearfully oppressive and was enveloped in a cloud of distrust, faultfinding, and hate.[1]

And not only were the people who cultivated the land thus bound, but the very soil itself was in fetters—tied up, as to sale and cultivation, by feudal restrictions which had become absurd. Under the old system, the three castes—the nobility, the burghers, the peasants—had been carefully kept each to itself. The rule, resulting from the theory underlying the whole, was that the nobility must not engage in the occupations of the burgher class; that burghers must be kept well separated from the peasant class; and that, to this end, all three classes should be hampered by a network of restrictions upon their power to hold land. Barriers of various sorts had been built between these three classes. Broad tracts of

---

[1] For a very clear detailed statement regarding the condition of the Prussian peasantry, and the German peasantry generally, see Häusser, *Deutsche Geschichte*, vol. iii, pp. 123 and following.

land were lying waste because their noble proprietors
had not the capital with which to till them, and yet were
forbidden to sell them; great amounts of capital were
lying idle because burghers who had accumulated it were
by the laws and customs hindered from applying it to
land owned by nobles; trade was stagnant and multitudes of young nobles idle because they must not engage
in trade. All this and many kindred masses of evil were
now largely swept away, yet not without opposition;
political philosophers and declaimers filled the air with
arguments to prove these reforms wicked and perilous;
nobles of the court, high officers of the army, and landed
proprietors in great numbers caballed against the reformer; General Yorck, one of the best and strongest men
of the time, declared the new measures monstrous; but
Stein persevered and forced through the edict which,
three years later, on St. Martin's Day, 1810, struck feudal
fetters from two-thirds of the Prussian people, and extinguished serfdom under Prussian rule forever.[1]

It is only just to say that for this great edict of 1807
and for the later legislation which supplemented it—
transforming serfs into freemen throughout Prussia—
various colleagues and assistants of Stein, and especially
Hardenberg, Altenstein, and Schön, deserve also to be
forever held in remembrance. They too had given long
and trying labor to it all. They had taken the better
thought of their time and brought it into effective form;
but the credit of giving life to what they thus produced,
of forcing their main ideas upon the conservatism of the
nation—beginning with the King himself—belongs, first
of all, to Stein. Others saw, as he did, the causes of the
Prussian downfall; others contributed precious thought in
devising this great restoration; but his was the eye which
saw most clearly the goal which must be reached; his,
the courage which withstood all threats and broke through

---

[1] See Treitschke, *Deutsche Geschichte*, vol. i, p. 281.

all obstacles; his, the mental strength which, out of vague beliefs and aspirations, developed fundamental, constitutional laws; his, the moral strength which, more than that of any other German statesman, uplifted three-fourths of the whole population, gave them a new interest in the kingdom, and a feeling for its welfare such as had never before been known in Prussia, and thus did most to create that national spirit which was destined to sweep everything before it in the Freedom War of 1813, in the War for German Unity in 1866, and in the Franco-Prussian War of 1870.

It may be objected to these claims for Stein that the fundamental thought in his reforms was derived from Adam Smith. That statement is true. It cannot be denied that Adam Smith, penetrating thinker that he was, set in motion the trains of thought which largely resulted in Prussian emancipation; yet this detracts not at all from the glory of Stein and the statesmen who wrought with him. All the more glory to them for recognizing, developing, and enforcing the great Englishman's thought, in a way which has proved a blessing not merely to Germany, but to humanity.[1]

[1] For a very full discussion of Adam Smith's influence, see Roscher in the *Berichte der Königlich-Sächsischen Gesellschaft der Wissenschaften,* 1867; and, for a careful statement as to the influence of Smith on Stein, see pp. 5, 6. Roscher's concession is all the more convincing since he is clearly inclined to minimize Smith's influence on German thought in general.

II

ANOTHER great work now begun by Stein was the REFORM OF THE CITY GOVERNMENTS. The enfranchisement of the serfs had been due, largely, to the spirit of reform aroused in general thought by Voltaire, Rousseau, and their compeers, and in economic science by Adam Smith; but this city reform was peculiarly his own. The need of it had doubtless been felt by many; good methods of promoting it had been seen by few; the practical measure for carrying it into effect was the work of Stein alone.

This system, which has been fruitful in blessings ever since his time, was in principle somewhat like that of England, but differed from it widely. It was the very opposite of the system fastened upon France by the French Revolution and by Napoleon. As Seeley very justly says: "The French Revolution began at the top, creating a central national legislature and giving all the power to that, leaving town and local organizations generally deprived of all life, making the prefects of departments and the mayors of communities mere functionaries appointed from the central government at Paris and representing the ideas of the capital." The reform of Stein began at the base, giving self-government to the towns, schooling them in managing their own affairs, in checking their own functionaries, in taking their own responsibilities. While keeping the central monarchy strong, his great exertion was to restore fitness for public life in the country at large: by his first reform he had converted the rural serfs into beings who could feel that they had an interest in the country; by this new reform he had sought to exercise the city populations in public affairs.

The old city system of Europe had, many centuries before, been a main agency in developing civilization: Guizot declares it the main legacy from Rome to the Middle Ages; Maurer asserts that it saved the Reformation. The Roman Empire was made up of cities. When all else save the Church was swept away and the country districts desolated, these cities remained, and in them was a continuity of much that was best in the old civilization, and a potency of vast good in the new. During the Middle Ages their vigor increased. The cities wrested from the feudal lords right after right; the city magnates leagued with the distant emperor or king against the feudal oppressors immediately above them; when the feudal lords wanted money to join the Crusades the cities brought it, and bought with it rights and immunities. The commerce of the Middle Ages developed many of these towns nobly, especially throughout Italy and Germany; but, Vasco da Gama's passage around the Cape of Good Hope having largely withdrawn trade with the East Indies from the Mediterranean, the commercial cities, not only in Italy but even in Germany, lost for a time a very large share of their prosperity.

During the Reformation period, many of the German cities having recovered strength and shown hospitality to the new thought, various leading reformers in Northern and Middle Germany took refuge in them, and there found protection against Pope and Emperor. In the League of Schmalkald, sturdily defying all efforts to crush out civil and religious liberty, we find territorial princes associated in a widespread confederation with warlike cities; but in the seventeenth century the Thirty Years' War ruined many of these city centres, and diminished the power of them all, so that after the Treaty of Westphalia, in 1648, the sway of the princes was greatly extended, and only a few of the greater cities could withstand them.

Especially did political liberty, that is, the right of citizens to take part in public affairs, die out in Prussia; the strong race of the Hohenzollerns might at times make use of local self-government, but as a rule they overrode it, and everything tended more and more to centralization, until finally the genius and absolute power of Frederick the Great seemed to remove from men's minds the last remaining ideas essential to city independence. The individual citizen was comparatively of no account; he became essentially a parasite, living upon a state whose real life was centred in the brain of the monarch. As a result of all this, whatever authorities there were in the German towns wrought at cross purposes: there was a medley of various sorts of municipalities, and in them royal tax administrators, municipal figureheads, guilds, privileges, customs, usages, exemptions, ceremonies, benumbing the whole organization, save when some genius like the Great Elector or Frederick the Great broke through them. The mass of dwellers in cities came more and more to consider public affairs as no concern of theirs.[1]

So far had this obliteration of city activities gone in Prussian towns that, although various guilds, corporations, and privileged persons were the nominal authorities, the paid offices were filled largely with old invalids of the army. And what, in a general national emergency, was to be expected from a nation made up of a city class like this, and of a rural class like the serfs in the fields? What wonder that Prussians seemed to look on the downfall of Prussia and Germany with stupid in-

[1] For a lucid account of the action of the Great Elector and Frederick the Great in at times breaking through these city privileges, or, as they were called, "rights," see Tuttle, *History of Prussia*.

difference, and applauded Napoleon at the Brandenburg Gate?

On this mass of unreason in the city organizations Stein had thought for years. Other patriotic public servants had also thought upon it, and at last, at Königsberg, afar off in the northeast corner of the Prussian state, in this its time of dire trouble, some of them prepared a tentative plan of self-government for their own city. This plan, largely under the influence of Stein, soon grew into a provisional system covering sundry neighboring towns, and this, under quiet suggestions from him, was finally sent to the King. His Majesty naturally referred the whole matter back to his great minister, who now began work upon it directly and energetically, and developed out of it a system applicable not only to the cities which had asked for it, but to all the towns in the Prussian kingdom. Thus, mainly under Stein's hands, came into being the great statutes for municipal reform.

By these statutes the municipal medley of Prussia was swept away, and the cities were divided into three classes: "great towns," with ten thousand residents and upward; "middle towns," with thirty-five hundred residents and upward; "small towns," all the others. Every town now took part in the election of its own authorities, and in all towns of above eight hundred inhabitants there was a division into wards, each with its own local powers.

As a rule, all were recognized as burghers who owned real estate or other property which insured a direct, tangible interest in the city; but soldiers, Jews, Mennonites, and criminals were excluded. Magistrates and town representatives were, as a rule, selected by the assembly of citizens, the number of councilors varying from twenty-four in the smaller towns to a hundred in the larger. Every elector must appear at the polls and

18

vote, under penalty of losing his citizenship by continued neglect of this duty. Two-thirds of the town councilors must be resident householders; they received no pay, and, as to the theory of their relations with their constituents, it is well worth noting that each represented, not his guild, not his ward, not any subordinate interest, but the whole city. At the head of the city was a paid burgo-master, and about him a small body of councilors, paid and unpaid; only those officials being paid who were really obliged to devote themselves to their official duties as a profession.

The burgomaster was elected by the representatives of the people and confirmed by an authority representing the nation; but the chief burgomaster in sundry great towns was selected by the king out of three named by the city representatives. Various features in the develop-ment of this system are worthy of note. Take as a con-crete example the recent history of Berlin. Whenever the chief burgomastership of that city, perhaps the best governed city in the world, has become vacant, those elected and submitted to the king for approval have been men who have distinguished themselves in the administration of other cities, some of these far from the capital. It has been my good fortune to know two of the chief burgomasters of Berlin thus selected; both were eminent, and one of them, who became and re-mained a very influential member of the Imperial Parlia-ment, especially so. The tenure of the chief burgomaster is virtually during good behavior, with a good salary, a suitable residence, a high position, and a retiring pen-sion—the man thus chosen, first by the electors and finally by the emperor, being expected to give himself entirely to the welfare of the city; this is his whole business, into which he is to put the expectations and ambitions of his life. The result of this system is seen to-day in the magnificent development of that great capital: everything carefully thought out; everything managed on business principles; and all the affairs of the city conducted, with the aid of the burgher councils, quietly and with an efficiency and economy such as in American cities is rarely, if ever, seen.

The official terms of citizen functionaries under the legislation of Stein were generally long, varying from six years to twelve, the rule being continuance in office during good behavior. Generally speaking, every citizen was liable to serve in unpaid offices for six years, though he might, for sufficient reason, secure permission to retire after a service of three years. State officials, ecclesiastics, university professors, schoolmasters, and practicing physicians were largely excused from active state duties; but any other citizens refusing to serve might be punished by loss of citizenship and by fine.

On the 19th of November, 1808, Stein's plan became a law. One feature in it which strikes us in these days as absurd, and which has in the main disappeared, is that by which Jews, Mennonites, and soldiers were classed with criminals as unfit for citizenship; but there is another feature which, while it may seem surprising, is well worth close study, especially by any one taking an interest in American politics.

To be a burgher in Prussia, one must, as a rule, have a definite and tangible interest in the community. Here was a principle running through the whole theory and practice of city government in Europe, ancient, mediæval, and modern: a city was considered a corporation,—a corporation which had business to conduct and property to administer. This theory is widespread among civilized nations to-day: a distinction being made between what may be called the *civil right* to enjoy protection in the natural rights of man and the *political right* to take part in general public affairs, on one side, and, on the other, what may be called *municipal right*,—the right to take active part in administering city property and determining city policy. As to the latter right, it was generally felt that the people exercising it should have some evident "stake" in the corporation whose affairs they were called upon to control or administer. We in America have tried the opposite system fully. We have applied universal suffrage to the whole administration of our city corporations, and the result, in most of our cities, has been not merely disheartening, but debasing. Least of all can we be satisfied with its results in our large seaport towns, with their great influx of people whose whole life has unfitted them to exercise public duties, and who have had no training or even experience of a kind calculated to fit them. The distinction recognized in Stein's system, between the proletariat and men having a direct tangible interest in the town, has deep roots in human history; and a better system than that which now exists in the majority of our American cities seems never likely to come in until some account is taken of this distinction, founded in the history of liberty-loving peoples and based on an idea of justice: the idea that, while *civil liberty,* which implies protection in natural rights, must be guaranteed to every citizen, and *political liberty,* the right to take part in the general political government, shall be as widely diffused as possible, *municipal liberty,* the right to exercise some effective initiative and control in municipal affairs, which are principally practical business affairs, shall be reserved for those who have won a direct, tangible interest or valuable experience in such affairs. A perfectly just and even liberal compromise between political and civil liberties on one hand and municipal liberties on the other would seem to be given by a fundamental law requiring in all our cities above a certain size that a mayor and board of aldermen, each of them representing the whole city, be chosen by universal suffrage, but that a board of control, whose affirmative vote shall be necessary in all financial appropriations, all questions relating to the management of public property, and all grants of franchises, be elected by the direct taxpayers.

The system proposed by Stein was met as we should expect. The nobles and the old school of officials denounced it as radical, and even as savoring of Jacobinism. Moreover, there was considerable disappointment in its first workings. People of the towns showed at first no desire to go into it; they had become listless and indifferent, and preferred to go on in the old way; the new system, also, at first increased expenditure. But Stein carried it through, and, as time went on, it began to produce the effects which he had expected: the town populations began to take an interest in national affairs; began to think upon them; began, a generation later, to take efficient part in a Prussian parliament; and, a generation later still, in a parliament of the German Empire. The municipal system of Prussia and of Germany has, indeed, been largely developed to meet new needs since Stein's time; but its cornerstone, then as now, is the right of the people to think and act upon their own local interests.

It is worthy of note that, while this idea was thus taking shape in reformatory statutes thought out by the great German statesman, one of the greatest of American statesmen was dwelling upon it and urging it in our own country. For it had deeply impressed Thomas Jefferson. In his latter days he often dwelt upon the popular vigor of New England in dealing with questions internal and external as compared with the apparent indifference of the Southern States, and he attributed this vigor to the New England town meetings, declaring that in the struggle between Democrats and Federalists he had felt the ground shake beneath his feet when the town meetings of New England had opposed him, and that the county assemblies of Virginia gave no compensating strength.[1]

It has been urged that a part always large and sometimes controlling in the great reforms which began the regeneration of Prussia and, indeed, of Germany, was taken by Stein's sometime friend, sometime enemy, Hardenberg. This is certainly true: Hardenberg, with his longer service and his diplomatic nature, had opportunities which Stein, with his uncompromising zeal, had not. While Hardenberg had, perhaps, a stronger belief in freedom of trade and manufactures, it was Stein's energy, fearlessness, and skill, and, above all, the weight of his character, which embodied the fundamental reforms in laws and forced them upon an unwilling sovereign and an apathetic people.

While pressing forward these great reforms needed to start Prussia upon a better career, Stein dealt no less thoughtfully with a vast multitude of petty abuses. These were largely feudal survivals, of the sort which had driven the French peasantry mad twenty years before; but instead of proceeding against them with fire and sword, after the Celtic manner, he studied each carefully and dealt with it rationally. There was no wild plunge into chaos and night, but each evil survival was dealt with upon its demerits.[2]

But Stein and his compeers saw that something vastly more general and powerful was needed than reforms in detail, and hence it was that there now began a better era in Prussian, and indeed in GERMAN EDUCATION. Into

[1] See, especially, Jefferson's reference to this in a letter to John Adams, in his later correspondence. For a clear and thorough account of city government and administration in Prussia and in Germany generally, see Albert Shaw, *Municipal Government in Continental Europe*, chap. v; also, W. B. Munro, *The Government of European Cities*, chap. ii, one or both of which works every thoughtful dweller in an American city should read.

[2] For the remedies administered to a large number of these abuses, see Pertz, as above, vol. ii, pp. 142 and following.

the whole system of national instruction a new spirit now entered; slowly, at first, but doubtless all the more powerfully. Occupied though Stein was in a different field, one feels his influence in all this movement. In the great spoliation by Napoleon at Tilsit, the old Prussian University of Halle, founded a hundred years before by Thomasius, which had given so many strong men to the Prussian state, was lost. But this calamity was the harbinger of a great gain. Thoughtful men began to plan a university for Berlin. Strong men began to be secured for its professorships. The rule that a university is made, not by bricks and mortar, but by teachers, was fully recognized. Stein had, indeed, the instinct, so strong in America, against sending undergraduates into large cities for their education; but he recognized the importance of a new educational centre to send fresh and vigorous life through the renewed educational system, and his activity did much to inspire this great movement, which was destined to work miracles, not only throughout Prussia, but throughout Europe.[1]

It will presently be seen that to carry out all these great reformatory efforts Stein had but little more than a year in office. Could he have had more time, he would doubtless have created a national parliament. But, as we shall see, fate was against him; the struggle with Napoleon and the reaction after the Napoleonic downfall caused the creation of representative bodies to be long deferred. Still, when at last they were created, they had a basis of political experience for which they were mainly indebted to him. It has been my fortune to be

---

[1] For a very thoughtful comparison of the merits of Stein and Hardenberg, see Zorn, *Im Neuen Reich*, pp. 216 and following. For Stein's relations to the educational movement in Prussia, see Pertz, vol. ii, pp. 162 and following; also Kuno Francke, *Social Forces in German Literature.* For probably the best that has ever been written regarding the relations of university life to patriotism, see Paulsen, *Die Deutschen Universitäten*, bk. iv.

present during discussions in the principal parliaments now existing: the British, the French, the Italian, the German, as well as our own; and as regards quiet, thorough, sober discussion, free from the trickery of partisans and the oratory of demagogues, the parliaments of the Prussian kingdom and of the German empire have seemed to me among the very foremost. My belief is that they have before them a great future, and all the more so because their roots draw vigorous life from principles of self-government which were called into action by Stein.

While laying foundations for a better civic system, Stein was obliged to give immediate and intense thought to THE MILITARY SYSTEM. The old Prussian army organization had been, under Frederick the Great, the wonder of the world; and its supremacy had become a tenet of military orthodoxy on both sides of the Atlantic, but above all in Prussia. In spite of the revelation of power given to an army by national feeling and by the awakened consciousness of personal rights, as seen in the French Revolution,—in spite of the new light and life thrown into military science and practice by Napoleon,—the leaders in Prussia clung to the old system, boasted of it, and threatened to overwhelm Napoleon with it.

But things had changed since the great Frederick conquered Soubise at Rossbach. The French soldiers of the new revolutionary epoch, feeling themselves citizens of a great republic and apostles of human rights, were very different from the poor creatures of the previous century, who had been sent out to die in battles demanded by the intrigues of Louvois or the whims of Madame de Pompadour; the French marshals, trained in the campaigns of the republic and empire, were very different from poor Soubise; the commands of Napoleon were different indeed from orders issued by Louis XV.

All this had passed unheeded in Germany, and the whole Prussian military fabric, which it had taken nearly two centuries to build, collapsed at Jena. The fact was that, judged by any good modern standard, the old Prussian military system had become vicious. The fatal weakness of absolutism was shown in it no less than throughout the civil administration: a genius like Frederick the Great could do wonders with it, but the men who succeeded him were powerless to use it to any good purpose.

The officers were chosen, with rare exceptions, from the nobility; military talent and ambition in the rest of the nation were virtually excluded; promotion went by seniority or favor; birth went before merit; the better class of officers were thwarted by pedantry; the ordinary class were ignorant; the soldiers were either peasants' sons, torn from their homes, or the scum of continental cities, huddled together by recruiting officers; the soldier's career was hopeless,—the usual term of service twenty years, and no promotion above the ranks. Degrading punishments were in constant use; blows with a stick could be inflicted on any veteran at the whim of a petty lieutenant, and for such offenses as a misplaced strap or broken button.

The whole formed an organized system of injustice which touched the vast majority in their dearest interests. This injustice in the time of Frederick the Great was of little account; his people regarded it as the inevitable and natural condition of things; but ideas of right were now in the air, and had even reached the cottages of German boors. The peasant class, which paid the bulk of the taxes, paid also the main tribute of blood; the middle class, which also bore heavy burdens, was excluded from all military honors; the least honor was to those who labored most, the most to those who labored least. Old exemptions of districts, towns, and persons— exemptions which once had some reason, but now had none—only added to the general sense of injustice. And substitution was allowed: the rich man's son could buy exemption; the poor man's son could not escape. The great mass of antiquated peculiarities in army organization were retained as sacred,—the stiffness, the martinetism, the brutality; the only wonder is that soldiers so treated and trained did not come to regard their country as their worst enemy.

The first feeling after Jena was that somebody had blundered, but it was soon clear that everybody had blundered. Scapegoats were of course sought, and they were near and plenty; the first step universally demanded was vengeance upon indifferent, incompetent, beery, sleepy, cowardly officers, who had delivered up important commands, fortresses, towns—sometimes without striking a blow. Many were disgraced; some sentenced to imprisonment and death; but thinking men soon saw that the fault lay deeper, and among those who searched into the causes of the catastrophe most deeply was Stein. It was this search which led him to propose the measures calculated to develop a people no longer to be treated as "dumb, driven cattle."

The immediate need was for military reform: the whole military system must be recast, and at once. For this, Stein had the best ally possible—General Scharnhorst; and about Scharnhorst stood a body of exceedingly able and patriotic men, like Gneisenau, Boyen, and Grolmann.

Scharnhorst seemed to have stepped into those worst days of Germany out of the best days of Rome; he was a divine gift, like Carnot in the dire trouble of France, like Lincoln, Stanton, Grant, and Sherman to the North, or like Lee to the South, in the dark days of our own Civil War. He was broad in views, simple in tastes, quick in discerning essentials, firm, incorruptible, and, above everything, devoted to his country. By the general body of officers about him he was looked down upon, for he was one of the few Prussian officers of peasant descent. More than this, he was considered a theorist, his real worth being known to few,—but among these few was Stein.

Into his plans for military regeneration Scharnhorst threw not only his mind, but his heart and soul. Plan after plan he carefully elaborated and discussed:—plans for reconstructing the army, for providing a reserve, for developing a militia; all this in the face of enormous difficulties,—the indecision of the King, the suspicion of Napoleon, the poverty of the country, and the inertia of influential people wedded to the old system by self-interest or dread of change.

The fundamental idea of Scharnhorst's whole system was that every citizen is bound to defend the state; that there should be few exemptions and no substitutes; that the state has a claim on all the talent within its borders. From this followed the duty of all young men to bear arms; the advancement of officers and soldiers not through influence, but by enterprise, bravery, and character. The recruiting of soldiers abroad was given up: only on rare occasions was a foreigner admitted to service in the army. The plan of Scharnhorst and Stein was that the army should be a school for the whole nation,— a school in the virtues of soldier and citizen. The germs of the whole military system as it exists to-day, with its active service, its reserve, its Landwehr and Landsturm, now began to appear.

But to carry out this whole idea at once was impossible, for the spies of Napoleon were everywhere, and no one noted the slightest indication of desire to regain liberty and independence so keenly as he. Seeing this movement, which showed the German feeling for liberty aroused by the Spanish uprising, Napoleon forced on Prussia a new treaty, supplementary to the Treaty of

Tilsit, which new treaty, besides other degrading conditions, bound Prussia to keep down her army to forty-two thousand men.

Tyranny had now to be met by cunning. Many of the exterior features of the old system had to be preserved as a disguise. The plan was adopted of giving soldiers leave of absence after a period of thorough drill, and taking fresh recruits in their places, so that the whole body of young Prussians might pass through the army. Everything was done to evade the keenness of the French spies: regiments were marched to exercise, leaving large numbers of sound men in barracks or hospitals, and at last, while nominally keeping up an army of only forty-two thousand men, Scharnhorst had trained and inspired a hundred and fifty thousand.

Troubles arose, too, from the suspicions not only of the French, but of the Prussians themselves. Nervous men, impatient men, frivolous men, were constantly in danger of precipitating a catastrophe. Selfishness and prejudice were also active, and the pressure of individual and family influence against the new system was at times enormous; the routine men in the army raged against Scharnhorst, and to show the depth of their scorn called him "schoolmaster." [1]

The poverty of the country was also a great hindrance, and for months the artillery in Silesia could not exercise effectively because Napoleon's satraps had carried off their powder. For five years, Scharnhorst, one of the most manly and frank of men, had to double and turn, concealing his plans and acts, like a hunted criminal, until, at the beck of Napoleon, the King was forced to disgrace him, and virtually to drive him from the service. But the great work could not then be stopped, and to

[1] For most interesting and instructive details of this struggle, see Treitschke, *Deutsche Geschichte im 19. Jahrhundert,* Erster Theil, Zweiter Abschnitt.

these beginnings are due, in great measure, not only the glories of Leipsic and Waterloo, a few years later, but of Düppel, Sadowa, St. Privat, and Sedan. Scharnhorst, with Stein advising and strengthening him, thus began the military system which Moltke and Roon completed.

But while Stein stood firmly and hopefully by his great colleague, providing for the wants of the nation and laying plans to baffle Napoleon, he was still occupied with the civic system and with the reorganization of the general administration. Having taken measures for the abolition of monopolies,—the mill monopoly, the millstone monopoly, the butcher, the baker, the huckster monopolies, and a multitude of others,—and having rooted up, as far as possible, all barriers against the admission of women to various trades and occupations for which they were fit, his main strength was thrown into ADMINISTRATIVE REFORM. This, in many respects, was the greatest work of all, though he did not remain in office long enough to complete it.

The general administrative system of Prussia had become a muddle like all the rest. There were councils, chambers, directories, departments, cabinets, ministers administrative, ministers territorial, generally working in accordance with outworn needs or ideas, or with the appetites or whims of the persons who happened to sit on the throne. A strong king, like Frederick the Great, did mainly without them; a luxurious king, like Frederick William the Fat, left them to lumber on chaotically; a mediocre king, like Frederick William III, unable to see his way in this jungle, knew no other plan than to lean on a little coterie of favorites, and to avoid any decision as long as possible.

The local administrations were of like quality. Out of these Stein began developing something better. He made no attempt to change suddenly the nature of the people: whatever had helpful life in it, he endeavored to preserve, and he especially sought to restore some features introduced by Frederick William I, which, under Frederick the Great, had been lost sight of.

The edict drawn up under his direction proposed to give to the whole administration the greatest possible energy and activity, and yet to put all in direct relations with the central government. The plan was wrought out carefully and logically; large as a whole, precise as to details, it combined all Stein's experience—his knowledge of men, his boldness, his caution.

Preliminary to all this was the creation of a Council of State, made up of fitting men from the royal family, ministers, privy councilors of distinction, former ministers, heads of bureaus and of departments; but a far more important change was one which in these days seems exceedingly simple, but which in those seemed almost impossible,—the assignment of a small number of ministers to the main subjects of administration throughout the whole monarchy. These ministers were mainly of the interior, finance, foreign affairs, war, and justice; and, with a few other officials of great experience, formed a cabinet to decide on various weighty and general matters,—with the understanding, which now seems axiomatic, but which then seemed chimerical, that no clique of favorites should stand between cabinet and king.

Various departments, each with a minister at its head, have been added since Stein's day,—a Ministry of Trade and Commerce, a Ministry of Agriculture, a Ministry of Ecclesiastical, Educational, and Medical Affairs; but his simple system, as a whole, remains as he planned it.

For historical and patriotic reasons, he rejected the example of the French Revolution, and allowed the old territorial divisions to remain, with proper officers, each with functions which could be discharged for the good of the country, but without injury to the new system. The general local system was also carefully studied, and reforms were begun in accordance with experience and sound sense. Stein had expected to go further into the lower local organization, but he was too soon driven from office. His successors attempted to deal with it, injuring it in some respects, improving it in others; but, taken as a whole, his was a great and fruitful beginning, and it has grown into that system which has made Prussia the most carefully and conscientiously administered nation in the world;—doubtless with sundry disadvantages— with too much interference and control, with too little individual initiative, but, after all, wonderfully well managed. At the present time, one of the most interesting of studies for a close political thinker would be a comparison between this system, which seems to hold that government best which governs most, and our own, which, in theory, holds that government best which governs least.

Stein's object was to secure, in the whole administration, unity, energy, and responsibility. His correspondence and his papers show that he intended later to propose a parliamentary system, with two houses, in which the better national spirit could be brought to bear on the discussion of general affairs and on the enlightened support of the monarchy. Royal edicts put in force his plans, as far as he had developed them, during the latter months of 1808, but anything further was prevented by a catastrophe. During the whole year Napoleon was striving to free himself from the fearful complication of his affairs. Up to this time, his conquests had been comparatively simple and easy. Austria, Prussia, and Italy were beneath his feet, and he had now attempted a policy of conquest in the Spanish Peninsula. Here came the first capital folly of his career. Spain was ignorant, corrupt, priest-ridden, but it was not a collection of ill-compacted governments like Germany; it was, with all its faults, a *nation*, and its

uprising against Napoleon's effort was the beginning of
the anti-Napoleonic revolution. At every important
point in Spain Napoleon's marshals were worsted, and
at Baylen came a great disgrace: for the first time in
his history, one of his armies was forced to capitulate.
In the Portuguese part of the Peninsula, where the
British forces aided those of the population, he encountered the same desperate resistance. The Emperor's
brother was obliged to flee from the Spanish throne, and
finally the great conqueror himself found it necessary to
put himself at the head of his army against the Spanish
people; but, though for a time he broke down all opposition, this revolt in Spain gave a new idea to all Europe,
—the idea that, after all, a people, if united, could throw
off his tyranny. Nowhere did this thought spread wider
or strike deeper than in Germany, and among those most
profoundly influenced by it was Stein.

In the midst of his labor for municipal reform, administrative reform, military reform, Stein devoted himself
to impressing this Spanish example upon the leading
men of his country, especially by letters, and finally one
of these letters fell into the hands of Napoleon. It had
become especially dangerous for any man, no matter
how high in place, to incur the wrath of the great conqueror; but how great the danger of Stein became has
only recently been revealed. For, within the last ten
years, the world has received a revelation of the Napoleonic tyranny, in Germany especially, which enables us
to see what unbridled autocracy means and to what dangers Stein exposed himself in opposing it. Under the
second French empire, there was formed, about the
middle of the nineteenth century, a pretentious commission, presided over, finally, by Prince Napoleon, the son
of Napoleon's youngest brother, King Jerome, which
published, in a long series of volumes, what claimed to
be Napoleon's complete correspondence. But it was

soon found that this correspondence had been carefully expurgated, and since that time various investigators have given to the world letters which the official committee omitted. There could be no more fearful revelation of the tyranny engendered by unlimited power. The conqueror had come to regard any resistance to his plans, or even to his wishes, as a crime worthy of death. The whole world knew how he had ordered the Duc d'Enghien to be executed at Strasburg for a crime of which he was guiltless, and how he had ordered the bookseller Palm, at Nuremberg, to execution, for having in his possession a simple and noble patriotic pamphlet; but these letters recently published by Lecestre, Brotonne, and others have shown that this cruelty had become, especially after his reverses, a prevailing principle with him.

In these letters we find the great conqueror treating his brothers, whom he had placed on thrones, as mere lackeys,—with utter contempt, and with not the slightest recognition of their duties toward the people whom he had called them to govern. His letters to them are frequently in terms such as no self-respecting man ought to use toward a lackey. Among the letters also appear simple offhand instructions to his commanders in various parts of Germany which are really orders to commit murder. As a rule, at the moment the spies of the Emperor report any person as troublesome, there comes back a virtual order to punish the offender with death. Orders to shoot this or that troublesome patriot in Germany or Spain are frequent, but perhaps the climax is reached in a dispatch to Junot, to whom Napoleon writes that no doubt the General has disarmed Lisbon, and adds, "Shoot, say, sixty persons." [1]

[1] For examples of these letters showing Napoleon's rage provoked by opposition, see Lecestre, *Lettres Inédites de Napoléon* (*An. viii—1815*), Paris, 1897, *passim*, and especially for the letter to Junot, p. 136. Also de Brotonne, *Lettres Inédites de Napoléon*, Paris, 1898.

19

It was in this frame of mind that Napoleon read Stein's intercepted letter, and his wrath became at once venomous. At first it was somewhat dissembled, probably with the hope of bringing the culprit more easily within striking distance. The notice of it in the *Moniteur,* on September 8, 1808, was merely contemptuous, but this was the prelude to more severe measures against Prussia, and, three months later, Napoleon, from his camp at Madrid, issued his decree placing the German statesman not only under the ban of the Empire, but under the outlawry of Europe.

Beginning with a contemptuous reference to him as "a person named Stein," this decree proceeds with a notice that his property of every sort in all parts of Germany and in France is confiscated, and it ends with an order to seize him "wherever he can be caught by our own troops or those of our allies." This edict was posted in every part of Germany, and even in Poland. Though Stein, from the first discovery of his letter by Napoleon, must have seen its inevitable result, he braved all dangers. His heart was set on the edict for administrative reform, and to this he devoted himself, until, on the 24th of November, the King was at last induced to sign it. And still Stein lingered to render other administrative services, until his family and friends, in utter distress, prevailed upon him to consider his own safety, and possible future services to his country. On the night of January 5, 1809, he took flight in a sledge from Prussia into the snowy mountains of Bohemia, and for three years, amid privations, illness, and suffering, though constantly active, he was, by the world at large, unheard of. There seemed to come to him as complete an effacement of personality and influence as to Luther during his stay in the Wartburg.

Stein's escape was made none too soon. The simple fact was that Napoleon recognized in him a man who understood the Napoleonic policy thoroughly; who knew, down to the last details, the whole story, not only of the Treaty of Tilsit, but of Napoleon's violations of it, and of that wholesale plunder, without warrant of the treaty, which Germany was forced to endure during the years which followed it. More than this, the conqueror recognized in Stein a man whose German patriotism was invincible; one who saw the vulnerable point in the Napoleonic system of conquest, as Napoleon himself must have begun to see it at Madrid when the official proclamation against his enemy was issued;—one who had the gift, also, of inoculating others with his patriotic spirit. Therefore it was that Napoleon, who had at first urged him upon the King of Prussia as a man whose financial talent and genius could develop the nation for the better support of the French armies, now made him an outlaw, and would certainly, could he have laid his hands upon him, have put him to death.

This was no ordinary case of outlawry, and it brought results which the conqueror little foresaw. It gave Stein a hold on the German heart which all his vast services had failed to gain. It secured him recognition as a leader throughout Europe, from royal palaces to the huts of peasants. It inspired phlegmatic men with indignation, and prosaic men with eloquence. Of this there is a striking example to be found in every good historical library. About the middle of the nineteenth century, Privy Councilor Dr. Pertz, eminent for close historical research, director of the Royal Library at Berlin, gave to the world his *Life of Stein*. It was in seven octavos, closely printed, a collection which Carlyle would have blasphemed as the work of the arch-fiend Dryasdust, but which, though minute and painstaking almost to a fault, betrays a wholesome enthusiasm. Throughout the whole seven volumes the erudite Privy Councilor restrains himself; but, when he reaches this period in Stein's history, there comes the one outburst of eloquent indignation in the whole vast work. Having given the text of Napoleon's edict, dated in his camp at Madrid, the historian gives scope to his feelings as follows:—

"At the quarters of the French troops at Erfurt, at Magdeburg, and at Hanover, the population read with astonishment and sorrow this declaration of war whereby the conqueror of Marengo, Ulm, Austerlitz, Jena, Friedland, and Tudela, the sovereign of France, Italy, Holland, Switzerland, half of Germany, and the whole of Spain, singled out one defenseless man from the innumerable numbers of his contemporaries and branded him as his enemy for life and death. But this measure of blind passion, far from reaching its purpose, turned against the man who devised it. Napoleon's hate pointed out to his enemies their main hope. Innumerable men then read Stein's name for the first time, but this outlawry at once surrounded his head with the halo of a martyr. The hearts which in all parts of Germany longed for freedom had found their living leader. He became instantly a personage on whom downtrodden peoples far outside the boundaries of Prussia placed their hopes and expectations; and, that the mightiest of this earth might stand in awe of eternal justice, from this 'person named Stein,' six years later, went forth that thought of a European outlawry to which the Emperor of a hundred days was to yield." [1]

[1] See Pertz, *Leben Steins*, vol. ii, pp. 319, 320. It is a curious fact that Pertz himself first heard of Stein when he read Napoleon's proclamation placing him under the ban.

III

BUT a dark veil hung over this retributory future. The mighty of the earth, whether French or German, considered this outburst of Napoleon's hate as a decree blasting Stein's entire future. Yet this Napoleonic hate was by no means the worst thing that Stein had to encounter; even more galling to his spirit was the opposition of the German courtiers and nobles, and especially of those who had taken positions under the Napoleonic régime. By these the bitterest epithets were now lavished upon him. It became an every-day thing among the court and government officials to declare him the worst foe to monarchy. From time to time, Napoleon followed up the decree of outlawry by charging him with Jacobinism; and not only in Prussia, but throughout Germany. At the Austrian capital, Stein's efforts to uplift the lower orders of the Prussian people gave strength to this charge. His idea of appealing to the national feeling was declared to be more dangerous than the worst tyrannies of Napoleon; a large body of influential men and women devoted themselves to everything which could thwart his efforts, and some of them kept Napoleon informed regarding him, thus helping to bring on the catastrophe. Seeley, in his *Life of Stein,* hesitates to believe this, but no one can study the pages of Pertz and Treitschke without becoming convinced that many of Stein's German enemies were capable of going to any length in betraying him.

In the midst of this personal catastrophe, he was constantly meditating not merely means of raising the German nation against the Napoleonic tyranny, but new reforms which should strengthen the people for the coming struggle. Just before leaving office, he presented to the King a summary of his views which has passed into history under the name of "Stein's Political Testament." In this his wish to crown the whole edifice with a legislative system, and to bind the whole together with a constitution, is made clear. As he had changed the rural population from serfs to freemen, the dwellers in cities from ciphers to citizens, and the whole administration from a worn-out machine to a vigorous, living organism, so it now became clear that he wished to change the old Prussian despotism into a limited monarchy, tempered by a national representation, such as came to Prussia forty years later, after the revolutions of 1830 and 1848.

For the time being all these patriotic efforts were brought to naught by what Napoleon considered Stein's unpardonable sin: his crime in detecting and discussing the vulnerable point in the Napoleonic system,—the heel of Achilles. He it was who, more than any other, had detected and accentuated in his private letters to leading German patriots the significance of that Spanish national uprising against Napoleon in 1808, and thus for the first time had given Europe an idea of the way in which Napoleonic tyranny could be overthrown. To meet this action by Stein, Napoleon was by no means content simply to drive him from office and threaten his life; the next move was to extort a new treaty from Prussia, grinding down the North German people more wretchedly than ever before.

During Stein's flight, and, indeed, during his whole outlawry, he remained, in spite of the ruin of his family and the fate which menaced him, calm, thoughtful, and determined as ever. His confidence that the masses were ready to resist foreign aggression and eager to secure their political independence remained unshaken. It was at this crisis that he wrote: "The spirit of the people is excellent; in all classes prevails a self-sacrificing devotion to the good cause which is truly affecting and beautiful (*wahrhaft rührend und schön*)." The three years which he passed in Moravia and Bohemia he used to the best possible purpose: though never noisily active, he continued to be the trusted guide and counselor of the men who were to bring in a better future for his country. The influence of his invincible patriotism steadily increased. Napoleon's new war with Austria, that of 1809, was now clearly drawing on. Had Stein remained in the ministry at Berlin, Prussia would probably have acted energetically and promptly with Austria against the invader, the course of European history would have been different, and six years more of war on the largest scale, and myriads of lives would doubtless have been spared; but, though Stein left many good men and true in the ministry at Berlin, they had not that strength with which he had been wont to overcome the King's fatal indecision, and Austria was left to her fate.

There was, indeed, one moment when his own distress and the apparent hopelessness of Germany and of Europe before its oppressor led him to other thoughts. Interesting to an American is a letter written by him in 1811, in which he says, "I am heartily tired of life and wish it would soon come to an end. To enjoy rest and independence, it would be best to settle in America,—in Kentucky or Tennessee; there one would find a splendid climate and soil, glorious rivers, and rest and security for a century, not to mention a multitude of Germans— the capital of Kentucky is called Frankfort."

But this mood seems to have been only momentary, and he soon returned to patriotic work as earnest as ever, always without haste, but without rest, in unison with the best men in Prussia and Austria,—still their most influential leader.

Great men, animated by his example, rebuilt the foundations of the Prussian state at many points. William von Humboldt reorganized the whole system of public instruction, gave new life to higher education, welded together the best ideas of the foremost thinkers of his time, and crowned all with the University of Berlin, which remains to this day the foremost in the world. Fichte issued his *Addresses to the German Nation* (*Reden an die Deutsche Nation*), which gave new heart to the whole oncoming array of manly youth. Schleiermacher preached his sermons, which, casting aside the mere husks and rinds of ordinary orthodoxy, developed not sickly cowards, merely or mainly anxious to save their own souls, but men willing to strive for good as good,—willing to die for their country. Arndt wrote his *Spirit of the Times* (*Geist der Zeit*), which ran through fifteen editions, and, at a later period, his great song, "*Was ist des Deutschen Vaterland?*" stirring an enthusiasm for German unity and liberty which would-be oppressors have ever since found irresistible.

More and more, Stein, proscribed and a fugitive, became a centre of thought; "where he was, was the head of the table." His famous successor in the Prussian government, Hardenberg, went to meet him secretly in the Silesian mountains, advised with him, and soon Stein's ideas took shape in new reforms, constitutional and financial. The old religious endowments, Catholic and Protestant, which had absorbed so much treasure, were subjected to heavy forced loans; dead capital was thus made living, and trade and industry relieved from a weight of taxation which was crushing out all business life. A representative system, local and general, was more and more distinctly foreshadowed, and, animated by Stein's example, Hardenberg even outran Stein's counsels: in all of Prussia where he had direct control, he exerted himself to transform the peasants from renting tenants into owners of the soil.

Meantime, new catastrophes came. Austria, unsupported by Prussia, endeavored to stand against Napoleon, and, at last, despite official stupidity and sloth, exhibited, especially in the Tyrol, a resisting force never before seen in her campaigns, a national spirit akin to that which had struck Napoleon so severe a blow in Spain, an energy which inflicted upon him, at Aspern, his first great defeat by Germans. Had Stein been at the side of the wavering Frederick William III, Prussia might now have joined in the struggle; but, before the Prussian King could make up his mind to give his help, Austria was overcome at Wagram, and Stadion, as prime minister, was forced to give way to the archintriguer, Metternich. Now comes apparently the culmination of the Napoleonic epoch. Metternich marries a daughter of the Austrian House to Napoleon, and thus ushers in upon Europe another long series of sacrifices and sorrows, with that heartbreaking policy of intrigue, political immorality, and reaction which outlasted Napoleon by more than thirty years.

In these darkest hours Stein never lost heart, but one great change was wrought in him,—he became less and less a Prussian and more and more a German. He would not yield to the oppressor of his country, and, being no longer safe in Austria, he again became an exile.

In Napoleon's hand were now all the great nations of Continental Europe save one. Alexander of Russia, despite his shameful concessions at the Treaty of Tilsit, shrank from the further iniquities into which Napoleon attempted to draw him, and, as Napoleon allowed no dissent from his plans, war drew on between these two great powers. Therefore it was that, just as King Frederick William had sought Stein's aid after the downfall of Prussia, so now Emperor Alexander sought Stein at what Europe generally considered the approaching downfall of Russia. Personal prudence counseled Stein to lie quiet, to allow himself to be forgotten, to wait for better days. It was dangerous indeed for him to throw himself against Napoleon, even in Russia. Russia then, as now, was poor, her policy tricky, her officials corrupt, her ruler weak. Napoleon, the greatest conqueror the world ever saw, was at that moment passing over her frontier with more than half a million soldiers, apparently invincible, and, should Stein engage himself actively against Napoleon in Russia, a French triumph would bring him to the scaffold, or at least to long exile. How Napoleon treated those who troubled him—whom he affected to despise—was seen in the orders for drumhead court-martials, which were now sent more frequently than ever to his agents throughout Germany: how he would certainly have treated Stein could he have laid hands upon him is seen in the Emperor's letters to his minister, Champagny.

But with Stein this weighed nothing. He immediately joined Alexander at his headquarters, and the Emperor at once tendered him high position in the administration of finance or of public instruction. But all this Stein declined, declaring frankly that his main purpose was to act in the interest of Germany. His mission as regarded Russia was to keep up the courage of the Russian Emperor; his special effort as regarded Germany was to arouse her to arms, so as to cut off Napoleon's army from France. Stein took the lead in this effort, corresponded more actively than ever with German patriots in every part of Europe, spurred or curbed patriotism, as there was need, answered sophists, summoned Arndt to his side and inspired him to write those appeals to patriotism which stirred the hearts of the whole German people.

Yet still, throughout Germany, a large party at the various courts, though they dreaded Napoleon much, hated Stein more. His appeals to the people still seemed

to these so-called conservatives revolutionary. Their
necessary result was an infusion of life and thought into
the people which would first, indeed, be directed against
the new French oppressor; but which might afterward,
perhaps, be directed against their old German oppressors. Foremost in holding these views was the old
Emperor of Austria, and his most trusted minister,
Metternich.

In Russia the opposition to Stein was of another sort,
but hardly less serious. Napoleon's successes had spread
terror through the court. The awful sacrifices of Russian soldiers during the French invasion, which were
hardly less than those of Napoleon's own troops, filled
the leading Russian families with dismay. The steady
march of the French, winning battle after battle, and
finally entering Moscow, gave the party of peace at any
price most cogent arguments. Led by the Dowager Empress and others of the imperial household, this party
became clamorous. Napoleon, foreseeing his own danger, and knowing Alexander's wavering character, sent
him the most seductive messages and used the most entic-
ing arguments; again he held out the lure of a virtual
division of the civilized world between the two Emperors.

Against all this pressure Stein stood firm, and, more
than any other, kept Alexander firm. His statesmanlike
eye saw Napoleon's real position, and he made the Russian Emperor see it; he roused the courage of the Russian
patriots, and chilled the ardor of the sympathizers with
France. But, important though it was to leave no stone
unturned against the enemies of his country, he was still
the sturdy baron of the old German Empire—utterly
refusing to become a mere courtier. Such frankness,
straightforwardness, and fearlessness as his has never
been seen in Russia before or since. On one occasion
the Empress Dowager, the mother of Alexander, received
a lesson from him, in the presence of the court, which

to this day remains one of the wonders of Russian history. After the battle of Borodino, the Empress, in a temporary fit of enthusiasm, cried out in Stein's presence, "If now a single French soldier shall escape from the German borders, I shall be ashamed to confess myself of German descent." The court chroniclers tell us that Stein immediately became red and white by turns, marched up to the Empress, stood firmly before her, and said, in the hearing of all present, "Your Majesty is most unjust to speak in this manner of so great, so true, so bold a people as that to which you have the good fortune to belong by birth. You should have said, 'I am ashamed, not of the German people, but of my own brothers and cousins, the German princes. Had they done their duty, never had a Frenchman come over the Elbe, Oder, or Vistula.'" Any one acquainted at all with the Byzantine submission exacted at the Russian Court can understand the consternation spread by these plain words; but, fortunately, the Empress, having something left of her better German ideas and training, answered, "Sir Baron, you are perhaps right. I thank you for the lesson."

The whole conduct of Stein at this period, and indeed throughout all the last years of his official life, was due not merely to his hatred for the oppressor of his country, but to a deep faith that Napoleon's career was a challenge to the Almighty, and that therefore it could not continue. Stein noted well the sacrifices which Napoleon, without fear or remorse, had demanded of the nation which worshiped him. The number of his subjects who during his reign had laid down their lives to exalt him was something over two millions. This devotion meant the annihilation, during every year that the Empire continued, of nearly two hundred thousand lives, and these the most vigorous and promising lives which France could offer. This, Stein saw, could not last; and he had a deep conviction that, even if it could last, it was so monstrous a crime against the Divine Majesty that it must surely be punished.[1]

There can be no doubt that to Stein, more than to any other human being, it is due that, after the burning of Moscow, Alexander refused to enter into any further negotiations with Napoleon; and this refusal it was that brought Napoleon to ruin. The conqueror relied on the pliancy of Alexander, as he had seen him at Tilsit and elsewhere, but he had not reckoned on the firmness inspired by the greatest of German patriots.[2]

Now came the great question of questions, What shall Russia do? It was the supreme moment—the time of all times. The advice of the elegant diplomatists about the Czar, headed by his Imperial Chancellor, was that she should patch up a peace, curry favor with Napoleon, and thus secure large additions of territory at the expense of Prussia and Turkey. The danger of Germany was imminent—the danger of a renewal of that old alliance between the French Emperor and the Russian Czar at Tilsit, made more effective than ever to plunder the German people and to blot out German nationality—in fact, to make Prussia a second Poland. Stein, more than any other man, averted this danger; drove the leading

---

[1] For other striking examples of Stein's boldness of speech before the mighty of the earth, see Pertz, vol. iv, pp. 152, 153. For the reckoning of French lives lost under the Napoleonic Empire, see a careful statement in Alison, *History of Europe*.

[2] It seems to me clear that Professor Seeley, admirable as is his *Life of Stein*, wrote under academic limitations which prevented full appreciation of Stein's influence at this crisis. His argument that "public opinion" kept the Emperor Alexander up to the required pitch of firmness must seem to one acquainted with official life in Russia utterly inadequate. Two official residences in Russia during trying times have shown me that "public opinion" in that country, down to the present moment, has always been the opinion of the Czar, if he is man enough to have an opinion; and if he is not, "public opinion" is the feeling of some exceptionally strong man or clique. At the period now referred to, Stein was by far the strongest man in Alexander's councils.

intriguers out of the Russian councils; filled the imagination of the Czar with the idea of becoming, not a robber of Germany, but the savior of Europe. Since Richelieu made the weakling Louis XIII a champion of French unity and a leader against Austrian tyranny in Europe, never until now had a statesman exhibited such power to turn a great sovereign to his own noble purposes. Events conspired to aid him. Stein's worst enemy in Prussia, General Yorck, who, with a Prussian auxiliary army, had been dragged by Napoleon into Russia, took advantage of the Moscow catastrophe; and, in spite of the King's loudly proclaimed disapproval, turned against Napoleon, risked death for high treason, and for a time bade defiance to the nominal orders of his own sovereign, Frederick William III.

Stein was no less bold than Yorck. The Russians having conquered that large region centering at Königsberg, all so dear to Prussia, Stein took a Russian commission to go, virtually as a Russian viceroy, into those Prussian frontier provinces; ruled them, raised them, in defiance of their Prussian sovereign, against Napoleon, who was that sovereign's nominal ally; and, worse than this, committed a sin unpardonable in the Prussia of that time by calling together, without orders, or even the permission of the Prussian King, a parliament which should provide for war against the French oppressor.

This was a crowning audacity. King Frederick William and his bureaucrats, though they profited by it, never forgot it. Stein received honors afterward from Prussia, but was never recalled into the Prussian service. To Frederick William he seemed the most dangerous of Germans. To Napoleon, he was certainly the most dangerous; for never, even at the climax of his power, did the Emperor omit a chance to cast a slur upon him, to express his hatred of him, to call him a

Jacobin reformer, as dangerous to Hapsburgs and Hohenzollerns as the French Jacobins had been to the Bourbons.

So it came that, while the German monarchs, their ministers, and their favorites, were obliged to avail themselves of Stein's vast abilities as an organizer, they never forgave his appeals to the German people and his efforts to uplift them. Even during the days after the King and his greatest statesmen were once more nominally united, his Majesty of Prussia took pains not to invite Stein to dinner; and, when the old statesman lay in the garret of a hotel at Breslau, apparently at the point of death from fever, did not even take the pains to inquire after his health, or even to send him a kindly message.

The first struggles of Prussia and Russia against Napoleon after the Moscow collapse resulted doubtfully. Austria and Saxony stood aloof, doing everything possible to bargain with Napoleon at the expense of Prussia. The most amazing offers were made him by Austria and her allies, if he would give up his idea of reëstablishing the empire of Charlemagne. At the Treaty of Reichenbach, Austria in concert with Russia, and, indeed, Prussia, offered to leave him at the head of an empire greater than any other in Europe by far,—an empire comprising France, Italy, Belgium, Holland, German kingdoms and principalities on the Rhine, and much beside. But Napoleon refused, and now not only Russia and Prussia, but Austria, turned against him, Great Britain aiding them effectively. The world was weary of Napoleon's despotism, and in 1813 all Germany rose in alliance with the three great military monarchies on the continent outside of France. Stein and those who wrought with him had created a German people; Scharnhorst had given it military training; Arndt, Schleiermacher, Fichte, Jahn, and hundreds of others, nay, thousands of others, had inspired it with determination to conquer or die. Napoleon, having refused the very moderate terms of Austria, and having invaded Germany with a new army, was at first successful, but this renewed Germany pressed on against him: "the battle of the nations" was fought at Leipsic, and the end began.

To unite Europe for this effort, Stein had to make a great sacrifice. He had urged on Germany a levy *en masse;* but the Austrian government would not listen to him. For there was still dominant the old fear that the people, once called to rise against the French Emperor, might learn its strength and rise again later against the Austrian Emperor; therefore it was that Stein's counsels, just at the moment when they were most valuable, were set aside, and he was obliged to see the lead given to creatures like Metternich.

But while the allies would allow him no place where his counsels could be heard, they were forced to give him a more important place in administration than any other minister had ever held in Europe. They created a great central commission to administer the provinces of Germany outside of Prussia and Austria, and to restore order and good government in them just as fast as they were retaken from Napoleon. At the head of this commission they placed Stein. His administrative work now became colossal; he was even nicknamed "the German Emperor"; indeed, there were those who seriously proposed to restore the old German Empire and place him permanently at its head. He was called upon, not only to govern Central Europe and France as they were reconquered, but to reorganize all this territory; to divide it into manageable provinces; to appoint its rulers and counselors; to draw from it supplies of money and troops for the allies; and, among ten thousand other things, to care for those wounded in the struggles which now ensued, of whom thirty-four thousand were left on his hands after the battle of Leipsic.

Reigning princes waited in his ante-chamber, but the sturdy old baron treated them with scant courtesy: he could never conceal his contempt for most of them, and, as a rule, his treatment of them was much like that which Bismarck gave their successors fifty years later at Versailles. The German princelings of Stein's time had mainly preferred luxury to honor; had shown themselves ready to serve Napoleon or the allies, as might be for their comfort or advantage: Stein's manly dignity permeated all his thinking, in small things as in great; a territorial magnate ranking next to royalty, the Grand Duke of Weimar, attempting to make a filthy joke in a company where the great minister was present, Stein rebuked him with severity and directness. All present were appalled at his boldness, but his "High Transparency" of Weimar was thereby forced to change his style. On another occasion a lofty personage whom Stein had caused to be thrown into prison on account of fraud in dealings with the government, having obtained a pardon of the King and come to Stein in order to show the pardon to him, Stein drove him forth from the house with his uplifted stick. At a dinner in Berlin, a great noble whose name was soiled with scoundrelism being announced, Stein, in spite of all remonstrance, left the house, declaring that he would never sit under the same roof with such a creature.

Outside of Austria and Prussia, his nickname of "Emperor" was, during that period, the expression of a reality. New dangers arose. Napoleon's heir was the Austrian Emperor's grandson, and at various times Austria showed a willingness to preserve Napoleon's sway in France, restricting him within her natural boundaries, which were then supposed to reach to the Rhine; but Stein's influence, absent though he was from the central

20

council which seemed to control policies in those days, constantly kept the Emperor Alexander firm against all this, and, when Paris was at last taken by the allies, it is not too much to say that no other man had done more to promote this result. Yet no great man at that period was mentioned so little: Europe resounded with the names of the three monarchs, of Metternich, and of Talleyrand, but this sturdy old statesman, infinitely higher in character and in service than any other, was hardly ever heard of.

Afterward, indeed, as thinking men and impartial historians reflected upon the events of that great period, justice began to be done him. Well does one of the greatest of modern jurists declare, in words carefully weighed, that "the heroic determination in 1812 and '13 to bring a victorious Russian army from the frontier to unite it with the unchained might of the German people, to push it, with the rejuvenated Prussian army, toward the West, and by these and the allied armies to drive Napoleon from position to position and out of Germany was the work of a genius: for history it is no longer a secret that the genius which brought this expedition of Alexander from the boundaries of Siberia to the hill of Montmartre was the genius of Baron vom Stein. Thereby he reached the summit of his historical mission." [1]

At the Vienna Congress, which followed the abdication of Napoleon, Stein exerted himself for German unity and a proper position for Prussia, and, of course, was opposed by Metternich, Talleyrand, and all statesmen of their sort. At Napoleon's return from Elba, Stein's voice was potent among those who put him under the ban, and, at last, ended his career. During the whole Vienna Congress Stein labored on as best he might for a substantial German unity resting upon a constitution;

[1] See Gneist, *Die Denkschriften des Freiherrn vom Stein.*

he would have restored the German Empire, would have introduced deliberative assemblies, and would have brought into these the germs of something very different from the old "Holy Roman Empire of the German Nation," which had, indeed, come to naught before Napoleon had given its quietus. But Metternich was too firmly seated, and the influence of Austria on the petty interest of the lesser German princelings was irresistible: the Federation was created, which dragged on through years of humiliating politics, until it was ended by Bismarck. Stein also tried to have Alsace-Lorraine restored to Germany, but in this also he failed, and it was reserved for Bismarck to realize his idea, at the cost of myriads of precious German lives, half a century later.

French tyranny having at last been driven from Germany, Stein was no longer listened to, and retired from politics,—regretting the great work left undone, but happy in the great work done; seeing clearly that serious evils were to follow from the reaction, but with a calm faith that better counsels would finally prevail. To the end of his life, he continued to maintain that same independence and fearlessness which led Scharnhorst to say that Stein and Blücher were the only two men he had ever met who feared no human being. One high position was indeed offered him by Prussia,—that of its delegate to the Frankfort Diet; but his strong good sense forbade him to accept it: he saw that with reactionary forces then dominant, and especially in view of Austrian jealousy of Prussia, no further progress was at that time to be made. Instructive is it to reflect that in this position, which Stein refused, Bismarck first gave to the world an earnest of the powers by which, finally, he was to acquire for a new German Empire those provinces of Alsace and Lorraine which Stein had sought to restore to the old Empire.

Another tribute to the old statesman seems strange indeed. I⁓ was perhaps the greatest of all testimonies to his character and ability, for it was nothing less than an offer of the presidency of the German Diet at Frankfort; and, of all men in the world, it came from the man who had been his most troublesome German enemy,— Metternich. Needless to say that Stein declined it, as he declined various other honors coming from sources which he distrusted.[1]

To the end of his days he remained the same determined hater of all whom he thought evil or unpatriotic, the constant friend of all whom he considered true and intelligent lovers of the country. His old house near the ruins of his ancestral castle still stands, and its most interesting feature is the tower which he attached to it as a monument to the great triumph of right and justice in which he had aided, and as a receptacle for the portraits and other memorials of men who had stood by him in the great war for German freedom.

Two houses has the present writer visited which have revealed to him what a true patriot, cherishing justice and right reason, may accomplish even when apparently deprived of all power. The first of these is this old house of Stein at Nassau. From it, in his latter days, went forth his letters to Von Gagern and others who were leading in the struggle for right reason in Germany. The other is the house at Monticello from which Thomas Jefferson, during the long years after he had laid down official power, sent forth to James Madison and others those letters which did so much for right reason in the United States.

There was much to stimulate these final efforts of Stein. King Frederick William III of Prussia, in his

---

[1] For Metternich's offer, see Seeley, vol. ii, pp. 409, 410, where will be found also a most curious letter from Metternich to Von Gagern, written after Stein's death and containing a remarkable tribute to him.

time of trouble, had given a solemn promise to establish
a constitutional government; but, when peace and prosperity returned, reaction set in, and the royal advisers,
entangling him in sophisms, led him virtually to break
his word. Against this line of action Stein wrote constantly and earnestly. The assassination of Kotzebue
by Sand aided reaction, as assassinations generally do;
but Stein remained moderate and liberal, still urging a
constitution and representation for Prussia, with a beginning, at least, of free institutions in Germany. He
was not, indeed, a liberal in the modern sense. The constitution which he then urged would have been monarchic
and aristocratic; but embedded in it would have been
provision for a large representation of the people, and
in this would have been germs sure to develop into a far
broader system of self-government. He was no "fool
reformer." He knew how to estimate the facts and possibilities about him. He did not expect fruit on the day
the tree was planted; enough for him to plant a good
tree—sure to bear good fruit.

It became clear to him that his counsels were, during
his time, not to be followed, and he returned in his last
years mainly to historical studies. But he found important sources inaccessible, and so came into his mind
the idea of establishing a society to care for the records
of the German past, to rescue these precious documents
of history, and to preserve them from oblivion by publishing them. Thus was begun by German scholarship,
some years before the death of Stein, the publication of
the greatest historical work which any nation has ever
undertaken, the *Monumenta Germaniæ;* to this he sub-
scribed a sum very large in proportion to his modest fortune, and from 1819 to the present hour this great work
has been continued, in furtherance not only of scholarly
research, but of German patriotism.[1]

[1] For a full and interesting statement of the worth of the work upon

Although he had resigned all hopes of leadership in German or Prussian counsels, and indeed, in view of the limitations imposed by men then dominant, all wish for leadership, he was, from time to time, called upon to make important reports and to give weighty counsels; and in one of these, to the Crown Prince, afterward King Frederick William IV of Prussia, the old statesman made an admirable argument for provincial institutions and administration, as opposed to a centralized bureaucracy. Even in his modest dwelling, so remote from courtiers and men temporarily great, he never ceased to serve his country, and in his last years he took a useful part in the deliberations of the states of Westphalia.

His religion was simple and manly. As his eminent English biographer remarks, "There is no cowering, no terror, no fear of the future. Everything that relates to the saving of the soul is absent." He was a sincere Christian and took it for granted that if his soul was worth saving it would be saved. On the 29th of June, 1831, he died—died as he had lived, a great, true, Christian man; not what is usually called a philanthropist, not a partisan, not the banner-bearer of any momentary outburst of sentiment, but a clear-headed, strong-hearted laborer for right and justice as the foundations of national greatness.

As a legacy to the German people, and indeed to mankind, he left the record of his labors; but, even more effective than this record, the remembrance of his character. Perhaps in no human being save our own Washington has the value of *character* as a great force, not to be described but to be felt, been proved so quietly yet so evidently. The same great jurist who in carefully measured terms has shown us that to Stein, more than

the *Monumenta Germaniæ* in training eminent German historians, see Paulsen, *Die Deutschen Universitäten*, pp. 67, 70.

to any other German, and, indeed, more than to any other man, was due the final removal of the Napoleonic incubus from Europe, speaks of Stein as follows: "His greatest service in the reform of the administration was derived from his high character and his morally clean, unselfish, experienced, and forceful convictions. This carried his measures against the opposition of the provincial nobility and the great body of courtiers. Even Frederick William III had accepted Stein's ideas before Jena, but his adhesion to these ideas, when they were carried out, was due to his trust in Stein, a trust which Hardenberg could not arouse." [1]

No less due to his character was the confidence which led the autocrat of all the Russias to confide in him against all the power and all the temptations of Napoleon, and which caused the leaders of Europe, even though distrusting Stein's belief in popular rights, to unite against the universal tyrant. More than to any other, the ideas which began the new Germany were due to this quiet, strong, faithful, persistent, self-respecting statesman, and they were due him by virtue of one of the noblest characters which human annals can show.

The old state servant was buried near the rock from which he had taken his name. Over his grave was written an epitaph as follows:—

HEINRICH FRIEDRICH KARL, IMPERIAL BARON VOM UND ZUM STEIN,

born October 27th, 1757,
died June 29th, 1831,
lies here:

The last of his knightly race, which had ruled
on the Lahn for seven hundred years;
Humble before God, high-hearted before men,
an enemy of untruth and of injustice,

1 See Gneist, as above, p. 16.

highly gifted in truth and honor,
unshaken in proscription and exile,
the yielding Fatherland's unyielding son,
in battle and in victory a soldier for German
freedom.
"I have a desire to depart
and to be with Christ." [1]

Some forty years later, at that old rock, in the presence of leading statesmen, thinkers, historians, and poets of Germany, and among them the King of Prussia, who, now that Stein's main ideas had at last done their work, had become the Emperor of a united Germany, there was unveiled a statue of the great statesman; and upon its base was the old well-known play upon his name which had long before been a popular saying: *"Des guten Grundstein; des Bösen Eckstein; der deutschen Edelstein* (A corner-stone of goodness; a stumbling-stone for evil; a precious stone to Germany)."

Suitable honor was also done him, at last, in the capital of the Prussian monarchy, destined to become the metropolis of the German Empire. In front of the palace of the Prussian legislature stands, in bronze, a noble monument by perhaps the greatest of modern German sculptors. It represents Stein at his best—firm, foursquare to all the winds that blow. About him stand colossal statues typifying the virtues which he summoned to the uplifting of his country, and about the base are sculptured a series of the greatest scenes in that life by which he wrought so powerfully to save Prussia, Germany, and European civilization.

Nor was this all. These two monuments had been erected under Frederick William IV and William I, two sons of Frederick William III; but it was reserved to the

---

[1] For the translation given by Seeley, the present writer has substituted the above, taken down on the spot, which seems in some particulars more exact.

great-grandson of the ungrateful sovereign to erect a
final memorial. For, in these later days, the present
Prussian King and German Emperor, William II, having
given to the city of Berlin the long line of statues on
either side of the Avenue of Victory, which represent the
succession of princes—thirty-three in all—who have
ruled his territory during the past thousand years, each of
these sovereigns having on either side colossal busts
in marble of the men who did most to strengthen his
reign—he has placed at the side of the statue representing Frederick William III the bust of the great statesman to whom that King owed so much and gave so little.

But, better than monuments of marble and bronze,
better than eulogies which the foremost German orators
have been proud to deliver, is the monument which will
ever stand in the heart, and the eulogy which will ever
rise to the lips, of thoughtful Germans whenever the name
of Stein shall be spoken.

He was the second, in point of time, of the three
great German statesmen since the Reformation. The
first of these was Thomasius, mainly a publicist, between whom and the other two it is impossible to make
any comparisons, his work being in fields and by methods
so utterly different from theirs. In any comparison
between the latter two, the world at large will doubtless award the first place to Bismarck. His work was
on the whole more amazing and his triumph more impressive; but, on the other hand, it must be said that
Bismarck had at his command forces which in the Freedom War against Napoleon were wanting to Prussia, and
among these a sovereign, William I, standing firmly by
him from first to last, despite all intrigues and opposition,—Moltke, the greatest soldier since Napoleon,—
Roon, the greatest of army organizers,—an immense
army in the most perfect condition,—and, finally, an uprising of German feeling fully equal to that which Stein

had done so much to arouse against the Napoleonic tyranny.

But against the vast and impressive victories of Bismarck should be arrayed the fact that Stein's work was really more profound, more varied, more devoted to all sorts and conditions of men. In Bismarck's work, while there is at times a foresight and force almost preternatural, there is nothing which shows such depth of philosophic insight into the very heart of modern politics as Stein's idea of creating self-respecting men out of downtrodden serfs, self-respecting citizens out of despised burghers, and endowing a vast nation with parliamentary institutions. In this respect Stein is the superior of Bismarck; the only Europeans who have equaled him in this depth of thought and breadth of vision as regards the foundations of modern society are Turgot and Cavour.

Moreover the characters of the two great modern Germans present striking differences. Both could, on occasion, be irritable, and even overbearing; both could be humorous, witty, and even fascinating; but as regards straightforwardness, directness, and respect for popular rights, Bismarck is not to be compared with Stein. Nor is there anything which shows in Bismarck such wonderful powers of administration as those which Stein exercised when, in the rear of the great combined armies of the allies, he organized the territories as they were gained, first in Germany, and then throughout France, gathering troops, raising money, caring for the wounded, settling vexed questions between territorial rulers, and proving himself to rank, in administration, with Cæsar and Napoleon. It must also be confessed with some regret that the final years of Bismarck were infinitely less worthy of a great man than were those of Stein. Quietly settled upon his ancestral estate on the river Lahn, doing everything possible to promote quietly the better development of Prussia and Germany, dignified, thoughtful, accepting neglect without complaint, Stein seems, it must be confessed, infinitely more dignified than Bismarck, who displayed, after his retirement, defects of his qualities over which those who admire him most will most gladly draw a veil.

While, then, Bismarck, by the extent of his work, by its variety, by the evident result of it in the creation of the new German Empire, and by its boldly dramatic character, will long be exalted in the popular mind as the greater statesman, no thinking man who has studied closely the decline and rise of Germany during the nineteenth century can fail to award to Stein a place close beside him—equal as regards services to German nationality, superior as regards services to humanity.

CAVOUR

CAVOUR

I

OF all great prophecies ever made to a credulous world, the most futile and woeful was uttered toward the end of the eighteenth century by Aurelio Bertola.

Having visited many countries, in various capacities—at times a monk, at times a soldier, at times a man of letters and "philosopher"—flitting at times between the lecture-rooms of two renowned universities—always an optimistic phrase-maker, he published what he called, *A Philosophy of History,* and, as its culmination, summed up the condition of humanity on this wise: "The political system of Europe has arrived at perfection. An equilibrium has been attained which henceforth preserves peoples from subjugation. Few reforms are now needed and these will be accomplished peaceably. Europe has no need to fear a revolution." [1]

And this in 1787!—the year in which the French Assembly of Notables opened the greatest era of revolution and war in human history—an era which has now lasted over a century and which still continues; which, between that year and this, has seen every people on the European continent subjugated by foes foreign or domestic, every continental dynasty overturned or humiliated, and an infinite number of liberties crushed, or reforms wrested, by conspirators or soldiers; an era which, not only to every European nation, but to America, Asia, and Africa, has brought deluge after deluge of blood; which is blackened by thousands of battlefields, and, among these, by

[1] See Cantù, *Histoire des Italiens,* vol. xi, p. 23; also vol. x, p. 449.

Marengo, Austerlitz, and Borodino, by Leipzig and Waterloo, by the Alma and Inkerman, by Magenta and Solferino, by Antietam and Gettysburg, by Sadowa and Plevna, by Gravelotte and Sedan; by the naval slaughters of the Nile, Trafalgar, Navarino, and Sinope, and by the Japanese annihilation of Chinese and Russian armies and navies; by the storming of Badajoz, of the Malakoff, and of Düppel; by the sieges of Genoa, of Saragossa, of Sebastopol, of Paris, and of Port Arthur; by thousands of vast and bloody encounters besides, costing millions of lives; by a ghastly series of massacres, extending from those in the name of liberty, in 1792, to those in the name of throne and altar, in 1815, and from those of the Commune, in 1871, to those throughout Russia, in 1906; by scaffolds innumerable, and by the remodeling of every European nation, save Great Britain—some of them twice or thrice.

The world at large, which loves those who prophesy smooth things, took this utterance of Bertola complacently. To the warning of a very different tenor, given by Lord Chesterfield, it gave no heed.

Most of all was this optimistic prophecy enjoyed by Italians; for, of all great peoples, they had most reason to long for a future better than their past. During more than a thousand years Italy had been trodden down by foreign rulers and soldiers—Germans, Saracens, Frenchmen, and Spaniards. She had been torn also by feuds between countless tyrants of her own; between her city republics; between classes; between demagogues— all howling for "liberty" or "religion"; so that, despite her vast achievements in literature, science, and art, her people had sunk more and more into superstition and skepticism. Their main reliance was apparently upon such helpers as St. Januarius at Naples, the Bambino at Rome, St. Antony and his pigs at Padua, Buddha—transformed into a Christian saint—at Palermo, and ten

thousand fetiches besides. Faith in anything worth believing was mainly gone. The mediæval city liberties
had long been a vague remembrance. The utterances of
Dante and Michael Angelo were, to the vast mass, as if
they had never been.[1]

Their lay rulers were, mainly, frivolous and sensual,
their priestly rulers largely bigoted and cruel, their nobles given to futilities, their people groveling below
these—ignorant beyond belief.

But, shortly after Bertola wrote, the French Revolution made itself felt in Italy.

It raised many hopes, and, in 1796, came an apostle
from whom Italians expected much—Bonaparte—an
Italian who never spoke French until out of his boyhood;
and, knowing this, Italy saw some reason for believing
in him. Bringing his army over the Alps, he promised
to the Italian people an end of the miseries which had
been accumulating since the destruction of their municipal liberties, more than two hundred and fifty years before. He pledged to them the fulfillment of their wildest
dreams—liberty, fraternity, prosperity, glory. Some of
these promises he redeemed, for he brought better ideas
of liberty and justice; roads along which better ideas
could travel; a system of taxation, which, though taking
more money out of the country than it had ever yet paid,
was better than any it had ever known before. He reduced some fifteen petty despotisms to three, cast out
Bourbon, Papal, and Hapsburg administration, gave bet-

[1] For a most striking and convincing revelation of the complete moral
and religious debasement of Italian life during the "Ages of Faith," see
From St. Francis to Dante, by G. G. Coulton, London, 1906. This little
book, a translation of all that is of primary interest in the Chronicle of
the Franciscan Salimbene, is one of the most valuable contributions to
Mediæval History and to sane religious thought published during the last
twenty years. For the Italian devotion to Buddha as St. Giosafat, the
"St. Rosalia relics" and the examination of them by Dr. Buckland, and
the Januarius fetich, see A. D. White, *The Warfare of Science with
Theology*, vol. ii, chap. xiii.

ter laws, scared off Jesuits, discouraged monks, shot
bandits, restored vigor to states which had seemed mere
carcasses, and, best of all, gave an impulse to the idea
of Italy as a nation.[1]

But at his downfall Italy, of all countries with which
he had dealt, was left the most abject and distraught.
Liberty he had never given it; he had played with Italian
rights as suited his interest or fancy: had distributed the
whole Italian territory as his private estate; had, more
than once, thrown its liberties to the worst enemies Italians had ever known. While affecting veneration for the
Republic of Venice and admiration for the men who represented it, he had tossed it over to Austria as a mere
bagatelle at the Treaty of Campo Formio, just ten years
after Bertola's prophecy. He had carved out of Italian
territories a kingdom for himself, with principalities and
dukedoms for his family, his satraps, and his courtiers,
much as any ordinary brigand might have distributed
the plunder of a petty village. Works of art which were
to Italians the proudest trophies of their past, he had
sent to the contemptible Directory, at Paris. He had
left the bones of Italian youth scattered on hundreds of
battlefields, from Madrid to Moscow.[2]

[1] For a remarkable summary of Bonaparte's methods on arriving in
Italy, see A. Sorel, *L'Europe et la Révolution Française*, vol. v, pp. 198 and
following.

For examples showing the beneficial side of the Napoleonic system in
Italy, see Colletta, *History of Naples*, English translation, book vi, chaps.
iii, iv, and v.

For an admirable short statement regarding the good and evil in Bona-
parte's dealings with Italy, see Lemmi, *Le Origini del Risorgimento
Italiano* (1789–1815), Milan, 1906, cap. iv and v. Also Aurelio Saffi,
Ricordi e Scritti, vol. iv, p. 394.

[2] Of all who have ever unveiled the cynical treatment of Italy by Napoleon, and especially that masterpiece of treachery, the Treaty of Campo
Formio, none has surpassed Lanfrey, in his *Histoire de Napoléon*. See,
especially, vol. i, chap. ix. The number of Italian soldiers forced into the
Napoleonic wars between 1796 and 1814, Lemmi gives as 358,000, and the
number of lives lost as 120,000. The losses were especially fearful in

Hence it was that, when after his treachery in Italy, his infamy in Spain, and his folly in Russia, his throne tottered and fell, the Italians began listening to the Hapsburgs and Bourbons, and the race of princelings who returned in their train after the Peace of Vienna. In the anxiety of these old enslavers to recover Italian territory, their pledges were as splendid as any Napoleon had made; and especially alluring were their promises of liberties, constitutions, and reasonable government. But they, too, as soon as they were established, forgot all these fine pretenses, and the old despotism of the days before the French Revolution settled down upon the country more heavily than ever. Throughout the whole peninsula the influence of Austria now became supreme. The highest conceptions then applied to Italian development were those of the Austrian Emperor Francis, typical of which was his announcement to sundry delegates of the University of Padua that he required of them not enlightened scholars but obedient subjects. Typical of his practice was his command to the jailers of Spielberg to shorten the diet of his Italian prisoners and to make them feel every day—more and more—the bitter results of their patriotism.

Acting through him was Metternich, the great apostle of reaction, whose contempt for Italian independence was expressed in his famous utterance, "Italy is simply a geographical expression." Back of both was the Holy Alliance—especially Russia and Austria. Romanoffs, Hapsburgs, and, for a time, Hohenzollerns united in the effort to quench instantly in Italy every spark of freedom, every beginning of constitutional government—the Bourbons, in France, Spain, and Naples, applauding and helping them.

At the northern extremity of the peninsula, in Lom-

---

the insane Spanish and Russian campaigns, which touched no conceivable interest of Italy.

bardy and Venice, Austria had established a kingdom peculiarly her own—honest in a way, but brutally stupid. All traces of earlier independence and liberties were uprooted. The reforms of Napoleon were, as far as possible, brought to naught, and from Milan, especially, radiated the new gospel of Hapsburg despotism; its apostles the hierarchy of the Church, and its disciples the whole army of place-holders and pelf-seekers.

Adjoining this territory, on the northwest, was the realm of the House of Savoy, to which had been recently attached the Republic of Genoa. Everything like constitutional liberty was blotted out from this territory also. As regards education, the Church, and especially the Jesuits, were given complete control; but in one thing this Piedmontese kingdom was vastly superior to any other part of Italy: it had a peasantry, hardworking, honest, and conscientious; a nobility, which, though often narrow-minded and even bigoted, was self-respecting and patriotic; a monarchy differing in its whole spirit from that of the Hapsburgs and Bourbons; for, though the royal house had been, and, indeed, remained for some years after its restoration by the Treaty of Vienna, bigoted and despotic, it was straightforward and truthful, and, therefore, was respected by its subjects as Bourbons and Hapsburgs had not been for ages.[1]

Going southward, the next main division was Tuscany —ruled by a branch of the House of Hapsburg, but this branch the best in all Hapsburg history. Its people were hard-working and generally contented; its beauty, its fertility, and the glories of the arts there developed had made it, for several generations, the most attractive part of the peninsula. Its rulers, indeed, resisted every-

---

[1] For statements regarding the despotism of the House of Savoy during the early years of the 19th century, see Stillman, *The Union of Italy*, chaps. i, ii, and iii; and, for some better features, Cantù, *Histoire des Italiens*, vols. x and xi.

thing like constitutional government, but they devoted themselves to the welfare of their subjects paternally.

Neighboring Tuscany were a number of small states, like Parma, Lucca, and Modena, governed by petty despots, as a rule Austrian by birth or education, and among these, worst of all, the Duke of Modena, Francis IV. Even in that bad age he was despised and abhorred for his cruel cunning. No blacker stain rests upon the history of any modern man than his treacherous murder of Ciro Menotti and the patriots who had trusted in the ducal promises.[1]

Next southward, among the main divisions, came the States of the Church, ruled from the early years of the nineteenth century by men of little force: one of them, indeed, Pius VII, beautiful in character and ennobled by adversity; others, like Pius VIII and Gregory XVI, narrow and intolerant. As to moral and religious traits they were lifted by the spirit of their time far above the level of such pontiffs as Sixtus IV and Alexander VI, but as to ability they were infinitely below such as Sixtus V, and Benedict XIV, and Leo XIII. None of them were strong enough to make headway against the political absurdities that had been so long developing throughout their dominions. To each and all of them anything like constitutional government was unthinkable. None knew any way of governing save by despotism, and just as little could any one of them think of conceding any effective part in administration to laymen. All rule must be entrusted to priests—and these, the Monsignori, mostly young ecclesiastics, who had won their way by family connection, or old ecclesiastics, cynical and sluggish; some, indeed, well intentioned, but, for the most part, giving the cities they ruled governments as degrad-

[1] For details of this episode, so frightful but so instructive, see N. Bianchi, *I Ducati Estensi*, etc., Turin, 1852; also Gualterio, *Gli Ultimi Rivolgimenti Italiani*, Florence, 1852.

ing as any that modern civilization has known—save, possibly, those to be seen in our own day in some of our American municipalities. To the whole Napoleonic tradition of public works they were, as a rule, invincibly opposed. When railways came, these functionaries, from the Pope downward, mainly abhorred them: for they saw but too well what Buckle afterward stated, that better systems of internal communication bring in new ideas. So bad was their government, in all its practical details, that even Austria remonstrated, and Metternich complained, "The Papal Government cannot govern."

Last of all came, at the southern end of the peninsula, the Kingdom of Naples, or, as it was known after the Peace of Vienna, the Kingdom of the Two Sicilies. In no part of Europe was the whole life of the people so degraded. The Roman states were possibly more wretchedly administered, but the popes who ruled them had been, since the Renaissance period, at least outwardly decent. Not so the Bourbons who ruled at Naples. Throughout their entire dominion crime was rampant and murder almost as easy and carelessly treated as it is to-day in many of the states of our American Republic. The ignorance of the country was beyond that of any other which called itself civilized, save Russia. The court was the lowest, as regarded morality, in Europe; the palace, under the lead of the Hapsburg Queen Mary Caroline, hardly better than a brothel; the vileness of the Neapolitan populace proverbial.

The same city mobs which had committed every sort of cruelty, a few years before, in the name of liberty, had, at the return of the Bourbons, with the connivance of the Queen and under the lead of the Cardinal-Archbishop Ruffo, committed even worse crimes in the name of religion. Noble and thoughtful men, here and there in Naples, as in every part of Italy, strove to better this condition of things, but, by doing so, immediately fell under the ban of the court, lost all chance of promotion, and were fortunate if they escaped imprisonment or even death. On the other hand, spendthrifts and rakes, being considered not likely to conspire against the government, received the honors. The Neapolitan Bourbons also, like the popes, discouraged all public improvements of a sort likely to promote the circulation of ideas; and, several years after the middle of the nineteenth century, when Great Britain and Northern Europe generally were already enjoying extensive railway systems, there was hardly a mile of railway in the whole peninsula south of Genoa.[1]

To maintain this state of things, popular education was, throughout Italy, systematically discouraged. In Naples and Rome there was virtually no provision for the education of the people at large, and even in Turin, the capital of the most enlightened of all the Italian states, Piedmont, there were, as late as 1846, only fifteen hundred children in the public schools, in which to-day there are over thirty thousand. How dense popular ignorance thus became may be judged from an official report published as late as 1873, with a careful map giving the percentages of popular education in all parts of Italy. In the most enlightened regions the number of those who could neither read nor write was from forty to fifty per cent, but, in the greater portion of the country the number of illiterates far exceeded this, until, in the States of the Pope, it reached from seventy-five to eighty-five per cent, and, in Naples and Sicily, above eighty-five per cent.

[1] The statement regarding railways is based upon observations made in Italy by the present writer in 1856, when things were little if any better. For the character of the Italian governments at the outbreak of the French Revolution and afterward, see Sorel, *L'Europe et la Révolution Française,* vol. i, livre iii, chap. iv; and especially, for the Neapolitan Court, see pp. 386 and following. For the cruelties during the reaction, see Colletta, book v, chap. i, and book viii, chap. i, and especially Sorel as above, vol. v, pp. 421 and following. Also Lemmi, *Le Origini del Risorgimento Italiano.*

Such was the intellectual condition of the people after their education had been cared for by the Church during nearly two thousand years.[1]

The higher education had been reduced by the same influences as nearly to nothing as public opinion would permit. The warning of Kaiser Franz to the Pavia professors was enforced to the letter. The Jesuits, who had been expelled by Clement XIV, and by various sovereigns of Europe, half a century before, were, in 1814, readmitted by Pius VII, and speedily secured control of higher schools and universities. These institutions had been among the greatest glories of Italy. They had, indeed, been interfered with by the Church, at former periods, in various ways, notably in the days when Galileo tried to teach astronomy and physics at Pisa and Florence. Under control of local governments not especially in fear of the Church or of revolution, there was then some liberty. But all higher teaching was now more and more alloyed with Jesuitism and directed by the bishops and the Vatican. Sundry studies—Latin, mathematics, scraps of Greek, a little rhetoric, and concoctions of a suitable philosophy—were taught with skill. Manners also were attended to: as late as 1883, an Italian marquis at Milan informed the present writer that he sent his sons to the Jesuits "because they teach a young man how to enter a room." But studies which taught men to think, and, above all, history, political economy,

---

[1] For the condition of general education in Italy before the establishment of the Italian Kingdom, see *L'Italia Economica*, vol. ii (Tavole), Rome, 1873,—map entitled "Numero degli Analfabeti." For various striking facts showing the studied neglect of education in the period before Cavour came, see F. X. Kraus, in *Weltgeschichte in Karacterbildern* (Cavour), Mainz, 1902, final chapters. For very interesting comparisons between the educational system above referred to and that of the present time, see King and Okey, *Italy To-day*, p. 234 (London, 1901). For exact statements regarding education in Turin in 1905–06, I am indebted to Professor Dr. Peroni, of the university in that city, formerly a Member of Parliament.

and the like, were reduced to nothing. History, indeed, was apparently taught, but it was absurdly and comically distorted to meet the needs of theology and ecclesiasticism. Research in science, in spite of the great achievements in this field by Italians, was more and more discouraged, and the reading of Dante and other great writers who might suggest ideas of Italian nationality was, in many places, forbidden.

In the Kingdom of Naples all this was at the worst. Among the multitude of repressive measures, King Ferdinand II issued, in October, 1849, two edicts relating to education: the first required all who sought to be masters in teaching any science to undergo an examination in the Greater Catechism and to answer questions in the presence of the royal theological faculty on the relation of Christian doctrine, as taught in the Catechism, to the science which they proposed to teach.

A month later came another edict on the qualifications of students. In Naples and in each provincial city was established a commission "made up of four priests and a commissary of police" who should see to it that all students take satisfactory religious instruction. Students not conforming were to be taken back to their homes by the police, and all directors and masters neglecting to put the rule in force were to be excluded from the schools. The university continued to exist and strong men occasionally arose in it, but, as a rule, its best professors were humiliated, and finally, for utterances which, in these days, would be thought harmless, imprisoned or set at work in the chain-gang. To keep out the higher thought and scholarship, there was issued a Neapolitan edition of the Roman *Index*.

In Tuscany things were better; for in that state lingered traditions of culture which could not be put down by papal fulminations or even by Austrian armies.

In the Papal States the repression of thought was carried out logically. At the University of Bologna, once a great centre of enlightenment, the dangers of research or publication of thought were warded off most carefully: any book, before it could be printed, must run the gauntlet of no less than seven censorships; it must have the approval, first of the literary censor, secondly of the ecclesiastical censor, thirdly of the political censor, fourthly of the Inquisition, fifthly of the archbishop, sixthly of the police, and seventhly a second verification by the Inquisition.[1]

Rome, too, as the spiritual centre of Italy and of the world, continued to issue the *Index*, which forbade the reading of nearly all books which represented any triumph of modern thought, and among them those of Galileo, supporting the movement of the earth around the sun, and of Grotius, supporting arbitration. Even as late as the latter half of the eighteenth century, when Beccaria, a deeply religious churchman, wrote his great work *On Crimes and Punishments*, reasonable and mild to a fault, but taking ground against torture in procedure and penalty, that, too, was placed upon the *Index* of books forbidden to Christians, and to this decision infallibility was guaranteed by a Bull signed by the reigning pontiff. As regarded the Italian people at large, most things which reminded them of anything higher than futilities seemed forbidden. Typical was the fact that, when the opera "I Puritani" was given, the word "loyalty" was substituted for the word "liberty," and

[1] For striking examples of this debasement of higher education in Italy, see F. X. Kraus, a Catholic author, as above, citing especially Minghetti's *Memoirs*. A special Neapolitan *Index*, of which a copy is in the Cornell library, was published at Naples, in 1853. For the system repressing publication at Bologna, see Minghetti, cited in Kraus, *Weltgeschichte in Karacterbildern* (Cavour), p. 18. For copies of Edicts of King Ferdinand II of Naples, 1840, requiring instructors and pupils to be examined on the Catechism by four priests and a policeman, see Zini, *Storia d'Italia*, vol. ii, pt. i, pp. 164–166.

a singer who happened to forget this was imprisoned. The word "Italy" was as much hated as the word "liberty"—school children were at times punished for using it, and the word "Ausonia" was frequently substituted for it.

Nor was this all. The action of the various governments was not merely negative but positive. Patriotism and even the principles of morality underlying it were to be extirpated. For this purpose there were prepared political catechisms, and these were taught in the schools in the name of religion. One of these, issued from Milan, in 1834, by the Austrian government, entitled *Duties of Subjects toward their Sovereign,* contained things like the following:—

"Question: How should subjects behave toward their sovereign?"

"Answer: Subjects should behave like faithful slaves (*servi*) toward their master."

"Question: Why should subjects behave like slaves (*servi*)?"

"Answer: Because the sovereign is their master and has power both over their possessions and over their lives."

"Question: How does God punish soldiers who forsake their lawful sovereign?"

"Answer: By sickness, want, and eternal damnation." [1]

Most famous of all these catechisms was that prepared by Monaldo Leopardi—father of the poet-patriot who afterward wrought so powerfully for free thought in Italy. This catechism was enforced especially in the Kingdom of Naples, being republished by Archbishop Apuzzo of Sorrento, the tutor chosen by King Ferdinand II for his successor Francis II, better known as "King Bombino." The Neapolitan edition was entitled, *A*

---

[1] See Probyn, *History of Italy from 1815 to 1890,* p. 46, and F. X. Kraus, in the *Weltgeschichte in Karacterbildern,* as above.

Philosophical Catechism addressed to Princes, Bishops, Magistrates, Teachers of Youth, and to all Men of Good Will, and it remains one of the most precious monuments of the counter-revolutionary reaction. Its main effort was nothing less than an attempt to root out from the mind of a whole people all that the modern world knows as patriotism, right reason, justice, and civic morality.

The first chapter is entitled "Philosophy," and, after a diatribe against modern philosophers in general, it winds up with the following touching question by "The Disciple": "Do all such persons wear beards and moustaches?"—to which "The Master" answers that, while wearing beard and moustache is not necessarily evil, it is to be regarded with suspicion.

The third chapter is entitled, "Liberty." The first part of the dialogue runs as follows:—

"Disciple: Is it true that all men are born free?"

"Master: It is not true, and this lie regarding liberty is only one more piece of deceit that modern philosophers use in order to seduce people and upset the world."

The fifth chapter is devoted to "The Rights of Man," and in it occurs the following:—

"Disciple: Is it true that the supreme power resides in the people?"

"Master: It is not true. It would be absurd to affirm that by the disposition of Nature the people can control or moderate themselves."

The disciple then asks: "May it not be, as the liberal philosophers say, that the sovereignty resides in the people but may be exercised through their representatives?"

The master shows that this idea is utterly delusive, that the people cannot delegate a power which they have not.

Chapter seven treats of the constitution, and, in its defiance of political morality, is, perhaps, the boldest in the book. It is clear that, in some of the answers to the

questions of the disciple, the archbishop was not unmindful of the famous perjuries of various kings of
Naples, and, especially, of his royal master, in swearing
to constitutions and then openly violating them, for during the dialogue occur the following questions and answers:—

"Disciple: Can the people establish the fundamental
laws of the State?"

"Master: They cannot, because the constitution and
fundamental laws of a state are a limitation of sovereignty, and sovereignty cannot receive any bounds or
measures except from itself."

"Disciple: But, if the people, in the act of choosing the
sovereign, have imposed upon him conditions and agreements, are not these conditions and agreements the constitution and fundamental law of the State?"

"Master: They are not so, because the people, which
was made for submission and not for command, cannot
impose any law upon that sovereignty: it receives its
power not from the people but from God."

"Disciple: Is not a prince, who, in assuming the sovereignty of a state, has accepted and sanctioned the
constitution or fundamental law of that state and has
promised and sworn to observe it, obliged to maintain
his promise and to observe that constitution and that
law?"

"Master: He is obliged to observe it in so far as it
does not infringe the foundations of sovereignty, and
in so far as it is not opposed to the universal good
of the state."

"Disciple: Who, then, is to judge when a constitution
infringes on the rights of the sovereignty or injures the
people?"

"Master: The sovereign has to judge, because in him
exists the supreme power established by God in the
state."

Chapter eight is devoted to "Government," and begins as follows:—

"Disciple: What is the best of all governments for a state?"

"Master: The best government for any state is that under which it is at the present moment legitimately ruled."

"Disciple: But, considering things in the abstract, what is the best of all governments?"

"Master: Hereditary monarchy, that is to say, that in which the sovereignty resides in the monarch alone and passes from him to his descendant."

Chapter nine is devoted to "Legitimacy," but, though it is, in some respects, the most subtle of the book, it is one of the most inconclusive. The archbishop evidently labors under difficulties. In view of the fact that the Church had sanctioned the usurpation of Napoleon in France, against the Bourbons, and of other rulers of the Napoleonic period, elsewhere, against the old ruling houses, nothing was possible here save to raise a cloud and escape in it.

But the charge of obscurity cannot be brought against the tenth chapter, which is entitled "Revolution." The archbishop adopts a view as clear as the day and shows the courage of his convictions. Being asked by the disciple whether the people have not the right to resist "when the prince loads his subjects with enormous taxes and wastes the treasure of the state," the master answers: "The people have not the right to judge regarding the needs and expenses of the monarchy; the Holy Spirit, by the mouth of St. Paul declares to the people, 'Pay tribute,' but does not declare to the people, 'Examine the accounts of the king.'"

After arguments in this strain through thirteen chapters, the disciple says, "Then, according to your judgment, for the good of a state it would be well to favor ignorance rather than education?'' to which the master, after various platitudes, answers as follows:—

"I have already said to you that it is necessary to follow a middle course. . . . For servants and ploughmen, a proper moderation consists in knowing the catechism and prayers to be said aloud, and nothing more; in other classes, moderation consists in knowing how to read, write and cast accounts a little, and nothing more; for other classes, moderation consists in studying that which regards the proper profession of each,'' etc.

Reading this, one ceases to wonder that the official map, issued shortly after this system had ended, showed that, throughout the whole extent of the combined kingdom of Naples and Sicily, the proportion of persons unable to read or write was over eighty-five in every hundred.

Later occurs an especially curious question:

"Disciple: Tell me, do you believe that the newly invented savings-banks are the carnal brothers of general instruction, and that philosophy is preparing, by means of them, to accomplish the diffusion of property and goods?''

"Master: Although few suspect it as yet, I am absolutely certain of it.''

The fourteenth chapter is entitled "Our Country,'' and it reveals a desperate effort to root out from the Italian mind everything like patriotism.

The master tells his disciple that, if similar degrees of the thermometer make men fellow-citizens, then the Romans and the Tartars are of the same country; that, as to similarity of language, the people at the two ends of Italy hardly understand one another, and that, if similarity of appellation gives fellow-citizenship, and all those are fellow-citizens who are called Italians,—

"Then, because you are called Bartholomew, you are a fellow-citizen of all the Bartholomews throughout the world."

The book is at times witty and shrewd, and has in it, here and there, suggestions which look like wisdom. There is in it much historical allusion, but, of course, as in most cases where ecclesiastics write for the supposed benefit of religion, the author manipulates history to suit his necessities.

As to Italian independence, he insists that in three-quarters of Italy, Italian independence is already established, and that those who deny it are, to use his own words, "simpletons who are looking round for their hats when their hats are upon their heads." He defends the rights of Austria in Lombardy and Venice as sacrosanct, and winds up by declaring that "the independence of Italy . . . is simply a cabalistic phrase, used by thieves and scoundrels."

In this work culminated an effort long and earnest. To its earlier stage belongs the *"History of France for the Use of Youth, with maps, A. M. D. G.,"* published to uphold the French Bourbons, in 1820 and 1821, by the Jesuit Father Loriquet. Father Loriquet's effort had been simply to efface all knowledge of the Napoleonic Empire from the French mind, and his history, therefore, made Louis XVII the immediate successor of Louis XVI, and Louis XVIII the immediate successor of Louis XVII, virtually leaving out Napoleon as ruler, mentioning him as little as possible and always under the name "Bonaparte."

Exquisitely naïve, also, was this Jesuit historian's attempt to discredit "Bonaparte" by falsified history. Perhaps of all the innumerable Jesuit attempts to manufacture history to suit ecclesiastical purposes, the most comical is the account given by Father Loriquet of the Battle of Waterloo. In the crisis of the battle, which the world knows by heart, he represents the Old Guard as a mass of madmen, firing upon one another while the British look upon them with horror.

The final effort of Archbishop Apuzzo to save the Neapolitan Bourbons turned out to be as futile as the effort of Father Loriquet to save the French Bourbons. Each book became a laughing-stock and was suppressed as far as possible by the reactionary governments in whose supposed interest it was written. Like some similar attempts in our own day to further ecclesiastical interests, each recoiled fatally upon those who prepared it.[1]

To maintain the system thus supported, stood Austria, the agent of the Holy Alliance, and, whenever there seemed special danger of any movement for independence or constitutional government, international congresses were called, as at Troppau in 1820, at Laybach in 1821, at Verona in 1822; and the Bourbons in France showed their sympathy by sending an army to put down constitutional government in Spain.

[1] The original of the *Catechismo Filosofico* was written by Monaldo Leopardi, the reactionary father of the liberal philosopher, Giacomo Leopardi, and published in 1832, and again in 1837. A careful comparison of these two early editions with the reprint above referred to, published at Naples in 1861 by the liberal enemies of the Bourbons, shows that they are substantially alike. It is of this later edition that I have a copy, for which I am indebted to the Reverend Father Casoli, of Sorrento. For an opportunity to examine the earlier editions of the book and various works bearing upon them, I am indebted to H. N. Gay, Esq., now residing at Rome. The work is ascribed by various leading writers on Italian history, such as Montarolo in his *Opere Anonime*, 1884, p. 12, King, in his *Italian Unity*, vol. i, p. 367, Gladstone and others, to Apuzzo, as they evidently had known only the Neapolitan edition.

For a more extended presentation of the questions and answers of this catechism, see a paper entitled "A Catechism of the Revolutionary Reaction," by the present writer, in the Proceedings of the American Historical Association, vol. iv, p. 69.

A copy of the famous *History of France*, by Father Loriquet, published at Lyons, 1820–21, may be found in the library of Cornell University. For his amazing account of the battle of Waterloo, see vol. ii, p. 374.

22

Was any concession to more reasonable ideas made in any Italian state, large or small, Metternich's emissaries were speedily upon the spot, using bribes, threats, or pressure. Austrian, Papal, or Neapolitan spies swarmed in churches, cafés, and throughout private society; they wrought steadily, at the post-office and in the confessional, to discover every man's political ideas. No family so high or so low as to be exempt from police interference. The slightest suspicion led to arrest, the pettiest utterances against despotic methods led to the chain-gang or to long, solitary imprisonment, and anything like effective resistance brought the best and bravest to the scaffold.

Such was the system which the great powers, assembled at Vienna,—Great Britain now and then halting and, at last, ashamed,—had developed in the most beautiful territory and for the most gifted people in the world. But one thing European rulers had left out of their calculations,—the great body of thoughtful and patriotic Italian men and women. Over all this misery and shame they brooded in every city and hamlet, in castles, in shops, in professors' chairs,—even in sacristies. To them Dante, Michael Angelo, and the long line of their inspired countrymen had spoken. More and more these men and women dreamed of independence, of unity, of liberty. These were, indeed, troubled dreams, always fitful, often absurd, sometimes criminal, but they were unceasing and foreshadowed much.

But all this the men who profited, or supposed they profited, by the existing state of things, could not or would not see or hear. When have men profiting by unreason and wrong, ever, in any country, really seen their own true interests? The ruling classes in Italy were as blind to their own interests, at the beginning of the nineteenth century, as were sundry great American political leaders regarding slavery, in the middle of the same century, and as are sundry great American financial leaders in our own time. Both those and these have been and are really the most dangerous fomenters of revolution, sure to bring disaster upon their country and punishment upon themselves and their children.

The first main effort to realize something better in the Italy of that period was seen at Naples in 1820. The Bourbon king, Ferdinand I, was finally forced to grant a constitution, and this he again and again swore to maintain. Pathetic, at the time, were his profuse public thanks to God for permitting him to aid so great and good an action,—and to the leading revolutionists for showing him his duty. Especially dramatic was his oath in the chapel of his palace, when, with tears in his eyes, he, in the presence of a great assembly, swore to maintain the constitution and invoked the curse of Heaven upon his head if his oath should be broken.

The Holy Alliance took up the matter at once, and the three sovereigns of Austria, Prussia, and Russia wrote letters to King Ferdinand, identical in character, pointing out his duty to violate this oath. A little later he went to meet these advisers at Laybach, there took back his oath, thence returned heralded by an Austrian army, abolished the constitution, and sent to dungeons, galleys, and scaffolds the men to whom he had rendered such profuse thanks for advocating it.[1]

In the next year came a revolution at the other end of Italy, in Piedmont. Its population was far more sound and moral than that of Naples; its rulers, of the House of Savoy, far higher in character than the Bourbons. Deeply religious, even bigoted, many of them had been. Against their fearful persecution of the Waldenses, Milton had testified, nearly two hundred years before,

---

[1] For a careful account of this period by a Catholic historian, see Cantù, *Histoire des Italiens*, tome xi, livre 17. See also Probyn, as above, p. 26.

in verses that have echoed through human hearts from his day to ours. The governmental creed of these rulers was absolutism; but, at least, they were brave and true, and this was destined to count for much—indeed, for everything—in the history which followed.[1]

The demand of the Piedmontese revolution was for a constitution, but against this the Holy Alliance was so firmly set that, feeling unable to grapple with the difficulty, the King, Victor Emmanuel I, abdicated, giving over the succession to his brother, Charles Felix. As this brother was living in retirement at Modena, the regency was given to his nephew and heir-presumptive, Charles Albert, who, after much wavering, reluctantly promised a constitution. Against this constitution, Austria and the Alliance took ground at once: the regent's uncle, King Charles Felix, was made to repudiate the concessions of the young regent, to banish him to Tuscany with bitter reproach and insult, and at least to pretend to favor an intrigue for transferring the right of succession to the vilest and most despotic branch of the family, that of the murderer Duke Francis of Modena.

Austria now pursued at Turin the same policy as at Naples. She sent an army which supported Charles Felix in annulling the constitution, in restoring absolutism, in sending constitutionalists to dungeons and scaffolds.[2]

These examples served as powerful deterrents to every open effort for liberty, and there now came ten years of slumber, with dreams more feverish than before. No

---

[1] The poem referred to is Milton's sonnet "On the Late Massacre in Piedmont," beginning with the words:

"Avenge, O Lord, thy slaughtered saints, whose bones
Lie scattered on the Alpine mountains cold."

[2] For the Piedmontese Revolution, see Santa Rosa, Costa de Beauregard, and Masi; but for an English-speaking student there is ample information, admirably presented, in W. R. Thayer, *Dawn of Italian Independence*, 1893, vol. i, chap. vi.

great demonstrations took place, but everywhere was seen and felt an active and even poisonous ferment of liberty. An early symptom of this was the secret society of the Charcoal-Burners: the *Carbonari*. With ceremonies somewhat resembling those of Masonry and with vows against tyranny, this society spread throughout all the Italian-speaking peoples, and embraced vast numbers of devotees of freedom, from the highest classes to the lowest. Even Louis Bonaparte, who afterward became Napoleon III, was, in his youth, one of those who swore fidelity to it. Its fanaticism knew no limit; outrages and assassinations were everywhere, and this provoked successive rulers at Naples and elsewhere to oppose it with every sort of cruelty. Torture was freely used to detect it, and, in the Austro-Italian dominions, any connection with it was punished by death. Every expedient was tried, and a rival organization, in behalf of absolutism, the *Sanfedisti*, with vows and secret ceremonies equally fanatical, was created to ferret it out and fight it. The natural result followed. Absolutism pointed to these societies as its justification, and by their excesses general European public opinion was first made cool toward Italian liberty and, finally, hostile. These associations rapidly deteriorated and, in various regions, became banditti, glorying in outrage and murder, as do "the gangs" in some of our great American cities of to-day. Typical was one of these bands—the *Decisi*—whose leader, an unfrocked priest, being brought to trial and asked how many persons he had himself murdered, answered, "Who knows? Sixty or seventy, perhaps." [1]

Supported by the public opinion thus caused, Austria and her subordinate despotisms went further. Great numbers of thoughtful and serious men were seized and con-

[1] On the Carbonari see Johnston, *The Napoleonic Empire in Southern Italy and the Rise of the Carbonari*, London, 1904. An example of a Carbonari discourse may be found in the Appendix, p. 153.

demned, among them the heads of some of the most eminent Italian families at Milan, who were arrested and dragged to Austrian dungeons or scaffolds. Notable was the case of Silvio Pellico, a gentle, religious soul, known widely and favorably as a man of letters. Arrested at Venice for hostilities of a very mild, scholarly sort, he was kept, for nearly twenty years in an Austrian dungeon, during part of the time chained to a fellow-prisoner who was suffering from a repulsive disease. His final account of his prison life, entitled *My Prisons,* with his simple recitals of sufferings and consolations, ran through Christendom, touching all hearts and inflaming all with a hatred of Austrian tyranny. Throughout Italy matters grew worse and worse, until even the most determined reactionaries, largely responsible by their theories or their acts for this state of things, found it necessary to express their horror and to throw blame on others. Chateaubriand, committed though he was to Bourbon despotism and the Church,—Metternich, yet more devoted to Hapsburg despotism and reaction,— and even Joseph de Maistre, hating liberty and devoted to the most extreme theories of papal authority, denounced governments responsible for this cruelty and folly.[1]

And yet the surface of things was charming: as free from forebodings as was the surface of society in the American Republic in 1860, when drifting toward the abyss of Civil War which swallowed over half a million

---

[1] For an account of the severities exercised in Northern Italy toward the Carbonari, see *An Epoch of my Life: Memoirs of Count John Arrivabene,* London, 1862. For pictures of the cruel struggle in Southern Italy, see Settembrini, *Ricordanze della mia Vita,* Napoli, 1886. As to the easygoing life of the time, see Silvagni, *La Corte e la Società Romana nei Secoli XVIII e XIX,* English translation by MacLaughlin. For the better side of Italian scientific and literary development under the old régime in Italy, see Cantù, *Histoire des Italiens,* vols. x, xi, xii; also, for a very interesting short statement, see H. D. Sedgwick, *Short History of Italy,* Boston, 1905, chaps. xxxii and xxxiii.

of the best lives our country had to give. Italy at large was immoral, superstitious, and happy. From the whole world pleasure-seekers were attracted by its "fatal gift of beauty," scholars by its monuments of former greatness, devotees by its pomps and ceremonies at the capital of Christendom.

II

BUT beneath this surface the political disease grew more and more virulent. In 1830 broke out the second stage of revolution in France, and in three days the French Bourbon monarchy was lost forever. Revolutions in Italy rapidly followed. The murderer, Duke Francis IV, was soon driven out of Modena; Maria Louisa, the worthless widow of Napoleon, fled from her Duchy of Parma; a provisional government declared the Pope's temporal power ended in Bologna; rebellion was seething in Naples; and, most ominous of all, Charles Albert, with his tendencies to constitutionalism, succeeded to the throne in Piedmont.

Again came intervention by Austria. Every effort for freedom was suppressed, every worthless Italian sovereign was replaced; constitutionalists were again sent to dungeons and scaffolds. More than this, France, under pretext of jealousy of Austria, sent troops to Ancona, in the Papal States, and thus began a policy of French intervention to match Austrian intervention,—the policy of supplying "bayonets for the popes to sit upon." Beyond supplying this doubtful seat, the powers could really do nothing. Austria and France, whatever their cruelties and absurdities might be, had at least developed and observed decent rules in ordinary administration. Though they hanged lovers of liberty, they did not systematically foster sloth, poverty, and knavery; but the various governments throughout Italy, with the exception of those in Piedmont and Tuscany, seemed utterly given over to vicious administration, and among the worst, in this respect, was the Papal Kingdom. Under all save

344

a few of the greatest popes it had been, and continued to be, a scandal to Christendom. All really important offices were filled by cardinals and Monsignori, and, while a few of these, like Consalvi, Lambruschini, and Antonelli, were statesmen, the vast majority were sluggish reactionaries. Against this state of things, as leading to revolution, Austria and France protested again and again; but all to no purpose; the Vatican would go on after the old, bad way, and, finally, it received its reward.

Still another government which gave constant trouble to the great powers banded against constitutional freedom, was Piedmont. Its new king, Charles Albert, was, indeed, strongly religious and inclined to the old ways, but more and more it was seen that he hated foreign intervention and that, to put an end to it, he might accept the aid of constitutionalists; but Austrian pressure was put upon him and, to all appearance, his patriotism ended.

So began a new period of eighteen years, hardly less sluggish than the old,—its hero Mazzini. Hardly out of his boyhood, he launched every sort of brilliant and cogent attack against the oppressors of his country. Imprisoned in the fortress of Savona, he pondered over the great problem even more deeply, and, on his release, wrote a letter to King Charles Albert, urging him to head the movement for independence and liberty. This letter became a vast force in arousing a national spirit. Private letters and published articles rapidly followed from his pen, each a powerful blow at tyranny. In 1831 he created a new weapon. He had entered fully into the work of the Carbonari, had risked his life with them again and again, but having now ceased to believe in their system he founded the society of "Young Italy."

His activity seemed preternatural. He appeared to be in all parts of Europe at once, and did his work under every sort of disguise and stratagem. His power over the Italian youth was amazing: obedient to his call they rose in cities, villages, regiments, everywhere,—going to death joyfully. ⸔ From London, where, after 1837, he made his headquarters, he inspired every kind of Italian conspiracy and revolt; but gradually it dawned upon thinking friends of Italy everywhere that these costly sacrifices of the most precious lives were not adequately repaid. From a practical point of view they availed little. His right to sit in his English retreat and send the flower of the Italian youth to be shot or hanged began to be widely questioned. His ideal was an Italian republic, but there were so few republicans! Republican government to him meant freedom, but even the simplest students of history could remember that the old Roman republic, and every one of the mediæval Italian republics, had resulted in the tyranny of illiterate mobs, always followed by the tyranny of single despots as a lesser evil. Men had learned the truth that a single despot can be made in some degree responsible to public opinion, but that a mob cannot.

The uprisings inspired by Mazzini, notably that of the Bandiera brothers, were mercilessly trodden down in blood. Nor did more quiet efforts fare better. Tuscany tried to give moderate freedom of the press, but Austria intervened and forced the Grand Duke to appoint ministers who ended it.

Yet forces were at work, more powerful by far than Austria and the Holy Alliance. Political activity being checked, genius and talent had long been mainly directed to literature, and the spectacle of Italy in the hands of her oppressors made this literature patriotic. There had come the poetry of Alfieri, Niccolini, Rossetti, and Giusti; the philosophy of Rosmini; the prison reminiscences of Silvio Pellico; the romances of D'Azeglio, Guerrazzi, and, above all, the *Promessi Sposi* of Manzoni, the most perfect historical novel ever written. These were not all revolutionary by intention; some, like the writings of Pellico and Manzoni, were deeply and pathetically religious, even inculcating submission to wrong; but all served to create Italian ideals, to stimulate Italian patriotism, and to give more and more life to the idea so hated by Austria and the Holy Alliance,—the idea of Italy as a *nation*.

The patriotic thought, thus gradually evolved as a vast elemental force, was now brought to bear upon events by three great books.

First of these was the *Moral and Civil Primacy of the Italians,* by Vincenzo Gioberti. This was a glorification of Italy as a nation, displaying eloquently her greatness in the past and the possibility of her greatness in the future, and urging a confederation of the existing Italian states, with the Pope as perpetual president, and the King of Piedmont as the "Sword" of Italy's regeneration. Though in three large volumes, it was read and pondered by every thinking Italian, man or woman.

Closely following this was a treatise of a very different sort, by Cesare Balbo, entitled *The Hopes of Italy.* Though hardly more than a pamphlet, and though it gave up the idea of an Italian kingdom as chimerical, it pictured constitutional liberty and Italian independence with a clearness and strength which brought conviction to all patriotic hearts. Statesmanlike was its suggestion that Austria might find compensation on the lower Danube.

The third of these works was a small treatise by Massimo d'Azeglio, entitled, *The Latest Cases in the Romagna.* Of all the three writers d'Azeglio was the most fascinating as a personality: a genius in painting and poetical fiction, a statesman who had traveled quietly through various governments of Italy and who reported what he saw with amazing lucidity and force. The latest cruelties of the papal subordinates in suppressing the uprisings in the Romagna had aroused him, and he made the world see and understand them. His work was not at all declamatory or hysterical; perhaps its most striking feature was its self-control; it was plain, simple, straightforward, and clear as crystal, but with a quiet and restrained eloquence which carried all before it.

Others writers of genius or talent followed these,— among them, Durando, Capponi, and their compeers,— each aiding to undermine the whole existing régime.

The votaries of science also wrought for the same ideals. The Science Congress at Genoa, in 1846, inevitably discussed Italian independence, freedom, and progress. The Agricultural Congress at Casale, in 1847, took the same direction, and to it came a letter from King Charles Albert which set all hearts throbbing with patriotic emotion. For it contained these words: "If Providence sends us a war for Italian independence, I will mount my horse with my sons and will place myself at the head of my army. . . . What a glorious day will be that in which we can raise the cry of war for the independence of Italy!"

Meantime, in 1846, an event of vast importance had occurred. There had come to the papal throne Pius IX. His nature was deeply religious, kindly, given to charitable effort, and his aversion to cruelty was, doubtless, a main cause of his desire to break away from the methods of his predecessors. His manner was most winning and he held wonderful sway over devout imaginations, for in great religious functions and ceremonies he was supremely impressive, and his blessing, chanted forth from the balcony of St. Peter's, with his dramatic action in bestowing it, appealed to the deepest feelings even of those who differed most from him. But, as a sovereign, he was the last of men to carry out Gioberti's great programme,—to preside over an Italian confederation, or, indeed, to govern his own states. As a statesman he failed utterly,—beaten, in all attempts at reform, by the *Monsignori,* thwarted in all his good intentions by Jesuits and other intriguers, more or less religious. The times called for a Hildebrand, or an Innocent III, or a Sixtus V, and, instead of any one of these, there had come this kindly, handsome bishop, vacillating, fitful, superstitious, dreaded most by those who loved him best.

At first he mildly opposed Austria and appointed a quasi-constitutional ministry, but he could not rise above the old tradition, and in this new ministry there were no laymen.

In January, 1848, a new constitutional movement began throughout Italy. Revolution broke out in Sicily, and Ferdinand II granted a constitution. This movement extended rapidly to all parts of Europe. The Grand Duke of Tuscany promised a constitution, the Pope showed an intention to grant reforms, and even called a new ministry in which, for a wonder, there were three laymen. An occurrence at one of the early meetings of this ministry threw a curious light on the character of Pope Pius. Presiding over this body, his eye happened to light upon the comet then appearing in the Roman sky. Rushing to the window and opening it, he fell on his knees and called on his ministers—among them such men as Mezzofanti and Marco Minghetti—to kneel also and to implore the Almighty to turn away the calamities of which the comet was the forerunner. The pontiff might well be pardoned this superstition, for everywhere throughout Europe were signs of coming political catastrophes. Under popular pressure various reforms were granted in Piedmont, among them more liberty to the press,—a condition of things under which the Piedmontese could at last discuss public questions to some purpose.[1]

---

[1] For Pope Pius's fear of the comet, see Minghetti's *Miei Ricordi,* vol. i,

And now Europe begins to hear of Cavour. While as writer in magazines and reviews he had long been known and prized by many statesmen and economists in Italy, and by a few thinkers in England and France, Europe and the people at large in Italy as yet knew him not. But it happened that, just at this time, Genoa, true to its old republican traditions though incorporated into the Kingdom of Piedmont, began to be restive and to demand loudly various reforms of a petty sort,—among these, the banishment of the Jesuits and the creation of a national guard. This subject being brought up for discussion in a meeting of publicists and journalists at Turin, Cavour rises and compresses the needs of Piedmont and of Italy into a single sentence. Casting aside all petty demands for changes in detail, he insists that the king be asked "to transfer the discussion from the perilous arena of irregular commotions to the arena of legal, pacific, solemn deliberation." The audience and the country, thinking upon this utterance, soon recognized its demand for a constitution, with a free parliament, as wholly to the purpose,—as the solution of the first great Italian problem,—and during the great discussions which followed in the press Cavour led triumphantly. His advice was at last followed, and, on February 7, 1848, King Charles Albert promised a constitution which, a month later, took shape in a royal statute, the "Statuto." Thus began a great new epoch in which Cavour was to be the leader, and, to this day, the anniversary of this grant is celebrated throughout Italy as the date most significant for her Independence, Unity, and Freedom since the Fall of the Roman Empire.

Camillo Benso,—Count Cavour,—who now, in 1848, rose rapidly above Piedmont and Italy, attracting the

pp. 347, 348; and cf. also the *Deutsche Rundschau*, August, 1893, p. 210. The statement regarding his dramatic power in the great ceremonies at St. Peter's is based upon the personal recollections of the present writer.

attention of all Europe, had been born in 1810, under the Napoleonic supremacy. Curiously connecting him with that period was his baptism, when Camillo Borghese, Napoleon's brother-in-law and representative in Piedmont, consented to be the child's god-father and to give him his name.

The family of the young count was ancient and honorable, his father a marquis in high public employ and a sympathizer with the old régime; his mother, though a Catholic, descended from Swiss Protestants. Of his near relatives, uncles, aunts, cousins, some were among the highest nobility of Paris and some among that body of liberal thinkers who gave distinction to Geneva. Among the former was the ducal family of Clermont-Tonnerre; among the latter, the De La Rives. Among his remoter kinsfolk were men eminent in science and in official life, some conservative, some radical, but all respected as patriotic thinkers: his constant intercourse with them, and their debates on current questions in which he joined, counted for much in his development, moral and intellectual.

As a second son, his rights to rank and fortune were greatly limited, and this fact evidently stirred him to exertion. At ten years of age he was entered at the military academy at Turin, and at sixteen was graduated with special distinction, receiving a lieutenancy of engineers, an honor rarely bestowed on one so young. An aristocrat in any evil sense he was not. Though never a demagogue in his utterances, his tendencies were, in the truest sense, democratic. Though made a page at the royal court at the age of fourteen, he so disliked court etiquette and made this feeling so evident, that he was soon discharged. His tastes were for mathematics, which, both then and in his after life, he pursued far, and also for history, political economy, and social science, and for the English language, as giving, at that time, one of the best keys to these. French he spoke with ease from his childhood, and English he came to speak, at a later period, with fluency, if not with elegance.

As an engineer he was assigned to various duties,—first at Genoa,—and, though devoted to mathematics and social science, he did his practical work thoroughly well. But now came trouble. It was the period of the lowest debasement of Italy, and the period also of the second French Revolution, in 1830, which relieved France forever from the elder Bourbons. Naturally he brooded over the iniquities and absurdities which he saw about him, jotted down his reflections from time to time, and let his thoughts be known; as a result he was banished to nominal duties in the mountain districts, and, finally, to virtual imprisonment in the Alpine fortress of Bard, where, during eight months, his companions were of the rudest.[1]

Returning from his captivity, he abandoned his military career, despite the bitter regret of his family. Charles Albert had just come to the throne of Piedmont, and, in view of his mysticism and vacillation, no chance of any public career for a man of liberal views was visible; indeed, the new king had already indicated his hostility to Cavour, declaring him the most dangerous man in the kingdom. Cavour therefore asked permission to take charge of one of the family estates, and became a farmer. At the beginning he was ignorant of the simplest rudiments of agriculture; but his power of thought and work now showed itself, and, before long, he attracted attention far and near by his success in this new profession. From the first, he applied scientific methods, but always under the control of that sound, strong common sense which afterward became so important a factor

---

[1] For very interesting details of Cavour's early life and for especially significant extracts from his note books on his reading, see Berti, *Il Conte Cavour avanti il 1848*, especially pp. 87 and following.

in his political and diplomatic activity. To the end of his life he cherished the love for farming thus begun, and, even in the midst of his most active political services afterward, he continued the steady improvement of agriculture, and thereby deserved well of his country.

But this was by no means all. His activity seemed boundless. While managing great estates and bringing under cultivation large districts hitherto worthless, he established manufactories, mills, a railway, a line of steamers on the Lago Maggiore, a bank at Turin, and much besides. For a wonder, his enterprises succeeded: nine men out of ten, taking up so many vocations, would have ruined themselves and all their friends; but in all this work his foresight, his insight, and, above all, his keen, strong common sense carried him through triumphantly. Though caring little for money, refusing, in one instance, a great bequest which he might have accepted most honorably, he accumulated in his various enterprises a large private fortune.

During seventeen years—the years between the resignation of his position in the army, in 1831, and the great revolutionary outbreak in Europe in 1848—he threw himself fully into this practical work. Political life there was none which he cared for: he was excluded from state service by the prejudices of the king, the aristocracy, and the clergy, but, most of all, by his own self-respect. His high rank, connections, and abilities made him eligible for the foremost offices of the monarchy, but an office-seeker he could not be; for office in itself, or for its emoluments, he cared nothing; for power as such he cared nothing; and this was his spirit to the last hour of his life; for office and power he cared only as a means of enforcing his ideas.

Despite his attention to work remote from political activity, he was constantly under grave and annoying suspicions, both from the government of his own country

23

and from that of Austria. In 1833 the Director General of Police at Milan issued instructions to public officials at the frontier, warning them to be on the watch against one Camillo di Cavour, who "in spite of his youth is already deeply corrupted in his political principles."

Still, even under the ban thus laid upon him, both by his own country and by its enemies, and in the midst of all this practical work so remote from politics, he had prophetic dreams. At this very time he wrote a letter to an intimate friend, in which he said, "I can assure you that I shall make my way. I own that I am enormously ambitious, and when I am minister I hope to justify my ambitions. In my dreams I see myself already minister of the Kingdom of Italy." And this was written when he was twenty-four, when a "Kingdom of Italy" seemed utterly impossible, and the very mention of it was treason.

Yet, during all those seventeen years, he was preparing himself for far higher service. In the intervals of business he made extended journeys and long stays in Switzerland, France, and England. Visiting Paris, he entered fully into the society of the foremost thinkers, writers, and statesmen, discussed current political problems with them, frequented the parliamentary bodies and studied closely their procedure, attended lectures by the foremost men of science at the Sorbonne and elsewhere, examined thoroughly farms, factories, mines, prisons,—every sort of man or place likely to give him knowledge of value to his country.

In England, also, he made vigorous studies, especially of parliamentary procedure, methods in agriculture, manufactures, and commerce, dealings with pauperism, crime, and every branch of national economy. He also devoted himself, early and late, to British history,—studying carefully, not only the dealings of living statesmen with large questions, but the struggle of Pitt with

Napoleon, of Chatham with the Bourbons, and even the
policy of Cromwell and the Stuarts in its relations to
British freedom and power.

Thus he absorbed ideas of Anglo-Saxon liberty, and
strengthened his faith in free government; in after
years this became of vast value to his country, but it
brought at first some obloquy, and, especially, the nickname of "My Lord Camillo." Though there was never
a nobleman who cared less for distinctions of rank, and
prized more highly eminence in character and attain-
ment and patriotic service, this nickname, for a time,
served well the purposes of knaves and fools: they called
him a "reactionary in disguise," caricatured him in a
pig-tailed wig, and, for a considerable period, made him
one of the most unpopular men in his country.

Returning home, he redoubled his efforts to improve
agriculture, manufactures, and commerce, and, what was
yet more important at that epoch, to promote discussion,
economic and political. To this end he founded an agricultural club and even a "whist club,"—mainly for the
purpose of bringing together thinking men,—published
articles in reviews, and, among these, studies on agriculture, pauperism, and, above all, in 1846, in the Paris
Revue Nouvelle, a masterly review of a book on railways
which in Piedmont had been forbidden. That was the
period when railway development on the continent was
beginning, and very slowly. Franz List, one of the most
gifted of political thinkers, who had urged it in Germany, had failed, and died impoverished and broken-
hearted. But Cavour was of sterner stuff; he aroused
thought throughout Europe, but especially in Italy, for
he dwelt upon the value of railway communication as an
agency in the conveyance, not merely of bales and boxes,
but of ideas. That which led various Italian princelings
and, above all, the Papal Government, to dread railways,
led him to promote them, for he recognized in them a

power not only for the introduction of better ideas but for the unification of his country.[1]

In the midst of all this work, which required an amazing activity, he found time to cultivate some beautiful friendships and to keep up correspondences which remain among the treasures of literature. His letters to the elder De La Rive, wise, witty, suggestive, are among these; but most striking perhaps of all is his correspondence with the Countess de Circourt. She was of Russian birth, married to a man of eminence in France, and, though she was a hopeless invalid, her *salon* at Paris was the centre of a large circle of eminent men of various nationalities, among whom was Cavour. With her he found time to discuss all sorts of subjects, grave and gay; and their letters, as given to the world by Count Nigra (in his early life one of Cavour's secretaries, since so distinguished as ambassador to France and to Austria, and, more recently, as president of the Italian delegation at the Peace Conference of The Hague), throw a beautiful light into the depths of Cavour's character.[2]

In December, 1847, he founded, at Turin, a newspaper, *The Resurrection,—Il Risorgimento,—*and he pressed into the service with him a majority of the leading thinkers of upper Italy, chief among them being Cesare Balbo, who had already done so much for his country with his famous treatise, *Delle Speranze d'Italia.*

As a writer, Cavour felt himself lacking much. He confessed that he had never had any adequate training in literature, and his writings certainly lacked the beauty which made so many of his contemporaries famous; but

[1] For a very striking passage regarding the early foresight of Cavour in promoting railways, and its effect upon Italian unity, see Zanichelli, introduction to *Gli Scritti del Conte di Cavour*, Bologna, 1892, p. 55.

[2] For the De Circourt correspondence, see the English translation by Butler, London, 1894.

his patriotism broke through all obstacles. His style, rough at times but always clear and forcible, held his readers; his knowledge of events and his experience among men convinced them, and his earnestness, rising at times into fervent eloquence, inspired them.[1]

At first he wrote mainly on large subjects, economical and social, of general value to his country; but more and more he turned to political questions, and was soon recognized as a leader. He was neither a demagogue nor a doctrinaire. He avoided revolution and revolutionary methods; but he believed in revolution when nothing short of it would do, and when it could be controlled by men of thought and knowledge. He believed in the steady development of better institutions rather than in vociferation, in open discussion rather than in conspiracy, and in right reason rather than fanaticism. He hated the despotism, not only of tyrants but of mobs, and he disbelieved hardly less profoundly in Carbonarism and the plots of Mazzini than in the methods of Francis of Austria and Ferdinand of Naples.

Opposed to him were extremists on both sides,—men calling themselves "Monarchists," who had ruined or were destined to ruin every monarch who trusted to them; and men calling themselves "Democrats," or "Republicans," who had brought to naught every effort in Europe for rational liberty. Revolution was to him the last remedy in the most dire extremity.

Therefore it was, as we have seen, that, when the revolutionary leaven of 1848 began working throughout Europe, and revolutionists in Genoa and elsewhere began declaiming in favor of this or that quackish panacea, Cavour, to save liberty from mobs on one side and monarchy on the other, threw all his power into an effort to

[1] For a brief but excellent statement regarding the influence of Cavour's life as a journalist upon his life as a statesman, see Zanichelli, *Cavour*, pp. 166 and following.

secure a constitution. His success was immediate, and
the *Statuto* advocated by him and issued by King Charles
Albert became at once the cornerstone of Piedmontese
liberty, and, finally, of Italian liberty and unity.

The *Statuto* was no mere makeshift, no worthless
promise made by a despot in trouble. Promises made by
the Bourbons had come to count for nothing, and promises made by Hapsburgs were little better; pledges
from either of these houses had come to be regarded
much like those made two centuries before by Charles
the First of England, who had lied to all parties until it
was found that putting him to death was the only remedy.
But a promise from the House of Savoy was of sterling
value, not only in the eyes of Italy, but of Europe. How
much it meant was to be seen later, not only in Italy but
in Spain and throughout Europe.

The revolutionary movement in Europe spread rapidly
and irresistibly. Louis Philippe fled from his throne in
France, the King of Prussia was humiliated by the mob
in his capital; from every part of Europe despots, great
or small, rumbled along the high-roads toward England.

In this general scramble for safety, absolute rulers now
began to offer reforms and even constitutions, but, ere
long, nearly all the petty princelings of Italy fled from
their states. Even Rome moved. Pope Pius offered,
finally, as we have seen, various reforms, among them a
ministry containing, for a wonder, three laymen, and even
a parliament,—but this parliament subject to a secret
committee of cardinals.

Best of all for Italy was the revolution at Vienna.
Milan and Venice rose immediately, and each drove out
the Austrian oppressor; Italian patriotism seemed irresistible, and the whole nation rose in aid of these two
city-centres of effort for national independence.

Up to this time Cavour had in all his work sought to
develop Italian resources, to promote education, to stim-

ulate the arts of peace, to resist everything like revolution. Now comes a sudden change. In all his utterances he is now for war; he declares that, no matter how inferior in forces Piedmont may be, she must march to the aid of Milan and Venice.

To this pressure King Charles Albert yielded, marched his troops against Austria, was in the first main battle—Goito—successful, and entered Milan as a conqueror. As he had promised, his sons supported him bravely. Of one of them, the world was destined to hear much,—as Victor Emmanuel II. The world now began to hear also of one Joseph Garibaldi, fighting in the mountains at the head of volunteers.

But King Charles Albert was no general; his first victory was not vigorously followed up, and calamities came on all sides. Pope Pius, having yielded to the Roman people so far as to send troops to keep the Austrians out of his dominions, began to show an utter unwillingness to do more; he would give no further help to his fellow Italians rebelling against his old friend Austria. Ferdinand of Naples, who at first, after the Neapolitan-Bourbon fashion, made every sort of patriotic pledge and proclamation, and had sent ships and troops against Austria, now turned traitor and secretly issued instructions to his admirals and generals, nullifying all their patriotic efforts; other Italian princelings followed his example; in the minds of all these rulers there was working not only a hatred of constitutional liberty, but a jealousy of Piedmont as the head of the new movement,—as the kingdom whose monarch had begun to lead Italy to victory and who might profit by it.

But there came things worse by far than these,—political fooleries of the sort which have generally ruined revolutions. At Milan, the great centre of Lombardy, after days of heroic bravery, came a reign of utter folly, —long and bitter discussions as to what sort of government should be established when Italian liberty should be finally achieved, demands for a Constituent Assembly, for a Convention, for all the fine things which had hitherto brought every European revolution to ruin. It was a folly only comparable with the scenes at Constantinople, nearly five hundred years before, when the leaders gave their time to impassioned debates on theological points, while the Turks were storming the walls of the city. Nor was this all. At Rome things were even worse. Pius IX had wisely selected, as the head of his cabinet, Pellegrino Rossi, a political thinker whose abilities had received the highest recognition in Switzerland and France, a statesman who, though a refugee from Italy, had been made an ambassador at Rome by the government of Louis Philippe. No thinking man denied Rossi's high character and great ability, and it was certain that all his influence would be thrown in behalf of constitutional liberty; but meantime had come declarations of schemers and dreamers, demanding fruit on the day the tree was planted, stimulating every sort of outbreak, glorifying every growth of quackery, demanding "government by the people"—by which they meant the sovereignty of the city mob—and denouncing Rossi as an incarnation of evil.

The natural result of such denunciations followed,— the same result of unbridled calumny which our own Republic has seen in the deaths of Lincoln, Garfield, and McKinley. Rossi was assassinated at the door of Parliament; and the Pope, a prisoner at the Quirinal, insulted, terrified, gave up all hope or effort for liberty and fled to Gaëta. From that date, through his entire reign, the longest in the history of the Papacy, Pope Pius remained an utter disbeliever in free government; and not only this but a disbeliever in all freedom of thought, destined, in his famous "Encyclical," to make the most reactionary declaration against everything like human freedom which the world has ever known until that of Pius X in 1907.[1]

Thus it was that "the fool reformer"—the worst plague of thinking statesmen, in all times—had done the work of Austria and the Italian tyrants thoroughly,—as thoroughly as did similar "reformers" in Russia thirty years later, when they assassinated Alexander II, the Czar Emancipator, in the midst of his efforts to give his people constitutional liberty,—and as they have done it since, under Nicholas II. At this cruel murder of Rossi, all Europe, and, indeed, all the world, was disheartened and even disgusted.

In northern Italy Charles Albert had tried to fight on, but, in July of 1848, at the battle of Custozza, he was overcome and there came a truce. Now was the time to call in Cavour; but the king still distrusted him, the people misunderstood him, the Turin mob had its way, another period of political mistakes set in, and, as a result, the Piedmontese army marched once more against Austria, and in March, 1849, at Novara, was soundly and thoroughly beaten. The king abdicates his throne, even on the battlefield, takes refuge in Portugal, and soon dies. Full reaction succeeds throughout Italy, and, indeed, throughout Europe. Austria, in spite of her own troubles elsewhere, is jubilant in Italy. Again her

[1] For interesting and brilliant descriptions and statements of the various episodes in the struggle before and after the battle of Novara, see W. R. Thayer, *The Dawn of Italian Independence*, Boston, 1893, vol. ii, chap. ii.

For a convincing exhibition of these revolutionary follies, see Cantù, *Histoire des Italiens*, vol. xii, livre xviii; also Ottolini, *La Revoluzione Lombarda del 1848–1849*, Milan, 1887. For some redeeming characteristics of the Italian revolutionists, see Countess Martinengo Cesaresco, *Italian Characters*, especially the chapters on Bassi, Bixio, and others.

For a succinct but striking picture of the earlier political follies of the mob at Milan in Bonaparte's time, see Lemmi, *Le Origini del Risorgimento Italiano*, pp. 118 and following. For curious details regarding the earlier patriotic activity of Rossi in Italy, see same, pp. 427 and 437.

troops enter Milan and, finally, Venice; still worse, if possible, a French garrison enters Rome, nominally to control reformers of the sort who had murdered Rossi; and there it remained for nearly twenty years.

All seemed lost. Piedmont, under its new king, Victor Emmanuel II, seemed utterly at the mercy of Austria. The material distress of the little kingdom was of the greatest, but, in spite of it, she showed a moral elevation which from the first indicated that she would finally rise above all this calamity; and the main agent in this new effort was Cavour. Up to this time, though recognized as a powerful journalist and man of affairs, he had taken no official part in political life. He had been a candidate for election to Parliament and had been beaten; but the people, taught by adversity, seeing that his counsels had been prompted by patriotic foresight, finally elected him. The new king's ministry was led by D'Azeglio, but, at last, after various ministerial changes, came a personal catastrophe which ended in a way most unexpected.

Holding the Departments of Agriculture, Commerce, and the Navy in the ministry was Santa Rosa, a patriotic writer and scholar, respected and beloved throughout the kingdom. Suddenly, in the autumn of 1850, he was taken with mortal illness. As a writer he had been one of Cavour's main colleagues in the editorial work of the *Risorgimento;* as a minister he had aided to carry out one of Cavour's main ideas, by bringing into Parliament a bill abolishing the mediæval powers of ecclesiastical tribunals. Against this, though the Church had long before agreed to a similar reform in France, there came fierce ecclesiastical protests, and, in his dying hours, Santa Rosa, though a devout Catholic, was refused the last sacraments, by order of Monsignor Fransoni, the Archbishop of Turin. To most men of these days such a matter would seem of little consequence, but, to the devout populace of Turin, it seemed an awful catastrophe and they held the archbishop responsible for it. The hatred thus engendered lasted long. It was brought to bear in various ways upon those whose petty spite had caused it and upon the Church at large, but its most noteworthy immediate result was that patriotic pressure now obliged the young king to name Cavour as Santa Rosa's successor. The king yielded gracefully, but with the jocose warning to all the other ministers that Cavour would some day occupy all their places. As we shall see, this prediction proved virtually true: with the exception of one ministry, that of Justice, Cavour was destined, at various periods, to occupy all the positions in the royal cabinet, and not infrequently several of them at the same time.

Various difficulties followed; but the country soon recognized him as its leader. The special work of his new office was done admirably. Agriculture he developed as never before; manufactures he strengthened by the best scientific and practical methods; commerce he extended by special treaties; as to the navy, there came a stroke of genius, for he founded the great naval arsenal at Spezzia:—people complained that it was on the extreme edge of the Piedmontese dominions; but he made little if any reply, treasuring in his heart of hearts the fact that for a future united Italy it was the best site possible.

A dissolution of the ministry having come in 1852, Cavour gave up office for a time, visited France and England, made a closer acquaintance than ever with their leading statesmen, and, most important of all, met for the first time Napoleon III, and had an opportunity to impress his ideas regarding Italy on that monarch, formerly a Carbonaro, now in all his glory as Emperor of the French,—not yet shown to the world by Bismarck as "a great unrecognized incapacity."

Returning to Turin and again entering the ministry, Cavour's work became greater than ever. There were more and more trying questions to be settled with Austria; difficulties even more subtle with the Vatican and the clerical party, who sought to save every old ecclesiastical abuse which Cavour wished to remedy.

Nothing could be more unjust than their attacks upon him, for from first to last, against all provocations, he was singularly faithful to the Church. When he felt that the old monkish abuses must be stopped and sundry revenues of bishops diminished, he used the revenues then obtained, not for civic purposes, greatly as they were needed by the state, but to increase the stipends of the poorer clergy. No maltreatment by the Church ever succeeded in provoking him to take anything like revenge.

The annoyances from the clerical party were, indeed, vexatious. The bad harvests, the coming of the cholera, which science had not yet disarmed, and the death of the queen, with two other members of the royal family, all were exhibited by clerical orators as a divine punishment of Cavour's government for its crimes against the Church.

But he presses on none the less vigorously. He begins the new system of Italian railways, makes commercial treaties with the leading European powers, alleviates the suffering of the poor by wiser adjustment of tariffs, visits the cholera hospitals, cheers the patients and sees that the best care is given them, and in the midst of ten thousand matters of business, great and small, carries on continuously his negotiations with France and England looking to the driving of Austria out of Italy.

Three serious difficulties beset him ever more and more. A strong industrial party, vexed by his commercial treaties, which had interfered with their profits, insisted that he was ruining the country financially; the extreme revolutionists, vexed by his coolness toward fanatics, insisted that he was ruining the country politically; the all-pervading clerical party, vexed by his suppression of sundry monasteries and church abuses, insisted that he was ruining the people religiously. Calumnies of every sort were invented: he was making a vast fortune out of the people; he was wrecking the liberties of the people; he was destroying the souls of the people.

He took it all cheerily and pressed on, taking it for granted that the sober second thought of the country would do him justice.

The calumny regarding his self-seeking cleared itself away when the fact became known that on his accepting office he had sold all his stocks and shares which could be affected by legislation or by government policy.

His method of working through the various parties in Parliament also exposed him at times to attack, and even to obloquy. From first to last, he utterly refused to violate the constitution of his country, but he never hesitated to break over party lines and precedents. If he could not work with one party, he made alliance with another; if he could not carry the whole of any one party with him, he found his supporters in various parties. To a man of less genius this would have been perilous, but it was by this means, especially, that he carried through many of his most important measures, and it was soon felt that his aims were those of his country, and that he rose superior to all parties.[1]

[1] For an able discussion of this characteristic in Cavour's statesmanship, see Zanichelli, Introduction to his *Scritti di Cavour*.

III

IN January, 1855, Cavour made the first in a series of
great moves, not only as an Italian, but as a European
statesman. The Crimean War had come. Nicholas I
of Russia, a fanatical absolutist, had brought together
vast and showy armies and navies, had concentrated
great power in the Black Sea, and had, in various ways,
shown a determination to take possession of the Turkish
Empire in Europe and along the eastern Mediterranean.
Against this, France, England, and Turkey had united
and had sent their armies into the Crimea. Suddenly,
in January, 1855, Europe was amazed to find that Cavour
had leagued Piedmont with the three powers against
Russia, and had pledged his country, with its four millions of inhabitants, to send 20,000 troops to aid them.
Never was there a bolder stroke of policy. Against it
were arrayed all his old enemies in Parliament and press,
and, with them, many who had been his oldest and best
friends. The aristocracy naturally favored autocratic
Russia; the democracy naturally dreaded imperial
France. In the debates conservatives and radicals bitterly attacked him; indeed, the argument seemed against
him. How absurd to plunge his country, with its four
millions of people, into a war against Russia, with her
hundred millions! How wicked to join in a war with
which Piedmont had nothing to do! How slender the
chances that the little Italian army could accomplish
anything! How certain that the only possible result
would be the impoverishment of the little kingdom!
How inevitable that the great powers, having used Pied-

mont, would, in any treaty which might close the war, ignore her claims and fling her aside!

Against these the argument of Cavour seemed slender. His main reasons—the necessity of obtaining recognition of Piedmont as a European power, of securing an alliance with the two great powers of Western Europe in order to counter-match Austria, of training an Italian army for a new struggle for independence—he could not avow. Those which he could avow were anything but convincing. Of what avail to say that little Piedmont did not wish Russia to become too strong in the Mediterranean?

But, despite all this, Cavour defeated his adversaries. Having won over King Victor Emmanuel and a majority of the Parliament, he sent the little Italian army to the Crimea. At first Europe was inclined to laugh at it. The fable of the Frog and the Ox was recalled in countless satires and caricatures. Ill fortune came; the cholera sadly depleted the little force; there was much delay in its operations; but, finally, came news that it had won a real victory, demanding skill and hard fighting, at the Tchernaya. The effect was magical. The pride of all Italy was aroused; more widely than ever Cavour was now recognized as the Italian leader; the people at large began to divine his reasons and to do him justice; more and more the idea spread throughout Europe that Italy was determined to have her independence and freedom, and that somehow Cavour would secure it.

At the close of the war, in 1856, came a first open triumph of his policy: Piedmont, with Cavour as her representative, despite all the opposition of Austria, was admitted to the Congress of Paris.

To many, his position as representing so small a state, among colleagues who represented great empires, seemed ridiculous, and he, knowing that it must be so, was at first very quiet,—not interfering while English, French, Russian, and Austrian statesmen discussed their main interests. But, as these questions went deeper and grew broader, his opinion was sought; and, joining in the debate, he was soon seen to be a master. This recognition obtained, he secured a sort of personal alliance with Napoleon III; forced the hand of his minister, Walewski, and so brought the condition of Italy and the conduct of Austria before the Conference. Naturally Austria protested bitterly; naturally, also, nothing decisive for Italy was then done; but the great thing was that Cavour had spoken, through the Conference, to all Europe. More and more it was seen that the condition of things in Italy was a menace to European civilization; that every town in the Italian peninsula was a centre of fanaticism, and that revolution might spring forth at any moment, to plague all the great powers.

This work done, Cavour returned to Turin and opened a new era in the industrial history of southern Europe by beginning, in 1857, the first of those great tunnels under the Alps which now connect Italy with the north,— that of Mont Cenis.

But in January of the following year came a calamity. Certain Italian fanatics, at their head Felice Orsini, enraged at Napoleon III, who, in his youth, had taken the oaths of the Carbonari, and at the height of his power had forgotten them, flung a bomb beneath his carriage. The immediate result was that many innocent people were killed and wounded, while the emperor escaped. The remote result was a decided check to the better feeling toward Italy, a bitter distrust of Italians, a feeling that, after all, Austria might be right in aiding to keep down a people which resorted to such cruelty and folly.

There was a sequence of events and a change in sympathies such as the world at large experienced during the early years of the twentieth century regarding Russia: at first, strong sympathy with her people and its representatives, but finally disgust at their folly and cruelty, and a preference for the old despotism over the new. To meet this feeling Cavour felt obliged to bring into the Piedmontese Parliament strong laws against conspirators and assassins. This brought upon him increased hostility from the fanatical element in Italy; but one thing served powerfully to recover the confidence of Europe, and that was the distinction which Cavour drew most powerfully and clearly between a rational evolution of freedom, on one side, and a wild plunge into revolution, on the other. In this he was thoroughly honest. Even in his youth, sketching in an essay his hopes for liberty in Italy and his ideas as to the best means of realizing them, he had declared against sudden and revolutionary changes; to put it in the language of our day, he supported evolution rather than revolution, and, in this new declaration of his creed, Europe recognized him as a true statesman; more than ever it was felt, even by conservatives, that an epidemic of destructive and sterile revolution could best be avoided by releasing Italy from her oppressors.

Six months later came the turning-point. Very privately—indeed, under an assumed name—Cavour visited Napoleon III at the little French watering-place of Plombières. There he brought to bear on the emperor all his skill, in showing that the existing order of things was a menace to the Napoleonic throne as well as to European order, and so cogently that the French monarch entered into a secret agreement with him against Austria.[1]

Returning to Italy, he met at Baden-Baden the Prince

---

[1] Cavour's letter giving Victor Emmanuel full details of the eight hours' interview with Napoleon III is printed in Chiala, *Lettere*, vol. ii.

24

Regent of Prussia, one of the most thoughtful of men, who had every reason to dread and hate revolution, and who afterward became William I, Emperor of Germany. Probably, in the conversation which then took place, an impression was made which, at the critical moment during the struggle which followed, did something to delay the interference of Prussia in behalf of Austria.

Of course, in all this effort by Cavour, especially with the Emperor Napoleon III, the Italian statesman had to encounter the open hostility and the secret intrigues of the clerical party in France as well as in Italy. Through the Empress Eugénie, a Spanish woman devoted to the Church, they had a hold upon the French court, and in a thousand ways were able to promote what they considered the interests of Austria and of the Vatican.

But, on the first of January, 1859, a speech made by the Emperor Napoleon in the presence of the ambassadors at the Tuileries foreshadowed war with Austria, and, in a similar speech at Turin, King Victor Emmanuel, some days later, showed the same intention. Warlike preparations followed, on both sides, Cavour being especially active. His greatest trouble now came from the vacillation of Napoleon III. The emperor had many misgivings, and did not know his own mind. At times he was bent on peace. England blunderingly interfered and offered her good offices. Worst of all, Russia interposed and urged a special conference of the European powers, thus influencing the emperor so far that he telegraphed Cavour, insisting that he must agree to this. Probably, of all the moments in his life, this was to Cavour the most trying. He telegraphed to the emperor his agreement; but so bitter was his regret that his friends feared his suicide.

For a moment all his plans seemed wrecked; but he now made a master stroke. Skillfully he provoked Austria to insist that Piedmont should disarm before the assembling of the council, and to declare that if she did not disarm Austria would begin war. Then Cavour simply refused to disarm—put Austria in the wrong, forced her to fight, and forced Napoleon III to lead French troops into Piedmont against her. Fortunately, too, the generalship of Austria proved as bad as her diplomacy. By a rapid movement the Austrians might have occupied the Piedmontese capital; but there was delay, the allied armies made the most of it, and, on the fourth of June they won the terrible battle of Magenta, and the allied sovereigns entered Milan as conquerors. Shortly afterward came the battle of Solferino, and, while Napoleon III showed none of the military qualities of the man whose name he bore, King Victor Emmanuel gained especial credit for bravery. Austria was beaten and it seemed certain that she would now be expelled from the Italian Peninsula. Suddenly came a catastrophe. In his proclamation at the beginning of the war, Napoleon had declared that Italy should be set free, from the Alps to the Adriatic, but, after these tremendous battles, he halted. He evidently feared that Prussia, with her great power, might interfere. He also saw that his army had, probably, gained more prestige in the battles of Magenta and Solferino than it was likely to secure thereafter. There was a vein of sentiment in him also, such as the first Napoleon had never shown: the heaps of dead and wounded sickened him, and he dwelt plaintively on the fact that he had lost ten thousand men. The Austrians had retreated within the strong "quadrilateral" formed by their four great fortresses in Northern Italy, and thenceforth war must be a slow, painful effort against Austria, the Papacy, Naples, and, possibly, Prussia.

Therefore it was that suddenly, without notice to Cavour, Napoleon III arranged a meeting with the Austrian emperor at Villafranca, and patched up a peace. In this he set Lombardy free from Austria and virtually gave it,

with Milan as its centre, to Piedmont, but he allowed
Austria still to retain her hold upon Venice, agreed that
the principal petty despots of Central Italy might return to their dominions, and provided for a Central Italian Confederacy, to be presided over by the Pope.[1]

For a time, Cavour felt that all was lost. He seemed
stunned and dazed. He had, indeed, taken Lombardy
out of the clutch of Austria; but he had expected far
more. He had relied upon the emperor's word that Italy
should be "free from the Alps to the Adriatic." In a
stormy interview with Victor Emmanuel he denounced
the whole procedure, protested against the treaty, begged
the king to refuse to sign it, and to press on with the
Italian army alone. Fortunately Cavour was in this unsuccessful; and now, sooner than attach his signature to
the treaty, he retired from the ministry and, apparently,
gave up political life. He even left his country, went to
Switzerland, and settled down for a time with his old
friends on the shores of Lake Leman. But soon his old
vigor—indeed, his old cheerfulness—returned. We
have the testimony of those who were then with him, to
the effect that he soon recovered all his elasticity and
devoted himself, even more earnestly than before, to
thinking out new ways and means of accomplishing his
great purpose—despite what he and the Italians regarded
as the emperor's treachery.[2]

[1] For letters and dispatches of Cavour and his agents, revealing his
skill in disentangling and solving the enormous difficulties before and
during the war of 1859, see Bianchi, *La Politique de Cavour*, pp. 334 and
following.

For a thoughtful statement of the motives of Napoleon III, in negotiating at Villafranca, see Zanichelli, *Cavour*, cap. ix; also Mazade.

For curious details, see General Fleury's account of his secret mission
from Napoleon III to the Emperor Francis Joseph, *Souvenirs*, vol. ii, chap.
li.

[2] For an intensely interesting account of Cavour's retirement to
Switzerland at this time, written by one almost constantly with him
there, see De La Rive, *Cavour*, cap. xiii.

At the Zurich Congress which followed, Napoleon III made proposals utterly incompatible with Cavour's idea of a united Italy. The emperor, evidently affected by the need of conciliating his French priesthood, suggested various plans, differing from one another in details, but all containing hints, more or less vague, at carrying out his version of Gioberti's old idea and establishing a confederacy mainly of four states: namely, Piedmont, including Lombardy; Venice, with the minor principalities put back under Austrian slavery; the Papal dominions; Naples, with Sicily; and, possibly, in addition, a little kingdom to be carved out of Tuscany and its neighbors for his wretched cousin, Prince Jerome Napoleon—the Pope to be president over the whole.

Curious was it, in connection with this, that Gioberti himself, the renowned author of the confederation idea, had now fully renounced it, had, indeed, avowed a sort of loathing for it, and, in his *Rinnovamento,* published shortly before his death, had demonstrated that in his old plan there was no longer any hope, but that Italy must be united as a single kingdom, with Piedmont at its head.

Happily, events in the Italian Peninsula were now far beyond Napoleon's reach. Though the Villafranca arrangement had contemplated the restoration of the Austro-Italian princelings, it had provided no means of accomplishing this, and the people throughout Middle Italy—indeed, throughout the whole of Italy—had determined that they would not be put back under the old tyranny and would never allow the Austrian satraps to return: the masterful influence of Cavour prevailed again Napoleon III on one side and the Red Republicans on the other.

Events followed fast. Cavour was soon drawn out of his retirement. In March, 1860, eight different districts elected him to the approaching preliminary Parliament,

and again he began his labors.   There was much difficulty
in keeping the hands of Napoleon III off the growing
movements for independence and liberty in Middle Italy,
but Cavour was skillful and vigorous, and the main districts of the Papal Kingdom, Tuscany, and adjacent divisions of Italy, by overwhelming majorities, voted themselves out from under Austria, the Pope, and their
various princelings, and into the new Kingdom of Italy.

This came as an embarrassing argument to Napoleon
III.   For when, as President, he had sought the imperial
power in France, he had appealed to the French *people,*
and his title to sovereignty rested upon just such a great
popular majority as this which the people of Central
Italy now gave Victor Emmanuel.   The *plébiscite,* in
these regions of Italy which Napoleon III sought to give
back to their old masters, now did its work thoroughly
against him; in every case the vote against the old order
of things, and in behalf of annexation to the Italian Kingdom, was virtually unanimous.

Meantime, in the spring of 1860, symptoms of revolution appeared in Palermo, and Bourbon power was
clearly waning in Sicily.   On the 11th of May, Garibaldi,
with his famous "Thousand," landed in the island, and,
after a series of brilliant victories over the Neapolitan
king, declared himself dictator in the name of Victor
Emmanuel.

In this matter, without doubt, Cavour swerved exceptionally from his fundamental creed, for, while he did not
promote the beginnings of Garibaldi's invasion of Sicily,
he had not opposed it, and, when it was under way, he
had aided it.

More than this, he now promoted insurrection in Lower
Italy, partly to prepare the way for Garibaldi, partly, no
doubt, to make good the claims of United Italy against a
Garibaldian dictatorship.

Southern Italy was fully ripe for revolution; every

sane mind in Europe must have expected it. As far back as 1850 and 1851, Mr. Gladstone, making a long stay in Naples, closely studied the methods of King Ferdinand II, and revealed them in his "Two Letters to the Earl of Aberdeen," which, in pamphlet form, were circulated throughout Europe and America. Gladstone had attended the treason trials, visited the prisoners, talked with men of light and leading, and his revelations were damning. The administration of the law was a cruel farce, the government freely bribed witnesses, the prisons were filthy and crowded with men merely suspected of liberalism. Former members of the king's cabinet, professors in the University, respected citizens of all professions, were languishing in dungeons or working in the chain gang. Among these, one who attracted especial attention was Baron Carlo Poerio, a former minister, whom Gladstone characterized as "a refined and accomplished gentleman, a respected and blameless character," and who was imprisoned, with fifteen others, in a room less than fifteen feet long and only eight feet high; and there these men lived night and day, always chained two by two. Still another was Settembrini, one of the most beloved and respected professors in the University of Naples, who had sat with the king in council, but who, having incurred the monarch's dislike by his liberalism, was, at this time, brought out to work in the chain gang in front of the Royal Palace—His Majesty occasionally going out upon the balcony to enjoy the sight of him.[1]

[1] Of all the memoirs of this period, those of Settembrini seem to me to throw the clearest light into the methods of Italian tyranny. The account of his rescue by his son is one of the most fascinating recitals in all history. See Settembrini, *Ricordanze della mia Vita*, vol. ii, pp. 356 to the end. For an elaborate account of the reigns of "Bomba" and his son, 1855–60, see R. de Cesare's authoritative *La Fine di un Regno*, Città di Castello, 1895.

As to Gladstone's revelations and their effect, see John Morley, *Life of Gladstone*, vol. i, chap. vi. The *Two Letters to Lord Aberdeen*—in Italian translation—are given in Zini, *Storia*, etc., vol. ii, p. i, pp. 247 and

Gladstone's denunciations of this whole system culminated in his declaration that it was "the negation of God, erected into a system of government." But all opposition was unheeded by Neapolitan royalty. The Holy Alliance found no fault with it, and the Emperor Nicholas of Russia especially honored it, petted its envoy at the Winter Palace, and sent the king two colossal statues in bronze, representing powerful steeds conquered by strong men and typifying the curbing of resistance to authority. These were placed at the entrance of the Royal Palace and there they remain even to this day. It may be added that within a short distance of them now stands a noble statue of Carlo Poerio.[1]

In 1859 Ferdinand died and there had come to the throne his son, Francis II, a poor creature, moulded as nearly as possible in his father's image by his eminent tutor, Archbishop Apuzzo, and by his Jesuit instructors; and, during his reign of two years, he proved himself their apt pupil.

In the summer of 1860, he gave a famous exhibition of tragedy and farce. Garibaldi, with his "Thousand," having conquered King Francis's realm of Sicily, despite the 30,000 troops stationed in the island, invaded the

following. The present writer, being in Naples five years after Gladstone, heard his strongest statements fully corroborated by the American minister at that post—Robert Dale Owen—a man of the highest character.

[1] A similar pair of statues was sent by Nicholas to his brother-in-law, Frederick William IV, of Prussia, in approval of that monarch's opposition to constitutional liberty. To one of these statues the Berlin wits gave the name "Progress Checked," and to the other, "Retrogression Encouraged"; and they have adorned the entrance of the Royal Palace at Berlin from that day to this. The originals, by Clodt, stand on the Nevsky Bridge at St. Petersburg.

The favor shown King Ferdinand's minister at St. Petersburg was a matter of jocose remark in the diplomatic corps during the first official residence of the present writer in that city. The representative seemed intellectually well suited to his duties, which were, apparently, little more than to keep the Czar assured of King Ferdinand's fidelity to the most extreme theories and practices of despotism.

mainland, and the young despot attempted to make headway against them by time-honored Bourbon methods.
Bringing out one of the old constitutions which his father
and grandfather had sworn to and violated, he avowed
his willingness, nay, his wish, to swear to observe it.
But, alas for him! his fathers had taught the people of
Southern Italy the worthlessness of Bourbon promises.
More than that, it was speedily made known how this
poor young king had been educated. The *Catechismo
Filosofico,* as edited by his tutor, Archbishop Apuzzo, was
republished and circulated far and wide, and it called the
attention of Italy and the world to the fact that the king,
with the approval of his father, had been taught by this
ecclesiastical tutor that no oaths sworn by a sovereign to a
constitution are binding, not even those made to secure
a throne; that the moment a man is made king he is responsible to God alone, and that no oaths to his people
can hold him. Jesuit casuistry now recoiled upon its
authors; the movement for Italian liberty in Naples carried all before it. In the first days of September, 1860,
King Francis fled to the fortress of Gaëta; and, while he
there showed himself to be feeble and worthless, his
young Bavarian queen won the admiration of Europe by
virtually taking command and holding that fortress during six months. Then the royal couple escaped, and, having for a time settled in Rome, were able to punish their
former subjects by sending bands of brigands among
them, robbing, burning, and murdering; but, this being
finally ended, they retreated to Paris, and were heard of
no more save in a romance which exhibited them to the
mingled derision and pity of the world.[1]

---

[1] As to the Apuzzo Catechism, the edition in my possession is that of
1861; the title-page, however, speaks of it as a reprint from the edition of
1850. For the authorship of the work and for illustrations of its teachings, see pp. 332–337 above.

The romance referred to is by Daudet, *Les Rois en Exil.*

On September 7, 1860, Garibaldi entered Naples; and now began a new complication—for Cavour perhaps the most wearisome of his whole life. With the Garibaldian army had come Italian extremists of every sort, who were now reinforced by many others, in the midst of them Mazzini, and these, in the interest of their vaguely dreamed republic, did their worst against the annexation of Naples and Sicily to the Italian Kingdom, and won to some of their most troublesome ideas the support of Garibaldi.

The Pope, too, gave great trouble. He obtained an army by summoning foreign volunteers, among them many dismissed from the French army, put them under Lamoricière, who had won respect as a French general, and did his best to make Italian unity impossible. It was serious, indeed, for Cavour to find arrayed against him this triple foe—the Pope, appealing to the religious world, Mazzini, appealing to lazzaroni republicans, and Garibaldi, flushed with his great victories; but with each and all these foes he at once grappled vigorously. Next to the French alliance it was his greatest stroke of policy. Not waiting for Garibaldi to come northward, he sends an Italian army into the Papal States, and, at Castelfidardo, defeats Lamoricière and disperses the last of papal armies. He strikes no less boldly at Naples— pushing on Italian troops, with Victor Emmanuel at their head, to coöperate with Garibaldi, but, at the same time, to assert, against the great adventurer, the claims of united Italy, to disperse anarchic forces, and to establish the claims of right reason. Unmindful of the pretended republican or democratic proclivities of the Neapolitan lazzaroni, who had shown themselves as ready to murder and plunder with hurrahs for liberty as with cheers for King Bomba, he carries through Parliament measures incorporating into the new nation Naples, Sicily, the main part of the Papal territory, Tuscany, and the rest, until he has brought into it all Italy save Venice and Rome.[1]

And now, in February, 1861, having assembled in Turin the first Italian Parliament, he fully committed it to all his great measures, and, above all, to a United Italy and to Victor Emmanuel as its constitutional king.

The rapidity, vigor, and inspiration of Cavour's measures carried everything before them. He was now president of the new Ministry of the Italian Kingdom, and summoned to his side as colleagues the foremost men of the whole peninsula, among them such men as Minghetti, Peruzzi, and de Sanctis.

There was, indeed, a painful side to all this, for Cavour had, by some of the measures which he had felt obliged to take, separated himself from many old and devoted friends; and especially had he given offense to some of the best of these by his apparent relinquishment of his old ideas against revolutionary methods.

Even more painful to him was the course of Garibaldi, who bitterly resented various things in Cavour's statesmanship, and, above all, his surrender of Nice to Napoleon III. In that town Garibaldi was born, and he complained that Cavour had made him a foreigner in his own birthplace. Garibaldi urged the king to dismiss Cavour from the ministry, issued letters against him, and finally entered Parliament in order to attack him.

All this was, indeed, disheartening. Nearly a year before, Cavour, in one of the most powerful and brilliant speeches in parliamentary history, had shown why the cession of Nice and Savoy to France was an absolutely necessary condition to the establishment of Italian unity. At times pathetic, at times humorous, at times eloquent, he had defended his policy and convinced the country.

[1] For the masterly letter of the king (Cavour) to Pope Pius—and the bitter reply of the latter—on the Italian invasion of the Papal territory, see Zini, *Storia d'Italia*, vol. ii, pt. ii, pp. 574–577.

He indeed lamented the necessity of ceding these territories, and this feeling he expressed most nobly; but, as a matter of fact, both Savoy and the city of Nice had long been more French than Italian. In both, French was the language mainly spoken, and many of their deputies in parliament could speak no other. The commerce and the sympathies of both were largely, if not mainly, French. Savoy, though the cradle of the royal house of Italy, was largely in the hands of priests, and constantly in opposition to Italian aspirations. Nice was rapidly becoming a French pleasure ground. That speech of Cavour had, to all appearance, settled this question and opened the way for other questions far more pressing; but now all must begin again and in a way that was discouraging and even exasperating.[1]

Despite all this, the triumphant general now loudly denounced the triumphant statesman as one who had flung away Italian territory, had made war between brothers, had betrayed liberty; and he united with those who denounced Cavour for selling to France Savoy, the cradle of the new Italian monarchy. Parts of the debate were very painful; but Cavour thoroughly controlled himself and rose quietly above all passion and bitterness. He admitted that the resentment of Garibaldi for the sacrifice of his birthplace was natural, declared that he could not blame him for it, and, at the crisis of the attack, he remained silent. But others came to his defense. The cruel injustice of these charges was manifest to every thinking Italian. The speech of Ricasoli, discussing the whole situation and Cavour's part in it, has

[1] For Cavour's main speech in full, with indications of his sway over his audience by his wit, humor, knowledge of affairs, and eloquence, see Artom and Blanc, *Cavour in Parlamento*, pp. 557 and following. For Cavour's reasons for the cession of Nice and Savoy, as presented diplomatically to Europe, see his despatch to Nigra, given in Zini, *Storia d'Italia*, vol. ii, pt. ii, p. 587; also Countess E. Martinengo Cesaresco, *The Liberation of Italy*, chap. xiii, New York, 1894.

taken its place among the masterpieces of Italian eloquence; and among those who followed him on the same
side were men who had long differed with Cavour.

It looked for a time as if civil war between Northern
and Southern Italy might ensue; but leaders on both sides
showed a determination to allay this bitterness, and
finally, in April, 1861, there came a reconciliation—Cavour and Garibaldi continuing to revere, and to distrust
each other.

Now drew on Cavour's final struggle—his effort to secure Rome as the national capital; but the Vatican rejected every proposal, and the emperor, to please the
clerical party in France, interposed obstacles to every
measure tending to make Italy united and independent.
There constantly rose in the emperor's mind the old
vague dreams of an Italian confederacy with the Pope
at its head, with a restoration of Bourbons here and
Hapsburgs there, and, perhaps, a Bonaparte in Tuscany
—all keeping the country disunited and weak, making it
for ever an easy prey to French intrigue or force. But,
against both Pope and Emperor, Cavour steadily maintained his policy of a United Italy under a single head
and with a liberal constitution, and he gained constantly
upon his adversaries.

While the steady opposition of the Vatican to every
proposal for placing the national capital at Rome was
vexatious, and the attitude of the emperor still more so,
there came a piece of great good fortune to the Italian
cause. This was an occurrence apparently most trifling,
and in a Roman provincial city; yet of all things that ever
alienated public opinion—Jew and Gentile, Catholic and
Protestant, throughout the world—from the Papal policy, this proved the most powerful. On the 24th of
June, 1858, a devout servant, Anna Morisi, entrusted
with the care of a little child, Edgar Mortara, in a Jewish family of Bologna, and anxious to save the child's

soul, had entered into relations with the Holy Inquisition —the result being that a priest was sent who baptized the infant and then carried off both the maid and the child.

The agonized parents begging for the return of their son, the pontifical authority threatened to put into force against them certain obsolete laws which punished Jews for employing Catholic servants. The parents were not allowed even to see their child. These facts were concealed until about the end of August, 1858, when the story came out and ran like wildfire throughout Italy and, indeed, throughout Christendom. Everywhere the press protested against this monstrous iniquity, save in Austria, where the government forbade any public mention of it. In France the remonstrances became especially bitter, and Veuillot, the most eminent of French ultramontane editors, made matters still worse by defending the abduction of the little Mortara as in conformity with the traditions of the Church, and by calling attention to the fact that this right of abduction had been claimed, as against Protestant children, by some of the most eminent authorities of the French Church, under the old Bourbon monarchy.

All this but served to increase the indignation of Christendom, and public opinion became so strong that both France and Great Britain made remonstrances at the Vatican. All to no purpose. The Papal Government simply inserted in its official organ—the *Civiltà Cattolica*—a note declaring the question "purely spiritual"; the Pope had no response to make to foreign powers. This increased the general indignation, crippled the French clerical party in its efforts to prevent the union of France with Italy during the following year, and vastly increased the number of those who hoped and prayed that the war of 1859 might result in the substitution of lay for clerical government at Rome.

Two years later the Mortara family brought suit against Anna Morisi for the abduction. To this the Papal Court simply answered that the young woman had entered a convent, and that the whole matter was "purely spiritual." Finally Prussia showed a disposition to intervene. This seemed so serious that, in some mysterious manner, the Mortara family were persuaded to withdraw their suit, and were even offered restitution of the boy if they would consent to be baptized. Meantime the boy had become fully converted and the matter ceased to occupy public attention; but probably nothing did more than this apparently petty matter to produce the feeling which at last enabled Italy to make its capital at Rome, without the slightest effective remonstrance from any human being. Nor was this the only result. Whenever any European nation since that time has established unsectarian public schools and the priesthood has protested against them, in the name of the "Rights of Parents" as regards the education of their children, the Mortara case has been cited as a sufficient answer.[1]

But in these efforts for Italian Unity Cavour sacrificed his life. His daily work was a wonder to all who knew him. During various periods he held several of the most important ministries at the same time, and constantly had to deal with intricate problems in every part of Italy and in many parts of Europe. At these he wrought night and day—in his bed-chamber, at his work-table, in the audience rooms, in the King's Cabinet, at the various ministries, in the parliamentary debates—everywhere; but so easily, so cheerily, that he and all about

---

[1] For the Mortara case, see Vollet, in *La Grande Encyclopédie.* Also Zini, *Storia d'Italia,* vol. i, pt. i, pp. 978–984. Also, as revealing the impulse given by it against the temporal power of the Papacy, Tivorani, *L'Italia degli Italiani, 1849–1859,* tome i, p. 198. The best résumé of the whole affair is in R. de Cesare's *Roma e lo Stato Romano, 1850–1870,* Rome, 2 vols., 1907.

him were for a time deceived as to his physical condition.[1]
Arrived at the age of fifty, in full middle life, he suddenly found himself unable to go on. There was a painful illness of a week—his powers had at last completely
failed him. Pathetic were his attempts to grasp again
the various pressing Italian questions. Touching were
his final interviews with his dearest friends and with the
king. Italy and its future were in all his thoughts.
During the last visit of Victor Emmanuel to his bedside,
the dying statesman dwelt long upon the difficulties yet to
be encountered, but always hopefully.

He was upborne by his faith in eternal justice. Just
before this final illness Castelli had asked him how much
time he would require for bringing Rome into the new
Italy. Cavour turned—looked Castelli full in the face—
"stood silent a full minute and said, 'Two years.' "[2]

In all his last conversations he held steadily to
his declaration, "Italy is made"—"L'Italia è fatta."
Most earnestly he urged that no despotic measures should
be used under any pretext. Especially touching was his
reference to the Neapolitans, his plea for patience with
them, corrupted as they had been by centuries of despotism.

Most touching of all was the final scene. Some years
before, in the time of the cholera, bearing in mind the
refusal of the Archbishop of Turin to grant the last consolations of the Church to Santa Rosa, Cavour had secured from a kindly friar, "Brother James," a promise
to attend him in his dying hours. This promise was re-

---

[1] The present writer knew personally three of Cavour's colleagues, Minghetti, Peruzzi, and Count Nigra, and was informed by each of these that
Cavour very frequently summoned between four and five o'clock in the
morning those who worked with him. Each of these statesmen dwelt on
Cavour's enormous capacity for work, on his quickness, his skill, his
thoroughness, and on the fact that, toward the last, he virtually gave no
time to rest

[2] For the reply of Cavour to Castelli, see the latter's *Ricordi*, p. 37.

deemed, and, in the final moment, Cavour grasped the friar's hand and uttered his last words—"Brother, brother, a free Church in a free State" (*Frate, frate, libera chiesa in libero stato*).

Thus, in leaving the world, he asserted the great principle for which he had so long labored and which he felt sure gave the best of guarantees to religion as well as to patriotism. His words are still the religious watchword of Italian patriots.

In thus showing his respect for the religion in which he had been born and bred, he was, undoubtedly, actuated both by patriotic and by religious motives. During his last hours he had said, "I die as a good Christian; I have never done evil to any one."

Sad is it to record the fact that the good priest was severely punished for his kindly act—was summoned to Rome, removed from his little church, and sent to end his life in a distant monastery.

The completion of Cavour's work for the unity of Italy followed as if under a natural law. He was succeeded by noble men, who, in their turn, were succeeded by men sometimes of high and sometimes of doubtful character. During the nine years following his death, the struggle for complete unity continued and became a fearful tangle of motives and events—at times heroic, at times scandalous, but all tending toward Cavour's ideal. During this whole period Garibaldi continued to play his astonishing part, sometimes brilliantly, sometimes absurdly, but ever determined to set Rome and Venice free. Though defeated by the Italians at Aspromonte and by the French at Mentana, he finally saw his dream of United Italy fully realized. For, in 1866, by an alliance with Prussia, Italy won Venice, and, in 1871, owing to the prostration of Napoleon III by Bismarck, was able to make Rome her capital. The work and the prophecy of Cavour were thus fulfilled.

25

Not merely by what was done in his lifetime, but also by what followed it, his place in history was made secure. Well was it said by one of the most broadminded, skillful, and truthful of English diplomatists in the nineteenth century—a statesman who had known Bismarck and Cavour most intimately, and who had studied their careers from every possible point of view, near and distant—that, of the two great statesmen of Europe in the nineteenth century, Cavour was the greater.[1]

Not at first sight so imposing a figure as Bismarck afterward became, not, apparently, gifted with such prodigious force to make all men bend to his will, not a dictator to the nations about him, crushing all opposition, Cavour's was a nobler will and power, the will and power to lay the foundations of Italian unity in Italian liberty; to work by means of reason rather than by force; to preserve faith in freedom and justice; to fit the nation for freedom by education; to inspire Italians to win liberty by sound thinking, and to preserve it by political sobriety. All this combined to give him the foremost place not only among Italian statesmen, but among the statesmen of

---

[1] The English diplomatist referred to was Lord Odo Russell, afterward Lord Ampthill. He had long diplomatic service in America, in many parts of Europe, and, especially, in Italy and Germany. Both Cavour and Bismarck he knew intimately, and was beloved and trusted by both; but, on being asked at Berlin by the present writer which of the two men he considered the greater in his character and work, he made the statement above referred to.

For a masterly development of the reasoning which proves Cavour greater in true statesmanship than Bismarck, see W. R. Thayer, *Cavour e Bismarck*, Rome, 1905.

I may add to Mr. Thayer's exhibition of Bismarck's scorn for popular rights and hatred for parliamentary government that, having heard the great German statesman address the German Parliament on various occasions, I cannot remember one of his speeches which did not, on the whole, betray contempt for his audience and dislike, if not hatred, for its most distinguished thinkers. How far all this differed from Cavour's feeling may be seen by any one who will take up his parliamentary speeches, as given in Artom and Blanc and elsewhere.

the European Continent during the nineteenth century. Two great peculiarities of his statesmanship may here be mentioned. First: in his dealings with the Church Cavour enforced a distinction between the religious and the political—thus he withstood and thwarted the Vatican, which sought to prove to Italy that the *political,* by which the Roman Curia had worldly power, wealth, distinction, was the *religious.*

Secondly: from 1850 on, Cavour's policy steadily tended to bring as many Italians as possible together. Mazzini, for example, cried "Unity! Unity!" and then excluded everybody who was not in his particular faction: in 1859 and 1860 Cavour had Mazzinians, Giobertians, Guerrazzians, and virtually all the other factions of liberal intent, working together (though they hardly realized it themselves) for the great cause which he was directing. Well does our foremost American authority on the events of Cavour's time say: "In his ability to get as many as possible, even against their will, to fight under his banner, he has had no equal save Abraham Lincoln." [1]

Since Cavour's death Italy has taken him to her heart as during his lifetime she never did. His services were of a sort which, while he lived, won respect rather than popularity. He was obliged to injure many interests and to offend many men. He never sought popular plaudits, and, at times, was exceedingly unpopular; more than once his speeches in Parliament were drowned by hisses from the galleries. Beloved he indeed was,— deeply beloved by a wide circle of friends; admired he was by a large and ever increasing circle of political thinkers; but other men, during his lifetime, won far more of unthinking applause. Just at the end of his life there did, indeed, come a rapid change. All men of patriotic instincts recognized more and more his supreme service. More and more it was seen that what

[1] W. R. Thayer, as above.

other statesmen, generals, philosophers, poets, could not do, he had done. More and more the nation came to understand him and, therefore, to love and revere him

This newer growth of feeling has continued since his death, ever deepening in the convictions of the newer generations. Throughout all the greater districts which he brought into United Italy, now stand noble monuments to his memory; but, among all these, the most impressive is the simplest.

Several years before his death, in the thick of his labors and struggles for his country, he had visited the Campo Santo at Pisa; and there, standing upon sacred earth brought from Palestine, amid the frescoes of Orcagna and the memorials of great Italians, he had mused over the future of Italy, and his relation to it. He was not destined to be buried there; his body lies in the little church at Santena, near the homestead he loved so well. But, in the Pisan Campo Santo, among far more pretentious monuments, has been placed his simple bust in marble; and upon the ancient walls behind it have been festooned the colossal chains with which Pisa once prevented the access of Florence and Genoa by the Arno. Having been torn away after fearful struggles and displayed for centuries as trophies at Genoa and Florence, they have in these latter days been returned to Pisa, and a simple inscription records the fact that they are restored to United Italy, in token that the ages of disunion are past. No better place could have been found for them, and no more worthy tribute could have been paid to the man whose great genius ended more than a thousand years of internecine struggles among his countrymen, and who, more than any other, finally established Italian independence, unity, and freedom.

BISMARCK

I

COULD there have come in Germany an evolution of right reason from the work of Stein, what long years of heart-breaking disappointment, of precious lives wasted in dungeons, in exile, on scaffolds and on battlefields, had been avoided! But revolutionary excesses had inevitably provoked reactionary retaliations equally severe: the feverish cruelty of Danton, Marat, and Robespierre was, under a law of nature, followed by the chilling cruelty of Bourbons, Hapsburgs, and Romanoffs; conspirators on one side provoked tyrants on the other and thus came a rule of unreason, with successive reactions and revolutions, which lasted more than fifty years.

As long as the German monarchs were summoning aid for their final effort against Napoleon, their promises to their subjects were dazzling, and especially so were their pledges of constitutional liberty and national unity. But, Leipzig and Waterloo having been fought, and Napoleon no longer feared, there was ominous delay: even at the Congress of Vienna, which was expected to bring in a golden age of peace and good-will, there came, especially between the two greater German powers, a scramble for territory which, for a time, seemed likely to end in fraternal bloodshed.

Austria, with Metternich at her head, fell back upon her old despotic methods. The Austrian emperor, haranguing the German professors at Laybach, gave them another version of his famous address to the Italian

professors at Padua. His words were: "I do not need
savants, but sturdy subjects. It is your duty to educate
the young to be such. He who serves me must learn
what I order: he who cannot or who brings me new ideas
can go, or I will dismiss him." In accordance with this
spirit in Austria and various other parts of South Germany, not only private tuition but public instruction was
kept in the hands of the priesthood; history and literature
were subjected to strict censorship; under suspicion of
liberalism imprisonments were meted out to the noblest
of men—to scholars and thinkers who, believing in the
promises of rulers, had risked their lives in the wars
against Napoleon. The Elector of Hesse became so
fanatically reactionary that he alarmed even extremists
on his own side: as far as possible he undid every reform, restored every abuse, and even reverted to the
uniforms, wigs, hair powder, and military tactics of the
period before the Revolution. Prussia was in some
respects better, but here too there bloomed forth the old
theory of the "right divine of kings to govern wrong":
from the Prussian university of Bonn professors suspected of favoring constitutional liberty and national
unity were expelled with as little compunction as at
sundry times and in divers manners professors were
threatened with expulsion and even expelled from sundry
American colleges and universities for beliefs regarding
infant baptism or apostolic succession or free trade.

The leading German monarchs assembled from time to
time to denounce liberal ideas and to devise new methods for suppressing them. Various political inquisitions
were established, and yet, despite proscriptions, confiscations, banishments, there remained a great body of
patriots throughout the whole German territory, from
the Alps to the North Sea and from the Rhine provinces
to Russia, who held high an ideal of well-regulated free-

dom. Most evident was this at the great city centres and, above all, at the universities.

In the cities rose vigorous writers who, in spite of paid adversaries, strengthened this feeling. At the universities there continued to appear, despite the apparent certainty of banishment or imprisonment, professors who inculcated ideas of constitutional right and of a united German nation. Then came into being the *Burschenschaft*—a widespread student organization with speeches and songs glorifying liberty and unity. Notable was the great student assembly on October 18, 1817, at the Wartburg. There, in the heart of Thuringia, in the old castle of the Minnesingers and of Luther, student enthusiasm seemed to carry all before it;—but inevitably with many noble utterances there were extravagances. As usual in such movements its worst enemies were of its own household: fanatics arose, and one of these, the student Sand, assassinated the reactionary writer Kotzebue. No better pretext could have been offered to reaction. Sane and sober people were alarmed. To their fear of anarchy monarchs appealed anew and there came measures of repression more and more cruel, —among these the imprisonment and impoverishment of Arndt, whose songs had aroused Germany for the Freedom War, and of Jahn, who had sacrificed all to the redemption of the country.

In sundry minor states rulers did, indeed, grant constitutions or charters more or less valuable; the Duke of Weimar, the friend of Goethe and Schiller, winning the honor of being the first to make an honest attempt to keep the promises made by German sovereigns in trouble.

As to Germany at large, the thirty-nine separate sovereignties remaining after Napoleon had dealt with the old Empire had formed a confederation. Its national congress, which met at Frankfort-on-Main, was made up of representatives not selected by the peoples of various states, but by their rulers, and its functions were therefore not legislative but diplomatic—the representatives sitting around its green table simply as envoys of their respective sovereigns and its sessions being secret. It became at its beginning and remained until its end a nest of intrigues:—Austria against Prussia, Prussia against Austria, the minor states taking sides as each thought most profitable, but Austria generally securing a majority. This Federation Diet was foredoomed to impotence as regarded any good purpose; its whole influence made for despotism and disunion.

Now came the French Revolution of 1830 which dethroned the Bourbons, and this with various other efforts, more or less successful, at throwing off tyranny in Italy and elsewhere, and the passage of the Reform Bill in Great Britain, aroused new hopes everywhere. But now came attempts of hot-headed men to arouse revolution;—as at the castle of Hambach in 1832, and at Frankfort-on-Main in the year following. Thence inevitably resulted reactionary measures equally absurd, among them the abrogation of the constitution of Hanover by King Ernest August and the expulsion of the "Göttingen seven"—seven of the most eminent men in Germany driven from their professor's chairs for believing in constitutional methods. Everywhere was the see-saw from revolution to reaction and from reaction to revolution, nowhere, apparently, evolution in obedience to sober judgment and right reason. The result among thinking men was mainly discouragement and apathy: the philosophy of Kant, the supreme call of duty, which had inspired the mighty thoughts and deeds of the Freedom War, was succeeded widely by the philosophy of Hegel—in its popular interpretation, "Whatever is, is right."

The whole economic framework of German institutions was as preposterous as its political condition. It was the same condition which Turgot had endeavored to reform in France, but which had only been destroyed by the great Revolution of 1789. In 1815 Germany was divided between thirty-six commercial districts, each with its own custom-houses and tariff schedules. And yet it was out of all this unreason that there came beginnings of fruitful thought for German liberty and union: for gradually there was developed a Customs Union, a *Zollverein*, Prussia taking the lead and other states joining her. This proved more and more strikingly successful and it suggested quietly to every thinking mind two great questions:—if rational freedom is good in commerce why not in politics, and if commercial union is possible why not political union.

Meantime constitutional assemblies, generally poor and petty, and for advisory purposes merely, had been created in various German states and these kept alive some germs of rational liberty. Even an assembly of this wretched sort was prevented in Prussia for more than thirty years after representative government had been promised. But in 1840 there came to the throne of Prussia Frederick William IV. Though given to mediæval dreams and theories he was a man of many gifts and much was expected of him. His first doings were greeted with joy. He set free patriots who had been imprisoned, he returned to their university chairs professors who had been ejected—among them Arndt,— and in 1847 he allowed the eight local diets in the various provinces of the kingdom—feeble bodies under complete royal and police control—to be represented in what was called a United Prussian Diet at Berlin, the first parliament which represented the whole of Prussia.[1]

But this body was carefully tethered and fettered. Its

[1] On the significance of this body, see Bryce, *Holy Roman Empire*, p. 463. As to its composition, see Matter, *Vie de Bismarck*, chap. i.

functions were not legislative, but advisory, and in opening it the King gave forth a most disheartening gospel: "No power on earth," he said, "shall ever succeed in persuading me to exchange the natural relation between king and people for a conventional, constitutional one; neither now nor ever will I permit a written sheet, like a second providence, to thrust itself in between our God in Heaven and this land, to displace the old sacred fidelity."

By various other rulers, occasional concessions were made to the longing for sane liberty, some effective, some farcical; but the evident purpose of every crowned head in making these concessions was to glorify the sovereign and depress the subject.

Adding enormously to the general difficulty was the aristocracy: it held to its mediæval position and privilege as if Stein had never abolished serfdom nor given city liberties. As a result the ferment increased. Outbreaks by mobs continued, alarming the moderate, steadygoing population, and thus giving to absolutist rulers the pretexts they needed.

In February, 1848, came a new French Revolution which dethroned the house of Orleans. Never was an outbreak more causeless or useless; never was one which revealed more folly on both sides; never one more sure to result in a reaction paralyzing both liberty and national self-respect. Yet, futile as it was, it set all Europe in flames: Metternich fled from his Vienna post forever; the old Emperor Ferdinand was driven out of Vienna, and a new Emperor, young Francis Joseph, was enthroned; at Berlin, King Frederick William IV was humiliated by a mob which forced him to swallow his mediæval theories, to dismiss his guards, to grant a constitution, and to call a Prussian national assembly which was to be a very different thing from that poor evasion, the United Prussian Diet. The King of Bavaria was

forced to abdicate in favor of his son, and German rulers
generally were obliged to submit to indignities and to
grant constitutions. On the highways of the Continent
princes and their ministers were flying for their lives
toward England, and among these Prince William of
Prussia, afterward the first Emperor of the new Germany. On all sides war was threatening;—in Austria,
in Hungary, in Italy. In Denmark war with Prussia was
begun.

Yet another effort was now made for a united Germany. To take the place of the wretched old Federal
Diet at Frankfort-on-Main, representing the princes, a
National Parliament was now elected, representing the
entire German people, and in May it met in that city.
Rarely has any public body contained so many men of
profound thought and high ideals; rarely has any public
body contained so few members of practical experience;
never was there a more discouraging failure.

The assembly had begun well. Its president, Von
Gagern, seemed a most happy choice; but soon came disappointment. With wars threatening on all sides; with
the mob spirit seething in every city; with desperate
efforts, open or secret, by the old governments to regain
their power; with attempts throughout the nation, sometimes contemptible, sometimes ferocious, to abolish absolutism; and with the whole German people, indeed the
whole world, longing for practical measures, the assembly became simply a debating club. Professors and
jurists discussed, day after day and week after week,
their theories of the state, of the origin of sovereignty,
of the nature of popular rights,—everything save practical measures necessary to secure national liberty and
unity. Soon sophists, satirists, and caricaturists were
at work, many of them doubtless well paid by the supporters of absolutism. Popular confidence waned. But
at last the Diet seemed to make efforts of a more

practical sort: after a world of metaphysics and rhetoric, a popular Austrian Archduke was made Administrator of Germany, and, after nearly a year more, came the climax: on March 28, 1849, the Assembly chose King Frederick William of Prussia to be German Emperor, and a delegation of the foremost men of the Parliament went to Berlin and solemnly offered him the crown. The gift was utterly refused, and soon the world was informed that the King could not take it from the people, that it must come from their rulers.

To the national parliament this was a killing blow. Anarchy became worse everywhere. A rebellion broke out in Baden; a revolt was sprung in Saxony; Hungary was in the throes of a mighty revolution, threatening the very existence of the Austrian Empire; assassinations of generals, of rulers, of publicists, were reported, and not only in Germany, but in France and Italy. The Administrator of the Empire, Archduke John, gave up his office in disgust, and more than a hundred delegates to Frankfort resigned their seats,—among them the president and a large number of the most trusted leaders; a week later about a hundred members transferred themselves from Frankfort to Stuttgart and there fell again to debating, outbidding each other in proposals wild and futile. Less than a fortnight of this sufficed to disgust all Germany, and, on the twelfth day of their session, a Würtemberg minister, formerly one of its members, closed the riding school where it met, and, by the aid of soldiery, dispersed it. Thus ended forever, after a little more than a year of service, the great National Parliament of Frankfort.

Other events depressed German patriots yet more. In Berlin a constitutional convention apparently went mad and was turned out of doors by Marshal Wrangel. From Italy came news that the efforts in Naples against the Bourbons had failed; that the movement for constitutional liberty in the Roman States had resulted in the triumph of a ferocious mob, and in the assassination of Rossi,—the only statesman from whom Italian liberty and unity could at that time expect anything; that in upper Italy the heroic effort of Piedmont to establish national liberty and unity had been crushed by Austria at the battle of Novara. From France came news that the republican constitution had been discredited by the squabbles of orators and factions and that Louis Napoleon Bonaparte had been elected president of the new French Republic: what that meant every lover of liberty knew instinctively. Then, too, after a long series of Absolutist triumphs in various parts of Germany, word came that the Russian Emperor, Nicholas I, the high priest of absolutism, had marched his troops to save the Hapsburg dynasty, had overcome the Hungarian army, which up to this time had carried all before it, and that a foretaste was given of the ultimate treatment of liberals throughout Europe—extensive confiscations, with banishments and executions of liberal leaders. Everywhere absolutism seemed triumphant. During this long, dreary period many of the noblest Germans yielded to discouragement and departed for other countries,—especially for America; and, among these, Francis Lieber, Carl Follen, and Carl Schurz,—all of them destined to render high service to the United States. In Germany there seemed no hope. In every part of the country men of the purest character were in prison or in hiding; the old tyranny loomed up more threatening than ever; and it was at this time, at the very worst, when constitutional liberty and national unity seemed at the last gasp, that there appeared,—apparently to make a complete end of them,—a young apostle of reaction, absolutism, and disunion, Otto von Bismarck-Schönhausen.

His qualities came from far. The family name and history show that his ancestors were frontiersmen,—living in the lower Elbe region of Germany, perhaps on the "*mark*," or border, of the bishops trying to maintain their footing there, or, as sundry antiquarians insist, on the local border marked by the little river Biese:—hence the name, Bischoff's mark, or perhaps Biesemark, which became in popular speech Bismarck.[1]

The first of these ancestors on whom historic light appears is one Herebord or Herbert von Bismarck, who about 1270 was Master of the Clothiers' Guild at the market town of Stendal. More clearly is seen, half a century later, his grandson Ruloff, or "Rule,"—a man of substance and strength, who put himself at the head of the Stendal citizens, fought the neighboring bishop on questions regarding public schools, and was excommunicated.

Far more vividly is revealed to us Ruloff's son, Nicholas, better known as "Claus" von Bismarck, who, having become rich and powerful, made peace with the Church, led the Stendal aristocracy in fighting the city democracy, and, though driven from the city, secured finally a strong feudal castle and rich estates hard by. He was the precursor of his great descendant, not only in war but in statesmanship. During the middle years of the fourteenth century his fame spread far; he allied himself with the lords of the land—the Margrave of Brandenburg and the Bishop of Magdeburg; gained rank among their leading councilors; showed skill in large finance; took part in war against the Duke of Brunswick, against the German Emperor, and finally against the Church, and, like his father, achieved excommunication. In the following centuries, members of the family are frequently heard of, fighting or negotiating. In the sixteenth century, at least one of them fought against the Turks; in

[1] For this question between Biese-Mark and Bischoff's Mark threshed out at great length, see Dr. J. Langer, in the Horst Kohl *Bismarck Jahrbuch*, iv, pp. 289-298.

the seventeenth, several of them took part in the Thirty
Years' War; early in the eighteenth, one of them, after
exile in Siberia and diplomatic service in England, laid
down his life fighting against the Swedes under Peter
the Great at Poltava. Later in the same century, a great
grandfather of the future Prince Chancellor fell fighting
under Frederick the Great against the Austrians at
Czaslau; a grandfather took part in the famous victory
of Frederick over the French at Rossbach; and the father
was wounded in battle under the Duke of Brunswick
against the French Revolution. In the nineteenth, two
were in Schill's Free Corps, which persisted in fighting
Napoleon, even after the Peace of Tilsit; and seven of
them fought in the Freedom War of 1813, of whom three
were killed and four won and wore the Iron Cross for
valor. Bismarck in his old age summed it all up by saying: "During the last three hundred years, I have no
ancestor who has not fought against France."[1]

In its various abiding places on the lower waters of
the Elbe, certain characteristics made the family widely
known; it was largely represented by rough riders, fierce
hunters, hard hitters, sturdy trenchermen, heavy
drinkers.

The father of the future Chancellor, though for a time
a soldier, seemed of a milder type, and settled down at
Schönhausen as a worthy country squire. The mother
claims notice as the first Bismarck not of noble blood.
Though she came of a line which had produced eminent
scholars and professors, and though her father had won
approval in the civil service under Frederick the Great,
the title of Privy Councilor under Frederick William II,
and the praises of Stein under Frederick William III,

[1] For lists showing that collateral branches of the Bismarck family
were also exceedingly fruitful in public servants, both military and civil,
see H. H. V. von Bismarck, *Stammbuch des Geschlechts Bismarck*, Berlin,
1900, throughout.

26

she could not write the "von" before her name until after her marriage. So far as Berlin knew her, she was brilliant—read much, talked well, loved city society and travel—and spent too much money. Her children knew her but little, for she had learned, probably from Rousseau, to keep them much away from home and to have them treated as young Spartans, but it was doubtless through her that there came into the Bismarck family the love of great literature, the frequent passion for hard study, the penetrative thoughtfulness, which appeared in her son, Otto Eduard Leopold.

Born on Saturday, the first day of April, 1815, Otto was the fourth of her six children, of whom there survived, beside himself, an elder brother heard of afterward honorably but not widely, and a younger sister, bright and devoted, to whom he was deeply attached, and who received from him many of the letters which throw so pleasing a light over his family life and his political experiences. In his seventh year he was sent to a preparatory school in Berlin, and remained there for six years. It was a trying time for him: the rules were severe, the instructors harsh, the diet thin. The school claimed to train young Spartans, but its methods resembled those of Mr. Squeers. Even at this period, that love for country life and interest in rural affairs, which became at a later period his passion, had taken strong hold of the boy, and it made confinement in a city cruelty to him. At the close of this early school period, his family having taken an apartment in Berlin, he was transferred, first, to one of the great gymnasia in that city, and, later, to another, and the instruction in these seems to have been of much use to him: toward some of his more friendly teachers he cherished an affection which ended only with their lives. During all this preparatory period, though a leader in sports among his fellows, he was scholarly and thoughtful; his school work was undoubtedly good, though there were some oddities: a tradition has come down that, having a choice between languages, he learned English, in order to avoid the class of a French professor whom he disliked. Not only at this time, but always afterward, he showed great facility in acquiring languages: both French and English he learned to speak with remarkable correctness and fluency, had during his stay as Ambassador at St. Petersburg obtained a serviceable knowledge of Russian, and had some knowledge of Dutch, Polish, and Lettish. His favorite study was history—first that of Greece and Rome, next, that of his own country and of England.[1]

His talents were recognized as excellent by his more observant masters; one of his Latin essays at the gymnasium appears to have been marked very favorably, and apt references in his speeches during after years show that this early school training had impressed him: to the end of his life he was wont to make pithy Latin quotations.

In his sixteenth year he was confirmed by Schleiermacher in the little Trinity church at Berlin and one interesting reminder of this event remains. The text then placed in his hands by the great theologian was from the Epistle to the Colossians, "Whatsoever ye do, do it heartily as to the Lord and not unto men." There are various evidences that this mandate impressed him. It survived the roystering, the doubts, the cynicism, which at various times eclipsed it, and it is now written in golden letters above his tomb at Friedrichsruh.

Early in his eighteenth year he was ready to enter the

[1] The present writer once asked Bismarck how long he had remained in England to gain his remarkable facility in English. He answered: "Two or three days, and one of these was Sunday." This was a humorous understatement; he made two visits to England during his life, one in 1842, one twenty years later, but each of them very short. For a very sprightly letter written from England by him to his father, dated July, 1842, see Horst Kohl, as above, vol. i, pp. 4–6.

University. There had been differences between his parents regarding this step: the father, thinking that family influence could not fail to secure him a Church living, favored his adopting the clerical profession; the mother favored preparation for a diplomatic career; but both feared university dissipation—so that they sent him not to Heidelberg but to Göttingen.[1]

His first three months at the university were largely given to study and he was especially attracted to the lecture room of Heeren, then eminent as a historian; but soon the old wild Bismarck spirit broke out irresistibly. He remained but three terms at Göttingen, and many days during this period were spent by him in the university jail for duelling and general insubordination. Duelling seems to have been a passion with him; he took part in twenty-eight student combats, one of them with pistols, and to the end of his life he carried on his face a scar, broad and deep, then gained. His university life was, to outward appearance, mainly swaggering and roystering, but in reality he read much and well; he attended very few lectures—his professors during his whole university life generally complaining that he did not come near them. Heeren seemed the only one among them who impressed him. His evil repute spread far: the authorities of the University of Jena, hearing that he was about making a visit to that city, at once foreordained his expulsion.

In his "Reflections and Reminiscences," dictated late in life, he declares that he became in his school days a pantheist and a republican; but a moderating influence upon him appears to have been now exerted by a small knot of New England students, the foremost of these being John Lothrop Motley, eminent afterward as an

---

[1] It was from Bismarck himself that the present writer received the statement regarding his father's preference as to his choice of a profession and the reasons for it.

envoy of the United States at Vienna and London, and as the historian of the Dutch Republic.

After a year and a half of this life at Göttingen, his heart and mind seemed to revolt against his own folly, and, having decided to apply himself more vigorously to legal studies, he went to Berlin, and there rejoined Motley; the association between the two men became close; in after life they corresponded, and whenever Motley appeared in Germany he at once became Bismarck's guest; to the end of his life Bismarck was very fond of talking to Americans, and especially to American envoys at Berlin, of his happy relations with this friend of his student days.[1]

In spite of this friendship with a man averse to roystering and swaggering, Bismarck appeared in Berlin under an academic cloud, since by the understanding at his departure from Göttingen one of his first duties after arriving at the capital was to make up part of a sentence to the university prison. He now went on with his legal studies, but for a considerable time showed little earnestness in them. Though the greatest of contemporary law professors, Savigny, was then teaching there, Bismarck appeared but twice or thrice in his lecture room.

Yet he was by no means intellectually idle: during this scholastic period, even during his excesses and roystering, he continued vigorously his reading in Spinoza,

[1] For reminiscences of the life of the two friends together, dictated by Bismarck himself, see Oliver Wendell Holmes, *Memoir of Motley*, Boston, 1898, pp. 17–19. For other details, and for portions of the correspondence between them, see G. W. Curtis, *Correspondence of Motley*, New York, 1889. For a much more complete presentation, see *Drei Briefe, 1855–1858*, in Horst Kohl, *Bismarck Jahrbuch*, Band iii, pp. 97 and following; and *Sechs Briefe, 1864–1874*, *ibid.*, iv, p. 209 and following. For a curious evidence of Bismarck's pride in his acquaintance with Motley, see *The Correspondence of William I and Bismarck*, Eng. translation, London, 1903, vol. i, p. 136. Some additional matters connected with their relations, learned from Bismarck, are given in the Autobiography of the present writer.

SEVEN GREAT STATESMEN

Hegel, Goethe, Shakespeare, and other great thinkers,—giving himself much to history, and continuing to show, as Stein had done, especial liking for the history of England. More than two years had thus been spent, apparently aimlessly, when he began to show that power in work which became later the wonder of Europe. For in spite of his neglect of lectures he grappled heroically with his law books, and by working, night and day, pushed his way through all barriers, became Auscultator, or legal attaché of a court, and in this capacity tried sundry cases with an originality, not to say impudence toward witnesses and judges, which nearly ended his legal life then and there.

Then came another of the many sudden changes in his career. He announced a preference for administrative work rather than legal, rapidly prepared himself, astonished the local jurists by the brilliancy of his examination, and became a *Referendar,* or official law reporter, at Aix-la-Chapelle. In this new career he again learned to despise the bureaucracy about him; but he continued to read much, cultivated largely the society of foreign visitors, appeared at the Royal Palace at Berlin and was presented to Prince William of Prussia—afterward the Emperor William of Germany. But here there was a new outbreak of dissipation which later in life he bitterly regretted, and which began a period of unrest lasting nearly ten years. The young man seemed "everything by turns and nothing long." He became a petty bureaucrat at Potsdam, began his military service in the Royal Guard and flew among the highest; but suddenly there came a shock,—news that the family fortunes were wrecked, that the passion of the mother for high life had led to neglect of the estates and to wretched financial entanglements.[1]

[1] For Bismarck's theses, on taking his examination as Referendar, given

The better Bismarck now asserts himself. He realizes the situation at once, acts promptly, breaks away from Potsdam and all its court attractions and extravagances, goes to the little university of Greifswald, resumes his military service in a comparatively humble company there, and devotes himself to study at the neighboring agricultural college of Eldena, and to practice at his little estate in Pomerania.

The death of his father in 1845 increased his responsibilities and we now hear of him as a country squire at the most important of the three family estates,—Schönhausen. His passion for rural life deepened; in his great days afterward his wife told visiting statesmen, "He cares more for a turnip than for all your politics."

In redeeming the estates he applied the scientific theories he had learned at Eldena, but with that practical common sense which was always his main trait. He learned much from the men about him. To the end of his life he loved the rude ways and shrewd talk of the peasantry. He knew them through and through, became one of them, and this mingling of science and practical observation brought success and won respect. Erelong he was made Captain of the Dikes upon the Elbe. This suited his character well, for it demanded prompt decision in emergencies, sudden grapples with danger, forceful assertions of authority, and persistent fighting with trespassers and marauders along the coasts and in the courts.

Like so many of his ancestors he at times broke over conventionalities and proprieties. As the hero of various reckless adventures he became widely known as "crazy" Bismarck—*Der tolle Bismarck*. There were wild night rides, with falls and rib-breaking which cost him weeks in the hospital,—carousals worthy of the

in full, see Horst Kohl, *Bismarck Jahrbuch*, Band ii, pp. 3–47. They show wide reading, close reasoning, and much Prussian patriotism.

Thirty Years' War,—visits to boon companions whom he awakened by pistol shots through their windows, and to ladies whom he once sought to amuse by letting loose a fox in a ballroom.

Great as was his liking for rural life, he went often to Berlin, and saw much of society in all its phases,—from court to barrack. Throughout his sayings and doings at this period, and especially through his letters, there runs an exuberant vein of humor; but he was wont to pass rapidly from exhilaration to melancholy—these moods being especially evidenced in his copious home letters, above all in those written, now and later, to his sister and his future wife. Both from a psychological and a literary point of view these letters are among the best ever written: witty, humorous, shrewd, exquisitely appreciative of events and characters, constantly revealing acute thought and profound reflection, and all perfectly natural—every utterance in them direct from his heart and mind: the letters are the man himself.

He remained a voracious reader—giving long winter evenings to history, philosophy, and poetry—German, French, and English; and his memory seemed to retain everything—even the ponderous German Geography, in twenty volumes, whence came largely that minute acquaintance with Central Europe which in after years so surprised his opponents in Parliament and in diplomatic conferences.[1]

But this physical and mental dissipation was not at the cost of steady application or of production. Then and ever afterward he was able to *study,*—to master thoroughly a given subject,—to write profoundly and pun-

---

[1] His passion for miscellaneous reading seems to have continued even to his last hours. The present writer saw at Friedrichsruh in the autumn of 1908, on the table at which Bismarck had been wont to work and adjoining the room in which he died, a pile of miscellaneous books which he read in his last days, and among them a brilliant English novel attacking New York City life.

gently,—in his early days for the newspapers and at a later period in his reports and despatches.

He greatly loved travel,—visiting England, France, and Switzerland, and later Russia, Hungary, Italy, Spain, and the Scandinavian countries. His letters show that he kept his eyes open; he seems to see everything,—and not merely things material. In his letters chronicling family and farm affairs his drollery is irresistible; in characterizing men and picturing scenery he is masterly. Were the letters not so good they would at times seem whimsical: he spreads upon his page the softening shades on the mountains, the shimmer of the sea, the coloring of the strata along the road, the play of the sunlight on the herbage, the character of the farming and its yield. He shows himself capable of deep moral impressions, as when he visits the Wartburg, recalls the work done there by Luther, and ponders its deep meanings; or later, when, sitting by the Rhine at Bingen, he reflects upon his earlier follies.[1]

Gradually there came a new evolution in his religious and political theories. Cynical and caustic as he frequently was, there can be no doubt that this was an honest change. The political change was entirely natural: it was the reaction which came over so many sound, strong minds as they reflected upon the follies, the crimes, the cruelties, the idiocy, and the nauseous cant of the

[1] For the family correspondence, see the collection authorized by Prince Herbert Bismarck entitled *Briefe an seine Braut und Gattin* (of this an English translation by C. T. Lewis, Harper and Brothers, New York, 1901); also various friendly letters to those near him given in Keudell, *Bismarck et sa Famille*, translated by Lang, Paris, 1902. For special letters, personal and political, see Poschinger's *Bismarck-Portefeuille*, and other works edited by him. For the confidential letters from Frankfort to ministers at Berlin, see *Lettres Politiques Confidentielles*, translated by Lang, Paris, 1885. For his letters to his sovereign, see *The Correspondence of William I and Bismarck, with Other Letters from and to Prince Bismarck*, English translation by Ford, London and New York, 2 vols., 1903.

Revolution in France and of the various attempts at mob rule in Germany. A religious change was also natural. The Rousseau ideas of the eighteenth century which he had heard in his mother's drawing-room were outworn; association with sundry thoughtful friends, and, especially, conversations with a very lovely and brilliant Christian woman, a neighbor and friend, as she consciously approached death, wrought a change in his views of life—a deep change. Now, too, he became engaged to the daughter of a neighboring squire,—a woman whose native strength of character and religious intuitions were to exercise a very deep influence upon his whole career. Thereby all his original tendencies to reaction were strengthened; the history of Prussia, including especially the work of the Great Elector and of Frederick the Great, whom he had always revered, took on yet deeper meanings for him, and he became known among his friends as a desperate reactionary.

To end this period came a series of events which opened to him a new career. As we have seen, there had been created eight provincial Diets in Prussia, petty assemblies where local affairs might be discussed by the squirearchy, not in a legislative, but in an advisory way; and in 1847 Frederick William IV, yielding to the pressure for some sort of central deliberative assembly, had called a United Diet at Berlin, made up of representatives from these local assemblies. To this came Bismarck. Nothing could be more unpromising than this entrance of his into politics. He had not been elected to this legislature, but, the person chosen being ill, the young squire went as a substitute; nothing was expected of him: he tells us that at his first election speech he was pelted with stones, and the only recorded parliamentary speech of his at that period was a protest in a little provincial assembly "against the excessive consumption of tallow in an almshouse."

Yet it should be noted that, although widely considered a mere noisy declaimer, he had already shown himself something better. He had seen the necessity of improving the procedure in certain courts and had drawn up a project of reforms which showed patriotic purpose and constructive power. But nothing of this better side of his activity was known beyond a very limited circle; and during the first part of the session he seemed to make no impression.[1] Not until larger politics were discussed, did he begin making known his views to better purpose; then his fellow-members, and, indeed, the world outside, began listening to him. His oratory was wretched, but his perseverance was invincible. Never was there a more defiant reactionary. He held fast to the divine origin of kingly right; on constitutionalism he poured contempt; Prussia, in his view, had become powerful under men like the Great Elector and Frederick the Great,—rulers with a rod of iron,—and it could only remain powerful under absolutism. To those who praised constitutional monarchy in England, he insisted that the circumstances of the two nations were entirely different; English ideas of divine right, he said, had been rooted out by revolution and civil war, whereas in Prussia the idea of kingship by the grace of God was the mainspring of popular political thought and the centre of the whole governmental system. In his view neither parliament nor any court of justice is the source of law, or its interpreter, but the king. He opposed all concessions to the modern spirit; he arrayed against the emancipation of the Jews the idea of the Christian state, insisting that "princes, intrusted with God's scepter, rule with it on earth in accordance with God's will, as revealed in his Holy

[1] See Horst Kohl, *Jahrbuch*, vol. iii, p. 36, and following. For the six points in the reform, very practically stated, see p. 37, with commentary preceding and following them, in the second of the letters addressed to L. von Gerlach.

Gospel, and this end could not in any way be promoted by the help of the Jews.'' All efforts to make the United Prussian Diet a legislative body, or even to allow it regular sessions, he fiercely opposed. He declared German unity a delusion; jeered and sneered at the flag which represented it; proclaimed his love for the flag and colors of Prussia—despotic Austria he regarded with reverence and even with affection.

In all this he gave evidence of that force which afterward became so potent in shaping the destinies of his country. In the ordinary sense he could never be called an orator: he stammered, stuttered, hesitated, not unfrequently insulted his audience, and on one occasion, when he had thus brought on a tumult, he turned his back to the assembly, drew a newspaper from his pocket, and stood reading it until order was restored. But he was deeply in earnest, he forced his fellow-members to listen to him, and, outside the Diet, Berlin, though it derided, remembered him.[1]

At the end of three months, it was seen that this Prussian United Diet could accomplish nothing, and it was dismissed. Now came Bismarck's marriage, and it proved happy. His letters to his wife are among the treasures of German literature; her influence over him was one of the fortunate things of his career; to the end of his days, his household life brought blessings to him, and these he at all times attributed to his wife's influence.

In 1847, while on his wedding journey, at Venice, he met King Frederick William and talked fully and freely with him. No two men could be personally more unlike; but the sovereign was evidently won by the young man's theories of carrying on the government with a high hand.

[1] The present writer, having heard Bismarck speak at various times in important debates, has given an account of his manner, in his Autobiography, vol. i, pp. 598, 599. For the exhibition of contempt for his parliamentary audience, see Keudell, as above, p. 7.

The revolution which broke out early in the following year took a peculiarly violent form in Berlin and its first outburst resulted in much bloodshed. Bismarck at once showed himself its resourceful enemy. In the village adjoining his estate he tore down the German flag and hoisted the flag of Prussia; under his inspiration the peasants of the region declared themselves ready to march on Berlin with scythes and pikes to rescue the king from the mob; and he overawed all his neighbors who took a different view.

He also wrought through the press. The so-called "Journal of the Cross" (*Kreuz-Zeitung*), was, and still is, one of the great reactionary newspapers of Prussia, the organ of high Lutheranism and of unbridled power in church and state; for this Bismarck wrote many articles, clear, pungent, and cogent; though at times whimsical, they were sure to arouse and bind together conservative ultraists.

But the revolution took its course. The king submitted to abject humiliation in presence of the mob which besieged his palace, allowed his troops to be sent away, consented to a constitution and called a Prussian Diet,— not, like the poor old United Prussian Diet, with merely advisory powers, but a parliament for actual legislation.

In the Prussian Diet, Bismarck, even while merely a substitute deputy, won speedy recognition as a leader. On the claims of the people to be represented, on the ballot box as a means of choosing legislators, on the decision of state questions by majorities, on establishing periodical sessions, he poured contempt constantly and loudly; Frederick the Great was still his ideal: not the Parliament, but the Army, was to uplift the country.[1]

[1] On all Bismarck's early parliamentary efforts an intensely interesting light is thrown by his letters to his intended wife. See *The Love Letters of Bismarck*, New York, 1901. For peculiarly engaging pictures of his family life, see especially Keudell.

It was not a case of bark worse than bite. Worse than his talk was his action. Never was intriguer more persistent. Night and day, when not stirring up resistance to constitutionalism in the Diet, he was rallying his friends on the lower Elbe, or at Potsdam, or at Berlin, against all efforts for constitutional liberty, whether rational or irrational. Nothing but his sincerity and force saved him from becoming ridiculous as a busybody. During the revolutionary days he went disguised into the mob and forced his way into the presence of generals, ministers, princes, and the king himself. On one occasion he so reproached His Majesty for concessions to the revolution that the Queen rebuked him for impudence. He drew tears from the eyes of the two future emperors by reciting reactionary verses to them. He was deeply in earnest: rising to speak in the Diet his voice at times faltered and once at least he shed tears. The extremists on the liberal side in the Diet gave him abundant texts and chances, for most of them were wont to take the second step before they had taken the first. In palaces and in barracks, he urged, with shrewd plans and bitter taunts, the most desperate measures, and, at last, seemed successful; for, with the king's permission, Marshal Wrangel, a tough, swaggering old soldier, turned the Prussian Diet out of doors. Even this did not satisfy Bismarck: he showed disappointment that there had been no bloodshed; his wish was that a lesson should be written in blood which would last for a generation, and his favorite plan was to stir the mob to madness and then to crush it with the army.

There was no need of bloodshed. The people at large were tired of talk and sick with uncertainty;—and, beside that, the king had won them over by again swallowing his feudal formulas, granting a fairly good constitution, and calling a new election. To the new Prussian Diet thus called His Majesty's loyal subjects gratefully sent a reactionary majority, and in the midst of it—at last as a full member—came Bismarck.

It was a triumph for him, but in spite of it the stars in their courses fought against his ideas: the king's new constitution seemed to betray them, and even the reactionary ministers, whom Bismarck had aided to bring it in, soon began making concessions to the modern spirit. During long years all was chaotic,—strong men fighting in clouds and darkness with no clear purpose and toward no definite end.

While this fiasco was taking place at Berlin, another was beginning at Frankfort-on-Main. At this ancient imperial city, as we have seen, there met, in May of 1848, a Federal German Parliament with aspirations to establish German liberty and unity. Toward all its activities Bismarck showed the same feelings as towards similar efforts in the Prussian Diet. All its efforts he opposed with scoffing and bitter irony, and, when the Parliament tendered the imperial crown to the Prussian king, he fought its acceptance passionately—his especial ground of opposition being that a crown coming from the German people represented popular sovereignty. In one of his speeches he said, "The Frankfort crown may be brilliant, but the gold which gives it genuineness must first be got by melting down the crown of Prussia," and, continuing his scoffs at the idea of accomplishing German unity by parliamentary methods, he expressed his "hope to God that Prussians would remain Prussians long after the Frankfort constitution has mouldered away like a withered autumn leaf."

The old federation having evaporated into thin air during the Revolution of 1848 and the national parliament then established having, as we have seen, gone to pieces at Frankfort and Stuttgart, chaos came again. There was an "assembly" at Gotha, an "alliance of three kings" (Prussia, Saxony, and Hanover), an "adhesion" to this of twenty-eight princelings inclined to Prussia, a *quasi* league of Bavaria and Würtemberg with sundry princelings inclined to Austria, and finally, in 1850, a new German parliament called by the Prussian king at Erfurt. This derived some prestige from sitting in the old church of the Augustines made memorable by Luther, and it was in one respect strikingly unlike its predecessor at Frankfort:—that sat over a year; this lasted hardly a month—its only important work being to consider a ready-made, cut-and-dried, spick-and-span constitution for the German nation, proposed by King Frederick William but entangled in manifold difficulties. To this body came Bismarck, simply to denounce every feature, and, especially, every liberal feature of the proposed instrument. Characteristic of him, as he then was, were his diatribes against the right of public meeting, which he stigmatized as "a fire-bellows of democracy," and against the German tricolored flag,—which he held up to scorn as a "badge of rebellion." Though the more liberal view nominally prevailed and the new constitution was then and there approved, Bismarck's sarcasms seemed to wither it; it disappeared in the gusts of political passion and was never heard of more.

Worse than this, his hatred of revolution made him, throughout this first parliamentary period of his,—from 1847 to 1851,—in whatever deliberative body he sat, not only the opponent of national unity but the champion of Austrian supremacy. Worst of all, when Austria, at Olmütz, with the aid of Russia, put upon Prussia the most shameful humiliation in her history—forcing her to cease all efforts toward national unity, to yield to Austrian threats and to go back submissively to the old Frankfort Diet, with its envoys sitting about the old green table and representing, not the people, but the reigning princes—Bismarck still supported Austria.

Although in his speeches and writings he did not spare

the weakness of the King and his ministers, spoke caustically against their policy, and voted at a session of the Prussian Diet in a minority of two against a vote of thanks to His Majesty for granting a constitution, King Frederick William now saw in him a man likely to be of use, and in 1851 sent him to the revived green-table Confederation Diet at Frankfort, first as Councillor of the Prussian Embassy, and shortly afterward as Ambassador. Here was to be the young statesman's work for the next eight years. It was an amazing promotion. At thirty-six years of age, an impoverished and widely discredited country squire, with no powerful connections and no diplomatic experience, he was thus given the most important position in the whole diplomatic service of Prussia.

OF all Bismarck's qualities revealed in his new position, most surprising were his insight and foresight, and most imposing were his courage in breasting opposition and his force in breaking it. His insight and foresight seemed due to intuition—to sudden flashes which lighted up his course and determined his conduct; but, in a very real sense, they were in most cases the outcome of study and reflection,—sometimes brought to bear upon the events of a year, sometimes focused upon the occurrence of a moment.

His courage never faltered. Whether in resisting the Parliament, or the press, or the mob, or assassins in the streets, or kings and emperors in their cabinets, it was ever the same. When, later in life, he told Europe, "We Germans fear God and naught beside," he but read into German history his own character.

Striking examples of these qualities were seen early. He had entered the Diet as a friend of Austria, as a supporter of its policy, as a believer in the value of its alliance with Prussia; indeed, he had defended Austria in the Olmütz matter, when she was really indefensible; his theory being that Austria was willing to support Prussia in German affairs and that Prussia should support Austria in foreign affairs.

But now came to him a revelation. He found that the old Austrian hatred of Prussia, which had begun in the early days of the Prussian monarchy, and which had been increased by the successes of Frederick the Great, was still venomous; that Austria opposed, openly or secretly, every measure looking to the better development of Prussia or to the extension of her legitimate influence; that the lesser powers cowered before her, and in the sessions of the Diet constantly voted for her against their own convictions: and he found, also, that Prussia had gradually become one of these lesser powers. Outward and visible signs of this Austrian supremacy in the Frankfort Diet were comical. The representative of Austria always presided, and seemed to think it his duty to magnify his office. At such pretensions Bismarck struck at once. In some of his conversations toward the end of his life, he enjoyed giving accounts of the farces in which he thus engaged. One well known story was of an Austrian presiding officer and his cigar. A precedent had grown up,—and the Diet was exceedingly tenacious of precedents,—that the Austrian president might smoke while in the chair, but that on no account might any other Ambassador follow his example: seeing this, Bismarck pulled a cigar from his pocket, went up to the president, asked him for a light, obtained it, and calmly smoked on during the sessions ever afterward. Gradually his colleagues mustered up equal courage, and soon all were in this respect equal. One very eminent Austrian president of the Diet, Count Prokesch, was also brought to his bearings. Having altered the record of the Congress in a way favorable to Austrian views, and attention having been called to this, Prokesch thought to overawe his colleagues by saying: "If that record is not correct, I am a liar": whereupon Bismarck, looking him full in the face, answered, "Exactly so, Your Excellency!" All present were aghast. A duel was expected. But Prokesch thought it best to set the matter right,—when Bismarck calmly continued to insist upon it. Prokesch's successor, Count Rechberg, next tried the same line of conduct, and in a bitter debate went so far that a challenge passed. Bismarck insisted that a protocol be drawn and pistols brought at once, whereupon Rechberg thought better of it and no harm resulted. Typical was

Bismarck's abolition of another custom implying Austrian supremacy. The Austrian president was wont, when any of his colleagues visited him, to remain sitting and to allow the visitor to remain standing. But, when this was attempted on Bismarck, he quietly seated himself, and so began a new custom. In all this his great personality, his reserved force, his perfect self-possession, his quickness in repartee, his humor, his readiness in every sort of resource, made him invincible.

His letters to his wife, his sister, and his intimate friends, as well as his despatches, now began to show utter contempt for the green-table Diet. He constantly complained of its pretentiousness, its uselessness, its pettifoggery, its quackery; and he uttered his growing conviction that the only solution of all the existing difficulties would be found in an agreement which should secure better treatment to Prussia, or in a war which should rid Germany of Austria. Among the many evidences of his feeling, one became widely known. At a public function, an Austrian officer, pointing to the few and scattered medals and crosses on Bismarck's coat, asked him sneeringly if he had won them in battle. "Yes," answered Bismarck, "in battle against the enemy here in Frankfort."

More and more he now insisted in his letters and despatches that the existing system could not last; that it gave no chance for a normal development of Prussia; that the votes of the minor states were directed by Austria against every Prussian interest and aspiration. Day after day he nagged the Austrians exquisitely,—and quarrels resulted which seemed at one time likely to force both nations into war. This attitude of his in the Diet brought upon him such personal unpopularity that stones were thrown at him and his wife in the streets of Frankfort; but his composure was not disturbed. Four octavos of Bismarck's despatches given to the world by

Herr von Poschinger show that, from first to last, he was completely master of himself: as literature, as practical political philosophy, humorous, witty, penetrative, convincing, they combine more striking characteristics than any other similar collection, and the best of them were written during this Frankfort period.

But, while the Frankfort Diet was dragging wearily along, there came the Crimean War, and this brought out anew Bismarck's foresight and courage.

In this struggle between Great Britain, France, Sardinia, and Turkey on one side, and Russia on the other, the three western powers put forth their utmost efforts to induce Prussia and Austria to join them. To these efforts Austria secretly yielded, her old dread of Russia prevailing over her gratitude for the rescue from Hungary which Russia had brought her during the Revolution year of 1849, and for the victory over Prussia which Russia had won for her at Olmütz in 1850. For a time Prussia also seemed likely to yield: the Chevalier Bunsen, minister at the court of Great Britain, one of King Frederick William's most cherished advisers, seemed likely to turn the King's mind against Prussia's powerful eastern neighbor. But now Bismarck intervened. In letters, despatches, conversations, he showed the King and his advisers that Prussia had no concern in the question at issue, but that it was her interest to strengthen friendly relations with Russia. Bismarck, of all men, saw here a great opportunity. Could he win the gratitude of the Russian Czar, Russia might allow Prussia, in what Bismarck regarded as the inevitable coming struggle with Austria, to fight without intervention,— might, indeed, possibly favor Prussia. This was not an argument he could avow, but it was none the less that which led him to exert himself to such good purpose that Prussia finally remained neutral during the war. Bitter hostility was brought upon him thereby, even in Germany; while in Great Britain revenge was taken by every form of attack, from parliamentary speeches and leaders in the *Times* to cartoons in *Punch*. From France came every sort of insult.[1] His reply to one of these French attacks became widely known. The French Ambassador, the Marquis de Moustier, in a heated discussion, charged him with leading Prussia to another Jena, whereupon Bismarck instantly replied, "Why not to another Leipzig or another Waterloo?"

The German statesman could afford to take all these attacks with equanimity; for from the first it was clear that he had secured the gratitude of the Russian Czar. One evidence of this was seen the day after the death of Emperor Nicholas—in the midst of the Crimean War— at the first reception of the diplomatic corps in the Winter Palace by the new Emperor, Alexander II. The young sovereign, having given the Austrian Minister a most cutting reproof, recalling bitterly the ingratitude of his country, turned to the Prussian Minister and thanked him effusively for the kindness which the Prussian King and his government had shown to Russia in this her hour of trial.[2]

More and more Bismarck's ability was now recognized at the Prussian capital. Partly in order to settle tariff

[1] For a very striking caricature in *Punch*, showing the bitterness of the time, see the cartoon, "Le Roi Clicquot," representing the Prussian King as drunk, maudlin, staggering, his crown falling from his head, and a bottle of champagne in his hand. In the Library of Cornell University are three folio volumes of German caricatures, covering the Revolution óf 1848; in these Bismarck figures rarely, but in the neighboring volumes of *Kladderadatsch*, beginning a little later, the young statesman has evidently become a man of mark. See also Walther, *Bismarck in der Karikatur*,—and Grand Carteret, *Bismarck en Caricature*. It may also be mentioned that in the Cornell library are five elephant folios containing caricatures collected at Paris during the Franco-Prussian War, and especially during the rule of the Commune, and that, in these, Bismarck figures largely and satanically.

[2] The present writer, who witnessed this scene, has given a detailed account of it in his published Autobiography.

difficulties, but mainly to make him better acquainted with the politics and statesmen of Prussia's great rival, King Frederick William sent him for a month to Vienna as a temporary Ambassador, giving him a letter of credence not of the usual perfunctory sort, but a personal epistle, impressing upon the Austrian Emperor Bismarck's loyalty to Prussia, and his reverence for Austria. This ensured courteous treatment; but, though he used this advantage fully in the endeavor to induce the Vienna government to pursue a more rational policy in German matters, he now satisfied himself finally that a peaceful solution of questions between Austria and Prussia would be impossible.

During all this Frankfort period he made the best possible use of his vacations, both as regarded his health and his knowledge of men and affairs: we hear of him at nearly all the courts of Europe; in danger of robbers in Hungary; swimming in the Danube, in the Rhine, and in the North Sea; hunting in the Scandinavian countries and in Russia; flitting between Frankfort and Berlin, and to other capitals,—always making good use of his observing faculties and of his acquaintance with leading men.

Of all these plunges into European life, the most important was his visit to the Paris Exposition in 1855, when he met Napoleon III for the first time—thus opening the way to the fruitful interviews of later years. On his return, always having in mind a future contest with Austria, in which it would be absolutely necessary for Prussia to secure French neutrality, he advised the Prussian government to cultivate the friendship of Napoleon III. For this policy he received much abuse—his old friends, who had adored him as a devotee of divine right and legitimacy, turning from him as a supporter of Bonapartism, the worst enemy of both; but he remained none the less firm in his opinion.

In 1857 came an apparent calamity. Frederick William IV under the stress of that troubled time having lost his reason, his brother, Crown Prince William, was given virtually royal power, and in the following year became Regent of the Kingdom. This change seemed especially injurious to Bismarck's interests; and all the more so when the new Regent recalled him from the Frankfort Diet and sent him as Ambassador to St. Petersburg. Of this period Bismarck was wont to say that the Regent, fearing his fervent hostility to Austria, "thought it best, for a time, to put him on ice." But before going Bismarck wrote to the Prussian minister of foreign affairs letters summing up the result of his observations and experiences at Frankfort, with a most bitter indictment of Austrian aims and methods, and openly declared that sooner or later the question at issue must demand treatment "with fire and sword": these despatches made a deep impression on Regent William, and caused Bismarck to be remembered; they were destined to become part of a new Prussian political gospel.

A good opportunity for a strong man to carry out this policy against Austria was now offered. The war promoted by Cavour was beginning between Austria and Italy. Had Bismarck then been called to the head of affairs in Berlin, he would doubtless have seized this occasion to give Prussia the supremacy in Germany; but, as it was, he could only exercise an influence through his despatches from St. Petersburg. The Crimean War had ended in 1856, but Russian resentment toward Austria and gratitude toward Prussia remained. This gratitude he did his best to increase; all ranks, from the Emperor down, received him with the greatest cordiality; in one of his home letters, he says: "Life here is like being in Abraham's bosom."

In his despatches to the Prussian government he constantly urges it to keep out of the war then going on between Austria on one side and France and Piedmont on the other, and to make the most of it in pushing Prussia's opportunity; so earnest was he in this policy that hostility at home against him was increased, and it became a common taunt against him that he was "more French than German."

In spite of all his advice, the Prussian government and people became more and more inclined to interfere in favor of Austria. The victories of the allied French and Italians at Magenta and Solferino over the Austrians naturally aroused a widespread pan-Germanic feeling. The German press stirred it vigorously. It was the old story. Hundreds of newspaper writers throughout the German states, sitting safely and snugly in their various dens, were exceedingly anxious to send other men to fight "for German brotherhood and honor."

Luckily, Austrian cunning detected in this a serious danger; squabbles arising between the two great German powers regarding the command of the proposed combination of Prussian and Austrian armies, Austria became more fearful of Prussia than of France and settled the whole matter by giving up Lombardy to Italy at the peace of Villafranca.

In 1861 Frederick William died and Regent William crowned himself at Königsberg as King of Prussia. Menzel, the greatest of Prussian painters, commemorated this event in a picture which attracted European attention at Paris and was finally given a place of honor in the royal residence at Berlin. King William in full robes stands before the high altar, takes thence his crown, and places it upon his own head. Of all the Prussian monarchs he was the only one thus consecrated, save the first, who had assumed the title of Frederick I a hundred and sixty years before, and the reason for this revived ceremonial was that the new King wished,—especially at the close of a revolutionary period,—to assert more earnestly than ever the origin of his sovereignty, as not in the popular will, but in the grace of God. Bismarck was present and doubtless was confirmed in his monarchical sentiments thereby; but a new feeling had arisen in him: while remaining a devoted Prussian, he had become more and more German, and, while holding strongly to his monarchical ideas, he had begun to believe more and more in popular support. His was the same feeling which had led Stein, fifty years before, to exert himself to make subjects into citizens; and at last we have a statement from Bismarck that Prussia's main alliance henceforward should be, not with the German rulers, but with the German people.

The new King, William I, though not possessing the graces of his predecessor, was a more manly and soldierly character, with infinitely more force, common sense, and penetration—one of his most marked qualities being his ability to choose strong men and to stand by them. He soon discerned the characteristics of his ambassador at St. Petersburg and after Bismarck's stay of three years in that capital recalled him to Berlin with the thought of making him a cabinet minister.

But there came delay. In after years Bismarck said that his royal master had dreaded him as "a political rowdy," and therefore it was that this period of uncertainty was tided over by making him Ambassador at Paris. This jumped well with Bismarck's humor: in view of eventualities he wished to know more of France and of Napoleon III,—evidently hoping to win the French Emperor over to his scheme for driving Austria out of Germany. His stay in France was short, only about three months; yet during this period he learned much. He studied the French Emperor closely, walking and talking with him, unfolding various plans to him, drawing various vague schemes and dreams from him, presenting skillful baits to his ambition, suggesting reasons why France should allow Prussia to have her way in German matters.

Curious were the estimates the two men made of each other: Napoleon insisted that Bismarck was "not serious"; Bismarck spoke later of Napoleon as "a great, unrecognized incapacity." [1]

Meantime King William had become uneasy at various weaknesses in the Prussian army. As far back as the attempted mobilization during the war between Austria on one side and France and Italy on the other, these weaknesses had become apparent, and the King and his war minister, Roon, were seeking to increase the army largely and to reorganize it. But the liberals in the Prussian Parliament opposed this: while willing to increase the army temporarily, they dreaded to do so permanently; and therefore it was that, while returning from a vacation in Spain, Bismarck suddenly received a summons to come home at once. Arriving in Berlin, he found the King in despair. Coming into the royal presence, he found His Majesty not only greatly depressed, but with his abdication already prepared. The King had done his best to oppose Parliament constitutionally, had even thought of opposing it unconstitutionally; but his family, including the Queen, the Crown Prince, and the Crown Prince's English wife, were strongly against him. They had presented to him their English theories, had drawn for him historical lessons from the revolutions in 1648 and 1688, which had put an end to the Stuart dynasty—especially they had pointed out to him that these revolutions involved the same principles, indeed the same lines of action, as those now contemplated in Prussia.

At first, Bismarck, supposing that the King would not

[1] For a very minute and interesting account of these and later interviews, especially at Biarritz, see Von Poschinger, *Bismarck-Portefeuille*, vol. i, pp. 143 and following.

SEVEN GREAT STATESMEN

support him in strong measures, refused to become Prime Minister; but, when the King asked him if he was ready to govern against a majority of the national representatives in Parliament, Bismarck promptly answered that he was, and the abdication paper was destroyed.

Thus it was that in 1862 Bismarck committed himself to a contest against the Prussian legislative body, which believed itself the savior of the national constitution. For a time, his main effort seems to have been to keep up the courage of the King, and, in a talk between them about the English Civil War and the fate of Charles I and Strafford, Bismarck avowed his willingness to suffer the fate of Strafford in support of the rights of the sovereign, whereupon the old Prussian feeling of Frederick the Great and the Great Elector asserted itself in William's breast, and it was determined between him and his minister to fight the lower house of the Prussian Parliament to the bitter end, constitution or no constitution. The King at once dismissed the existing ministry and appointed as his Prime Minister Bismarck, who now began ruling in defiance of the majority, and raising money without a parliamentary budget.[1]

Never has any parliamentary struggle so desperate occurred in any other modern nation. In his first speech after coming to power, Bismarck said: "Prussia must collect its strength for the favorable moment, which has already several times been allowed to pass; Prussia's borders are not adapted to sound health in the political body. It is not by speeches and resolutions that the great questions of the times are to be decided—that was the mistake of 1848 and 1849—but by blood and iron." For

[1] For a thrilling account of Bismarck's conversion of the King to extreme measures in the railway train at Jüterbogk and at the palace of Babelsberg, see Bismarck's *Reflections and Reminiscences*, Tauchnitz edit., vol. i, pp. 294–297, 313–317; also Busch, *Bismarck and Some Secret Pages of His History*, vol. ii, pp. 414, 415.

four years (1862–66) he governed in spite of the opposing majority; twice he dissolved Parliament and sent its members back to their constituents; at his own will he took from the treasury money for carrying on the administration, including the reorganization of the army. In Parliament he defied the presiding officer, and, when called to order by him, declared that he acknowledged no master save the King. When his opponents denounced him he often went out to smoke in the lobby. He gave an interpretation of the constitution which was thought an insult by all who heard it. He hurled at his enemies epithets which astounded Europe—among others the phrase, "Catilinarian existences." The press he muzzled or bribed. The judicious grieved, the doctrinaires raged, the mob insulted him in the streets, hatred against him extended so far and wide that from Spain came a threat to murder him. Even more serious were the efforts at Berlin to reach him by special law, and the fate of Strafford, which King William had foretold for him, seemed to some of his friends so probable that they advised him to transfer his estate to his brother; but he did nothing of the kind and only became more defiant than ever. Honorable to him was his care, while fearlessly exposing himself, to shield the monarchy. He took the responsibility. He seemed to feel that it might lead to his destruction—that he might be sent to the block as a second Strafford—but he was evidently determined that King William should not be a second Charles Stuart.[1]

Meantime, he was obliged to combat extremists on his own side. The old Elector of Hesse Cassel persisting in reactionary follies despite remonstrances from King William and disapproval even from Austria, Bismarck sent

[1] For Bismarck's refusal to transfer his property to avoid its confiscation, see his *Reflections and Reminiscences*, Tauchnitz edition, vol. iii, p. 78, and Keudell, *Bismarck et sa Famille*, p. 115.

a simple military courier with a peremptory summons, and brought him to terms at once.

In 1863 came a new outburst of hatred against him. The Poles arose in rebellion against Russia. Bismarck undoubtedly had a contempt for Polish revolutionists, based on his historical knowledge of the follies which had brought Poland to ruin. As to the great landowning class, he knew that, having had every advantage throughout hundreds of years,—with a vast territory, admirable seaports, and a brave people,—they had persisted, despite repeated warnings, in maintaining anarchy and had allowed their country to become the chosen seat of clerical and aristocratic tyranny. As to the tillers of the soil, he accepted the old Silesian proverb, "Where you find a peasantry hopelessly wretched, you find them hugging two masters—the priesthood and the whiskey bottle."

But what was far more to Bismarck's present purpose, he saw in this rebellion an additional chance to strengthen the Prussian sympathies of the Czar, so that there should be no interference when the grapple with Austria should come: he, therefore, arrayed the Prussian power in alliance with Russia against the whole Polish uprising.

At this, a cry of horror arose from millions of good and kind people throughout Europe, and, above all, in France and England. All to no purpose—Bismarck stood firm.

In the world-wide detestation of Bismarck Austria now saw her opportunity, and in the summer of 1863 summoned at Frankfort a meeting of the reigning princes and representative free cities of Germany to consider a new and, as was claimed, more liberal project of a German constitution. But Bismarck had in his mind a constitution for Germany widely different from anything that Austria would favor; under his compelling power, King William, sorely against his will, turned with affected contempt from his brother monarchs, declined taking part in this meeting, and so brought the project to naught.

And now, toward the end of 1863, the death of the Danish King, Frederick VII, brought on, in acute form, a danger which had long been brooded over in cabinets, fought over on battlefields, and wrangled over among the German people at large—what was known as the Schleswig-Holstein question.

Of the myriad subjects which had tormented German statesmen and diplomatists during the middle years of the nineteenth century, this had been the most vexatious. Its intricacies were proverbial. Lord Palmerston was credited with the saying that but two men had ever understood it,—himself and another,—that the other statesman was dead and that he himself had forgotten all he ever knew of it. There were rights to sovereignty under Danish Law and estoppels under Salic Law; rights under German Law and extinguishments by treaty or purchase; claims to the Schleswig duchy as adjoining Denmark and containing a considerable admixture of Danish blood; claims to the Holstein duchy as adjoining Germany and thoroughly of German blood; rights of each duchy, which implied their separation; rights of both duchies, which implied their union. There had been a settlement under the Treaty of Vienna, in 1815. There had been another under the Treaty of London, in 1852. There had been interferences from Prussia, from Austria, from Russia, from Sweden, and from Great Britain, and bloody battles between Germans and Danes, sometimes one being uppermost, sometimes the other. Throughout Denmark it was held fanatically that the control of the duchies should be Danish; throughout Germany it was no less passionately asserted that it should be German. Learned lawyers wrote convincing opinions on either side; on both sides orators moved men to desperation with the wrongs of ''our Schleswig-Holstein brothers''; poets wrote songs, both in Germany and Denmark, which ''got themselves sung'' with fervor, with rage,—even with tears. The King of Denmark, asserting his claims, was confronted by the German Prince of Augustenburg, asserting his claims no less stoutly. In some churches the official prayers were put up for one; in other churches, for the other.

After spasmodic struggles in council-chambers and on battlefields during nearly half a century, the agitation came to a climax in 1863–4, and Germany, acting through the Federal Council at Frankfort, sent Hanoverian and Saxon troops, which seemed to clear the way for "The Augustenburger" as the rightful sovereign. But this only made anarchy more virulent; Holstein was still dissatisfied and Schleswig in more hopeless confusion than ever.

The region concerned, including the two main divisions of Holstein and Schleswig and the little duchy of Lauenburg, was valuable: there was a territory of over seven thousand square miles, and a population exceeding a million—a population hardy, sturdy, brave, God-fearing; and the importance of people and territory was enormously increased by their great harbor of Kiel.

The claims of this region to cast in its lot with its neighbors having the same traditions and language were now recognized by a statesman who could do something: now came one of Bismarck's masterpieces. Though Austria and Prussia had long been quarreling at Frankfort and were especially jealous of each other regarding this region, and though he had been a main agent in provoking these quarrels, he suddenly, as by witchcraft, induced Austria to join Prussia in putting an end to all this anarchy and folly. Most skillfully he played on the two dominant characteristics of Austrian statesmen at that period: first, on their fear that, if the two great powers did not intervene, Germany might rise in revolution and seize the duchies; next, on their dread that Prussia might lead alone in the contest and thus increase her territory and prestige. Thus it came, to the amazement of all Europe, that these two powers, which had so long seemed ready to fly at each other's throats, took the whole question into their joined hands, marched side by side into the Danish peninsula, conquered the Danes, and occupied the whole Schleswig-Holstein region. But not without a fearful struggle. The Danes fought with desperation, and military history shows few pages as heroic as those which record their resistance against vastly superior forces at Düppel and Alsen; but, as a result came the Treaty of Vienna, in 1864, and by this Denmark gave up the territory so long disputed into the hands of Austria and Prussia.

But what to do with it? Their booty was embarrassing; the sweet reasonableness which had led them into partnership now evaporated. Austria became suspicious and Bismarck surly. Whatever either suggested, the other opposed. Austria proposed that the Prince of Augustenburg should be installed as Duke; a majority of the Schleswig-Holstein people longed for him; Germany was almost unanimously propitious to him; even Prussia was largely inclined to him as the legitimate sovereign—the royal family generally favoring him, the Crown Prince supporting him, and even King William thinking well of him. Outside of the two powers immediately concerned, the same sentiment prevailed: England, France, and Russia looking on the Augustenburger as the true prince. But against all these stood Bismarck. He had tried the Augustenburg pretender and found him incapable of recognizing the real issue,—wanting in fealty to a united Germany. One more princeling in the Bund, nominally independent but really a puppet of Austria, he would not have. As to the Augustenburger's "rights," Bismarck trumped up others, apparently quite as good— notably sundry claims of Oldenburg—and at his behest court lawyers ground out various weighty opinions, the

28

most cogent being that all the old rights and claims had been superseded by the recent victories. The majority of the German states, acting through the Federal Council at Frankfort, tried to settle the matter; but Bismarck promptly reminded them that the German Confederation had no longer any right to meddle,—that Prussia and Austria now held the disputed territory by right of conquest. France and Great Britain also sought to interfere; but he informed them in diplomatic language, more or less civil, that the matter was none of theirs.

The Augustenburg Prince himself pressing his claims upon Bismarck, there came a grim sort of comedy. The faithful chronicler, Busch, gives an account of it in Bismarck's own words, as follows:

"I remember an interview I had with the Augustenburger in 1864, in the billiard room near my study, which lasted until late in the night. First I called him 'Highness' and was altogether specially polite; but, when I mentioned Kiel harbor, which we wanted, he remarked that that might mean something like a square mile, or perhaps even several square miles,—a remark to which I was, of course, obliged to assent; and, when he also refused to listen to our demands regarding the army, I answered in a different tone, and addressed him merely as 'Prince.' Finally, I told him quite coolly, using an old Low-German proverb, that we 'could wring the necks of the chickens we had hatched!' "

But Bismarck did not long remain in this negative phase: gradually he became positive. He was determined that the duchies should not form one more satrapy of Austria; that Austria, being at so great a distance, had virtually no interest in them; that Prussia, adjoining them, had a direct practical interest—in their territory as adjacent to her own, in the harbor of Kiel as necessary to her proper naval development, in the right to dig a canal connecting her dominions on the North Sea with those on the Baltic, and in the extension of her railway system northward; and he therefore proposed that Austria give up to Prussia virtually all rights in the newly acquired territory. This proposal Austria, after first refusing and then shuffling, expressed a willingness to consider, but insisted on compensation: there must be restored to her a portion of those Silesian territories torn away from her a hundred years before by Frederick the Great. To this Bismarck would not listen; he refused to yield an inch of German territory and the Great Frederick's conquest he held to be especially sacred.

War between the two great German powers seemed likely to come at any moment; but, Bismarck being not quite ready, there came, on August 14, 1865, a temporary makeshift known as the Convention of Gastein. By this treaty Prussia took Schleswig, with the right to buy for a petty sum Austria's share of Lauenburg, also to control the port of Kiel, to dig a ship canal connecting the North Sea and the Baltic, to build railways through Holstein, and to draw the duchies into the Prussian Customs Union. Austria's share was Holstein, now to be surrounded by Prussian territory and permeated by Prussian railways. All this was recognized throughout Europe as a brilliant diplomatic victory for Bismarck. He was wont to boast of it in after years and in his talks with Busch he tells the story as follows: "When I was negotiating the treaty of Gastein with Blome (the Austrian Envoy) I played *Quinze* for the last time in my life. I gambled recklessly, so that the others were astounded. But I knew what I was at. Blome had heard that *Quinze* gave the best opportunity of testing a man's character, and he was anxious to try the experiment on me. I thought to myself, I 'll teach him. I lost a few hundred dollars, for which I might well have claimed reimbursement from the state as having been expended on His Majesty's service; but I got around Blome in that way and made him do what I wanted. He took me to be reckless, and yielded.''

To indicate Prussian gratitude for this exploit King William now made him "Count Bismarck." [1]

But the troubles were only increased. Bismarck's activity became greater than ever. To him, and indeed to many others, it was evident that war between the two allies was inevitable, and preparations for it were made on both sides—those of Prussia being much the more effective.

With Italy he now brought his long-cherished plan to a climax, by making a treaty giving her Venice, in case within three months she should assist Prussia in a war against Austria. Among the South German states, notably in Bavaria, and among the states of North and Middle Germany, notably in Hanover, he plied the old enemies of Prussia with arguments to show that it would be best for them not to oppose her in the approaching struggle; but in this he had little success—their old jealousy of Prussia became more virulent than ever.

Next came the question as to possible interference from Russia and France. As to the former, Bismarck's refusal to unite with Austria and the western allies against her in the Crimean War of 1854–56, his cultivation of close social and political relations during his embassy at St. Petersburg after 1859, his aid given to Russia against the Polish uprising in 1863, and his supposed willingness to stand by Russia in any future efforts to break the Crimean treaty which hampered her in the Black Sea,—all these removed the danger of interference from Prussia's great neighbor on the east. But how about the great power on the west? Napoleon III, Em-

---

[1] See Busch's *Diary*, English edition, vol. i, p. 140. Also, Poschinger, *Bismarck-Portefeuille*, vol. i, pp. 153 and following. For the details at length, given admirably, see Matter, *Vie de Bismarck*, vol. ii, chaps. vi and vii.

peror of the French, was then at the summit of his fame.
He had fought out successfully the Crimean War against
Russia, thus gaining the good will of Great Britain; he
had aided effectively in the war for Italian independence,
thus gaining the good will of the new King of Italy; he
had seated a Hapsburg Archduke on the throne of Mexico, thus gaining the good will of Austria; he had held
the revolution in check at Rome, thus securing, as was
supposed, the good will of the Pope; by his International
Exposition, in 1855, he had made Paris the capital of
Europe, and European crowned heads and statesmen who
had snubbed him in the first days of his power now
rejoiced to be his guests at the Tuileries, and with these
came Bismarck. Sundry European publicists then in
vogue declared the enthroned nephew greater than his
uncle; Napoleonism became a fashion not only in Europe
but in the United States; and the most absurdly fulsome
plea for it ever made came from the pen of an American.
The French Emperor had in reality passed the summit
of his power. Physical weakness had diminished his intellectual strength; he had become sluggish, even careless;
his great armies since the wars in Italy and in Mexico
had not been brought up to their earlier strength. The
world at large did not realize this, but Bismarck was not
long in discovering and acting upon it.

The great question now was: Will this supreme poten-
tate allow Prussia to extend her territories? Will he allow
a united Germany, on the borders of France, and, if so,
at what price? He had permitted various states of Italy
to unite; indeed, he had sent his armies to aid them, but
had exacted in return the cession of Nice and Savoy from
Cavour. What cession of territory would he now demand
from Bismarck? This question, and others grouped about
it, Bismarck had studied in his own way for ten years—
taking pains at various times to meet the French Emperor and to discuss burning questions with him. Espe-

cially had this been done in 1862, when Bismarck was
content to await for a time the position of Prime Minister
at Berlin and to be sent as Ambassador to Paris, in order
that before becoming Prime Minister of Prussia he might
study the French Emperor face to face. But also at
other times, and notably in October of 1865, he had made
visits to Napoleon III at Paris and Biarritz, and, in long
walks and talks, with that frankness which so often
amazed his contemporaries, discussed the relations of
France to his projects, avowing to the Emperor his determination to work for German unity, for the supremacy
of Prussia in Germany, and for the expulsion of Austria from German concerns. This amazing openness,
it is true, had led the French Emperor to speak of him
at first as "not serious"; but gradually Bismarck's
frankness invited something like similar conduct on the
Emperor's part, his dreams of the future were now
largely revealed, and all these might be summed up in
one statement—France must extend her boundaries to
the Rhine.

Yet in his efforts to this end he showed a strange lack
of activity: the Biarritz interviews seemed to throw a
spell over him. Though Bismarck and his emissaries
again and again sought to know what the French Emperor would definitely insist upon, all answers were vague
and dilatory, and so they remained until Prussia's
strength was fully manifested. Then Napoleon wrought
desperately. He proposed a European Peace Conference; but it was too late. He sought to take Luxemburg
from the King of the Netherlands, while pretending to
be his protector; to annex Belgium, while claiming to be
its best friend; to obtain large parts of Bavaria and other
South German States, while professing willingness to aid
them against the encroachments of Prussia; he was even
so imprudent as to allow his ambassador, Benedetti,
to put some of his schemes on paper and to leave them

in Bismarck's hands. These movements of Napoleon Bismarck generally humored: it has never been shown that he pledged himself to anything, but there can be no doubt that he again and again encouraged the French Emperor to expect, in case of Prussia's success, splendid additions to France,—not, indeed, from Prussian territory—on that point his refusal was always frank and final—but from the domains of neighbors.

But Napoleon plotted not merely with Bismarck against Austria, he constantly negotiated with Austrian statesmen against Prussia—holding out to them, among other lures, the restoration of Silesia. In any case, he seemed to command the situation completely. The general opinion in France was that, in the war evidently approaching, Austria must win. The present writer, being at that time in Europe, found on all sides, not only in France but in the lesser states of Germany, the belief that the Austrian troops, with the aid of the German states which dreaded Prussia, could not fail to be victorious. Especially was this the opinion of military men and ecclesiastics. Military men believed that Austria could put into the field at least six hundred thousand soldiers, and these of the best, with officers tried thoroughly in the Italian War. Ecclesiastics of the Roman obedience were convinced that the war could have but one end; that it was providential; that the Almighty could not permit the supremacy of heresy in the old Empire which had for centuries been the child of the Church;—and they found eloquent advocates at the French court, chief among them being the Empress Eugénie.

The French Emperor's policy, under all the conditions, real and supposed, seemed perfectly indicated. He must, while pretending to desire peace and outwardly advocating a conference to prevent war, quietly egg on both powers. Though, in his opinion, Austria was, perhaps, likely to win, Prussia was sure to make a good fight; this would exhaust both parties, and, when both were at the last gasp, he could intervene by throwing his army into the arena and give final victory to that government which should offer most to France: never was scheme more promising.

But Bismarck's most vexatious difficulties were at home. The feeling of Germany at large was bitterly against him, and nowhere more so than in the royal family of Prussia. The Queen, the Crown Prince—later to be known as the Emperor Frederick III,—his gifted wife —later to be known as the Empress Frederick,—with the cliques and parties grouped about them, steadily opposed him, and, worst of all, they at times influenced the King against him: the letters which passed at that time show an almost invincible reluctance on the part of King William to be dragged into war with his brother monarch of Austria,—a reluctance which on at least one occasion showed itself in an outburst of passion and floods of tears from the King and in a nervous crisis of his great minister. In Bismarck's memoirs and private letters, we constantly find evidence that overcoming the reluctance of the King was the task which most severely tried him.[1]

Trying beyond measure also was the Prussian Parliament. Its House of Commons was steadily arrayed against him, and some of its men of mark, utterly fanatical, were as much in Bismarck's way as were Wendell Phillips and men like him in the way of Lincoln during our Civil War. Eloquent parliamentary orators denounced Bismarck's policy unsparingly, and, as the lower House by enormous majorities steadily refused to vote

---

[1] The accounts given both by Bismarck and by Busch of theatrical outbreaks between King William and his great minister, both in regard to bringing on the war and as to the proper line of conduct after the victory, have been shown by recent investigations to be exaggerated; but that the struggle between them was in each case long and severe and at times accompanied by nervous crises and tears is amply proven.

supplies, he again and again sent them home and levied taxes unauthorized by law, and, as was claimed, in defiance of the Constitution.[1]

And fanaticism even more frantic now beset him. On the 7th of May, 1866, while walking along the Unter den Linden, at Berlin, he was attacked by a stepson of Carl Blind, the revolutionist, a young Jew named Cohen, who fired upon him at close quarters with a revolver. Bismarck was unarmed: he had, at times, so far yielded to the expostulations of his friends as to carry a pistol, but on that day he had left it at home and had not even a walking-stick. Yet the indomitable Bismarck spirit asserted itself: rushing upon his assailant, he overpowered him, but not until five shots had been fired at close quarters, one of them drawing blood and several of them burning his clothing. Though he fully believed himself mortally wounded, he still showed his invincible self-possession, and handed the assassin over to the police. He then quietly joined his family and guests at dinner, as if nothing had happened. None of these things shook his purpose: he pressed on, and now Austria, persistently and skillfully provoked by him, carried a motion, in the Federal Diet at Frankfort, against Prussia—Austria and the greater states of the German confederation being on one side and Prussia with sundry minor states on the other. At this Bismarck tore Prussia away from the confederation, and war began at once on a prodigious scale. Now were seen the results of that increase and reorganization of the army which during four years the courage of Bismarck had made possible, despite the Parliament. Thanks to Bismarck, Moltke, and Roon, four great Prussian armies were at once put into the field. The Kingdom of Hanover, not yielding

[1] For interesting details of the reformation of the army and the opposition of the Prussian Parliament, see Matter, *Vie de Bismarck.* For the effect of the struggle on Bismarck personally, see Keudell.

immediately, was subjugated within a week, her army overcome, and her King exiled; Saxony was immediately overrun and her King forced to flee with his army over the border into Austria; Hesse, so long malevolent, was overwhelmed in like manner, her troops beaten, and her Elector made prisoner; Nassau was taken and her Duke sent into exile; the free city of Frankfort-on-Main, despite its widespread political and financial influence, was reduced to complete submission; and the greater divisions south of the Main, like Bavaria and Würtemberg, were at once brought to a frame of mind very moderate and even very humble. Meanwhile, three great armies were pushed against Austria, steadily and victoriously, until finally, at Sadowa, they were united and gained one of the greatest victories in history. Four hundred and sixty thousand combatants were engaged: so far as numbers were concerned, it was the greatest battle of the nineteenth century and one of the decisive battles of all time.

What use should be made of the victory? The course proposed by King William and applauded by all the military leaders and by the vast majority of civil leaders was to wrest from Austria large tracts of territory, thus perfecting the Prussian frontier, and to insist on a great indemnity, thus strengthening the Prussian finances. The King, the chief commanders, the generals, the troops, were also determined that the army should march on Vienna. It lay fully open to the victors and to occupy it would exhibit to the world the greatest triumph since the occupation of Paris by the allies half a century before. Thus would the humiliation of Prussia at Olmütz and the long series of insults at Frankfort be atoned for. The German nation demanded it,—even Bismarck's wife and children urged it,—the whole world expected it.

But now, as at other times, it was Bismarck against his country and against the world. Fearless, uncompromising, he opposed all these measures. He saw that the war had strengthened Prussian territory by such vast additions from the northern and middle states that Austria could never again claim supremacy in Germany; but he also saw looming up in the immediate future something which his opponents did not see—a great war with France. He foresaw that France, disappointed, duped, enraged, all her calculations brought to naught, would never, without a savage struggle, permit the establishment on her boundaries of a united Germany. In such a war he saw that it was of infinite importance that Austria should not be Prussia's implacable enemy; that Prussia's true policy was not to arouse unappeasable hatred in the minds of the vanquished by seizing Austrian territory, by burdening the Austrian people with a crushing indemnity, or by occupying their capital. He saw that the true policy was to be content with the main result of the war and to avoid everything like revenge, punishment, or insult. His wisdom was that of the eminent American politician who said, "Never make your enemy so angry that he cannot get over it." There came a long struggle, in which the Emperor and his Minister were wrought up to the utmost, and to carry his policy Bismarck was at last obliged to make the threat of resigning, always so powerful with King William, and to ask simply for an officer's commission in the army to serve actively against the enemy. Thus it was that, at fearful odds, with no supporters save the Crown Prince—never a powerful advocate with his father—Bismarck was successful. The King most reluctantly decided in his favor; the policy of moderation prevailed; the army was turned away from Vienna; the preliminaries of peace were speedily agreed upon at Nikolsburg, to be ratified afterward at the Treaty of Prague.

This policy of Bismarck toward Austria is the more striking when compared with his course toward the defeated states of Western Germany. These states—Hanover, Hesse-Cassel, Nassau, the free city of Frankfort—had given Prussia no such cause for war as had Austria. They had but obeyed the parliament of the Confederation and followed Austria into the war, but their area was of priceless value to Prussia as giving her territorial unity and rounding out her frontiers; and heedless of their protest they were now—and with them not only Schleswig and Lauenburg, but Holstein—incorporated fully into the Prussian state. Such high-handed use of the fortunes of war in modern Europe only Napoleon had ventured; but so wisely were its victims chosen that the deed was to have a permanence unknown to the Napoleonic creations.

By these amazing achievements the whole world was dazed. In seven weeks Prussia had fought successfully through one of the greatest wars in history and had increased her domain by one-fourth, and her population by four and one-half millions, bringing it up to twenty-three millions: thus rounding out the Prussian dominion in a way better and larger than the greatest of previous statesmen had dared dream—giving her a great seaport, the possibility of connecting the North Sea with the Baltic, and a position among the maritime powers of the world. Best of all, she had driven Austria out of Germany, had made Prussia the directing state in a new German nation numbering nearly thirty millions, and had brought under Prussian command an army of eight hundred thousand men.

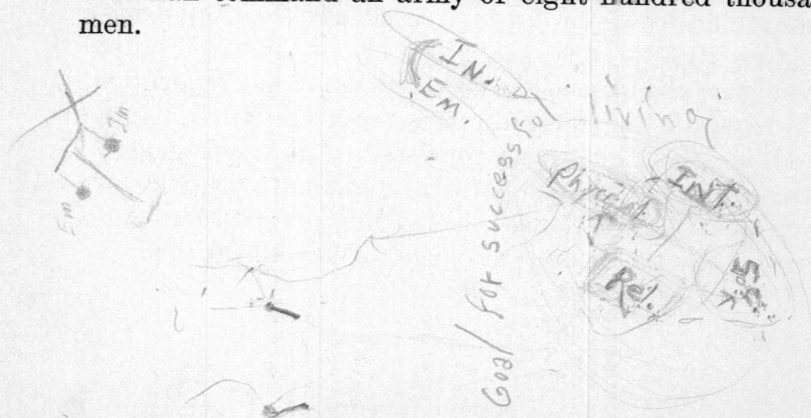

III

GREAT events followed rapidly: "Nothing succeeds like success." From being the most hated and abhorred man in Germany, and, indeed, in Europe, Bismarck had become the most popular. Personally he had long since become popular among most of his colleagues. Easy of access, whether to rich or poor; always keeping open house; original, quaint, shrewd, witty, jovial, fertile in illustrative anecdote, skilled in mimicry, he was sure, despite his occasional brutalities, to win a great following; and he was also sure to compel respect by his courage, clearness of vision, power of shaping events and controlling men. His success made him the idol of the nation. The elections gave him what he had not before had—a majority in the Prussian Parliament: the Prussian people were ready to give him anything. Now came another stroke of wisdom. Powerful as he was—able to bid defiance to his parliamentary enemies and even to crush them—he simply asked for a law of indemnity for his past defiance of Parliament. This was at once passed, and fifty millions of Prussian dollars were also voted toward further military operations, with a million and a half to the leaders in the great triumph: of this the lion's share fell to Bismarck, and with it was purchased the Pomeranian estate of Varzin, so closely associated with his later life.

Now was established the North German Confederation, embracing all the German states from the North Sea to the Main. Its Parliament consisted of an upper council, representing the various political divisions of North Germany, and a lower house, elected by universal suffrage, representing the people at large. Over the confederation, as its president, was the Prussian King, with great powers of military control, but without formal power of initiating laws or vetoing them.

In all this system, presented by Bismarck and agreed to by the German states, one sees a striking departure from his earlier ideas. His old hatred of parliamentary institutions, of the admission of the people to power, and of restrictions upon the God-given rule of the monarch, is gone, and in place of it has come a recognition of ideas formerly abhorrent to him. There can be no doubt that a strong influence was exerted upon him in this development by the American Minister at Berlin during that period, George Bancroft. Bismarck had shown, from his Göttingen days, a liking for the better sort of Americans, and Bancroft was in strong sympathy with him. The dispatches of the American Plenipotentiary at that period abound in references not only to the military but to the constitutional evolution of the new Germany: he takes pains to show to the Washington authorities various resemblances between the North German constitution and our own. Historian, statesman, diplomat in the best sense, as Bancroft was, and at the same time an intense lover of democratic government—with a personality which impressed deeply all who knew him, and especially the King—his reasonings undoubtedly had much to do with the development of Bismarck's opinions,—especially regarding a federative government, with a broad democratic representation. So marked was this development that many of Bismarck's old reactionary associates never forgave him. The extreme monarchical and aristocratic *Kreuz-Zeitung*, to which he had formerly been a frequent contributor, and with whose editor he had been on terms of intimate friendship, now turned bitterly against him and persistently waged war on him.[1]

[1] As to the strong impression made by Bancroft, the present writer,

Interesting also is it to an American that Bismarck broke from his old reactionary friends, not only on German, but on American affairs. While Germany was in strong and effective sympathy with the American Union during our Civil War, the Prussian reactionaries were bitterly against us: they longed for the downfall and disgrace of American republicanism; they gloried in the anti-American utterances of Gladstone and Carlyle; they besought the King to recognize the Southern Confederacy;—but all this Bismarck brought to naught,—he felt that no alliance between Germany and a nation based on slavery was possible.[1]

The four years following the Seven Weeks' War did much to consolidate the North German Confederation, and in this work Bismarck won victories no less rapid and decisive than those gained on the battlefields by Moltke and Roon. Though the French Emperor had been able by vague threats to force into the Treaty of Prague a clause declaring the South German states—Bavaria, Würtemberg, and the rest—completely independent of the North German Confederation, he had again

succeeding him after an interval of a few years, had abundant testimony from diplomatic colleagues and from leaders in German politics. Curious was it that the Prussian King, who had now become the Emperor William, until the end of his life, when he met the American minister, usually asked, "How goes it with your predecessor?" (*Wie geht es mit Ihrem Vorgänger?*)—always meaning by the "predecessor" Bancroft. As to Bismarck's feeling toward Bancroft it is noteworthy that, among the portraits of European sovereigns at Friedrichsruh, he placed the portraits of Bancroft and General Grant, with the busts of Washington and Hamilton. See Busch, *Diary* (English edition), vol. iii, p. 351. As to Bismarck's efforts to have Bancroft retained in Berlin, see a letter of his in Motley's *Correspondence;* also Lowe, *Bismarck's Table Talk*, p. 149. For special evidences of Bismarck's good will, see *Life and Letters of George Bancroft*, vol. ii, pp. 246, 247, 254, and elsewhere.

[1] On the refusal of Bismarck to recognize the American Confederate States, see Lowe, as above, p. 147. On Bismarck's sympathy with the Confederate leaders as an individual, but his opposition to them as a statesman, see his conversation with Carl Schurz, given in Schurz's *Memoirs*, vol. ii.

been duped; for just before the treaty was signed Bismarck had secured special treaties with these same South German states, pledging them, in case of war with France, to act with the North German Confederation. He now pushed on measures binding these states even more firmly to the confederation, and when any state, yielding to the old anti-Prussian jealousy, made trouble, he brought powerful weapons from his armory: especially effective were his threats of exclusion from the Customs Union, which meant financial ruin to the excluded states. This weapon he brandished at times with great effect over the South German states outside the confederation: as to Bavaria, deep as was the House of Wittelsbach's jealousy of the House of Hohenzollern, bitter as were the Bavarian ultramontanes against Prussia as a Protestant power, and ingrained as was the dislike of her people for everything Prussian, they could not but remember that exclusion from the Customs Union meant ruin to their brewers. Then, too, Bismarck used more subtle weapons: when Bavaria and Hesse showed signs of a liking for their old connection with France, he quietly revealed to the Bavarian and Hessian rulers and statesmen the fact that the French Emperor was ready to cede almost anything to Prussia, provided Prussia would allow him to swallow sundry choice morsels of Bavarian and Hessian territory. The old reactionary King of Hanover, for whom, in spite of much opposition in Parliament, Bismarck had secured an indemnity of sixteen millions of Prussian dollars, began a most determined opposition, maintaining a Hanoverian legion and employing journalists to attack Prussia in every point thought vulnerable. At him Bismarck struck a fatal blow by sequestrating the sixteen millions and using it largely, as he said, "in following these reptiles to their holes"; hence the "reptile fund" for subsidizing journalists, which played a notable but not always a creditable part in the ensuing struggles. Yet

Bismarck's ability to wait was as striking as his ability to labor. Many perfervid patriots made the strange complaint that he was not daring enough; that he did not push and pull the South German states, and especially Bavaria and Würtemberg, into the confederation at once. But all such efforts he discouraged: he wished the entrance of these states into the union to result from the deep convictions of the princes and peoples themselves. Our own American Civil War, which had just ended, and our wretched reconstruction period, with its hatreds, suspicions, and jealousies between South and North, and its scandals which echoed throughout the world, evidently taught him to hasten slowly; he realized, with Bishop Butler, that there may be "a possible insanity of states," and that for such a disease time affords the best cure. Even when the state of Baden then sought entrance, he refused her and bade her wait: he thought it not best to give a new cause of jealousy to France and he also wished the sentiment of nationality to mature. To those who upbraided him for this he used, as he was so fond of doing, a homely peasant proverb, saying, "To take Baden into the confederation from the German states outside, would be like skimming the cream from milk; the rest will sour all the more quickly." [1]

The labors of the Chancellor in consolidating the new

---

[1] It was one of these peasant proverbs with which he silenced the Augustenburg pretender. The present writer once heard another of them from Bismarck's lips. Walking in his garden and discussing German and American financial policy, the question came up as to sundry former finance ministers of Prussia, and of these he presently said, "I trusted them at first, but I soon found, as our peasants say of those who pretend to their neighbors that they are to have a good dinner, that they had nothing but water in their pots, after all."

Gustav Schmoller, in his very remarkable *Vier Briefe über Bismarcks socialpolitische und volkswirtschaftliche Stellung und Bedeutung*, refers very thoughtfully to this use of peasant wisdom by Bismarck. As a matter of fact, the great Chancellor drew so fully from no other sources save from Goethe, Shakespeare, and the pithy Latin of black-letter lawyers.

29

Federation became Titanic. Separate treaties had to be made with each of the states embraced in it, each treaty the result of a struggle between him and the local statesmen concerned. Night and day he was forced to grapple with questions of capital importance in each of three great parliamentary bodies—the Diet of the Confederation, the Prussian Diet, and the Customs Parliament—each requiring contests or compromises with leaders, cliques, or parties: complicated diplomatic questions beset him in every part of the world; but the thoughts deepest in his mind turned toward France. Napoleon III was not allowed by the French nation to forget the glories of the First Empire. If the sway of France could not be extended throughout the valley of the Rhine, it might at least prevail over portions of Southern Germany, Belgium, and the Netherlands. But the French Emperor had been dreamy and inconclusive. Again and again at various conferences Bismarck had endeavored to secure from him something definite, but in vain. The Emperor's theory had been that definite proposals from France could be better made after Austria, Prussia, and the other German states had been depleted and discouraged by a long civil war; but the victories of Prussia, sudden and vast, with the establishment of a German confederation on the French border, had changed the whole face of things. He now became urgent, and even before the preliminaries of peace were signed, after the Seven Weeks' War, his ambassador, Benedetti, had appeared in the Prussian camp pressing the claims of France. But Bismarck was not now so anxious as formerly, and the French ambassador was put off with the statement that nothing could be done until the terms of peace with Austria had been settled. Shortly afterward, Benedetti appeared again, and this time with virtual threats—nothing less than declarations that unless Prussia made large concessions to France Napoleon must declare war; but this Bismarck resented so effectively that the French government softened Benedetti's declaration, saying that it had been extorted from Napoleon during his illness. The effort was constantly renewed: Benedetti whimpering that, unless some concessions of German territory were made to France, popular resentment would endanger the Bonaparte dynasty, and then followed various definite proposals by him for pacifying French feeling at the expense of Germany, Belgium, and the Netherlands. The condition of the Bonaparte dynasty was certainly critical. The collapse of the French expedition to Mexico, with the execution of the Emperor Maximilian, whom Napoleon had placed on the Mexican throne, strong reminders of the Monroe doctrine from Secretary Seward, with the reunited American republic at his back, the increasing demands of the French radicals, the evident failure of the new liberal order of things which the French Emperor had conceded in his desperation, all made it necessary to secure some advantage which should propitiate the French mob. Moreover there was on the part of Napoleon III a personal feeling: it had dawned upon him that he had been outwitted by Bismarck,—that the man whom he had pronounced "not serious" had proved to be his master.

New and more splendid shows were now tried: the brilliant Paris exposition of 1867, with its visits of crowned heads and statesmen, among them King William and Bismarck,—the meeting of Napoleon with the Austrian Emperor at Salzburg, and with various minor German monarchs on the way,—every sort of venture to deceive or appease France; but still the opposition in the French Chambers, and especially Thiers, the most skillful of all French architects of ruin, were denouncing the shortcomings of the French Empire and prophesying its decline. These enemies were careful to point out that the French Emperor ought never to have allowed on its borders a united Italy or a united Germany; that formerly Cavour and now Bismarck had duped him. Still he resisted the pressure for war. When his efforts to secure Mainz and portions of Luxemburg, Bavaria, and Belgium had evidently failed, he still pressed for some concession with which he might oppose the mob opinion of Paris and the distrust of France. War he did not want; he was prematurely old, troubled with painful diseases and infirmities,—his one personal ambition was to finish his Life of Cæsar; he longed for peace.

But the opposing powers in France were far too strong for him. The mob mania for war, the ambitions of generals, the intrigues of priests, all goaded him on. To abase the Protestant supremacy of Germany, to restore by a new war the old order of things in Italy,—this had become, with the Vatican and its supporters throughout Europe, a passion; and unfortunately this ecclesiastical effort had the most efficient of political agents, the former Countess of Teba,—granddaughter of the Scotch wine merchant Kirkpatrick,—now the Empress Eugénie. Her Spanish characteristics having been developed by nuns and confessors and Jesuit preachers, she became the devoted agent of the hierarchy, and by expostulation, by ridicule, and even by menace she aided to drive her husband into war. She and the people about her watched most eagerly for a pretext,—as eagerly, indeed, as did Bismarck,—and at last it came—full orbed. The Spanish government, after the exile of the wretched Queen Isabella, was seeking a king; various candidates were approached in vain; but, at last, aided by the quiet efforts of Bismarck, unknown to King William, there was suggested a princeling of the family of Hohenzollern-Sigmaringen. His name was received in Spain with favor. He was a Catholic; his relationship to the Prussian monarch was very distant,—in fact, he was much more nearly related by blood to Napo-

leon III,—but he had the prestige of the Hohenzollern
name; and the Spanish leaders, in their despair, eagerly
caught at the prospect of so promising a ruler, called
him, and, after many hesitations and even refusals, he
accepted.[1]

No sooner had the news of this offer of the Spanish
throne been made public than the Parisian press attacked
the French Emperor for allowing it, and soon there was
a storm. It was insisted that Bismarck, having erected
a united Germany on the eastern border, was now about
to create a Hohenzollern satrapy on the southern border. The Duke de Gramont, French Minister of Foreign
Affairs, a showy incapable, soon joined the mob and
ordered Benedetti, the French Ambassador at the Prussian court, to see King William, who was quietly taking
the waters at Ems, and obtain from him assurances satisfactory to France. These assurances were, first, that
the young Prince should cancel his acceptance of the
Spanish throne. The aged King, shrewd but kindly,
while insisting that the whole matter was a family and
not a state affair, showed himself quite willing that the
Prince should withdraw, so willing, indeed, as to disgust
Bismarck, and to suggest ideas which led him to think
of tendering his resignation. Some days elapsed before

[1] Down to a recent period the general statement by Prussian writers
has been that Bismarck had nothing to do originally with the Hohenzollern
candidacy: even so great an historian as Von Sybel committed himself
to this view, but the revelations made by Busch and by Prince Charles
of Roumania in their respective memoirs make it certain that Bismarck
was among the first to urge the candidacy of the Prince, and that he sent
agents to Spain to press the matter; it is equally clear that King William
did not during its first stages have any adequate knowledge of his
Chancellor's action in the premises. As a member of the royal house
and as a Prussian officer, the Prince had sought and obtained the reluctant
consent of the King after the offer of the throne had been made, but in
the intrigues beforehand the King certainly had no share. See, especially,
Reminiscences of the King of Roumania, Tauchnitz edition, edited by
Whitman, pp. 100 and following; also the revelations regarding Lothar
Bucher's secret mission to Spain, in Busch's *Reminiscences*.

the Hohenzollern Prince could be found, for the family castle was in a distant part of Germany and the Prince himself absent from home.   This gave a great chance to French demagoguery: the sensational press, the mob orators, the partisans in the legislative body, vied with each other in denouncing this wrong to France, but finally the communication from the Prussian King took effect, and the French authorities speedily received from the Spanish government a notice that the Prince had canceled his acceptance.

King William, the Emperor Napoleon, the young Prince, and the world at large took it for granted that this ended the matter.   Bismarck seemed to lose the battle.   From the beginning King William and the Hohenzollern Princes had disliked the whole plan, all of them fearing complications, and the aged King's first wish was for peace.   Bismarck had been beaten in the matter again and again.   Again and again he had sent his most trusty confidants from the foreign office to Madrid and summoned most capable Spanish agents to Berlin, and only after three distinct struggles had he finally triumphed over the scruples of King and Princes.   His main arguments to them were based on the honor done to the Hohenzollern name, on the military prestige and commercial advantage to be derived by Germany from a friendly monarch at Madrid, and on the desirability of ending anarchy in the Spanish peninsula.   But behind all these was an argument which Bismarck avowed to none save himself, and least of all to the King or the Princes. Ever since the Prussian victory over Austria he had seen that a war with France was inevitable.   The only question with him was whether it should be brought on at a time favorable to France or to Germany.   He knew that France was all unready for war, but that the calling of a Hohenzollern monarch to Spain would provoke a conflict in spite of this unreadiness.   To his great disappointment King William had wrecked his whole plan. His disappointment was such that he was unable to sleep and renewed his threats to retire from office.

But who shall limit the possibilities of mob folly? Despite the fact that the French government, the Chambers, the people, had been amply informed from the most trustworthy sources that their army was utterly unprepared, they insisted on demands which could only lead immediately to war. From the strongholds of French demagoguery, from the sensation-mongers in the press, from public meetings, and from the Legislative Chambers came screams that the answer of the Hohenzollern Prince had but made the insult to France more deadly. "Why did the answer come from Spain?" "Why did it not come from the Prussian King?" [1]

Driven on by this tempest, the Duke de Gramont telegraphed additional orders to Benedetti. He must secure from King William not only the young Prince's renunciation but a declaration that no Hohenzollern would ever again, under any circumstances, become a candidate for the Spanish throne. Benedetti was not allowed to relax his efforts for an instant. Every day during that fateful week from the 6th to the 13th of July, Gramont was plying him with telegraphic orders to press the King harder and get more distinct assurances, in fact, to get evidences for the Paris mob that the King had been humiliated. And to make this still more sure Gramont wrote out with his own hand for the Prussian minister at Paris a sort of apology and pledge which the Prussian King should make to the French Emperor.[2]

[1] For choice specimens of mob oratory in the French Chamber, see Benedetti, *Ma Mission en Prusse*, appendix, pp. 428, 429, and elsewhere.

[2] For a striking specimen of De Gramont's efforts to humiliate the Emperor William, see the passage underlined by Gramont in his telegram to Benedetti July 12, at 2 A. M., marked *"très confidentielle,"* in Benedetti's *Ma Mission,* etc., p. 365. For accounts valuable because jotted down by a man of high character who was in constant attendance

King William's position had become difficult indeed. He had never liked the candidacy of the Hohenzollern Prince. He longed for peace, and his private letters show that he was glad when, as he supposed, the whole thing was ended. On the other hand, Bismarck during the whole week was telegraphing him from Varzin to stand firm, and, if any difficulty arose, to refer the matter to his Chancellor; in various ways also Bismarck hinted that the King should summon him to the scene of action. His Majesty was not so easily managed: he evidently feared Bismarck's warlike proclivities and preferred to deal with the matter himself. But it soon became too much for him and on the 11th he telegraphed for his Chancellor. It was too late—the crisis came before Bismarck could arrive. For on the morning of the 13th, as the King was taking his morning walk and sipping his warm soda amid the crowd of his subjects on the promenade at Ems, Benedetti, pressing him for a distinct pledge that he would never allow a Hohenzollern to accept the Spanish crown, was told by the aged monarch, courteously, though firmly, that he could not give it, and that, as regarded the renunciation of Prince Leopold, he had received no further news. To this the official who forwarded the King's account of the interview to Bismarck added that His Majesty, having afterward received a letter from the Prince confirming his renunciation, had decided not to receive Count Benedetti again, but to send the news to him by an aid-de-camp, who should state that His Majesty had nothing more to say. The official also added that the King left Bismarck to decide whether the matter should be communicated to the Prussian ambassadors and to the press.

upon the Emperor at Ems, see the life of *Heinrich Abeken* (by his wife), pp. 373–378. As to other unfortunate characteristics of Gramont, and especially his untruthfulness, see Rechberg, in Friedjung, *Der Kampf um die Vorherrschaft in Deutschland*, appendix, vol. ii, p. 526. It is to be noted that Rechberg was an Austrian.

The first effect of this telegram was to disgust Bismarck, utterly. Instead of continuing his journey from Berlin to Ems, he was inclined to return to Varzin. He was the responsible minister of the crown and ought to have been consulted, and the King had made concessions at which the French mob was shrieking with joy and demanding more. The Hohenzollern candidacy, for which Bismarck had labored so earnestly and so long, the King had thrown overboard, and the dispatch seemed to show that even with this the King had not ended the matter decisively, and that he might consent to continue negotiations still further. This was contrary to all Bismarck's ideas. He felt himself disgraced before his country and before Europe; and he found immediate support from Moltke and Roon, who met him in Berlin. They too had arrived at the conclusion that, as France was determined on war, there could be no better time for Germany than the present. The King seemed to them to have flung away the opportunity and enabled France to delay hostilities until she was fully ready: all three were greatly depressed at the turn things had taken, but presently, under the King's permission given in the telegram, Bismarck proceeded to edit it for the press. Running together the two parts of it—that which came from the King and the addition by the official—he simply took enough from the whole to make it appear that, Benedetti having demanded the irrevocable pledge, the King had refused it and dismissed him curtly and finally.

This new version of the dispatch being read by Bismarck to the two generals, both were pleased with it. As Bismarck afterward told the story, Roon said, "This is better"; Moltke said, "Now it has a different ring,—it sounded before like a parley, now it is like a defiance"; Bismarck himself said, "This will be like a red rag to the Gallic bull." Vastly significant was the fact that before sending it Bismarck questioned Moltke

once more regarding the chances of victory in case of
an immediate war, and that the great strategist answered,
guardedly, that they were in favor of Germany.[1]

The dispatch was now sent to the press and before
midnight reached Paris. The French passion for war
now became resistless: the Paris mob went wild for it;
the press demanded it; the Emperor's favorite generals
and courtiers insisted upon it. One eminent statesman
alone stood in the French legislative body against it—
Thiers. Though during his whole political life he had
been wont to exasperate France against Germany, and
had very recently insisted that no French government
should permit German unity, he now exerted himself to
hold the nation back from war. With his immense knowledge of political and military affairs, he saw the unreadiness of France and knew that she was approaching an
abyss. He was a judge in the matter of catastrophes
and revolution, for he had taken part in wrecking the
three preceding governments and had learned to read the
signs of the times. With tears in his eyes he besought
the legislative body to hold back. All in vain: the French
Senate approved the declaration of war by a unanimous
vote and the Chamber of Deputies by a majority of 245
to 10.

In reply to this, Prussia, and indeed all Germany,
showed a determination more sober, but quite as sin-

[1] Sundry recent writers, in view of slight discrepancies in Bismarck's
Reminiscences, and of an alleged letter in the possession of the family,
which has now disappeared, have seemed inclined to consider the general
account of the editing of the King's telegram by Bismarck and the two
generals as merely legendary, but by far the better opinion seems to
accept the facts as above stated. Horst Kohl has amply proved the
amazing tenacity of Bismarck's memory, as shown in the *Reflections and
Reminiscences*, and even Lenz, guarded as he is, concedes the general
truth of the statement as made. See Horst Kohl, *Wegweiser durch Bismarck's Gedanken und Erinnerungen*, pp. 117, 118; also the same in the
Regesta; also Lenz, *Geschichte Bismarck's*, pp. 349 and following; also
Matter, *Bismarck et Son Temps*, vol. iii, p. 60, note.

cere. On July 19 the French declaration of war was received in Berlin. In his speeches before the imperial parliament Bismarck now insisted that this declaration resulted from a French determination to make war on any pretext,—that it was, in fact, the first official communication in the premises from the French to the German government; and in a diplomatic circular he dealt with much emphasis on the haste of France to humiliate Prussia and her venerable monarch. Most effective manœuvre of all, he ere long revealed to Europe, through the London *Times* and other agencies, the previous French proposals to annex to France, in time of peace, territories belonging to Belgium, the Netherlands, and South Germany; and some of these proposals, on French official paper and in the handwriting of Benedetti, he circulated widely in facsimile. Thus he put France in the wrong before the whole world.

The war was pressed on by Germany with amazing vigor and precision: over five hundred thousand men being brought by her into the field, and her entire force, including reserves, numbering fully a million. Within a fortnight three great German armies were upon the Rhine, and two days later they began a vast series of victories; at Weissenburg, Woerth, Spicheren, Mars la Tour, Gravelotte, everywhere, the French were forced to yield; never did men fight more bravely than they, but it was soon seen that all their heroism must end in defeat. For, while the German armies were like instruments of precision, perfect in construction, management, coöperation, direction, distribution, the French forces were from first to last in dire disorder. The dispatches between the commanders and the government at Paris, afterward published, showed complete disorganization: the whole machinery dislocated; subordinate officers and soldiers groping for their regiments; commanders without maps of the country in which they were to operate; artillery without ammunition, and ammunition without artillery; troops without arms, and even without shoes; and soon Marshal MacMahon, having been terribly beaten in preliminary battles and skillfully prevented from uniting his forces with the principal French army, was pressed into the great amphitheatre of hills at Sedan on the Meuse and forced to make one of the greatest surrenders in history—the captives including the Emperor, Marshal MacMahon, forty generals, over eighty thousand troops, with the whole enormous equipment of MacMahon's army and of the fortress of Sedan.

During the war thus far Bismarck had taken a very subordinate part; he had been marching with the army, advising King William, keeping in touch with the cabinets of the world, and incidentally looking after his two sons, of whom one was severely wounded and the other unhorsed in a fearful charge of cavalry at Mars la Tour; but now he stands forth as the leading personage. He it is who first waits upon the fallen Napoleon, with profound respect, but sternly preventing any meeting between the imperial captive and the impressionable Prussian King until all the terms of the capitulation had been settled. Now came, on September 4, the formal dethronement of the Emperor by the Parisian authorities, the establishment of the Third French Republic, and this complicated Bismarck's problem vexatiously. Up to this time he had dealt with the Napoleonic government; that government now no longer existed and the Emperor was a captive on German soil. To find a French government or to establish one with which Germany could treat, became a problem long and intricate.

More German victories followed, clearly ushering in a new epoch. In September Strasburg capitulated and Bismarck saw realized his great dream of recovering Alsace and its historic capital, which had been taken away from Germany by Louis XIV two hundred years before.

A few days later Bismarck established himself in Versailles, and thence, from his modest lodgings at the house of Madame Jessé, he now directed events. His labors were prodigious: there came royal councils, negotiations with princes, generals, bishops, statesmen from various provinces, envoys from various nations, and, above all, with Thiers, Jules Favre, and others, who sought to bring about a truce, and, if possible, a peace. His first effort to establish a responsible government in France with which a binding treaty could be made proved especially difficult. Everywhere was confusion: a Government of National Defense, weak and distracted; adherents of the house of Bourbon, of the house of Orleans, of the house of Bonaparte, each plotting, in its way, a monarchical restoration; masses of anarchists seeking to carry out their wild will in the main French cities; and Gambetta, who, having escaped in a balloon from Paris, was trying to bring together in Southwestern France a parliament from which all but members of his party were to be excluded. Meanwhile German victories continued: less than two months after the capitulation at Sedan came a triumph in some respects more overwhelming, at Metz. This city was the chief bulwark of Eastern France, the great fortress of Lorraine, the most important of Western Europe, after Gibraltar. In its surrender were included three marshals of France, six thousand officers, over one hundred and seventy thousand soldiers, three hundred thousand stands of arms and a vast mass of war material. Now came a complication especially vexatious. Ever since the treaty closing the Crimean War, which had forced the Russians to give up their supremacy in the Black Sea over their own seaports and along their own coasts, they had borne that ignominy in silence; but now they held their peace no longer. In this time of confusion they pressed forward their proposal to annul that treaty. So far as Germany was concerned it was embarrassing, for Great Britain was, of course, bitterly offended, and Bismarck, who had before beginning the war with France favored this demand secretly, must now do so openly. But with this complication he grappled, Great Britain reluctantly yielded and all Europe thought it best to acquiesce.

To the vast mass of affairs thus brought upon Bismarck there was now added a problem in many respects more complicated and far-reaching than all the others, for there loomed large and portentous the old German aspiration for national unity and for a government fitly embodying it. The practical difficulties were enormous. Old rights, privileges, precedences, jealousies, distrusts, hatreds, personal, racial, geographical, religious,—differences in theories, in customs, in laws, in political philosophy, in readings of the past, in hopes for the future,—all combined to render the problem insoluble. The greatest difficulties of all were with the southern states. With two of them, Baden and Hesse, the work was comparatively easy, but with Bavaria and Würtemberg the contest was long and severe. Upon the rulers and statesmen of each of them Bismarck brought to bear all his skill and force. All his patience too was needed, for at times when he seemed to have convinced or conquered them, they suddenly broke away and he must begin again. After endless discussion Würtemberg was won, but Bavaria, foremost of all German kingdoms save Prussia, seemed hopelessly lost.

Yet the progress toward unity went on. In December a deputation from the North German Parliament arrived in Versailles, bearing to King William an offer of the Imperial crown, and at its head was Simson, the same who in 1849 had made the same offer to Frederick William IV and seen it rejected. That former rejection of the crown had met with Bismarck's hearty approval; but now all was changed. The former Prussian King had refused the Imperial crown because the offer had not come from his brother monarchs of Germany. They had opposed it bitterly, and most bitter of all had been the Wittelsbach monarch of Bavaria, who had passionately declared: "Never will I submit myself to a Hohenzollern" ("*Ich unterwerfe mich keinem Hohenzollern*"). To meet this opposition Bismarck had quietly labored for years with a skill and patience almost superhuman. In the Bavarian parliament prevailed the most bitter opposition to his policies; the Church abhorred them; the peasantry were trained to hate the very name of Prussia. Many counselors now urged that Germany dethrone the Bavarian King and dismember its territory; but against these Bismarck stood for Bavaria, as formerly he had stood against the Prussian King, the army, and the whole nation, for Austria. With the Bavarian King, half genius, half madman, he had long maintained, with infinite self-control, a friendly correspondence, yielding to that monarch's whims, but steadily leading him toward his duty to the German nation—pressing upon him the argument that, while a King of Bavaria might not accept as his superior a King of Prussia, he might accept an Emperor in Germany. Now came the reward. Though the Bavarian parliament still held back from entering the imperial union, there arrived a letter from the Bavarian King, virtually in Bismarck's own words, urging the reëstablishment of the Empire and the proclamation of the King of Prussia as German Emperor. The other rulers had already been secured. Thus was the old objection made by Frederick William IV of Prussia brought to naught: an offer of the crown had at last come from the princes.

There was no longer need to wait for the Bavarian parliament, and on January 18, 1871, was made the solemn proclamation of the Empire to the world. Simple as it all was, nothing could have been more historic-

ally fit or dramatic. It was in the great hall of Louis
XIV, the most sumptuous in the palace of Versailles.
Ranke had once said to Thiers, during the Franco-Prussian war, "Germany is fighting against Louis XIV";
now came the triumph over that inveterate enemy. In
that Hall of Mirrors, directly beneath its inscriptions
glorifying the invasion and humiliation of Germany by
the *Grand Monarch,* the Emperor stood on a simple plat-
form, in the midst of a delegation of German princes.
At his side were his son, destined to succeed him as the
Emperor Frederick III, and his son-in-law, the Grand
Duke of Baden, who had long labored for a united Germany; before him were the great generals, with Moltke
and Roon at their head, and leading statesmen, at whose
head stood Bismarck, who now read the proclamation
which established the German Empire. Thunderous
salutes, bursting forth from the army which was besieg-
ing Paris, echoing over German camps throughout
France, and thence repeated throughout Germany, announced the event. Nor was this all; the new nation was
ushered in by a wonderful series of new victories: Le
Mans on the 12th; the surrender of Belfort on the 17th;
St. Quentin and Mont-Valérien on the 19th; the capitulation of Paris on the 28th; and the disarmament of Bour-
baki's army, the last great army of France,—driven upon
Swiss soil,—during the fortnight following.

The great question of the treaties now drew on. After
a world of trouble, a legislative body had been secured
which had some right to speak for the nation. Here
again was shown Bismarck's skill and decision. Gambetta, in the wild hope of continuing the war, still
endeavored to exclude all who had supported the Empire
from any position in the new republic, and, indeed, from
voting for its representatives. At this Bismarck
stretched forth his arm, and brought all this folly to
naught. He declared against all proscription and insisted

upon a free election by the whole people. In a free election a national assembly was now chosen, which on February 12, 1871, began its sessions at Bordeaux. This body chose, as chief of the executive department, Thiers; and he, with his ministers, Jules Favre and others, speedily began negotiations for peace. In the tedious diplomatic struggle which followed, Bismarck showed the same masterly qualities so evident in his previous career: asking at first more than he probably expected to obtain, he demanded Alsace and German-speaking Lorraine, with the border fortresses of Metz and Belfort, and an indemnity of six thousand millions of francs. Of the two negotiators on the French side, Thiers had been prime minister of France and had won fame as an historian, debater, and financier; Favre, a former tribune of the people, was renowned for forensic oratory. And now there came a mixture of tragedy and comedy. The French representatives insisted passionately and even with tears that the indemnity named was utterly impossible; that France was wholly unable to pay it or any sum approaching it; and that, if counting it had begun at the birth of Christ, it would not yet be finished. To this Bismarck replied, "But I have provided for that very difficulty,—I have brought from Berlin a little man who begins counting long before the birth of Christ"; and upon this he introduced the Jewish banker, Bleichroeder, who found no difficulty in proving that France was so rich that the indemnity asked was really too small. Again, when the French envoys became wildly eloquent, protesting, haranguing, and orating upon the dishonor of France and her determination to die rather than yield, Bismarck objecting, as he afterward said, to being "addressed as if he were a public meeting," replied in German, of which neither Thiers nor Favre understood a word; and, when they answered that they could not understand him, Bismarck replied, "Neither can I understand you." And

30

again, when in this diplomatic struggle Thiers and Favre, representing the republicans, who dreaded Bonapartism above all things, halted and delayed, Bismarck simply threatened to recall the captive Emperor Napoleon, and to allow the myriads of Bonapartist soldiers from German prison-camps to put him again on the throne. Nor was this all. The French, trying to enlist European public opinion, spread impassioned appeals throughout the world. On one point they laid special stress: that Prussia had no right to continue hostilities against France, since the power which demanded the war, the Emperor, had fallen. To this Bismarck replied by a European circular reminding the world that the war had been demanded unanimously by the French Senate and with virtual unanimity by the popular representative body and by the French press.

Appeals for European intervention being still made by the French, Bismarck sent forth another circular, solemnly warning the European powers that anything like foreign intervention could only arouse false hopes among the French people and so prolong the horrors of war. To yet another appeal from France to Europe declaring that Germany had determined to degrade her to the rank of a power of the second grade by taking away vast territories from her, Bismarck answered in a circular showing that France had thirty-eight millions of inhabitants, or, including her leading colonies, forty-two millions, and the territory demanded included only about a million and a half.

In all these Bismarck circulars there was an undertone of defiance which all foreign powers thought it best to heed. Especially pithy as regarded the taking of Strasburg and Metz was Bismarck's argument that, as there had been twenty-three unprovoked invasions of Germany from France, in days gone by, and not one, save in retaliation, from Germany into France, Germany was hence-

forth determined to keep the key of her two western
doors in her own hands. The Treaty of Frankfort, which
followed and which Bismarck signed, not only restored to
Germany Alsace and a large part of Lorraine, including
Strasburg and Metz, but exacted an indemnity of five
thousand millions. Belfort, important as its conquest
had been, was thus relinquished, as were also one thousand millions of the indemnity originally demanded.

The constitution of the German Empire was now
adopted,—virtually as Bismarck had drafted it. Its
Parliament represented twenty-five states, exclusive of
Alsace-Lorraine, and was divided into an Imperial Council (Bundesrath) and an Imperial Diet (Reichstag). In
the first of these bodies the states were represented
mainly in rough proportion to their population, Prussia
having seventeen votes, Bavaria six, Saxony and Würtemberg four each, a few other states three or two each, and
the remaining states one each.

Though this constitution showed some resemblances
to that of the American Union, the differences were far
greater. The American idea of equality between the
states was cast aside. To secure national unity Bismarck gave up all mere doctrinaire uniformity: Prussia
was given a veto power on all changes in the constitution
and virtually on all fundamental legislation regarding
the army, the navy, and the taxes; privileges superior to
those of smaller states were also given to three or four
of the minor monarchies, notably to Bavaria, and in a
less degree to Würtemberg, as regards various military,
diplomatic, and fiscal matters; the central legislative
power was extended further than our own, but the central
administrative power was, from an American point of
view, strangely hampered by entrusting it largely to officials of the different states.

As to the military power, Bismarck recognized the facts
in the case and, above all, the fact that Germany has on

all sides hereditary enemies and on no side extended natural frontiers: therefore it was that the combined army was conformed to Prussian principles and kept under Prussian control.

Naturally, in his constitution-building, Bismarck saw the need of continuity in policy, and to this end he adopted an idea apparently American rather than European; for he avoided that imitation of English ministerial responsibility which has cost so many continental states so dear. He retained in the constitution the power of dissolving Parliament, but without requiring any accompanying dissolution of a ministry; as a result he sat serene at the head of German affairs and saw some forty different ministries win, waste, and lose power in the French Republic.

As to the executive branch, King William was made Emperor, but, curiously, the most serious struggle which arose on this measure concerned simply the imperial title. King William, who took pride in his Prussian kingship, made glorious by Frederick the Great, cared apparently little for the title of Emperor, and insisted that if he took it at all he should be styled "Emperor of Germany." This was objected to by the lesser German sovereigns, and, indeed, was disliked by thinking German statesmen generally, as indicating a more direct and complete territorial control than was needed for the maintenance of German unity. It was, therefore, decided that a mediæval precedent should be followed and that the title should be "German Emperor"; and this Bismarck supported steadily. As King William declined to yield, he was proclaimed simply as "Emperor," the style "German Emperor" being afterward gradually adopted in public documents.

Under the headship of the Emperor, sometimes nominal, sometimes very real, Bismarck was made Chancellor, and as to his office he stamped his theory and practice

deeply upon the constitution. He had never been able
to work well with equals. Even in his young manhood
he could not work with his brother in managing the
family estates; in the various legislative bodies to which
he had belonged he had constantly soared above his associates; at Frankfort his one great effort had been to
drive out the Austrian ambassador, his only equal at the
green table; in each of his embassies he had been surrounded only by subordinates; and when he became minister of the Prussian kingdom he must be Minister
President. Therefore it was that as Chancellor he was
the only Minister of the Empire. There was no other.
He would have no Imperial cabinet. He called about him
strong men, but they were known, not as Ministers, but
as "Secretaries": he would have "subordinates, but no
colleagues." There was for a time a Vice-President of
the Prussian Ministry who acted as a sort of Vice-Chan-
cellor, but after a brief service he retired and had no
successor. To the Chancellor was given the title of
Prince, with an estate valued at about a million of Prussian dollars added by the Emperor to those which had
formerly been given him, and there was appropriated as
his official residence the superb Radzivill palace and park
in Berlin. Sovereign and people vied with each other in
doing him honor. In the prime of life he had reached
a position such as had been held by no other man during
the nineteenth century, save during the ten imperial years
of the first Napoleon.[1]

---

[1] For Bismarck's mode of working on the constitution, especially through
Lothar Bucher, see his *Reflections and Reminiscences;* also Busch
and Keudell. For an excellent statement in detail regarding the Imperial,
Prussian, and other German constitutions, see A. Lawrence Lowell, *Governments and Parties in Continental Europe,* vol. i, chaps. v and vi.

IV

THE three wars—against Denmark, Austria, and France—being ended, and the German Empire established, Berlin became the centre of European political activity and Bismarck the leading European personage. In view of the war cloud hanging over Russia, Austria, and Turkey, his main effort was now for a general peace, and, obedient to his purpose, sovereigns and statesmen made pilgrimages to the German capital. First of all there met, virtually under his presidency, the Emperors of Austria, Russia, and Germany, who, finally yielding to his argument that their common interest in resisting anarchy was greater than the interest of any one of them in feeding grudges or extending territories, came to an understanding in behalf of peace and good will.

Then came also the Kings of Italy, Sweden, the Netherlands, Spain, various German monarchs, and a long train of lesser princes, all with their most eminent advisers. From Berlin, in return, went forth the German Emperor, the Chancellor, and the heir to the imperial throne, paying visits and thus consolidating the virtual alliance of Germany, Russia, Austria, Italy, and Spain, against the "international" evil revealed by the orgies of the Paris Commune. During all these journeys, while the Emperor William was treated with supreme respect, the outbursts of public feeling were for Bismarck; and, of all the capitals he now visited, the most emphatic in its welcome was Vienna—the centre of the empire he had so recently conquered.

Year after year these political pilgrimages continued

and frequent international conferences at the Chancellor's palace made it more and more a source of European political ideas.

During the period which now began, filled with a series of colossal achievements at home in remodeling and consolidating the new Empire, there came exertions of power abroad such as Europe had not seen since the days of Cromwell.

At the triumphant return of the German troops into Berlin from the French war, word was brought him that the French outposts were encroaching upon the space reserved in France by Germany. He was on horseback at the side of the Emperor, in the midst of frantic exhibitions of popular joy, but, quietly asking for paper and pencil, he telegraphed orders to Paris that, unless the French troops withdrew, the German army should immediately attack them: and to this France yielded.

His hand was felt heavily in another quarter. The Austrian Chancellor, Beust, who during long years at Frankfort, Dresden, and Vienna had done his best to thwart every Prussian effort, had sought to retain his position after the war of 1866 by abject submission and fulsome praise of the new order of things. But, peace having been made with France, Bismarck determined that there should be no risk of a return to the old treachery and trickery: the Austrian Chancellor was dismissed, and in his stead was placed a man of far different fibre, the Hungarian statesman, Andrassy, of whom Bismarck said:—"As to Austrian statesmen generally, their talk is to me as wind whistling down a chimney; but what Andrassy says I know to be true." And there was another reason for favoring Andrassy—the reason of a far-sighted statesman: previous leaders in the Austrian cabinet had generally been South Germans, and their eyes were constantly upon the North and West—upon Germany; Andrassy was a Hungarian and his aspirations were naturally for the extension of Austrian power toward the South and East.

Even more in the Cromwellian manner was Bismarck's dealing with Don Carlos and his adherents in Spain. Having captured a small Spanish force, the Carlists had found in it, to their great joy, a Captain Schmidt, formerly a soldier in the Prussian army, but now a correspondent of a German newspaper, and they indulged their hatred of Germany and of heretics by putting him to death as a spy. At an earlier period there could have been no redress; but times had changed: there had come a united Germany with a German citizenship to be held as proudly as was that of ancient Rome. Bismarck struck at once. Sending a squadron to blockade the port through which the Carlists obtained their supplies, and notifying the French government, which, for reasons of its own, was secretly aiding them, that this aid must cease, he called on the European powers to recognize the Spanish government at Madrid against Don Carlos, and to this call all the powers yielded save Russia. That wanton murder cost the Spanish pretender dear: up to that moment he had some chance of succeeding to the throne of Spain; thereafter he had none.

Closely related to this was another effective stroke. In 1874 sundry French bishops, vexed at the success of the new German power against the resistance of France and the intrigues of the Vatican, burst forth into seditious preachments and were evidently bent on goading the French people into religious war. To the diplomatic regrets expressed by the French government Bismarck gave no heed. To him the real point was that these denunciations gave new virulence to French hate and new stimulus to French revenge, and he therefore declared to Germany and to the world that his duty to his country forbade his waiting for war with France until she was fully prepared for it. The French government, and, indeed, the French people, saw the point at once: the fanatical pulpits were brought to reason.

Following this blow at Christian zeal came one equally crushing against Mohammedan fanaticism. Stirred by the approaching war between Turkey and Russia, a mob had murdered the German Consul at Salonica. The Turkish government was, of course, profuse in apologies; but Bismarck, paying no attention to them, straightway sent a squadron to Salonica, and did not rest until six of the worst ruffians were hanged, several careless officials sent to prison or the galleys, and the Sultan obliged to pay to the widow an ample indemnity.

Hardly less remarkable was a blow struck for due subordination in the civil service of the new Empire. Count Harry von Arnim was of a great Prussian family, a man of many gifts, attractive, persuasive, brilliant, efficient; and, having been trained in several important diplomatic positions, he had become German ambassador at Paris. To his mind the diplomatic dealings of Germany with France thus far were wrong in principle. He was a monarchist and felt that Prussia should for her own safety destroy republicanism in France and promote a revival of monarchy. Bismarck's theory was utterly opposed to this. The very strength of his belief in monarchical government led him to promote French republicanism. He frankly acknowledged that he did this in order to keep France weak, divided between factions, and unfit for war. Von Arnim, thinking that the German Emperor might incline to convictions like his own, at last began to cherish the belief that he might supplant Bismarck and change the policy of the Empire. The result was a struggle in which, first by skillful preparation and next by rapid blows, Bismarck crushed his opponent utterly,—imprisoned him, disgraced him, and drove him from the Empire.

It was in the midst of all these triumphs that Bismarck

received a check,—the greatest he ever met. The wonderful recovery of France from her reverses, the speed and ease with which she paid the vast indemnity, the skill with which she remodeled and enlarged her army, as well as the cries in the French press for revenge, evidently aroused in his mind the thought that he had failed to make the French nation incapable of doing further injury to the new Germany. This feeling seemed to become with him a sort of obsession. All Europe was soon convinced that he was planning a new war in which his purpose was to cripple France for many generations. Now was seen the force of a great and widespread moral opposition to injustice. Every great power quietly arrayed itself in this matter against him, and no head of a state showed himself more opposed to a new attack on France than the Emperor William. At the Emperor's side also, in full sympathy with his view, was his nephew, the Emperor Alexander II; and, the two monarchs having conferred together, an end was made to every possibility of a new war with France. Reluctantly and angrily Bismarck yielded.

Remembrance of this was soon lost in events of more pressing significance. In northern and central Europe Bismarck had made peace sure, but in southeastern Europe, the long-expected war storm having burst at last, there came a fearful struggle between Russia and Turkey, lasting nearly a year and ending in the San Stefano treaty, which seemed likely to blot Turkey from the map of Europe—thus bringing Russia into immediate collision with Great Britain and obliging the other great powers to make choice between them. Bismarck now intervened and at his behest there met at Berlin in June and July, 1878, the most important European conference since the Napoleonic wars were closed by the Congress of Vienna. In this body sat the most eminent statesmen of the time, and, as their president, the German Chancellor. The tangled results of the war were now taken out of the hands of Russia and Turkey, all concessions possible were made to aggrieved parties, and peace was restored. Throughout the whole proceeding Bismarck was not merely the nominal head, but the master spirit. When at one time Russia and Great Britain seemed on the point of breaking into open war, he restored quiet with a tact and mildness of which few had thought him capable; and, when Turkey seemed likely to plunge all into confusion, he brought her to reason by methods almost brutal.

His readiness and force continued even on an increasing scale. The Berlin Congress having adjourned, Russia retired from it in ill humor,—brooding over her loss of the vast concessions which she had extorted from Turkey at San Stefano. The ill feeling between the German and Russian Chancellors now became bitter. On one hand the course taken by Russia in thwarting Bismarck's plan for renewing the war against France, and especially the display made by Gortschakoff regarding his part in this, made Bismarck's ill feeling acute; and on the other hand Gortschakoff had accumulated griefs and grudges, the chief of them resulting from Bismarck's superiority. Although Bismarck, at the Berlin Conference, had done for the Russian interests all that was compatible with the interest of Europe, even to a degree which led him to say that during that time he had acted really as a Russian plenipotentiary, he had failed to satisfy the Russian government. Remembering the services they had rendered to Germany during her wars with Austria and France, by forbearing to interfere, the Czar and his Chancellor had expected more. Bismarck was now made a scapegoat. The Russian press joined in full cry against him as a traitor; the Czar complained of him to the German Emperor as an ingrate; Gortschakoff, passing through Berlin, ostentatiously shunned him; the Grand Dukes, on their way to a public exhibition of their

French sympathies at Paris, took pains to ignore him; Russian emissaries throughout Europe were loud in their denunciations; Russian tariffs on German goods were made especially onerous; Russian troops were massed near the German frontier, and there were signs of an approaching anti-German alliance between Russia and France.

A statesman of ordinary mold would have protested, explained, expostulated, apologized; not so Bismarck. He instantly recognized the realities in the case—the breadth of Russian unreason, the depth of official prejudice, the impossibility within any definite period of correcting these, and the dangers likely to arise in the meantime; he made no apologies or explanations; he accepted the situation, and mastered it. Going to Vienna at once, he speedily made a treaty which changed the whole existing system of European alliances, a treaty under which Prussia and Austria were to stand together against any attack by Russia and France. There had been one difficulty almost insurmountable. The old Emperor William, who was deeply attached to his nephew, Czar Alexander, could not bear the thought of a change in their life-long relations, and probably the most earnest letters he ever wrote were those in which he besought Bismarck not to break with Russia. But the sovereign was compelled to yield. Under the Chancellor's threat to resign, the imperial signature was obtained, and thus began a new guarantee of peace in Europe, far more stable than the old,—the dual alliance of Germany and Austria.[1]

Bismarck had also made assurance doubly sure in another way very characteristic. Quietly, in talks with the French representatives at the Berlin Conference, he had

[1] For light thrown into the heart of this treaty and its purpose, see two letters, one from Andrassy to Bismarck and its reply, in Ford's edition of *The Correspondence of William I and Bismarck*, vol. ii, pp. 200–202.

acknowledged the justice of their half-humorous, half-melancholy complaints that France alone, of all the powers, was securing no concessions. With sweet reasonableness he had asked, "Why does not France take Tunis? It is her close neighbor on the Mediterranean; it is a menace to her in the hands of its native population; why does she not annex it? No one will object." This winged word sped at once to the French government and ere long France proceeded to take Tunis; but in doing so secured for generations the ill will of Italy, which had long been coveting Tunis, yet had not dared to take it. The result was that France was soon far too busy with this new acquisition of territory to give any trouble to Germany, and Italy, in revenge, threw herself into the dual compact of Germany with Austria against France and Russia, thus forming the *Triple Alliance.*[1]

A curious change now took place in Bismarck's policy. Hitherto he had been very tender toward Russian sentiment; now he seemed a different being. The lesson he seemed determined to teach Russia was that the day of Olmütz,—when the Russian government regarded Germany as a brood of kinglets and princelings to be used as might be found most profitable,—was forever gone. His utterances now became defiant, and his policy drastic. Did a Muscovite grand duke or statesman stop over night at Berlin, the official organs became explosive with assertions of the new doctrine.[2]

Ere long it dawned upon the Russian mind that Bismarck was not to be scared into submission like an ordi-

---

[1] The Tunis episode is given from the traditions at the Berlin Foreign Office during the decade following the Conference. For Bismarck's rather cynical remark that "when they (the French) are busy in Tunis they cease to think of the Rhine frontier," see Busch, *Diary,* ii, 475.

[2] The present writer, who was then in Berlin, has in his Autobiography given examples of these explosive utterances which greatly amused all Europe.

nary statesman; and the old Russian Chancellor Gortschakoff, who was mainly responsible for the ill feeling,
was allowed to slip quietly out of office. His ambition
for many years had evidently been to pose before the
world as combining the qualities of the Prince de Ligne
and of Metternich: a critic has described him as "a
Narcissus who loved to admire himself as mirrored in
his inkstand." [1] A very different man was now put in
the Russian foreign office, De Giers, a man of business
who loved peace not merely platonically but with passion,
who was especially anxious to secure proper relations
with Germany, and who was never so eloquent as when
contrasting the gains of Russia by peace with her losses
by war. No more touching scene was presented in the
last decade of the nineteenth century than this patriot
minister evidently drawing near death, but using what
remained of his strength in advocating a change from the
old, haughty Russian war policy.[2]

And now, although the treaties which bound together
Germany, Austria, and Italy in the Triple Alliance against
any attack by Russia and France were still in force, the
Emperors of Germany, Austria, and Russia were again
brought together, skillfully wrought upon by the great
Chancellor, and as a result there was secretly devised a
supplementary system of diplomatic wheels within wheels,
so arranged that, if France attacked Germany, she would
find herself isolated from Russia and opposed by Germany, Austria, and Italy; that, if Germany were specially provoked into war with France, France was not to
receive Russian assistance; that, if Russia attacked Austria, Austria would receive German and Italian support;
but that, if any difficulties between Russia and Austria
should arise on the Eastern question, not from Russian

---

[1] "C'est un Narcisse qui se mire dans son encrier."

[2] For an account of some of these conversations between the dying
minister and his visitors, see A. D. White, *Autobiography*, vol. ii, p. 32.

aggression, Germany would not intervene and Austria would be left to herself in coming to terms with Russia.

The great Chancellor's hand was also felt outside of Europe. Very gorgeous in the north of Africa had been the career of Ismail Pasha, the Egyptian Khedive. Impressed by the opening of the Suez Canal, realizing the commercial possibilities of his domain as few Turkish or Egyptian statesmen had ever done, borrowing recklessly from all who would lend, pledging anything and everything, he had shaken off the gyves of his Turkish suzerain and had made a display which dazzled the world. His ambition finally rose even beyond the restraints of commercial honesty or international law. First to attack him effectively was Bismarck, whose protest led in 1879 to Ismail's downfall and made possible a new government under British control, which still remains the best that Egypt has known in all her thousands of years.

Significant of much was it that, in the complications resulting from this change in Egypt, no less renowned a statesman than Gladstone sought Bismarck's counsel and advice: had he taken it, he would have been spared one of the two great humiliations of his life.

The will of the Chancellor was also asserted in another part of Africa and in a part of Europe which, up to this time, had thought itself far outside his range,— even in Great Britain. The partition of the African Continent between various European powers had entered a phase new and vigorous, and between Portugal and Great Britain had been made an arrangement to control by treaty vast regions of West Africa,—especially those penetrated by the Niger and Congo rivers. Up to that time no human being would have dreamed that such a scheme had need of sanction by the powers controlling Continental Europe; but a new epoch had come and Bismarck was its prophet. Making proclamation that the world could no longer be thus seized and partitioned, he put the Congo Treaty beneath his feet. To this proclamation and action Great Britain modestly assented, and in them the other powers, including France, heartily concurred. Lord Odo Russell, British ambassador at Berlin, most moderate and trusty of counsellors, wrote Lord Granville, the British Secretary for Foreign Affairs, regarding Bismarck: "At St. Petersburg his word is gospel, as well as at Paris and Rome, where his sayings inspire respect and his silence apprehension"; the German ambassador Hatzfeldt boasted that Bismarck carried the Sultan in his pocket; the French Consul, M. de Courcel, having made a pilgrimage to the country seat of the German Chancellor, announced that between Germany and France there was "perfect identity of views." [1]

As a result of this condition of things the main European powers and the United States were early in 1885 invited to send delegates to a council upon African affairs at Berlin; and there, in the Chancellor's palace, during more than three months, the questions concerned were discussed, until finally there was made in Africa a new and broad partition of territories and spheres of influence—the German scepter being now extended over African realms of vast extent and possibilities.

It was in this matter that Bismarck showed most clearly his grasp of world politics. In his early utterances he had opposed German colonial aspirations, had even ridiculed them; but after the establishment of the Empire and the creation of a fleet his feeling changed. He had always regretted that the great surplus population of Germany passed, year after year, in larger and

---

[1] For interesting details regarding the change wrought by Bismarck in the dealings of Great Britain with African questions, see Lord E. Fitzmaurice, *Life of the Second Earl Granville*, vol. ii, chap. x, and elsewhere.

larger numbers, under foreign allegiance, and, brooding over this, he developed a wish for colonies which might retain some part of this population beneath the German flag.

His efforts to this end met at first with strong resistance: his proposals to develop colonies at Samoa and elsewhere and to subsidize steamer lines to the far East were thwarted in the German Diet. But opposition only increased his force, and a compromise by which he obtained in 1885 a subsidy of four millions of marks a year, for fifteen years, toward steamer lines to Asia, Africa, and Australia, laid the foundations for new extensions of German commerce.

And there was another opposition which even more deeply stirred his passion and drew forth his skill. Closely connected with "the scramble for Africa" was the scramble for new territories in the Pacific Islands, and, in his efforts to protect German settlers and to secure to Germany the proper control over them in both regions, he met opposition, sometimes brutal, sometimes subtle, which he speedily traced back to the Cabinet of Great Britain. His tactics now became interesting. Along the African coasts and through the Pacific Islands he pushed emissaries who soon planted the German flag over regions widely separated,—many of them desirable. The British government evidently sought to delay his projects, to tangle them, to erect barriers against them. All to no purpose: he cut through the entanglements and broke down the barriers. Revealing to the German Diet this foreign opposition to his policy, he gained strong support in the country at large and a majority in the Parliament which enabled him to maintain the German flag over the regions where he had placed it,—Lord Granville in the British Upper House and Mr. Gladstone in the House of Commons accepting the situation with an effusion of sweet reasonableness and an edifying recognition of Germany as a partner with Great Britain in carrying out the good intentions of Providence toward the heathen.

Characteristic of Bismarck was it that his sympathy was not won by these utterances of Mr. Gladstone. His antipathy to the British Prime Minister seemed thereby increased. Gortschakoff had given to a portrait of Gladstone a place of honor in his official residence at St. Petersburg, but the favorite English portrait at the Chancellor's palace at Berlin was that of Disraeli; pointing toward it, Bismarck was wont to say, "The old Jew: he is the man." Probably the most severe criticism ever passed upon Gladstone,—that which sped farthest and struck deepest,—was a reference, in one of Bismarck's speeches, to the injury and discredit the English Prime Minister had brought, by his foreign policy, upon British interests and the British name.

It must be confessed that during this struggle and others Bismarck showed the defects of his qualities. One dispatch to Count Münster, German ambassador at London, regarding the colonial aspirations of Germany and the methods by which she was willing to secure them, was so cynical that the ambassador suppressed it and the result was a comedy of errors—the German Chancellor acting upon the supposition that the British government had seen the dispatch, and the British Prime Minister acting without knowledge of it.

Even the United States was subjected to his displeasure. From the very beginning of his career he had treated Americans with especial kindness. His relations with Motley during his university days, with Bancroft during the formation of the German Federation and Empire, with Sheridan, Burnside, and the American officers whom he met at Versailles during the siege of Paris, and with a long succession of American ministers at the Court of Berlin, gave ample evidence of this feeling.

But suddenly all was changed: in an evil hour an American minister, a former Senator of the United States, wrote from Berlin a confidential letter to a high official of his government asserting that the Chancellor, having become a great landed proprietor, was naturally in sympathy with the landowning class in Germany and that it was, therefore, vain to hope for any lowering of German duties on foreign products of agriculture during his continuance in office. By some carelessness this letter became public, with the result that Bismarck's prejudice against the offending diplomat became bitter.

Closely connected with this was another exhibition of his determination that his policy should not be questioned. One of the most eminent parliamentarians during the formation period of Germany was Edward Lasker. He was an accepted leader of the National Liberal party; in his unselfish devotion to liberal principles, in his ability to sway thinking men, and in his influence over liberal-minded men throughout the Empire he was one of the foremost statesmen of his time. At the first elections to the Imperial Parliament, he had been chosen by half a dozen districts, and in the Prussian Parliament he represented the important constituency of Frankfort-on-Main. As a jurist, publicist, and debater, he stood among the foremost; his integrity was unimpeachable; he had won a victory over financial misdoing on a large scale, by which he had driven a finance minister out of office, and he had dared to attack the business enterprises of one of the proudest princes of the Empire. He had been, in various exigencies, one of Bismarck's most important supporters and notably one of his main aids in reforming German jurisprudence; but sundry other measures, dear to the Chancellor's heart, he opposed; he could not be reckoned on for thick and thin support, and Bismarck's antipathy toward him became passionate.

To the opening of the Northern Pacific railway across

the United States there came many eminent guests from Germany, and Lasker among them; but, returning from the excursion to the Pacific—worn with fatigue and excited by the novel scenes about him—he suddenly fell dead in a New York street.

Deep regret was at once shown on both sides the Atlantic, and in perfect good faith a resolution of sympathy with Germany in her great loss was immediately passed by the American House of Representatives and sent through the official channel to the German government. It was taken for granted that such a tribute would tend to produce kindly feeling between the two nations; but, to the amazement of all concerned, the Chancellor confiscated this resolution, cynically withheld it from the Diet, and returned it to America by the speediest channel, with a verbal message more curt than polite—its significance being, "Mind your own business!"

Nor was this all: Bismarck's wrath now fell, very illogically, on the American plenipotentiary and drove him to resign. It may here be chronicled to the honor of our country, that, while its President immediately offered promotion to our minister, its Congress, recognizing in Bismarck's conduct simply the weakness of a strong man, allowed the whole matter to be forgotten.

In the new relations of the Empire with distant regions, Bismarck gave constant evidence of his promptness and vigor. He had steadily enlarged the fleet and he now used it—sending armed vessels to collect debts in South America, to secure indemnity for injury from pirates in China, to protect Christians in Syria, to keep the peace in Greek waters, to secure apologies for an insult to a German Consul in Central America, to aid in destroying the slave trade in Africa, and, as we have seen, to avenge murders of Germans in Turkey and Spain.

Very characteristic of his foresight in paving the way for German commerce and of his determination to keep in touch with colonial needs and aspirations was it that, under his lead, the Diet now appropriated fifty thousand dollars a year for university instruction in six of the more important living languages of Asia.

It would seem that in efforts like these, having the whole world within their scope, he would have found full play for all his energies. Not so. Even more determined were his exertions to carry out his policy within the Empire. This policy was mainly twofold—both its parts, as he considered, necessary to the existence of the state: one part touching ecclesiastical and the other civil and economic questions.

As to the first of these, even at the time when he was carrying on his foreign policy with such breadth and daring, and his internal policy with a skill and vigor never before known in Germany, he was waging one of the most remarkable civil wars in modern history. While establishing the Empire he had recognized in the power centered at the Vatican a most subtle enemy of his country. In the "Syllabus" issued by Pius IX in December, 1864, he saw a condemnation of the best ideas which Germany had gained during the progress of her civilization, and especially a blow at that unfettered search for truth which was the proudest conquest of German thought. His main warning of this peril had come from the great Catholic patriot and statesman of South Germany, Prince Chlodwig Hohenlohe, who foresaw in the approaching council at the Vatican the assertion of papal infallibility, and in this assertion a plan for the subjugation of civil authority. Of this he warned Europe, and Bismarck gave heed to the warning. During the wars against Austria and France he had learned how bitter and deep was the opposition of the Vatican to German aspirations, and he noted as significant the fact that the solemn declaration of the infallibility dogma was followed, but one day later, by the declaration of

war by France against Germany. The matter was
serious, indeed; for one-third of the inhabitants of the
new German Empire belonged to the Roman branch of
the Christian church, and the question, as it shaped itself
in Bismarck's mind, was this: "Is this great body—one-
third of the entire German population—to obey, in civil
matters, laws made by the German Parliament or mandates issued by a knot of Italian priests?"

The championship of this latter view was speedily
extended from the Vatican to the bishops, and from the
bishops to their lower clergy and laity. From their pulpits came denunciations of a kind usually heard from
political platforms, and in the Parliament there now
appeared a "centre party," devoted to the interests of
the Vatican, with strong leaders, and, at their head, their
most formidable statesman, Windthorst. He had been
a fellow student of Bismarck at Göttingen, but, unlike
Bismarck, had given himself quietly and steadily to university work, plodding, untiring, with no aid from powerful family connections or high social position, and by
force of native ability and hard work had risen to leadership in the kingdom of Hanover. The incorporation of
Hanover into Prussia during the war of 1866 had deprived him of his commanding place in the Hanoverian
cabinet, and he had now come into the Imperial Parliament as simply a provincial member. His ambition and
his hatred of the new order of things combined with his
great powers as a parliamentary leader to make him
formidable. Probably no more singular parliamentary
picture was seen during the nineteenth century than the
great Chancellor, immense in size, commanding in movement, seated near the Tribune of the German Diet,—and
near him, in the Tribune itself, this most determined
opponent, dwarfish, unprepossessing in face and voice,
apparently insignificant, yet the most serious enemy
which the new imperial ideas ever encountered.

In the combats which followed, Bismarck at first exerted himself to keep within bounds, and, though from time to time he struck heavy blows, he showed frequently an inclination toward mild measures which surprised those who had watched his previous career. The struggle had been greatly embittered by the efforts of sundry ecclesiastics of the older church to drive out of pulpits and professors' chairs all those who had not accepted the infallibility dogma; and, as the men thus ostracized were salaried by the state, there came resistance by the civil authorities and this led to a violence in preaching which caused the enactment of the "Pulpit Laws."

Now came a colossal blunder on both sides. Bismarck, apt as he was in quoting homely German proverbs, forgot a favorite one just suited to this emergency—"Nothing is eaten so hot as it is cooked." This forgetfulness led to a sea of troubles in which both parties floundered long and evilly. The supposition that the infallibility dogma could be carried to its logical results in temporal affairs blinded both parties. A long struggle resulted, into which were drawn sundry high ecclesiastics, notably the Bishops of Ermeland and Paderborn and the Archbishops of Cologne and Posen. Soon, too, there appeared in the troubled waters the Jesuits: they had been active against Germany in her Austrian and French wars, stirring up not only religious differences but racial and provincial hates, notably in Poland and in Alsace-Lorraine, and now they redoubled their efforts. To meet the emergency Bismarck at first tried a combination of strength with mildness: on one hand appointing to the ministry of public worship the strongest man who ever held that position, Falk; on the other hand paying a nominal compliment to the Pope by proposing to send as ambassador to Rome no less a personage than Cardinal Hohenlohe, a younger scion of a house which was once a sovereign dynasty and which was still one of the great families of Germany. But, this courtesy being rejected at the Vatican, matters became worse, and in 1872 the whole body of Jesuits were expelled from the kingdom. This was all the more significant for the reason that the Jesuit order, from the days of Frederick the Great, even during the period when it had been expelled from all the Catholic countries of Europe and from Rome by the Pope himself, had been protected throughout the Prussian dominions. This expulsion was speedily followed on the other side by ecclesiastical denunciations of Bismarck and even by a solemn prophecy from Pope Pius that the vengeance of the Almighty would speedily overtake him. Reprisals were henceforth in order; the German diplomatic representative was withdrawn from the Vatican and there were passed what were known as the "Falk Laws," or "May Laws," which, with sundry supplementary enactments, were intended to put a curb on ecclesiastical encroachments throughout Prussia, and, indeed, indirectly throughout the Empire. The leading purposes of these laws were mainly four. First: to prevent the exercise of ecclesiastical power for civil or social oppression; the principle laid down being that involved in proceedings against those guilty of libel and slander. Secondly: to secure a better, broader, and more patriotic education for the clergy by insisting that, as they were salaried by the state, the whole of their education should not be taken in a succession of sectarian schools, primary, secondary, advanced, and finally theological—all, from first to last, entirely under the management of the priesthood and segregated completely from the world at large —but that a part of it, at least, should be more open to the world and should be taken at some one of the gymnasia or universities. Thirdly: to secure to every person the right of separating himself from any church, Catholic, Protestant, Jewish, or other, by declaring his intention before a judge and with security for himself and his family from any resultant degradation or stigma injurious to them as citizens. Fourthly: that the state might protect itself from zealots casting firebrands and arrows, —that, to this end, whenever the Church authorities were about to fill ecclesiastical vacancies, they should send to the civil authorities the candidates' names, and that, for the validity of such appointments, there should be confirmation by the civil authorities. Finally, it was required that, while a religious ceremony at marriages was not only permitted but encouraged, there must necessarily be a civil ceremony requiring state legislation and control. Most of these principles had been allowed by the Vatican in various other nations, but their assertion at this time in Germany vastly embittered the contest; the struggle in its worst phase lasted more than five years and each of its stages showed some new phase of unreason.

On the clerical side came new anathemas against those who had refused to accept the infallibility dogma, more and more stirring of racial hates in Poland and Alsace-Lorraine, of provincial jealousies in Bavaria and the Rhine provinces, and of sectarian fanaticism everywhere. On the government side came more and more expulsions of priests from their pulpits, of professors from their chairs, of high ecclesiastics from bishoprics, with fines and imprisonments scattered widely; and, as a rule, all religious orders not specially devoted to charity were driven from the kingdom. As the combat deepened, bishops and archbishops, for contravening the laws, were thrown into prison,—the Archbishop of Posen, Ledochowsky, for more than two years. Fanaticism was now at the boiling point, and in evidence of it there came, not only in Germany but in the surrounding countries, threats and plans to assassinate the Chancellor,—one of these very nearly succeeding. A youth named Kullman, who had been for a time in a clerical school, fired upon Bismarck on the promenade at Kissingen and came so near success that the bullet narrowly missed an artery—grazing the Prince's hand just at the moment when it was lifted to his forehead in the act of returning a salute. This act led to new severities by the civil authorities: the appropriation for the German legation at the Vatican was stricken out of the estimates, sundry Catholic members of Parliament were arrested, and civil marriage laws were extended over the Empire.

In February, 1875, Pope Pius having issued another encyclical, declaring the detested laws void and their makers godless, the contest entered an even more acrid phase, among its curious results being an increase in German pilgrimages to Lourdes, the very seat and centre of French hatred for Germany, and, in Germany itself, miracles at Marpingen,—supposed to indicate disapproval of Bismarck by the Almighty. Throughout all this period, the centre party, numbering one-fourth of the Parliament and led by Windthorst, fought indiscriminately all Bismarck's measures, of every sort, no matter how far removed from religious interests.

But in 1878 Pius IX died, and in his place was seated a man who, if less engaging, was much more gifted in breadth of statesmanship and in clearness of political vision: Leo XIII,—the greatest Pontiff since Benedict XIV. Both Bismarck and the new Pope now recognized their opportunity, and soon efforts were evident for compromise. Either side continued to show spasms of resentment at times, during which loud declarations evidently intended for European effect were made; but finally Bismarck, having conferred with Windthorst at Berlin, and with the papal representative, Jacobini, at Gastein, began more fruitful work,—the basis as laid down by the Chancellor being the understanding that, while the German government must remain firm in its assertion of the principles involved, their application could be made more mild and dispensations could be granted.

On the other side, in 1880, a letter of Pope Leo to the Archbishop of Cologne intimated a willingness that the nominations to vacant ecclesiastical positions be communicated to the Prussian civil authorities beforehand. This to Bismarck was an especially important point, and from this germ an agreement was gradually developed. It was felt on both sides that it was high time for the struggle to close. Thus far the religious interests of the people at large seemed to be forgotten by both parties. Eight out of the twelve Prussian dioceses were without bishops, and more than four hundred parishes were without pastors. The Prince Bishop of Breslau had fled to Austria, Cardinal Ledochowski had taken refuge in Rome, and the Archbishop of Cologne was wandering in disguise in Germany or concealed in Holland. The whole world was beginning to be scandalized at a conflict in which, mainly for questions involving the pride of the Vatican on one side and of the Chancellor's office on the other, so great a proportion of the humble, confiding Christian flock were left without shepherds. Evidences of a compromising spirit now increased: a new minister, Schlözer, who, as a confidant of Bismarck, had previously shown shrewdness and tact at Washington, was now transferred to the Vatican; the government was given more discretion in administering the Falk Laws; Falk himself, having been loaded with honors, gave place to a man less obnoxious; the special dispensing power of the King in relation to the laws was extended; and finally the Crown Prince, returning from Spain and visiting Pope Leo, was gladly received, and, of all surprises, his Holiness requested—Bismarck's portrait. This request was speedily granted, and the Chancellor himself, not to be outdone by the Vatican, extended to Pope Leo a courtesy which he, of all men, would appreciate,—by asking him to act as umpire between Germany and Spain regarding the claims of the two nations to the Caroline Islands. Meantime, from the

Vatican on one side and from the Chancellor's palace on the other came a succession of measures attenuating the severe laws and orders made on both sides, until the spectacle was presented of Bismarck relying on the German Catholic party's support for the main measures of his new financial and economical policy. The worst of the struggle was now over, and a *modus vivendi* was established. The Pope and the Chancellor were great enough to understand and appreciate each other; not only was Bismarck's portrait sent to the Vatican, but Pope Leo's portrait was sent to Varzin; denunciations and threats ceased, and Bismarck was enabled to concentrate his attention on the civil measures which he had been for some time bringing before the German Parliament.

For, knit into Bismarck's foreign policy and into the struggle with the Vatican was a domestic policy soon to attract the attention of the whole world. As far back as the opening of the first Imperial Parliament he had begun heroic endeavors to consolidate the realm which he had summoned into existence. This labor proved to be enormous; for the old centrifugal forces—local prejudices, state rights' theories, racial hates—continued and must be dealt with both energetically and tactfully. Besides this the newly annexed region of Alsace-Lorraine, with its million and a half of inhabitants, mainly German in descent, but French in sympathy, also developed tendencies and practices constantly annoying and sometimes dangerous. Against this new peril a statesman of less breadth and depth would probably have used threats or cajoleries, but from Bismarck came very different utterances: for, mindful of the truth that tact does not always consist in speaking evasively, he announced that Alsace-Lorraine had been taken back into Germany, not for the comfort and pleasure of its people, but for the safety of the Empire. On reflection, the population concerned saw the meaning of this defiant pronouncement, and they realized, as never before, that the decision of Germany to retain them was invincible. Yet a policy mild, though far-seeing, tempered this bluntness of speech. Under Bismarck's rule, the old University of Strasburg, which had fallen into decay since the days when Goethe sat on its benches, was reëstablished on a splendid scale, thus becoming inevitably a centre of living German thought; and in place of the lower schools, poor and scattered, conducted by the priesthood, was established a school system like that which had done so much for Prussia. Great wisdom was also shown in the Chancellor's election of viceroys for this new domain. First of these was Manteuffel, who during the war period had won high eminence as a general, and who now distinguished himself no less as a statesman—tempering Prussian rigidity with mild wisdom. No less happily inspired was Bismarck in choosing Prince Hohenlohe as Manteuffel's successor. His career as Prime Minister in Bavaria and as Ambassador to France had given him a European reputation, but that which had won him the respect of all thinking Germany was that in spite of his ancestral relations with Austria, the states of the South, and the Vatican he had remained faithful to his early patriotic ideal of German unity under the leadership of Prussia. It was as if during our own Civil War some preëminent statesman in one of our Southern States, realizing from the first that in the unity of the American republic is rooted all hope for liberty on the American continent, had taken his stand at the side of Abraham Lincoln,—had steadily asserted, with Andrew Jackson, "the Federal Union must and shall be preserved,"—had overcome family traditions, personal attachments, state prejudices, church demands, and had adhered, from first to last, to the Union cause, despite all opposition and obloquy.

The policy of Hohenlohe, somewhat more stern than that of Manteuffel, served to extinguish all hopes for a return of the provinces to French sovereignty, and it was a natural result that at a later period he became Chancellor of the Empire. It may be permitted to the present writer to say that, having been thrown into official and social relations with this statesman, he learned to respect him for his patriotism, his equity, his mildness, and his ever-present sense of justice. Loyal, too, the Prince always remained to his great predecessor: of all men of that period with whom the present writer has ever spoken, Hohenlohe threw the clearest and fullest light upon Bismarck's services to Germany and to mankind.

While the great Chancellor thus wrought at the circumference of the Empire, his power was no less evident at its centre. The five milliards transferred to Germany from France had proved a disturbing element; an era of wild speculation had begun and ere long came a financial crash which seemed to shake the Empire to its foundations. Worst of all, sundry men in high office at Berlin had been tempted into abuses of public confidence. Strong defenders of right now arose, and Bismarck's wisdom, regardless of party ties, allowed justice to be done, even against some culprits who stood very near him.

Another of his great services was in the maintenance of the German army, and in this he stood firm against an opposition earnest and powerful. He saw that France on one side and Russia on the other were steadily increasing their armaments; he remembered how after the victories of Frederick the Great a slothful optimism had brought the nation under the heel of Napoleon; he knew that Germany, having virtually no natural frontiers, must rely on the skill and prowess of her sons against powerful enemies on all sides: his motto therefore was not "Rest and be thankful"; he saw in past victories a reason for putting forth new energies. In the debates which now arose he stood firmly by the side of Moltke, the greatest strategist since Napoleon, who, in speeches sententious but weighty, declared that the provinces won in half a year could only be retained by military exertions extending through half a century. Bismarck was ready to compromise on minor matters, but on this main issue he was unyielding and finally overcame all opposition.[1]

During this epoch, under the guidance of the Chancellor, a succession of reforms was initiated, among them new codes of law and a supreme court for the Empire. Very vexatious had been the legal confusion existing in the new Germany. Petty states, and indeed petty cities, had their own codes and customs, differing from each other not merely in outward forms but often in their underlying principles: some being mainly outgrowths of feudalism, some of Roman Law, and some strange mixtures of both. Now were set at work jurists of the first order, and in 1877 appeared a criminal code for the entire Empire, in 1897 a commercial code, and in 1900 a civil code.

Noteworthy is it that in a minor feature of this legislation Bismarck was overruled: he had wished the supreme court to sit at the capital, but the Parliament, yielding to its fear of over-centralization, decided that it should sit at Leipsic.

Now also he wrought a change of the greatest moment in financial administration. From the first day of the Empire to the last of Bismarck's continuance in office he stood as the champion of a principle which was finally knit into all German legislation,—that of the financial independence of the Empire. Its revenues from customs and indirect taxes were inadequate and its deficits could only be made up by contributions from the several states.

---

[1] In 1880 the present writer heard Moltke virtually repeat his earlier argument on the renewal of the military grant. His speech was made in the presence of Bismarck, in the crowded Parliament House, and the sympathy of the two great men of the war period was most evident.

In this system he justly saw danger, for it afforded enormous possibilities of nullifying imperial laws by local refusals of appropriations. The situation was essentially that of the wretched Confederation which preceded the American Union; therefore it was that he was now drawn into a series of new projects which mark an epoch in the economic and social history of the whole world.

V

AMONG the first efforts of Bismarck in securing financial independence for the new Empire was to obtain for it the ownership of all railways within its borders. But here a majority in the Diet saw danger. They naturally asked what control the legislative body could exert over an administration thus gaining an assured income of hundreds of millions a year, with appointment and control of myriads of railway employés domiciled in every part of the Empire. Moreover, sundry large states—notably Saxony, Würtemberg, Bavaria, Baden—already owned their railways, and, finding power and profit in the management of them, had no wish to part with it. Bismarck's struggle to transfer this ownership to the imperial government was long and earnest; but, as it failed, he was obliged to seek new sources of imperial revenue, and finally, after various minor compromises and adjustments, he found them largely in indirect taxation.

The railways of Alsace and Lorraine came into the possession of the Empire, but as a rule those of the other states remained the property of their respective governments. Thence came great power to the various local bureaucracies; but it is especially worthy of note that in Germany, as in other European countries where state ownership prevails, the only great through railway trains which compare in efficiency with those of Great Britain and the United States are equipped and managed, under special contracts, by private companies—individual initiative thus demonstrating its superiority. It is also to be noted that the prices usually charged for passage and freight are much higher in Germany than those of the same class in the United States.

But, though Bismarck thus fell short of his main aim, he secured more fully than ever before coöperation throughout the whole German system of railways. While he could not secure imperial *ownership,* he brought all under an imperial *control* which has proved a great advantage.

The same tendency to identify the new Empire with great improvements in communication, both interior and exterior, was seen in his efforts to improve and increase the internal waterways and harbors by legislation carefully studied and steadily pursued.[1]

A new imperial coinage was also adopted. Those who knew Germany in the middle period of the nineteenth century, and among them the present writer, have vivid remembrances of the former circulating medium: Frederick Paulsen tells us that as late as 1860, when he arrived as a student at the University of Erlangen, though he had only made the journey from Hamburg, he found five different sorts of currency in his pocket, and he adds that they formed "an epitome of German misery."[2] The foreign traveler passing in those days through half a dozen different German states found, as a rule, not merely as many different coinages, but frequently two or three coinages, old and new, in each state, each of these with its own discount—if haply it was good at all. Nothing in its way could be more vexatious or wasteful, save perhaps the paper money system which prevailed in the United States down to our Civil War.

Regarding the basis of the new imperial coinage, though Bismarck consented to restrict it to gold, he retained strong leanings toward the double standard. The present writer twice heard him discuss the subject,—

---

[1] See Matter, as above, vol. iii, pp. 475–477.
[2] See Paulsen, *Aus Meinem Leben*, p. 138.

once in public, once in private,—and it was clear that he was dissatisfied with his decision and would have reversed it, had the double standard obtained the sanction of Great Britain.[1]   In the form of the new coinage, windy and wordy men infesting the various local legislatures, as well as the Imperial Diet, saw opportunities for party metaphysics and began to raise questions as to the rights of the Empire and the rights of the individual states to stamp the coins—each with its own arms and emblems; but a compromise very characteristic of Bismarck ended all this oratory at once: the imperial arms were stamped on one side of the coins and the head of the local sovereign on the other—it was like Columbus and the egg.

In the long series of measures which he brought before Parliament, Bismarck from time to time met with serious defeats, and these, acting on a body worn and sick and sore, galled him. Notably was this the case in his dealings with Socialism. From small beginnings it had developed rapidly, a most important force in its growth being the excesses of reckless promoters, swindling stock jobbers, and millionaire Epicureans, who brought on the great financial crash of 1873. The election to the first German Parliament, in 1871, showed a Socialist vote of about one hundred thousand; in 1893 it had become nearly eighteen hundred thousand, and the number of Socialist deputies had increased from two to forty-two. To meet this tendency Bismarck proposed severe repressive measures, which Parliament, insisting that they struck at the right of free speech and free thought, refused to pass. But aid came to him from the anarchists: in the spring of 1878 were made two desperate efforts to assassinate the Emperor—one by an illiterate tinker, and the other, which was nearly successful, by a

---

[1] This was made clear when the present writer, as American Minister at Berlin, brought the subject before the German government in 1879.

man of much higher acquirements. This aroused Bismarck's flagging strength. In the national indignation awakened by these outrages, and especially by the second of them, he saw his opportunity; dissolved Parliament; appealed to the nation; and obtained a majority which stood by him in legislation suppressing Socialist meetings and publications with great energy, made numerous expulsions of individuals, and authorized a state of siege in Berlin and other great cities.

But with repression of outrages went redress of grievances—and the measures which Bismarck now proposed have astonished the world to this hour. In the early days of his political activity, although he had accepted the *laissez-faire* theories then dominant, he had occasionally suggested state care for men worn out by labor; but his suggestions were thought mere vagaries and attracted little attention. Later he had been attracted by an erratic scholar and Epicurean agitator, Ferdinand Lassalle, to whose discussions of social problems he had listened with evident interest. These discussions, no doubt, aroused the Chancellor's curiosity, even if they did not influence his reason; the soil was ready for them; throughout his whole career the wish to strengthen the Empire which he had created grew upon him, with the result that the old *laissez-faire* theory became to him more and more offensive and sundry socialistic arguments for placing vastly more power in the hands of the central government more and more plausible. The ideas of Lassalle and his successors presupposed the centralization of all power in the state: the government becoming everything, the individual nothing. A similar order of ideas, coupled with the desire for larger imperial revenues, changed Bismarck from an indifferent free-trader to a convinced protectionist and caused him to propose the legislation which finally drove from him his earlier supporters and brought Germany under a high-tariff régime.[1]

This same train of thought finally led him to urge the most daring socialistic measure which had then been adopted by any modern nation,—compulsory state insurance for workingmen. There were in this system three main parts: first, compulsory insurance against sickness, with premiums one-third paid by the employer and two-thirds by the workingman—this he carried through in 1883; next, compulsory insurance against accidents, which was finally extended from mines and factories to every trade, the whole premium being paid by the employers—and this he carried through in 1884; finally came old age pensions, beginning at the age of seventy—premiums paid partly by the workingman and partly by the employer, with an added provision by the state—this was accomplished in 1889. During the whole course of this legislation enormous obstacles confronted him, greatest of all these being the opposition of those who up to this time had mainly supported him. His first bill they wrecked, but he returned to the charge, and to meet his new needs he now made perhaps the most striking change in the whole history of political parties. During the period of the Confederation and the early years of the Empire he had been supported by the National Liberal party, composed mainly of broad-minded men and containing a majority of the foremost thinkers of the Diet, while opposed to him had been the old Conservatives and the Centre, or clerical party, which had steadily obeyed the Vatican.

He now turned from those who had supported to those who had opposed him. He recognized new possibilities in his warfare. Among the Conservatives and Centrists

[1] A brief but very clear statement regarding Bismarck's opinion of Lassalle is given by Keudell, as above, pp. 161–163.

were leaders both of the landowning and manufacturing interests; and he determined to pay a price which would win them. Conciliating Conservatives by severity against the Socialists, and winning Clericals by mildness toward the Pope, he offered to both parties and to the great working population they represented a régime of protection. The offer was embraced, and, as a consequence, came a kaleidoscopic change: those who had been his partisan enemies now mainly standing with him, and those who had been his friends mainly against him.

At times, during this complicated series of struggles in Parliament and in the country at large, vexed, thwarted, disgusted, and suffering the bodily ills which beset him, he had threatened to leave office, and, in April, 1877, had gone so far as to lay before the Emperor a petition asking permission to resign. On this petition the Emperor wrote the word *"Never,"* and in this decision the nation, as a whole, heartily acquiesced. As a compromise the weary Chancellor was allowed to take a nominal vacation at his country seat, but even there his labors were constant, and on his return to active service in 1878 came perhaps the most important phase of his activity in internal affairs. He seemed now to rise above his discouragement and to forget all his ills. In his war on free trade his labor was colossal; the extent of his knowledge and the acuteness of his thought, as displayed in his speeches at this time, were a matter of marvel both to his friends and enemies, and none wondered at them more than men who had risen to professional eminence by life-long study of political economy.[1]

Here should be noted another development of his activity. He kept in his pay a great number of the men most skillful in directing public opinion through the press.

---

[1] As regards Bismarck's activity in this field and his wonderful characteristics revealed in it, see the very striking tribute paid him by the eminent economist, Professor Gustav Schmoller, in his *Vier Briefe*.

Summoning them at all hours of the day or night to the Chancellor's palace in the Wilhelm-Strasse or to Varzin or to Friedrichsruh, he laid before them sketches of articles for newspapers, for magazines, for reviews, not only at the capital but in other centres of German thought, and, indeed, in foreign centres. Sometimes these dictations took the shape of complete articles, thought out with great power and expressed with consummate skill; sometimes they were extended corrections of articles written in obedience to hints from him, and very curious are his annotations on them. Among the manuscripts in the library of Cornell University are three of these articles, written by others, but with copious changes, suppressions, and amendments in his own hand. Various things in these annotations are worthy of note, but perhaps most characteristic is his careful suppression of all compliments to himself, whether open or implied: there seemed in him a scorn for any such effort to extend his fame.[1]

But, as these last great measures were carried and as he seemed about to bring in a new epoch and to grasp power more tenaciously than ever, thinking men began to doubt and even to fear. The old Emperor William, who had stood by his Chancellor so long and so manfully, was evidently fading away, and when, in the spring of 1888, he died, doubts and fears increased. It was well known that the mother of the new sovereign, his wife, and many of his closest friends had for years hated Bismarck's policy, and that, at one time, sympathy with this opposition had caused Frederick while heir to the throne to abandon the capital. It was well known also that the old Prussian theories and indeed some of the new German theories of the Chancellor were at the opposite pole from

[1] For a large number of Bismarck's sketches and drafts for "reptile press" articles, see Busch's *Diary*, English translation, vol. i, pp. 36 and following.

those of the new monarch, whose ideas had been greatly influenced by his life in England, and, above all, by his wife, the gifted daughter of the British Queen. There was wide dread of a clash and final break-up between the new sovereign and his father's adviser.

But it was the unexpected which occurred. In spite of his theoretical preferences for English constitutional monarchy over German mitigated absolutism, Frederick had learned to value the great Chancellor, and in various emergencies, notably after the battle of Sadowa, had stood by him firmly when the old Emperor, the Court, and the generals were against him.

But there was now a special reason for retaining the Chancellor in power. The situation was one of the most pathetic in human history: the new sovereign was dying, and under constant torture from his disease. He knew well that he had neither time nor strength for a conflict with the old Prussian system, and, though during the ninety-nine days of his reign he made changes and bestowed favors among officers of the state which indicated his longing for a new era, he held fast to Bismarck.

The confidence thus shown was well repaid. Even during this short reign, the Chancellor had one striking opportunity to prove his patriotism. To all appearance this opportunity was a matter of little moment,—nothing more than the proposed marriage of a Hohenzollern princess to a prince of German birth, Alexander of Battenberg, former ruler of Bulgaria. It interested the world at large, for it was understood to be a love match, and "all the world loves a lover."

The women of the imperial family and most of the men wished it; all the women and most of the men throughout Germany and Great Britain who read the newspapers wished it; and certain great party leaders in Parliament and through the press, seeing in this an opportunity to embarrass Bismarck, poured scorn over all who opposed it. Had Bismarck been a statesman of the Beaconsfield sort—anxious to secure support among women at court and especially from the new Empress,—anxious to secure approval from the average family man and woman throughout the Empire,—anxious to be applauded in theatres and on the promenades,—he would have favored the alliance. But he realized the political danger in the case—the danger of complications with Bulgaria, and indeed with Russia, the possibility of new alliances which might interfere with his policy to restore good relations with the reigning house of Russia and to keep clear of Balkan matters. He therefore opposed the marriage resolutely,—winning over the new Emperor and even the Queen of Great Britain.

This undoubtedly brought upon him much unpopularity, but it showed thinking men how little he esteemed the applause of courts or mobs compared with the interests of his country.

At the death of the Emperor Frederick, in the midst of the general sorrow for the noblest occupant of an imperial throne since Marcus Aurelius, there was one thing which seemed of especially good augury. The young Emperor William II, who succeeded him, had received an admirable education and had profited by it. His original genius and talent, remarkable as they were, had been developed by studies and practical discipline rare indeed among the heirs to sovereignty. In the gymnasium he had sat among the sons of the plain people; had obtained profit in the university and in the military and naval schools; had gained actual and practical experience in the army and navy; was trained in the leading offices of administration; had kept abreast of progress in art, science, and literature. His knowledge of German and European history was good,—evidently inspiring him with a high patriotism; and it was especially as a German patriot that he recognized the Chancellor's greatness.

This recognition had been made known by the young Prince in ways which showed love and devotion for the old statesman, and it was universally felt that the Bismarck Era would be continued through the new reign.

But here also it was the unexpected which occurred. The young Emperor's activity was all-embracing. Every interest of his country he considered a direct interest of his own; the range of subjects which he studied and on which he delivered addresses eloquently, and indeed thoughtfully, was encyclopædic. Did any man do anything notable in any part of the Empire, the young sovereign took the earliest opportunity to know him; was any scientific or practical discovery of value made in any other country, competent professors were at once summoned to the Imperial Palace to explain it. He had, soon after his accession, visited not only most parts of his own Empire, but all the surrounding countries, save France, and had made acquaintance with their sovereigns and statesmen. To the Chancellor, broad as was his grasp of German and European affairs, this activity could not but be embarrassing: clearly the new imperial will was not prone to move in the old grooves. Sundry appointments also were made by the monarch without consulting the Chancellor: young aspirants were substituted for elderly officials. Moltke, the great "battle-thinker," having retired, was succeeded in the virtual headship of the army by Count Waldersee, to whom the new Emperor seemed to become greatly attached,—constantly consulting him, frequently taking long walks with him; and this fact, with a New York *Herald* interview which indicated that Count Waldersee felt that Germany was able to stand alone against her enemies, even without the aid of her allies, evidently aroused misgivings in the breast of the old Chancellor who had given so much time and thought to secure these allies.

From time to time came utterances which showed

this: Bismarck complained of interference in state matters by irresponsible persons; of appointments which he had not advised; of procedures which he would have had otherwise.

One thing was especially galling. The new Emperor showed a disposition to communicate directly with his ministers and to have them communicate directly with him. This was contrary to the Chancellor's fundamental ideas of proper government: he would have all communications between the sovereign and his ministers pass through the Chancellor, and he based his view upon rules adopted by the Prussian monarchy long before he came into office.

Yet, from time to time, there came matters on which in the face of the nation and the world the old agreement between sovereign and chancellor was maintained. Worthy of note is it, that when the eminent theologian and historian, Harnack, was called to the Berlin Faculty and bitter opposition had been aroused in the high orthodox party against him, taking shape in sermons, speeches, and newspaper articles, the young Emperor and Bismarck stood firmly together for him. Here may well be remembered a tribute to the Chancellor which meant much, though at first sight apparently comical. The University of Giessen, on the birthday of Luther, conferred upon Bismarck the degree of Doctor of Theology. He already held doctorates in philosophy and law, and this new distinction, completing the cycle of academic honors, he accepted in a letter showing a breadth of religious sympathy which in his early days would have been hateful to him.

But new subjects arose in which the Emperor and the Chancellor were not in equal accord, and among these Socialism.

Much alarm had been aroused by the gatherings of Anarchists, Nihilists, and adherents of the red flag, in

Switzerland, and more directly by a great mining strike extending over large parts of the Empire. This was a provoking return to Bismarck for his own series of state socialist ventures—state insurance against accidents, illness, and old age; and he was clearly purposed to return to his old plan of administering chastisement with one hand while bestowing benefits with the other.

But the bill which he brought into Parliament, giving extraordinary powers to banish individuals and to suppress newspapers, was wrecked as soon as launched; the Emperor preferred reliance on laws less drastic,—was clearly determined that his reign should not begin with bloodshed.

This was the first main break between monarch and minister; but soon there came another which proved to be the beginning of the end, and this was simply an interview granted by the Chancellor to his old opponent, Windthorst. Though it had been granted at Windthorst's request, the men hostile to Bismarck saw in it a proof that he was seeking clerical support against the Emperor.

Therefore it was that the Head of the Civil Cabinet was sent from the Imperial Palace to the Chancellor with a notice that, whenever he should receive members of the legislative bodies thereafter to discuss political matters, the Emperor must be informed beforehand. To this Bismarck sent answer that he "allowed no one but himself to control his threshold." On this the Emperor came early next morning, while Bismarck was still in bed, demanded an interview at once, and on Bismarck's appearance asked him what the conference with Windthorst meant. To this Bismarck answered that it was a private matter. Thereupon the Emperor rejoined that he had a right to be informed whenever his Chancellor entered into discussions with a party leader. This doctrine Bismarck at once rejected, insisting again that no one could interfere within his threshold. At this the Emperor asked: "Not even when I, as sovereign, command you?"—to which Bismarck answered: "The command of my master ends with my wife's drawing-room," and he added that it was only in obedience to a promise made to the Emperor's grandfather that he was still in service, and that he was ready to withdraw into private life whenever he became an embarrassment to his sovereign. Two days passed with no signs of a resignation from the Chancellor, and then General Hahncke was sent with a notice that the Emperor was awaiting it. To this Bismarck answered in substance that he would not end a career like his by virtual desertion,—that His Majesty could secure his resignation at any time by ordering him to send it. Thereupon there was forwarded a demand, in due form, that the resignation be sent by a certain hour. At this Bismarck demanded time for the preparation of a suitable document, and this he finally sent on March 20, 1890, with a full discussion of what he considered the main principles involved.

In accepting it, the Emperor made no mention of the circumstances which had caused it, but wrote an eloquent tribute to Bismarck's services, and sent with it a patent conferring upon him the Dukedom of Lauenburg, with verbal intimations of a grant of property suitable to so great a dignity.

The whole action of Bismarck in this crisis was certainly not in keeping with his character as the world had previously known it. Though he had long and earnestly declared his preference for private life and his desire for relief from public duty, he now showed a painful reluctance to give up his post and a most bitter feeling toward all who had, or had seemed to have, any part in the opposition to him: he evidently believed that Germany could hardly maintain its existence without his continuance in office.[1]

There was a strange alloy of strength and weakness in his course, both now and afterward. The dotation to accompany the Duchy of Lauenburg he rejected, declaring that services like his were not to be rewarded by a money gift like the drink money thrown to a postman at Christmas. As to the patent itself, while he did not reject it, he from time to time made it an object of ridicule, saying that he could use it should he ever wish to travel—*incognito*. Fortunately the general public knew nothing of the way in which his resignation had been brought about, or of the less dignified scenes which it had occasioned; Bismarck's letter was not published, but the Emperor's gifts, including his portrait at full length, were widely made known.

The result of Bismarck's retirement was an outburst of national feeling such as had scarcely been known in the history of Europe. During his drive to the Imperial Palace to take leave of the sovereign, and at his departure from the city, there came tributes of respect and affection by assembled myriads, such as no other German statesman had ever obtained. Bismarck wept, and from multitudes of strong men came floods of tears.[2]

The conduct of William II in demanding the resignation of the great Chancellor has been frequently and sharply criticised; but thoughtful men have more and more agreed in the opinion that the act was wise. To have taken any other course would have subjected the Emperor, his dynasty, and possibly the

[1] See Prince Münster's account of Bismarck's conduct at this period, as reported by Blowitz in the London *Times* and later in *Harper's Magazine*.

[2] The scenes at Bismarck's departure, in the Wilhelm-Strasse and on the Unter den Linden, have been described to the present writer by various persons who were present, and all testify to the widespread sorrow shown by the weeping of strong men, as well as of Bismarck himself.

Empire, to serious dangers. In the days of William I, Bismarck, under pressure of opposition, disappointment, and ill health, had often tendered his resignation, and at times in a way almost exasperating; but the old Emperor, who had won the respect of the world by force and decision during long years of war and peace, could afford to submit to all this. More than once when his great Chancellor sulked, the old monarch had driven to the palace in the Wilhelm-Strasse and by kindly remonstrances and entreaties had set him on his feet again. For this the right-thinking part of the nation felt grateful to the sovereign; but a young monarch just coming to the throne could not follow this example: to have begun by such concessions would have certainly been considered weakness and made him appear simply as a *roi fainéant*—a youth who reigned but did not govern— and would have subjected the whole monarchical system of Prussia and of Germany to the charge of decrepitude and decay. The resignation was doubtless a severe trial to the young monarch, but his courage in demanding it and his firmness in insisting upon it undoubtedly increased respect for him in the Empire, and indeed throughout the world.

Over the following period the admirers and best friends of the Chancellor would gladly draw a veil. Nothing during his long public life became him so ill as his leaving it. During the whole eight years following, his course certainly lacked the dignity which his best friends could have wished to see in it. Instead of wise counsels, unobtrusively tendered, there came from him constant fire of criticisms upon the Chancellor who succeeded him, and generally upon all measures taken by the new government, whether in diplomatic, internal, or colonial affairs. His residence, Friedrichsruh, became a special place of pilgrimage for scandal-seekers and sensation-mongers. To these he never hesitated to say things deeply embarrassing to the government. On the other hand, the conduct of the government was hardly less unsatisfactory. Official notice was sent out to the various representatives of the Empire, declaring the opinions of the former Chancellor unworthy of consideration; and when, on the marriage of his eldest son at Vienna, Bismarck visited that capital, such notifications were issued by the German government that Bismarck's old friends, the King of Saxony and the Emperor of Austria, refused to see him, and the German Embassy kept aloof from him. This in its turn provoking Bismarck's resentment, he at various places spoke wildly and almost treasonably. He constantly exhibited himself, even to casual visitors, as that pitiful being, a man with a grievance. Talking with Henry Villard, he spoke of himself as "kicked out of office"; and when Mr. Villard remonstrated, and tried to convince him that such a statement was unjust to himself, he angrily reiterated it.

Fortunately, during a severe illness of the old Chancellor, the young Emperor took occasion to send most hearty messages with tenders of kind offices, and named after him, with appropriate speeches, one of the great warships of the new navy, thus beginning a new era of mutual visits and better feeling.[1]

From time to time came tributes which showed that the nation, as well as its sovereign, had not forgotten Bismarck's services, and at his death, in 1898, there was an outburst of feeling which seemed to blot out forever all painful remembrances. Excepting a few ultraists in the Imperial Parliament, the whole nation, with the Emperor at its head, arose to honor his memory. When his body was conveyed to its last resting place in the Saxon Forest, when in various parts of the Empire memorials were erected recalling noted periods of his life or phases of his activity, and when finally the great national monu-

[1] See Horst Kohl, *Bismarck Jahrbuch*, v, p. 365.

ment to him was unveiled in front of the Imperial Parliament-House at the capital, innumerable evidences of gratitude and respect proved that his weaknesses were forgotten, that his services were inscribed on the heart of the nation, and that his place was secure as one of the two greatest state servants Germany had ever known.[1]

[1] For a very thoughtful comparison between Stein and Bismarck, see Dr. Neubauer, in Horst Kohl, *Bismarck-Jahrbuch*, vi, pp. 243 and following. Very wisely, resemblances are dwelt upon rather than differences, and no attempt is made to assert the superiority of either statesman.

VI

AS we look back over Bismarck's whole career there looms up before us his historic personality,—huge, portentous, like some vast figure hewn from the living rock in India or on the upper Nile.

In this figure appear various strata: mediæval ideas of feudal rule and duty, Frederician conceptions of the absolute monarch as a state servant, devotion to Prussian supremacy and German unity, German liberal ideas implying reliance on the entire people, American republican ideas necessitating local government and a confederation,—*laissez faire,* protectionism, absolutism, socialism, conservatism, radicalism. Veinings also appear,—permeating all strata alike: distrust of Rousseau sentimentalism and Manchester liberalism, contempt for marplots, hatred for demagogues,—degenerating frequently into dislike of constitutionalism, and even into scorn for rational freedom.

His physical qualities combined to give him Titanic force: his huge body, his brain (found after his death to be greater than that of any known contemporary), his easy dominion over the world about him, as a horseman, a hunter, a forester, a born leader of men.[1]

Looking next into his intellectual qualities, we recall first his insight,—his skill in discerning at once the central fact in any situation or combination—the germ of victory. And we note next his foresight,—the power of seeing how principles are to work themselves out or can

[1] On the size and weight of Bismarck's brain, as revealed by the *post-mortem* examination, see Gustav Schmoller, *Vier Briefe,* as above.

514

be made to work themselves out. It was this insight and foresight which, during the Crimean War, led him to oppose the general German tendency to take sides with the western powers against Russia, and which enabled him later to secure the neutrality of Russia in the Prussian war with France: these too were the qualities which in the Danish war led him to resist the Emperor, the ruling classes, and the German nation in their partiality for "the Augustenburger" and which enabled him to secure Schleswig-Holstein with the harbor of Kiel for Prussia and thereby to give a new stimulus to German patriotism, —the qualities which, when he had brought Austria to the feet of Prussia, led him to resist and conquer the Prussian king, army, and people in all their passion for a revengeful triumph, and enabled him to secure the acquiescence of Austria in the great war with France,— the qualities which led him during the entire war with France to resist everything likely to draw Germany aside from its one purpose—the establishment of its nationality.

Still another of his intellectual qualities was breadth of vision. The most learned of modern English historians, Lord Acton, in claiming that Napoleon was a greater man than Cæsar, dwelt especially on the fact that the French Emperor carried in his mind not only exact knowledge regarding every man of mark in Europe, whether supporting or opposing his policy, whether in the field or in the cabinet; that he had formed an estimate of each man's value, and a forecast of his action, and that, whether the great conqueror was in Paris or in Warsaw or in Vienna or in Berlin or in Madrid, all European affairs centred in him. The same quality is seen in Bismarck in all save military knowledge, and with a far more sane grasp of facts and an infinitely happier power of prophetic vision. Hence it was that, while the empire built by Napoleon came to naught in ten years and by a process inflicting infinite misery upon the nations who had trusted him, the empire which Bismarck built has stood through forty years of stress, has risen from strength to strength, and has brought prosperity to his country and peace to Europe.[1]

Glance next at some of Bismarck's moral qualities. As we have already seen, the foremost of these—that which was knit into his whole moral fibre—was his courage. From his boyhood this was especially noted. Whether leading his schoolmates into mimic battle, or plunging into deep water to save his orderly from drowning, or risking life and limb in his wild rides in the marches, or grappling instantly, at close quarters and unarmed, with the assassin, it was part of his nature. But it took higher forms—great historic forms—as when he entered into his contest with Parliament, braving the fate of Strafford and reconciling King William to the fate of Charles I, or when he braved the ill-will of courts and cabals, the loss of old friendships, hatred throughout Germany, and indeed throughout Europe, by pursuing policies which he believed patriotic,—or when he took upon his own shoulders the responsibility for the war with Denmark, and again for the war with Austria, and again for the war with France.

It must be confessed that, though he was never hot-headed, his courage rose at times to heights that were dangerous. Happy the nation that never needs this: for his was at times the courage of the desperado,—of the gambler who stakes all on a single throw. It is a question whether any statesman has, for anything save the national existence, the right to pledge a nation to such responsibilities as those to which Bismarck at times bound Prussia and the German people. And yet it must be said that another great quality of his, which

[1] Lord Acton's argument regarding Napoleon is given in the Autobiography of the present writer, vol. ii, pp. 414, 415.

must not by any means be lost sight of, was his caution,
—his *great* caution. His career exemplifies the warning—"Be bold,—be bold,—be bold: be not too bold."
Striking evidences of this are seen in his holding back
his King and country from wars until the psychological
moment,—in his holding back the adhesion of lesser
states to the empire until the greater states had ample
time to reflect,—in his forbearance regarding various
deeds of neighboring powers which must have tried him
sorely.

Here, indeed, is seen a characteristic quality of his
genius—in the proper admixture of boldness with caution,
—in his recognition of the moment when caution is to
cease and boldness is to begin, and when boldness is to
cease and caution is to begin. At such transitions the
working of his mind seemed intuitive, but it was doubtless the result of his amazing faculty for running out
lines of conduct in all their possible developments, keeping them before his mind and comparing them. Various
public utterances of his show his own consciousness of
this quality in his genius. He said: "I began very
early to be a hunter and fisher, and, in both pursuits,
waiting for the right moment is the rule, which I have
applied to politics." Evidence of it is seen in the fact
that every one of his great efforts of European concern
succeeded at all its important stages. In his career we
find no Spanish campaign, no march on Moscow, no
battle of Leipzig, and hence no Waterloo. Lord Acton
dwelt on Napoleon's ability to see European men and
things and conditions—in their entirety—at any given
moment; but the two most important things of all Napoleon failed to see: first, that during more than a decade
he had been steadily arousing the patriotism of his
enemies; and, secondly, that he had been as steadily
teaching them to beat him.

More than this, though Bismarck was a good hater,

he never planned or conducted great enterprises in obedience to hatred. There was nothing in his policy akin to the hatred for Great Britain which finally blinded Napoleon, led him on fanatically in his continental policy, and brought on the catastrophe, in his mid-career.

But as to another quality the judgment of contemporaries, and especially of Englishmen and Americans, has borne heavily upon Bismarck. He is charged with deluding his adversaries, especially Napoleon III, and an English essayist goes so far as to apply to his career Tennyson's famous verses, but to leave out their last four words:

> "Ah, God, for a man with heart, head, hand,
> Like some of the simple great ones gone
> For ever and ever by;
> One still, strong man in a blatant land,
> Whatever they call him, what care I,
> Aristocrat, democrat, autocrat—one
> Who can rule and dare not lie."

It cannot be denied that Bismarck at many periods during his career resorted to intrigue and strategy, and, when he did so, proved himself a master. And it is also true that some of his intrigues were hardly to his credit; but, as a simple matter of fact, never did statesman more thoroughly disdain falsehood, whether diplomatic or other. He himself proudly declared: "Lying have I never learned, not even as a diplomat." [1] His pride made falsehood repulsive to him. This is the secret of that frankness which so often startled his contemporaries. Publicly and privately,—in talks over the green table at Frankfort and in his despatches,—in discussions with Napoleon III or Alexander II or Francis Joseph,—in interviews with statesmen at Berlin and Vienna and

---

[1] *"Das Lügen habe ich auch als Diplomat nicht gelernt."* Cited by Dehn, *Bismarck als Erzieher*, p. 8.

Paris and London, and in his home letters, he frankly foretold the consequences of Austrian policy and foreshadowed his own intentions regarding it. He openly demanded at Frankfort and Vienna, as at Berlin, a change from the old Austrian contempt for Prussia, and openly pledged himself to drive her out of Germany unless she made this change. This frankness it was which led Napoleon III to speak of him as "not serious," and Disraeli to say, "Watch that man, he means what he says." Frankly, at all times and places, as long as speech was of use, he prophesied that if Austria did not make proper concession to the rights of Prussia and the aspirations of Germany, war must come, and to none did he tell this more openly than to the Austrians themselves. His ambition to build up a united Germany with Prussia as its leader he frankly revealed to Napoleon III, to Disraeli, to Alexander II,—to all the leaders of the time.

It has frequently been charged that he only used truth in order to deceive more effectively. Whatever alloy of this sort there may have been in his utterances, it is still true that his invincible pride made prevarication hateful to him. Perhaps a tangle of motives showed itself most curiously in his famous talk with Countess Hohenthal, the wife of the Saxon minister at Berlin, the year before the Austrian campaign. Sitting next him at dinner she asked him jocosely if he was intending to bring on war; he, though knowing that all her sympathies were with Austria, at once answered, "Yes," and vaunted the readiness of the Prussian army. She then said to him, "I have two estates, one in Bohemia, the other near Leipzig. To which would you advise me to take my family next summer?" Bismarck replied, "By all means to the estate near Leipzig; the great battle between Prussia and Austria will probably be fought near your Bohemian estate." And it turned out that Bismarck's prophecy was exactly true. That even his foes did not believe it made merely to mislead was shown by the fact that, when it was a little later dutifully communicated by the lady to the proper quarter, the Austrians concentrated troops in the neighborhood of her Bohemian estate. Bismarck's thought may have been that he would be disbelieved, and Austria thrown on a false scent, or his wish may have been to give additional provocation to Austria and insure war, but it is none the less true that the answer is, in some measure, an evidence of his colossal disdain for lying. The same thing was seen very generally in his conversations and especially in his own house and at his own table. His frankness regarding his own past life and the doings of his colleagues were a source of constant amazement.[1]

So too in his parliamentary struggles his truthfulness went frequently to the verge of brutality and at times beyond it. The utterance of half truths was not natural to him. His feeling is given in the Prussian peasant saying—"Ein Mann, ein Wort." His great contemporary, Mr. Gladstone, was constantly charged with leaving ambiguities in his arguments to serve as possible loopholes for retreat; well-worn jests based upon his alleged sophistries were always current and especially one in which a bigamist was advised to induce Mr. Gladstone to "explain away" one of his wives. Well worn, too, was the jocose saying of a London cynic that "Gladstone was capable of concealing four aces in his sleeve and persuading himself and others that the Almighty had placed them there." No one would ever have thought even in jest of imputing any of these things to Bismarck. Nor would any friend of Bismarck ever have felt it necessary to warn him, as Thomas Acland warned Glad-

---

[1] For a detailed account of Bismarck's conversation with Countess Hohenthal, see Keudell, *Bismarck et sa Famille*, p. 227; the present writer, in his Autobiography, has given sundry examples of similar frankness and, among them, the *"Affaire Kelly."*

stone, "for the sake of his personal influence to be sure
to deal with a question without refining and without dragging in some recondite view not seen by common men,—
in short, to be as little as possible like Maurice and more
like the Duke of Wellington." Nor have any of Bismarck's biographers ever felt it necessary, as have those
of Disraeli, to smooth over, decorously, public statements
widely known to be untruthful.[1]

As to the charge that Bismarck deluded Napoleon III,
it would be more just to say that Bismarck's sin, if sin
there were, lay in his allowing Napoleon to delude himself. At worst it may be considered as strategy in a war
already begun. No one will claim that there was in
Bismarck the sturdy truthfulness of Stein, and it is not
to be denied that at sundry points in his career, as, for
example, when he threw Count Eulenburg out of the
Prussian ministry, he showed a duplicity which Stein
would never have shown. But, taken as a whole, his
career reveals a colossal pride, which made for a diplomacy plain, open, straightforward.

To bring this into full relief we may contrast it with
the diplomacy of the first Napoleon,—with his letters
just before the Treaty of Campo Formio to the Venetian
Senate and the French Directory—full of lies to both,
—or with the preliminaries to the Treaty of Tolentino,
when the papal councilors at the Vatican found themselves, as compared with Bonaparte, mere novices in
falsehood,—or with his elaborate forgery of documents
by which he threw blame deserved by himself upon his
brother, King Joseph.

The far more usual charge against Bismarck as re-

[1] As to the Acland warning, see Morley, *Life of Gladstone*, vol. ii, p.
376.

For a very guarded, but none the less lucid, treatment of Disraeli's
ordinary attitude toward truth, see Bryce, *Studies in Contemporary
Biography*, especially in the essays on Gladstone and Disraeli.

gards his dealings with antagonists has been that of brutality. Delightful as he could be with his friends and with his moderate opponents, he sometimes pushed his resentment to extremes against those who crossed his path. Noteworthy in this respect was his conduct toward Von Rudhart, a representative of Bavaria in the Imperial Council. This representative of the most powerful of the German states save Prussia was a man of the highest character and of most attractive qualities, and he came from a family noted for its public services; but he had voted on one occasion, as he thought his Bavarian patriotism demanded, in a way contrary to Bismarck's ideas, and shortly afterward, appearing with his wife upon his arm at one of the Chancellor's receptions, was received with reproaches so bitter and threats so galling, in the presence of the whole assembly, that he immediately left the palace, sent his resignation to his government, and, despite all efforts of the German Emperor and the Bavarian King to appease him, refused to remain in Berlin. So deeply did the injustice of this treatment affect him that, although the Bavarian monarch showed approval of his conduct by sending him as minister to Russia, he lost his reason.

Such things are not to be defended, but we may remember that they resulted mainly from excess of patriotic feeling, and we may feel inclined to a more lenient judgment as we recall some of them. Noteworthy among these was a scene at the opening reception of the delegates to the Berlin Conference. They were, as a rule, the most eminent statesmen of the great powers. Of the Turkish delegates one was a German by birth who had gained distinction in the Turkish army, and doubtless by Turkish methods. Whatever he had been in his early life in Germany, he was now a Pasha of high degree, clad with all diplomatic rights and immunities, and he therefore came forward with his colleagues and offered his hand to the Chancellor: it was taken and shaken, but, this done, Bismarck immediately ordered water and a towel, and in the presence of the assembly washed his hands.[1]

It must be acknowledged that, as compared with his two great contemporaries in statesmanship, he had neither the full consideration for his adversaries shown by Cavour nor the nobly courteous bearing toward them always observed by Gladstone.

Here may be compared the general methods of these three great contemporaries in dealing with legislative bodies. Never were men more diversely endowed. Gladstone was of engaging presence, a manner that charmed and awed, and a voice that enthralled his hearers; his facts and arguments were wonderfully marshaled and lucidly presented. Cavour was stout, stumpy, his voice not usually pleasing, his manner that of the man of business, showing his training as a civil engineer, his arguments plain, matter of fact, enchained by a sort of mathematical logic—yet with rare bursts of eloquence all the more effective because so rare and so sincere. Bismarck was overpowering in stature, huge in bulk, with an air of military command, but his voice high-pitched and not strong,—his manner rarely showing any especial friendliness toward his audience,— his matter often loose, diffuse, grotesquely egotistical, frequently pungent, and at times insulting,—yet, in crucial periods, gathering his audience, as it were, in the hollow of his hand—as when he said: "We Germans fear God and naught beside." Compared with Gladstone neither Bismarck nor Cavour was, under ordinary circumstances, an orator. To the sonorous periods of Gladstone and his superb quotations from Virgil and

[1] A full account of this scene was given to the present writer by one of the delegates to the Conference, of the highest standing, who was present.

Lucretius neither of the two continental statesmen were equal, though Bismarck had a wonderful knack at quoting Latin maxims and peasant proverbs, and both Bismarck and Cavour were at times, in their differing ways, able to reach the depths of their hearers' hearts as surely as did Gladstone. Neither of the continental statesmen could at will throw such a charm around ordinary subjects and even into a budget as could the great Englishman; yet it may well be claimed that Gladstone never touched the heart of the whole nation as deeply as did Cavour in his defense against Garibaldi, or as did Bismarck in his indemnity speech.[1]

Take the next charge against Bismarck, based upon the variations of his political policy,—upon the change from mediæval devotion to Prussia and sympathy with Austria to support of German constitutional liberty and unity—the change which afterward made him the greatest advocate of all he had formerly opposed;—upon the break, still later, from his old political associates, and his passing from party to party to secure support for his measures. Yet all this is a necessary part of the same course. His own answers to this charge were pithy. He said, "The moment the interest of the country requires me to put myself in contradiction with myself I shall do it"; and again, "If anybody says to me, 'Twenty years ago you and I were of one mind; to-day I hold the same opinions which I held then, and you exactly the opposite,' I shall answer him, 'Yes; twenty years ago I was as wise as you are to-day; now I am wiser, for I have learnt something in the mean time.' " Nothing is more clear than that changes in his policy resulted from changes in his opinions as to what was best for the nation. It should

[1] For the parliamentary manner and methods and personal characteristics of Bismarck and Gladstone the present writer relies mainly upon his own recollections, with suggestions from those who stood near them. As regards Cavour he has relied entirely on the testimony of his immediate colleagues, especially of Nigra, Peruzzi, and Minghetti.

be kept in mind that he never, after he took the reins of power, was a party man. He was wont to say that the only members of his party were King William and himself. Like Gladstone, he made a complete change in his political opinions during his progress from youth to full manhood. Like Cavour, he used party combinations as seemed to him best for the state. His great change from the National Liberals and their free-trade theories to the Conservatives and their protectionist ideas was clearly the result of devotion to what he considered the highest interests of his country.

But there are other charges against him better grounded, namely, that at heart he disbelieved in rational liberty, that his chosen system was despotic and his preferred methods autocratic, that he was ready at any provocation to cripple or even destroy constitutional freedom, and that in all this he compared unfavorably with Cavour. Any believer in the development of liberty by liberty finds both in Cavour and in Gladstone a loyalty to constitutional rights, a repugnance to despotism, a faith in the evolution of better men and methods in an environment of rational freedom, which lift them above Bismarck. A recent writer refers to the well-known scene at Cavour's death-bed, when with his last failing breath he pleaded with his sovereign for constitutional methods against a state of siege and for patience with the populations of lower Italy and Sicily. It was, indeed, a noble and touching exhibition of faith, hope, and charity. That, as well as his whole career, shows Cavour far more in sympathy with the nobler aspirations of humanity than was Bismarck, and an antithesis is justly made between Cavour as an apostle of liberty and Bismarck as the champion of authority. But, while acknowledging Cavour's superiority in this respect, may not something still be said for Bismarck? In our own republic, where authority seems so little considered that the first of the

three rights asserted in the Declaration of Independence,
—the right to life—is violated more frequently and
with more impunity than in any other civilized nation,
and where in so many fields license masked as liberty has
uprooted so much of reverence for law, may we not look
even with some admiration upon Bismarck's sturdy assertion of authority? [1]

Take finally that which puzzled so many observers of
his career—his Religion.   To leave this out would be like
leaving out the religion of Cromwell.   It requires more
than mere mention, for it enters largely into the warp and
woof of his whole thought; it merits study at some length,
for in it was undoubtedly rooted that sense of duty so
evident throughout his life.

The definition of religion as "morality touched with
emotion" seems in his case futile.   His religion we know
more fully by far than that of most statesmen, for we
have pertinent revelations of it in his parliamentary contests, in his utterances in times of stress and trial, and in
his private letters to those who were nearest and dearest
to him.   In one of these he says regarding his early life,
"Many an hour did I spend in hopeless despondency, believing that my own and other people's existence was
aimless and useless, perhaps only an accidental emana-
tion of creation, rising and disappearing as dust from
rolling wheels."   Later we have frequent reference in
his letters to his wife to a complete change in his whole
way of looking at the world—manly expressions of con-

---

[1] For an admirable comparison between Cavour and Bismarck as regards political characteristics, see W. R. Thayer, in *The Atlantic Monthly*
for March, 1909.   For the statistics of capital crime in our own republic during the last fifteen years, showing an increase in the number
of homicides during that period from about three thousand to about
ten thousand a year and the severe punishment of less than one in
seventy guilty of homicide during recent years, see the statistical numbers of the Chicago *Tribune*, issued on the last day of each year during the
same period.

trition for the excesses of his early life and of aspirations for a better future.

With these he at times mingles theological discussions, notably one on "faith and works," quotes numerous passages to show the value of works, flatly takes ground against Luther, who in his zeal for faith had called the Epistle of St. James "a straw epistle," and says "I find the Epistle of James a glorious book." He had the courage of his convictions. In his reminiscences he gives a conversation between himself and the Prince Regent, afterward the Emperor William I. The Prince had applied to a certain prominent man the word "Pietist." Those who, like the present writer, remember Berlin social life in "the Fifties" will remember well how in good, sound German families the word Pietist connoted all that was unctuously hypocritical. On the occasion referred to, Bismarck instantly defended "Pietism," called His Highness to account, and put him to confusion.[1]

He never shows any of that reticence regarding religious belief and that tendency to fall back upon a single generality so common with Cavour. Much less did he show any of Gladstone's liking for fine-spun metaphysics.

In letters to his mother-in-law he constantly refers to his religious feelings in terms much like those used by the Anglican "Evangelicals." These letters show that, while during his university life he had given up the prayers of his childhood, he now resumed them. During a journey upon the Rhine he carried the New Testament in his pocket; during the French war he was wont to read the daily texts of Scripture published by the Moravians, and it was noted by those who went into his room immediately after he had hurriedly left his bed to meet the Emperor Napoleon, at Sedan, that at his bedside lay open a

[1] For Bismarck's dialogue with the future Emperor on "Pietism," see Bismarck, *Reflections and Reminiscences*, English translation, Tauchnitz edition, vol. iii, pp. 224, 225.

book of devotion which he had been reading the night before.

In one of his letters to his wife, he says, "Good night, my dear. It strikes twelve. I will go to bed and read yet the second chapter of Second Peter. I do this now systematically, and after I have finished Peter I am going to read the Epistle to the Hebrews." And here there is a characteristic Bismarck touch: speaking of his New Testament reading, he says, "I might be willing to feed mine enemy when he is starving, but to bless him—this would be merely perfunctory, if I could do it at all." Again comes a more intimate statement—"There is no need of reminding me to remember our dear little Mary in my prayers. I do so every day."

Even in the most trying periods of his life we note that it was his wont to partake of the Lord's Supper twice a year and to prepare for it by reading and prayer. And yet even in this was shown the old Bismarck temper. During one of his parliamentary contests came his duel with the Prussian orator, Vincke: his pastor sought to dissuade him from it, but Bismarck overcame him in argument and forced him, much against his will, not only to pray with him but to administer the Communion to him. Characteristic is the account which Bismarck himself gave of this duel in one of his letters to his mother-in-law. He says, "I believe it was truly wholesome for my entire life that I felt myself so near to death, and that I prepared for it. I know that you do not agree with my views on this point, but never did I feel myself so firmly believing and trusting and so fully resigned to God's will as at the time of this duel. My adversary offered to drop the whole matter, if I would declare that I was sorry for what I said. As I was unable to do this in accordance with truth, we took our places, fired and missed, both. May God forgive me the grievous sin that I did not at once recognize His grace; but I cannot deny that when I saw,

through the smoke, my opponent standing upright, a certain feeling of discomfort made it impossible for me to join in the general jubilation. I was ready to continue the fight; but, as I was not the offended party, I had nothing to say. . . . I never doubted for a moment that I had to meet my antagonist; but I was not clear in my own mind whether I should fire at him. I did it without malice, and missed."

Over ten years later he challenged Professor Virchow, the eminent pathologist, and, when a Christian friend expostulated with him, wrote as follows: "As regards the Virchow matter I have passed those years when men consult with flesh and blood on such things. If I risk my life for anything, I do it in that faith which I have obtained and strengthened in long and serious struggles, but in sincere and humble prayer before God, which cannot be upset by word of man."

Curious is it to note that, while at Frankfort he was fighting the Austrian ambassadors to the Confederation at every point, threatening war and meaning it, risking duels with Prokesch, Rechberg, and others, utterly fearless and apparently reckless, he was, to the religious monitions of his wife, as given in her letters, entirely docile. She had some doubts in regard to the sort of Protestantism he might find at Frankfort and therefore urged him to attend a strictly Lutheran church. He reassures her and says, "Day before yesterday I attended the Lutheran church here,—the pastor not a particularly intelligent man, but a believer. The audience besides myself consisted of exactly twenty-two women." More strange still sounds the name of one pastor whom he heard and with whom he conversed, though he tells his wife that he "found not much comfort in him." This pastor became one of the most famous men in Germany,—laughed at from the North Sea to the Alps, and from the Rhine to the Niemen,—the favorite quarry of the caricaturists,

—Pastor Knak,—as famous for his preachments on the necessity of believing that the sun moves round the earth, according to the Scriptures, as, at about the same period, was our eminent colored compatriot, the Rev. John Jasper, for his pulpit proofs that "the sun do move." Toward the end of his career Bismarck showed a tendency to broader churchmanship. He became rather unfavorable to the old Lutheran theologians: called them "little tyrants" and said that "each pastor was a little pope." He objected to Calvin especially on account of the burning of Servetus. He gave his adhesion to Frederick the Great's famous declaration, "Let every one go to heaven in his own way"—and, in defining Christianity practically, he spoke of it as "not the creed of the Court Chaplains." [1]

In comparing Bismarck's religion with that of the two other great statesmen of his time we find it very different from either. Neither in his arguments nor in his statements was there any of that fine-spun reasoning which made Thomas Acland caution Gladstone to avoid the methods of Maurice. Nor was Bismarck capable of any such intellectual process as that which led Gladstone to surmise some occult connection between Neptune's trident and the doctrine of the Trinity. As to Cavour, the mild deistical statements made in his early life and his nominal conformity to dominant opinion on his death-bed were as far as possible from the robust Lutheranism of Bismarck, even when, as in his last years, it had become "exceeding broad." [2]

[1] For an excellent summing up of Bismarck's religious opinions and relations, as presented in the letters to his wife and sister, and in various other documents, see Prof. Adolph Spaeth, *Bismarck as a Christian*, and, for some broader tendencies in his later life, see Busch, *Our Chancellor*, chap. ii.

[2] For Gladstone's suspicion of a mysterious connection between the doctrine of the Trinity and Neptune's trident, see the *Juventus Mundi*. For Cavour's early religious views and their later development, see a let-

His daily life was far from Puritanical. He said: "The Sunday observance in England and America is, after all, a fearful tyranny"; and, when Lothar Bucher defended the quiet English Sunday, Bismarck said: "I am not against observing the Lord's day. On the contrary, as a landed proprietor, I do for it whatever I can. . . . No work ought to be done on Sunday, not so much because it is against God's commandment as on account of the men who need recreation." As a matter of fact, Bismarck allowed no work upon his estates on Sunday that could be deferred, and, when Ambassador at Frankfort, he avoided using his carriage on Sunday in order not to keep his servants from church.

During the war with France, at the Rothschild seat, Ferrières, in the presence of a number of men, mostly sceptics, he spoke as follows: "If I did not obey my God and rely on Him, I would certainly not care for earthly matters. . . . Why should I worry and trouble myself and toil, exposing myself to embarrassments and ill treatment, if I had not the feeling that for God's sake I am bound to do my duty? If I did not believe in divine providence, which has destined this German nation for something great and good, I would at once give up my position as a diplomat, or I would never have undertaken it."

Three years later, in the Prussian Diet, he said: "Whenever the foundations of the state were attacked by the barricade and by republicans, I considered it my duty to stand in the breach. . . . This I am commanded to do by my Christianity and my faith."

Mention may here be made of Bismarck's family life. It was exemplary. Nothing in it clouded his career like that which stained the life of his eminent predecessor, Hardenberg. His relations with wife, sister, and chil-

ter written by him to his aunt, and other documents, given in Berti, *Cavour avanti 1848,* capit. xix.

dren, as revealed in his letters, were ideal, and his whole life at home, as known to his vast circle of friends, had a peculiar beauty which impressed every guest, and indeed influenced favorably the moral condition of the Empire.[1]

In the very thick of his Frankfort period, in all its turbulence, he wrote: "The happy marriage and the children that God has given me are to me like the rainbow, the token and assurance of peace after the flood of desolation and loneliness that covered my soul in former years."

In his temperament there was a strange mingling of the Stoic and the Epicurean. No one could meet more sturdily opposition, trial, and hardship, whether in war or peace; yet there were in him the appetites of his Baltic ancestors. Like them he was a valiant trencherman and held his own at table against all comers. For this he paid a heavy penalty. During the last years of his life he suffered from severe neuralgic pains in his face and especially in his mouth, so that it was almost impossible for him to open it; jestingly he used to say that this was quite natural, since with his mouth he had sinned most, in eating, drinking, and speaking. He was extremely fond of plovers' eggs, of which he was wont to consume fifteen at a single meal, and once he astounded the waiters of a restaurant by eating one hundred and seventy oysters. His excessive indulgence at table was so notorious that his estate, *Kniephof*, was spoken of as *Kneiphof* (tippling court). When he complained of illness and wretchedness to his old associate Gneist, and Gneist sent him a dozen bottles of strong Burgundy, advising him to take a couple of glasses of it daily with dinner, as a tonic, Bismarck later complained that it had done him no

---

[1] For striking pictures of his life at Frankfort and elsewhere, see Motley's *Correspondence;* also Keudell and Abeken everywhere.

good; and when Gneist asked him how he had taken it, he said, "Two bottles of it daily at dinner, as you advised me." Worthy of note perhaps, in connection with this, is the fact that among the effects sent, after his resignation, from the Chancellor's Palace in Berlin to his Friedrichsruh estate, were thirteen thousand bottles of wine,—mainly gifts,—from the choicest vintages in all parts of Middle and South Germany.

But there was survival in him of gentle traits. Nowhere was he more happy than in his woods. For his finest trees he had a personal affection, and for the birds among them he had an eye like Luther's—speaking quaintly regarding them, as did Luther. Coming in one day, at Friedrichsruh, he said: "The starlings held a public meeting to-day, probably in connection with the coming of spring," and then he described whimsically their doings and probable sayings. Another day, at Varzin, he chronicled the doings of the rooks in the tree tops—how they teach their children to fly—take them to the seaside for change of air and diet—and, "as people of position, take a winter town residence"—in the neighboring church towers. Comical was it that one morning at Gastein, sauntering in the park, he became so interested in the household economy of sundry birds which nested there that he utterly forgot and entirely missed an interview between the Emperors of Germany and Austria at which his presence was especially important.

Throughout his life within doors there was one especially soothing influence,—his love for music, and above all for the music of Beethoven. His wife's playing was good and he greatly enjoyed it. It seems to have helped him at some times when the strain upon his nerves was almost beyond endurance. Cynics were wont to say that the great hold which his eminent ambassador to Rome, von Keudell, had upon him was due not so much to Keudell's diplomacy as to his skill in interpreting the masterpieces of German music.[1]

A recent writer has somewhat brilliantly sustained a thesis that the only way of explaining Bismarck's life is by considering him a humorist. Quaint humor he showed when, speaking of Germans who hesitated to come under Prussian leadership, he said: "Prussian government is like a flannel shirt—unpleasant at first, but very comfortable afterward." Grim humor, also, he showed early, even in his old parliamentary struggles: to a revolutionary opponent who proposed—"If your party conquers you shall take me under your wing, and if my side gets the upper hand I will do as much for you," he answered, "If your party wins, life will not be worth living, and if *we* win, then hanging shall be the order of the day—but with all politeness, up to the very foot of the gallows." Caustic was his wit when he reminded "the Augustenburger" that "Prussia could wring the necks of the chickens she had hatched." Cruel was his humor when he made the treaty of Versailles, and especially when those two eminent orators, Thiers and Jules Favre, tried to overcome him with pathetic eloquence.[2] There was not unfrequently a melancholy chord in his utterances, which when swept by wit gave a humorous cast to proceedings otherwise dull or solemn; but the scene when Bismarck thought that he had failed to prevent the king from entering Vienna in triumph, as given us by the faithful Busch, reveals abysses of far deeper feeling.

Wit there was—coruscating especially through his letters and table talk; humor there was—glowing even through despatches; pungent sayings there were, which

[1] For his love of life in the open air, see Busch, Whitman, and others; for his fondness of music, see especially Keudell.
[2] See Chapter II of this essay.

flashed through the nation,—many of them cynical and some of them unjust, but not a few of them warming the hearts, clearing the eyes, strengthening the arms of patriots everywhere. (Yet beneath all, throughout his entire work, to the end of his service, was a deep seriousness which could only come from a sense of duty. This was the solid basis of that statesmanship which at last brought Germany, and indeed Europe, out of a chaos of unreason, and gave Bismarck his place in history as the greatest German since Luther.)

INDEX

INDEX